From the reviews of *Against Forgetting*

"Far from dispiriting, these poems on the century's various insults against humankind attest to an obstinate spirit, even a joyous insistence that something sane can be said, and in a lyric form. The book's range over time and place, and the many lesser-known poets alongside names we've grown up with, make this our fullest, truest access to the poetry of witness.

—John Felstiner

"This is a remarkable book. Not only in itself and for the poems it contains, but for the ideas that lie behind their selection as an anthology."

—*New York Review of Books*

"The anthology is dense with extraordinary outcries in the face of the unspeakable.... Certainly this book will be treasured by readers for whom it provides a first discovery of such work."

—*New York Newsday*

"What Forché instinctively knows, and what finally makes this volume so extraordinary, is the fact that even the lyric is ultimately political; perhaps, in extremity, it is the greatest political act of all."

—*Kansas City Star*

"Once read, the poems in this very moving anthology will not soon be forgotten. Together, they shed a harsh light as they witness the madness humanity has wrought upon itself during the course of this century."

—starred *Booklist*

"[*Against Forgetting*] exalts the power of the word, and the power of witness. It is a valiant act of remembering."

—*The Progressive*

Against Forgetting

Twentieth-Century Poetry of Witness

Edited and with an Introduction by
Carolyn Forché

W.W. NORTON & COMPANY
NEW YORK / LONDON

The text of this book is composed in 11/13 Garamond
with the display set in Caslon Open Face
Composition and manufacturing by the Haddon Craftsmen, Inc.
Book design by Jo Anne Metsch

Library of Congress Cataloging-in-Publication Data

Against forgetting: 20th century poetry of witness / edited and
    with an introduction by Carolyn Forché.
        p.   cm.
    Includes index.
        1. Poetry, Modern—20th century—Translations into English.
    2. Political atrocities—Poetry.   3. Military history—20th century—
    Poetry.   I. Forché, Carolyn.
    PN6101.A32   1993
    808.81'9358—dc20   92-26174

ISBN 0-393-03372-4 (cl)
ISBN 0-393-30976-2 (pa)

W. W. Norton & Company, Inc., 500 Fifth Avenue, New York, N.Y. 10110
W. W. Norton & Company Ltd., 10 Coptic Street, London WC1A 1PU

    5 6 7 8 9 0

For those who died
and those who survived.

Contents

THE HOLOCAUST, THE SHOAH (1933–1945)   357

REPRESSION IN AFRICA AND THE STRUGGLE AGAINST APARTHEID IN SOUTH AFRICA (1900–1991)   7 1 3

Motto

In the dark times, will there also be singing?
Yes, there will be singing.
About the dark times.

—Bertolt Brecht

Introduction

In 1944, the Hungarian poet Miklós Radnóti was sent to a forced-labor camp in what became Yugoslavia. While there, he was able to procure a small notebook, in which he wrote his last ten poems, along with the following message in Hungarian, Croatian, German, French, and English: ". . . [this] contains the poems of the Hungarian poet Miklós Radnóti . . . to Mr. Gyula Ortutay, Budapest University lecturer. . . . Thank you in advance."

When it was clear that they would be defeated, the Germans decided to evacuate the camp and return the workers to Hungary. Radnóti, assuming that the first column would be the safest, volunteered for the march and recorded it in his poetry. Once in Hungary, the soldiers in charge, unable to find hospital room for these prisoners, took Radnóti and twenty-one others to a mass grave and executed them. Had Radnóti not volunteered to return to Hungary, he might have been saved by Marshal Tito's partisans. However, the story does not end—as millions of such stories ended—with execution and the anonymity of a mass grave. After the war was over, Radnóti's wife was among those who found and exhumed the mass grave in the village of Abda. The coroner's report for corpse #12 read:

A visiting card with the name Dr. Miklós Radnóti printed on it. An ID card stating the mother's name as Ilona Grosz. Father's name illegible. Born in Budapest, May 5, 1909. Cause of death: shot in the nape. In the back pocket of the trousers a small notebook was found soaked in the fluids of the body and blackened by wet earth. This was cleaned and dried in the sun.

Radnóti's final poems are represented in this anthology, along with the poems of 144 other significant poets who endured conditions of historical and social extremity during the twentieth century—through exile, state censorship, political persecution, house arrest, torture, imprisonment, military occupation, warfare, and assassination. Many poets did not survive, but their works remain with us as poetic witness to the dark times in which they lived.

This attempt to assemble such work in a single volume is the result of a thirteen-year effort to understand the impress of extremity upon the poetic imagination. My own journey began in 1980, upon my return from El Salvador—where I had worked as a human rights activist—and led me through the occupied West Bank, Lebanon, and South Africa. Something happened along the way to the introspective poet I had been. My new work seemed controversial to my American contemporaries, who argued against its "subject matter," or against the right of a North American to contemplate such issues in her work, or against any mixing of what they saw as the mutually exclusive realms of the personal and the political. Like many other poets, I felt that I had no real choice regarding the impulse of my poems, and had only to wait, in meditative expectancy. In attempting to come to terms with the question of poetry and politics, and seeking the solace of poetic camaraderie, I turned to the works of Anna Akhmatova, Yannis Ritsos, Paul Celan, Federico García Lorca, Nazim Hikmet, and others. I began collecting their work, and soon found myself a repository of what began to be called "the poetry of witness." In thinking about these poems, I realized that the arguments about poetry and politics had been too narrowly defined. Regardless of "subject matter," these poems bear the trace of extremity within them, and they are, as such, evidence of what occurred. They are also poems which are as much "about" language as are poems that have no subject other than language itself.

This anthological history of our century begins with the genocide of the Armenians and follows extremity in its various forms. The volume is arranged in sections according to regions and major events, with historical headnotes. Within each section, poets appear in chronological order by date of birth, with biographical notes to illuminate the experience of extremity for each poet, and a selection of poetry from available works in the English originals or in translation. The criteria for inclusion were these: poets must have personally endured such conditions; they must be considered important to their national literatures; and their work, if not in English, must be available in a quality translation. The necessarily brief biographies included here provide information relevant to the poets' experience of extremity. In instances where it was possible to place poets in more than one section, they appear according to their first significant experience of this kind, even though their poems might reflect later experiences as well. Finally, not all poems address extreme conditions, nor do all appear relevant in terms of their subject matter. I was interested in what these poets wrote, regardless of the explicit content.

This collection reflects the abundance of works in translation from European languages, but unfortunately underscores the scarcity of works translated from Asian and African literatures. In addition, fewer women poets seem to have survived the horrors of our century than their male counterparts, and many fewer have been translated. Despite these limitations, the present volume makes available only about one quarter of the material I was able to gather. It is, however, not my intention to propose a canon of such works; this is, rather, a poetic memorial to those who suffered and resisted through poetry itself.

Poetry of witness presents the reader with an interesting interpretive problem. We are accustomed to rather easy categories: we distinguish between "personal" and "political" poems—the former calling to mind lyrics of love and emotional loss, the latter indicating a public partisanship that is considered divisive, even when necessary. The distinction between the personal and the political gives the political realm too much and too little scope; at the same time, it renders the personal too important and not important enough. If we give up the dimension of the personal, we risk relinquishing one of the most powerful sites of resistance. The celebration of the personal, however, can indicate a myopia, an inability to see how larger structures of the economy and the state circumscribe, if not determine, the fragile realm of individuality.

We need a third term, one that can describe the space between the state and the supposedly safe havens of the personal. Let us call this space "the social." As North Americans, we have been fortunate: wars for us (provided we are not combatants) are fought elsewhere, in other countries. The cities bombed are other people's cities. The houses destroyed are other people's houses. We are also fortunate in that we do not live under martial law; there are nominal restrictions on state censorship; our citizens are not sent into exile. We are legally and juridically free to choose our associates, and to determine our communal lives. But perhaps we should not consider our social lives as merely the products of our choice: the social is a place of resistance and struggle, where books are published, poems read, and protest disseminated. It is the sphere in which claims against the political order are made in the name of justice.

By situating poetry in this social space, we can avoid some of our residual prejudices. A poem that calls on us from the other side of a situation of extremity cannot be judged by simplistic notions of "accuracy" or "truth to life." It will have to be judged, as Ludwig Wittgenstein said of confessions, by its consequences, not by our ability to verify its truth. In fact, the poem might be our only evidence that an event has occurred: it exists for us as the sole trace of an occurrence. As such, there will be nothing for us to base the poem on, no independent account that will tell us whether or not we can see a given text as being "objectively" true. Poem as trace, poem as evidence. Radnóti's final notebook entry, dated October 31, 1944, read:

> I fell beside him; his body turned over,
> already taut as a string about to snap.
> Shot in the back of the neck. That's how you too will end,
> I whispered to myself; just lie quietly.
> Patience now flowers into death.
> *Der springt noch auf,* a voice said above me.
> On my ear, blood dried, mixed with filth.

This verse describes the death of his fellow prisoner Miklós Lorsi, a violinist, and remains the only trace of his dying.

Miklós Radnóti's poems evade easy categories. They are not merely personal, nor are they, strictly speaking, political. What is one to make of the first lines of "Forced March"?:

> The man who, having collapsed,   rises, takes steps, is insane;
> he'll move an ankle, a knee,   an errant mass of pain,
> and take to the road again . . .

The poem becomes an apostrophe to a fellow marcher, and so it is not only a record of experience but an exhortation and a plea against despair. It is not a cry for sympathy but a call for strength. The hope that the poem relies on, however, is not "political" as such: it is not a celebration of solidarity in the name of a class or common enemy. It is not partisan in any accepted sense. It opposes the dream of future satisfaction to the reality of current pain. One could argue that it uses the promise of personal happiness against a politically induced misery, but it does so in the name of the poet's fellows, in a spirit of communality.

We all know that atrocities have taken place on an unprecedented scale in the last one hundred years. Such monstrous acts have come to seem almost normal. It becomes easier to forget than to remember, and this forgetfulness becomes our defense against remembering—a rejection of unnecessary sentimentality, a hardheaded acceptance of "reality." Modernity, as twentieth-century German Jewish philosophers Walter Benjamin and Theodor Adorno argued, is marked by a superstitious worship of oppressive force and by a concomitant reliance on oblivion. Such forgetfulness, they argue, is willful and isolating: it drives wedges between the individual and the collective fate to which he or she is forced to submit. These poems will not permit us diseased complacency. They come to us with claims that have yet to be filled, as attempts to mark us as they have themselves been marked.

How do these poems try to remind us? The musical title of Holocaust survivor Paul Celan's "Todesfugue"—his "Death Fugue"—warns us that the poem will not represent the world "directly." And indeed it begins on the unexplained (and ultimately irreducible) vehicle of metaphor: "Black milk of daybreak we drink it at evening." There is no mention of who this "we" might be or what the milk is, nor is there any need to be explicit: the poem works through repetition and suggests meaning through juxtaposition. There are, of course, hints: the poem mentions Jews, and calls death "a master from Deutschland." In John Felstiner's translation, the German remains, and it remains out of terror. The German of the camps was an alien tongue, spoken gutturally to those who frequently knew no German, and who would have to construct its meaning out of their own fear and for their own survival. This poem, written by a Romanian Jew in France in German, is itself evidence of the experience it describes. "*Meister*" in German is not merely "master": in fact, *Herr* serves as Lord and Master as well. *Meister* also denotes mastery of a craft, the acceptance into a guild; to enter the poem, either in the original or in this translation, is to enter the world of death, to become a member of a guild whose language the poem can neither translate nor deny.

It is impossible to translate Celan into an accessible English, an English of contemporary fluency. Rather, to encompass Celan, we might have to translate English into him, that is, denature our language just as he denatured German. Benjamin argued that a poem brought into a new language had to transform that language: a good translation would enrich its adoptive tongue as it had changed the linguistic world of its original. Perhaps all the poems in this anthology—even those written in English—are attempts at such translation, an attempt to mark, to change, to impress, but never to leave things as they are.

To talk about a poem as the sole trace of an event, to see it in purely evidentiary terms, is perhaps to believe our own figures of speech too rigorously. If, as Benjamin indicates, a poem is *itself* an event, a trauma that changes both a common language and an individual psyche, it is a specific kind of event, a specific kind of trauma. It is an experience entered into voluntarily. Unlike an aerial attack, a poem does not come at one unexpectedly. One has to read or listen, one has to be willing to accept the trauma. So, if a poem is an event and the trace of an event, it has, by definition, to belong to a different order of being from the trauma that marked its language in the first place.

Not surprisingly, a large number of poems in this selection, written in conditions of extremity, rely on the immediacies of direct address. There are few writings as intimate as a letter to a spouse. Nazim Hikmet, the Turkish Communist who spent a large portion of his adult life in prison, writes from solitary confinement:

> It's spring outside, my dear wife, spring.
> Outside on the plain, suddenly the smell

> of fresh earth, birds singing, etc.
> It's spring, my dear wife,
> the plain outside sparkles . . .
> And inside the bed comes alive with bugs,
>> the water jug no longer freezes.

The poem depends on bare-boned simplicity, for it marks the differ-
ence between inside and outside, between prison and the world,
through small, disturbing details. Spring on the outside is easily evoked
by cliché, so Hikmet can cut his list short with an offhand "etc." On the
inside, however, spring is measured in the resurgence of lice and the
lack of ice in the water jug. Of course, the fact that the jug freezes
indicates just how cold the cell is. And so, while Hikmet is willing to
greet the spring, he does so in terms of prison's stark dichotomies. Life
there seems to consist of two seasons: the frozen and the vermin-
ridden. In spring, on the outside and the inside, a man dreams of
freedom. How does the poet know this? From experience. It is difficult
to read these lines. Does Hikmet only retrieve the "demon called free-
dom" from memory, or does the demon possess him, even now, in
solitary confinement? I am inclined to favor the second reading (al-
though both are possible), because in this way the final lines of the
poem have an added pathos. Out in the yard, in the sun, the poet rests
his back against a wall:

> For a moment no trap to fall into,
> no struggle, no freedom, no wife.
> Only earth, sun and me . . .
> I am happy.

The demon of freedom, like the pull of a wife, is a torment to a man
in solitary, who is alone and most distinctly unfree. Happiness comes to
the prisoner when he can forget his privations, his situation, and the
claims of the outside. The contentment he feels might be viewed as a
victory for his humanity, for his perseverance, but it contains a negative
judgment as well. It is bought at a very dear price: the fleeting forgetful-
ness of who and where he is.

The epistolary mode, while intimate and private, is also deeply pub-
lic. It has always been the poetry of the middle style, of a conscientious
communality, an attempt to speak for more than one and to engage all
others. So it is when Bertolt Brecht addresses *die Nachgeborenen,* the
generations that come after him. His poem is a self-laceration ("To
sleep I lay down among murderers") but also a demand for humility
from the future:

Remember
When you speak of our failings
The dark time too
Which you have escaped.

These lines might be read as an attempt at exculpation, but such a reading does not do justice to the rest of the poem. Brecht writes to the future to remind it of the ease of moral disaster and ethical complacency.

More modern, perhaps, than the traditional letter or address, is the postcard. Pithier than the letter, the postcard as it appears in this anthology is freighted with irony. Radnóti writes:

Bloody saliva hangs on the mouths of the oxen.
Blood shows in every man's urine.
The company stands in wild knots, stinking.
Death blows overhead, revolting.

This card is not backed by a picture: it is itself a picture. Its brevity cuts to the horror of the situation. If extremity produces a new kind of postcard, it can only view the traditional cards with a mixture of nostalgia and mockery. So Günter Eich's "Old Postcards" from before the war are shadowed by the war itself. The carnival atmosphere of the eighth postcard is undercut by the final figure, where the Renaissance staircase becomes an unspecified but evidently determinate number of prisoners' steps. The odd current of distress that runs through the poem, the hint of conflict and the motifs of war, leads to the final card:

Fine,
fine.
But when the war is over
we'll go to Minsk
and pick up Grandmother.

Let us assume that the war in question is either World War I or World War II. (We can make this presumption from the reference to Sedan Day, a now-forgotten German holiday to commemorate defeat of the French in the Franco-Prussian War.) The card seems to assure us of a German victory over the Russians, hence the writer's ability to pick up Grandmother in the city of Minsk. At the time of writing the poem, however, it would be impossible to "pick up Grandmother" in the Russian city: the course of history has made such ease of travel impossible. Hence the postcard comes to us (readers from the Cold War) as news from another time as well as another place: a time in which the world was so different as to be another place altogether. The poem also comments ironically on a certain chauvinism, and the belief in German military superiority and territorial hegemony. The victory that the poem indicates was nothing more than a vicious and dangerous dream.

It should come as no surprise that poets who urgently desire to influence a public have also used the news media as models, even if somewhat negative ones. Thus the Polish poet Zbigniew Herbert sends his "Report from the Besieged City," a fabular place that is an "everywhere." His is an "objective" report, a product of willed disinterest:

> I avoid any commentary I keep a tight hold on my emotions I write about
> the facts
> only they it seems are appreciated in foreign markets

There is despair in this flatness of tone: markets define the news, not the experience of the besieged. Foreigners want to hear nothing but the facts because they do not wish to be disturbed by their complicity in the sufferings of the city. In a similar way, writing about Vietnam, John Balaban explodes the myth of the impartiality of the media in "News Update," in which he celebrates the sometimes partisan heroism of the journalist (which does not make the news) and the silly stories that seem—to editors at least—worthy of public attention. In these two poems, Herbert and Balaban use the news media to stress the importance of poetry: what comes to us in the newspapers and on television is not necessarily factual, nor is it necessarily cogent. Determined by the market and by the tender conscience of the distant consumer, the news is is a degenerate form of art, neither wholly fact nor wholly fiction, never true to objective truth or subjective reality. The demands of modernist literary communication, with its stress on close reading, irony, and the fiction of textual depth, open up more complex visions of historical circumstance than are otherwise available.

Postcards, letters, and reports on the news—all these are communal forms, ways of writing that stress the interpersonal aspects of poetry, the public side of literature. They underline the collective urgency that propels a literature of the social. In Latin America we find the *testimonio,* the act of judicial witness. Bearing witness in such a poem becomes literal: the poet imagines himself or herself in a court of law. The *testimonio* casts a large shadow in this anthology (and on my conception of the poetry of extremity). In an age of atrocity, witness becomes an imperative and a problem: how does one bear witness to suffering and before what court of law? Such is the dilemma of Ariel Dorfman, in "Vocabulary":

> But how can I tell their story
> if I was not there?

The poet claims he cannot find the words to tell the story of people who have been tortured, raped, and murdered. Nevertheless, it is vitally important that the story be told. Who shall tell it? The poet answers:

> Let them speak for themselves.

It is not callousness that prompts Dorfman to write this line, but a sense that the story belongs to those who have undergone the extremity, and should not be determined, as in Herbert's poem, by foreign readers. Humility brings the poet before an ethical tribunal, a place where the writer must recognize the claims of difference, the otherness of others, and the specificities of their experience. Witness, in this light, is problematic: even if one has witnessed atrocity, one cannot necessarily speak *about* it, let alone *for* it.

The gap between self and other opens up the problem of relativism that has bedeviled modern philosophy, politics, and poetry. Respect for otherness seems always to release the specter of an infinite regress. The language of religion therefore becomes quite important in this supposedly secular century, for religion traditionally makes claims for universality and unimpeachable truth. Furthermore, some of the most flagrant forms of institutionalized violence in our era have been directed toward specific religions (during the Holocaust) or against religion in general (as in the Soviet Union and in Eastern Europe). Anna Akhmatova composes in the language of Christianity in her poem "Requiem," and even the title of this attack on both Stalinism and war becomes an act of protest, a religious form of memory that seeks to sanctify the dead and ease them on their way into the afterlife. Where Stalin erased the past and the present for the supposed good of the future, the poet asks the past and the present to stake a claim on that future:

> This woman is sick to her marrow-bone
> this woman is utterly alone,
>
> with husband dead, with son away
> in jail. Pray for me. Pray.

The appeal for prayer is both a request for help and a stroke against solitude: to pray for this woman is to express sympathy, to establish a communality through the medium of religion. It is to give help in the only way left to the powerless. Where there is nothing else, there is prayer.

If religion can provide a countersolidarity to the enforced communalism of the Stalinist era, it can also lend meaning to the desperate experiences of that time. The death of the son in Akhmatova's poem becomes a form of crucifixion: the apparent meaninglessness of terror is transfigured when it is mapped onto the story of Christ's Passion. Furthermore, it transforms that story by giving a special place to the Virgin Mary. Akhmatova's poem enters into a discreet dialogue with Christianity, a mutually informing interchange of meaning and pathos that indicates an enduring place for the explanatory possibility of religion: its ability to speak about us and to include us.

In countries where religion has been more firmly institutionalized, more central to the workings of the state, its conventions could provide an ironic counterpoint to the official version of extreme events. Wilfred Owen, himself killed in World War I, writes an anthem, a hymn of national praise and victory, for "doomed youth." Bells rung for the newly dead, prayers, candles—all the ritual accounterments of mourning—have been superseded by the realities of modern warfare:

> No mockeries now for them; no prayers nor bells;
> Nor any voice of mourning save the choirs,—
> The shrill, demented choirs of wailing shells . . .

The dead are mourned not by human song, but by the cacophony of new technologies and armaments. The comforts of religion seem to have no place in this poem. They only remind us of the lack of comfort of the present.

Religion in an age of atrocity, as Owen's anthem indicates, can itself bear a heavy responsibility for suffering. For Owen, the difficulty arises from the marriage of religion and the state, of the belligerent and nationalistic aspect of the very notion of the anthem itself. For other writers, religious qualms arise from the sheer prevalence of evil in this century, from the assault on theodicy that genocide, torture, and imposed misery present. This is perhaps most evident in the writings of Jewish poets, like Paul Celan and Edmond Jabès, where the reality of the Shoah (the Hebrew term for what is known as the Holocaust) seems to come into direct conflict with the traditional mission of the Jews. In "There Was Earth Inside Them" Celan writes of people who do not praise the Creator because He had willed their abjection. This refusal—apparently natural enough—leads to silence:

> They dug and heard nothing more;
> they did not grow wise, invented no song,

thought up for themselves no language.
They dug.

Theology, poetry, and words are all bound together—their antithesis, it seems, is the wormlike act of digging. The poem ends oddly, with an invocation to an absent other and the apparent inclusion of the poet among the silent diggers:

> O one, o none, o no one, o you
> Where did the way lead when it led nowhere?
> O you dig and I dig, and I dig towards you,
> and on our finger the ring awakes.

That "you" is both God and a loved one, God seen as a loved one and the loved one seen as God. The way to nowhere turns, through a difficult act of dialectics, into a road to somewhere, where the "no one" becomes a "someone" and that someone becomes a "you." Through this leap, the ring is not on one finger but on "our" finger: the same finger on different hands, or the one finger on a collective hand. It awakes because it has been asleep: the covenant, the troth, has been repledged. So for Celan (following perhaps the poetic precedent of Friedrich Hölderlin) the apparent absence of the Almighty leads us back to His presence. His absence is the mark of His presence. Divine absence in our time has two forms. One is the threat of the abyss, of the Death of God heralded by Nietzsche, and the other is the new technology of death presented by the death camps. To think religion through is to rediscover the holy in-between and in-spite-of this double negation, as Jabès has written: "I write in function of two limits. / On that side, there is the void. / On this side, the horror of Auschwitz."

The peculiar paradox, the insistence on God's existence in the face of His apparent disappearance, derives from the Kabbalah, the tradition of Jewish mysticism, in which the world in its imperfection is created by God's recession: He draws a curtain of darkness down before Himself in order to allow light to appear, darkness serving as the necessary foil for illumination. This thought rests at the center of Jabès's poetry, which turns on paradox and contradiction. Jabès writes in the final volume of his long work on the Shoah, *The Book of Questions*:

[G-d] is image in the absence of images, language in the absence of language, point in the absence of points.

The counterintuitive thrust of this thought leads to the imperative (in "Notebook II") that we have to "take the contradictions into our keeping. / At the edge of Emptiness." This is a religious thought without irony because it stems from a religion based on the indispensability of irony, of dialectic and dialogue. There is a secular version of this theology, figured in the rhetorical trope of prosopopeia, where an absent other is given voice, invoked, engaged in conversation. Milosz summons forth the dead in his early poem "Dedication":

> You whom I could not save
> Listen to me.

In contradistinction to Milosz's later work, however, these dead are not desired. They are a burden:

> They used to pour on graves millet or poppy seeds
> To feed the dead who would come disguised as birds.
> I put this book here for you, who once lived
> So that you should visit us no more.

Milosz calls up the departed only to banish them again. His poetry is both a magical way of bringing the dead to life and a talisman against that life. He can only create the new by expelling the old through a ritual act.

The poetry of witness frequently resorts to paradox and difficult equivocation, to the invocation of what is *not* there as if it *were,* in order to bring forth the real. That it must defy common sense to speak of the common indicates that traditional modes of thought, the purview of common sense, no longer *make* sense, or only make sense if they are allowed to invert themselves. In the face of our increasingly unreal reality, then, fabulation, the writing of the blatantly fictitious, becomes the recourse of those who would describe the everyday. This is the basis for the Polish poet Aleksandr Wat's bleak parable in "Imagerie d'Epinal" where a young girl, given a lollipop by her father's executioner, carries his head in a parade:

> With that pole she marched in a parade on a sunny, populous road,
> under her school placard:
> > "Happiness to all—death to enemies . . ."

It is clear here that the slogans of repression and enforced solidarity are the expressions of absurdity, the voice of the fictional. Surrealism in this circumstance marks not only the utopian desire for secular transfiguration but also the attempt to come to terms with an untransfigured world. Fabulation and the surreal are also good ways of masking intent, of circumventing the censor's stricture.

Irony, paradox, and surrealism, for all the interpretive difficulties they present, might well be both the answer and a restatement of Adorno's often quoted and difficult contention that to write poetry after Auschwitz is barbaric. Adorno wrote this just after World War II, and in the context of the essay in which it appears, his indictment extends to all forms of art. Art, Adorno felt, rested on the social inequities and objectifying tendencies that made Fascism not only possible but inevitable. Auschwitz, then, was contiguous with all the ornaments of Western art, for it stood as the culmination of culture where culture turned into its opposite. While the language of the everyday might appeal to Hikmet and Radnóti, it may not present an adequate language for *witness* in situations where the quotidian has been appropriated by oppressive powers. The colonization of language by the state renders that language inaccessible to a poetry that wants to register its protest against such depredations. The accepted languages of art might not be adequate either, for the sphere of art is frequently the first to be attacked: Hitler banished the work of the expressionists and celebrated Wagner. Socialist realism displaced all other forms of aesthetic expression under Stalinism.

The ultimate example of the cross-fertilization of culture and barbarity took place at Auschwitz, where the Jews were forced to play chamber music for their executioners. Art in such a world carries with it a dangerous complicity which it can neither refute nor ignore. Adorno did not wish to banish art from an ideal republic. He wanted art to become conscious of the sins it had to suffer and withstand. A better expression of his understanding of the task of poetry comes in an aphorism from his book *Minima Moralia*:

. . . there is no longer beauty or consolation except in the gaze falling on horror, withstanding it, and in unalleviated consciousness of negativity holding fast to the possibility of what is better.

In such a world poetry will yearn after truth through indirection—will speak, in the terms Jabès used to describe Celan, in wounded words. Jabès also maintains: "To Adorno . . . I say that we must write. But we cannot write as before." When we find eclogues by Miklós Radnóti, elegies by Johannes Bobrowski, and ballads by Ondra Lysohorsky, we are also forced to notice that these forms have been modified and transformed. Let us take another example, Robert Desnos's "Ars Poetica":

Across the snout
Picked up in the mud and slime
Spit out, vomited, rejected—

> I am the verse witness of my master's breath—
> Left over, cast off, garbage
> Like the diamond, the flame, and the blue of the sky
> Not pure, not virgin
> But fucked to the core
> fucked, pricked, sucked, ass fucked, raped
> I am the verse witness of my master's breath . . .

This is not the language of the "sweet and the useful," the *dulce et utile* that Horace prescribed. On the contrary, Desnos has written his own poetics of extremity, of situations where diamonds, flames, and the sky are reduced to refuse. Poetry, in order to be the witness of lived experience, of breath, will have to resort to a language more suitable to the time. The violence of Desnos's language, his willful assault on decorum, and his scabrous use of slang all attest to the violence of the age. In fact, Desnos chooses to leave the trace of extraliterary force by violating the codes of the literary. Thus Orpheus is turned into a "cold-blooded fucker." He has been translated—as has poetry itself—into a wild, nasty, and demotic modernity.

Extremity, as we have seen, demands new forms or alters older modes of poetic thought. It also breaks forms and creates forms from these breaks. The fragment is not new to poetry: it has a venerable history. Nor is it limited to the poetry of witness. Fragmentation is a standard feature of literary modernism. But the fragment gains urgency in the aftermath of extremity. It might well be the feature that binds this anthology together. Lines of poetry can be grammatical fragments, as in Desnos's poem. Poems themselves can be fragments. Or rather, they can be collections of fragments that indicate a whole, or a narrative that cannot be written. Dorfman's stuttering "Vocabulary" tells of the inability to tell a story. It evokes the story but leaves it unfinished, omits the details and the denouement. As in Eich's postcards, the reader is strangely aware of what has been left out, what cannot or has not been said. The French call this procedure *recit éclaté*—shattered, exploded, or splintered narrative. The story cannot travel over the chasm of time and space. Violence has rendered it unspeakable.

The psychiatrist Dore Laub has found that in the oral testimony of survivors of the Shoah, their accounts fragment as they approach the core of the trauma. The narrative of trauma is itself traumatized, and bears witness to extremity by its inability to articulate directly or completely. Hence the reduction of a century to a series of staccato images in Adonis's "Mirror for the Twentieth Century":

> A coffin bearing the face of a boy
> A book

Written on the belly of a crow
A wild beast hidden in a flower

A rock
Breathing with the lungs of a lunatic:

This is it
This is the Twentieth Century.

Our age lacks the structure of a story. Or perhaps it would be closer to Adonis's poem to say that narrative implies progress and completion. The history of our time does not allow for any of the bromides of progress, nor for the promise of successful closure. That this history can be retold in scattered images (while eluding them) indicates that the age repeats the same story over and over again, marking an infernal return of the same. In "Lines for Translation into Any Language," the contemporary British poet James Fenton offers the same bleak analysis: the story of war, of a shantytown in a cemetery and the plight of a noncombatant, has been broken down into discrete sections that can exist on their own or be organized into a narrative which seems to imply connections it does not state. The darkness of the vision is made clear by its title. The situation the poem describes can happen anywhere: it is not limited in time or space. For Fenton, as for Adonis, the tale of our time is one of infinite repetition.

The fact that extremity can be translated the world over—that institutionalized suffering has been globalized—means that fragmentation might also be global—that displacement has been rendered universal. Exile in this anthology is as much a linguistic condition as it is a question of citizenship. At the most obvious level, we find a number of poets writing in languages that are alien to the nation in which they write. Brecht wrote German poems in the United States. Milosz writes Polish poems in Berkeley, California. Vallejo wrote Spanish in Paris, and Faiz wrote in Urdu in the Arabic world. More interesting perhaps is a different kind of linguistic exile, where one comes to write in a foreign language or in a language that history has rendered foreign. We can compare here the different experiences of two Romanian Jews rendered homeless by World War II and its aftermath. Dan Pagis's native language was German. Pagis spent three years in a concentration camp and emigrated to Israel, where he became a leading Hebrew poet. His Hebrew was the result of history, of displacement—it was the very mark of his exile, a notion that is given great poignancy in his little graffiti poem "Written in Pencil in a Sealed Boxcar:"

here in this carload
i am eve
with abel my son

> if you see my other son
> cain son of man
> tell him that i

The language and the characters of the Bible have been translated into modern Europe: their Hebrew is the reason for their destruction.

For Celan, the task was different. He wrote in his native German in France. This first alienation from his language—the daily experience of his alterity, his foreignness—was augmented by his fractured use of that language. He attempted to purify the tongue, render up its Nazi contamination, mark it historically. His quest led him to write in a fragmented, idiosyncratic dialect of his own construction, whose grammar was as tortured as its words were often new. Thus he was exiled within his own mother tongue, and used his mother tongue to register that exile.

A similar sense of exile, of linguistic alienation, can be seen in writers like Quincy Troupe, who write some of their poetry in the vocabulary of Black English and seek to create their own poetic idioms:

> eye use to write poems about burning
> down the motherfucking country for crazy
> horse, geronimo & malcolm king
> x, use to (w)rite about stabbing white folks
> in their air-conditioned eyeballs with ice picks . . .

The thematized violence of Troupe's rejection of white America is repeated in the idiosyncrasies of spelling which seek to make visible the aural puns of the language, to uncover a depth in English which he can inhabit without undue self-sacrifice.

If modernity has established the norm of individual integrity which Troupe seeks to maintain, it should be obvious from much of the poetry in this anthology that the experience of this century has done much to undermine this norm. In *The Body in Pain,* Elaine Scarry has written eloquently about the way that torture seeks to destroy the language and the world of its victim; the way it tries to unmake the victim's ability to objectify himself or herself in language. Thus when we come across a poem in this book where the poet addresses himself or herself, this form of apostrophe speaks from and against a violent self-alienation, of a self-alienation born of violence. Claribel Alegría addresses her childhood self in "From the Bridge":

> Don't come any closer
> there's a stench of carrion
> surrounding me.

What separates the poet from the girl is precisely that smell of all the deaths the adult has witnessed, all the injustice the adult has seen. Similarly, Angel Cuadra writes of an inner split:

> The common man I might have been
> reproaches me now,
> blaming me for his ostracism
> his solitary shadow,
> his silent exile.

In this poem, "In Brief," the unimportant man the poet could have become is compared with the poet that the man has become. It would seem that Cuadra confronts himself with the possibility of a life not lived alone, not lived in exile. Had he not been a poet, the logic goes, he would not be ostracized. But as the poem unfolds, Cuadra claims that there is no difference between the common man and the poet. It is not poetry that has banished him from Cuba, nor is it fame that has made him an exile. It is exile that has alienated himself from himself, and its violence that has split him asunder. The "I" that speaks the poem, that begins and ends it, is a protest against such violence, an attempt to redeem speech from the silence of pain, and integrity from the disintegrating forces of extremity.

The poetry of witness reclaims the social from the political and in so doing defends the individual against illegitimate forms of coercion. It often seeks to register through indirection and intervention the ways in which the linguistic and moral universes have been disrupted by events. When I began this project, I was hard pressed to find a significant poet who could not be included, who in some important way or another did *not* bear witness to the ravages of our time. But clearly it was impossible to contemplate a book of such length. I was therefore forced to develop criteria for inclusion that would do justice to the poets I would necessarily have to exclude, criteria that would begin to describe the trajectory of our modernity. I decided to limit the poets in the anthology to those for whom the social had been irrevocably invaded by the political in ways that were sanctioned neither by law nor by the fictions of the social contract. The writers I have chosen are those for whom the normative promises of the nation-state have failed. They have not been afforded the legal or the physical protections that the modern state is supposed to lend its citizens, nor have they been able to enjoy the solidarity that the concept of the nation is supposed to provide. If my selection seems to include an inordinate number of writers whose human rights have been abused, it is because those rights, in the tradition of political theory, were supposed to police the boundaries between the government and personal self-determination, between citizenship and autonomy.

For decades, American literary criticism has sought to oppose "man" and "society," the individual against the communal, alterity against universality. Perhaps we can learn from the practice of the poets in this anthology that these are not oppositions based on mutual exclusion but are rather dialectical complementaries that invoke and pass through each other. Extremity is born of the simplifying desire to split these dyads into separate parts. It is the product of the drive to expunge one category in the name of another, to sacrifice the individual on the altar of the communal or vice versa. The poetry of witness is itself born in dialectical opposition to the extremity that has made such witness necessary. In the process, it restores the dynamic structure of dialectics.

Because the poetry of witness marks a resistance to false attempts at unification, it will take many forms. It will be impassioned or ironic. It will speak in the language of the common man or in an esoteric language of paradox or literary privilege. It will curse and it will bless; it will blaspheme against or ignore the holy. Its protest might rest on an odd grammatical inversion, on a heady peroration to an audience, or on a bizarre flight of fancy. It can be partisan in a limited sense but is more often partisan in the best of senses, that is, it speaks for what might, with less than crippling irony be called "the party of humanity." I do not mean this in an unreflective way, as a celebration of some mythological "inherent" goodness in man's "innate" nature. Rather, I take the partisanship of humanity as a rejection of unwarranted pain inflicted on some humans by others, of illegitimate domination. I am guided in this by Hannah Arendt's meditation on the self-justifications of collaboration with oppression, on the claim that the resistance of the single individual does not count in the face of the annihilating superiority of totalitarian regimes which make all resistance disappear into "holes of oblivion":

The holes of oblivion do not exist. Nothing human is that perfect and there are simply too many people in the world to make oblivion possible. One man will always be left alive to tell the story. . . . the lesson of such stories is simple and within everybody's grasp. Politically speaking, it is that under conditions of terror, most people will comply but *some people will not.* . . . Humanly speaking, no more is required, and no more can reasonably be asked, for this planet to remain a place fit for human habitation.

The resistance to terror is what makes the world habitable: the protest against violence will not be forgotten and this insistent memory renders life possible in communal situations. As Desnos wrote in a poem called "Epitaph":

You who are living, what have you done with these treasures?
Do you regret the time of my struggle?
Have you raised your crops for a common harvest?
Have you made my town a richer place?

If we have not, if we do not, what, in the end, have we become? And if
we do not, what, in the end, shall we be?

Carolyn Forché

Acknowledgments

This anthology was born of a desire to gather works of poetic witness to the sufferings and struggles of the twentieth century. I am indebted to the poets who survived its brutalities, who found strength within themselves to preserve the poetic spirit, and to the translators who assimilated their labors, thus blessing and enriching English with the riches of other poetries. During the years of research and gathering, I have always felt mysteriously and spiritually accompanied, and if this has been so, all the more have I been assisted by the many poets, scholars, critics, and translators who took an interest in this work. My deepest appreciation goes to my editorial associates, who worked selflessly, with grace and humor, during the past eight years. Daniel Simko lent me the breadth of his knowledge in making the selections; Andrea Gilats served as the angel of permissions. My colleague David Kaufmann bore the weight of historical and biographical research during the final year. Rebecca Wee proved indefatigible in proofreading, text preparation, and supportive goodwill. Diane Kohn, Evan Oakley, and Greg Grummer contributed to biographical research.

I have been particularly fortunate in the advice and support I have received from a number of distinguished scholars, writers, and librarians, among them Emery George, John Felstiner, Calvin Bedient, Ethelbert Miller, Sandor Goodhart, Anthony Brinkley, Peter Balakian, and most especially, the late Terrence Des Pres.

The Lannon Foundation, the National Endowment for the Arts, the Massachusetts Arts Council, and the District of Columbia Arts Council bestowed grants and fellowships which sustained me during the period of this work.

May my dear husband, Harry Mattison, and our son, Sean-Christophe, always know my gratitude for their patience and love during the long hours of this work.

Motto

This, then, is all. It's not enough, I know.
At least I'm still alive, as you may see.
I'm like the man who took a brick to show
How beautiful his house used once to be.

—Bertolt Brecht

The Armenian
Genocide

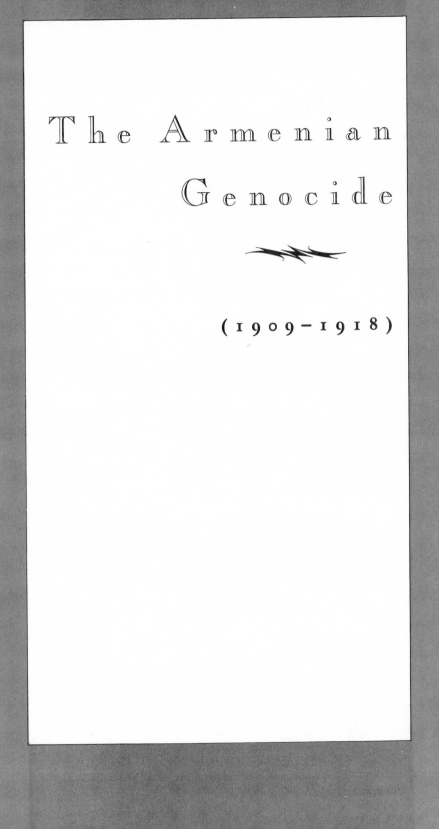

(1 9 0 9 — 1 9 1 8)

Any twentieth-century history of human rights and genocide must begin with the massacre of Armenians, then the largest Christian minority population of Turkey. Between 1909 and 1918, approximately 1.5 million Armenians were massacred by order of the Ottoman Turkish government. Under the Ottoman Turks, in the name of a nationalist movement known as pan-Turkism, the entire Armenian population of Anatolia, the oldest extant civilization in that part of the world, was annihilated.

Historians have called the Armenian massacre the first "modern" genocide, because it appears to be the first instance of political mass murder made possible by advanced technology and modern communications implemented by a centralized state bureaucracy. In time, as Michael Arlen points out in his *Passage to Ararat,* "Hitler's Germany would refine the process of railway deportation and introduce the gas chamber and the crematoria." The rhetorical question Hitler posed to his military cabinet days before his invasion of Poland in 1939—"Who, after all, speaks today of the annihilation of the Armenians?"—underscores the moral imperative of historical remembering.

During the second decade of the century, the Armenian genocide became, in Western Europe and the United States, a dramatic human rights issue. American newspaper coverage of the massacre, especially that of the *New York Times,* powerfully influenced popular opinion. Between 1915 and 1918, $100 million in relief aid was raised, at a time when a loaf of bread cost three cents. President Woodrow Wilson addressed Armenia's survival in the twelfth of his famous Fourteen Points, and urged the award of territory to Armenia in November 1920.

SIAMANTO (1878–1915)

Siamanto, born Adom Yarjanian in Turkish Armenia, was educated in Istanbul and at the Sorbonne, and during the first decade of the twentieth century traveled widely, including to the United States. A popular political activist with a bardic poetic style, he wrote *Bloody News from My Friend* as a response to the first massacre of Armenians committed by the Turkish government in 1909. Along with his friend the poet Daniel Varoujan and several hundred other artists, intellectuals, and professionals, Siamanto was executed on April 24, 1915.

≈ Grief

You, stranger, soul-mate,
who leaves behind the road of joy,
listen to me.
I know your innocent feet are still wet
with the blood of yours.
Foreign hands have come and yanked out
the sublime rose of freedom,
which finally bloomed from the pains of your race.
Let its divine scent intoxicate everyone,
Let everyone—those faraway, your neighbor, the ungrateful,
come and burn incense
before the goddess of Justice
that you carved from stone with your hammer.
Proud sowers, let others reap with your scythes
the wheat that ripens in the gold earth you ploughed.
Because if you are chased down by raw Evil,
don't forget that you are born
to bring forth the fruitful Good.

Walk down the avenues of merriment,
and don't let the happy ones see in your eyes
that image of corpse and ash.
Spare the passerby, whether a good man or a criminal.
Because Armenian pain
rises up in the eyes visage.
As you walk through the cross-road of merriment,
don't let a speck of gladness or a tear
stain grief's majesty.
Because for the vanquished tears are cowardly
and for the victors, the smile is frivolous, a wrinkle.

Armenian woman, with veils darkening you like death.
You, young man with native anguish
running down your face,
walk down the roads without rage or hate

and exclaim: what a bright day,
what a sarcastic grave-digger . . .
what a mob, what dances, what joy
and what feasts everywhere . . .
Our red shrouds are victory flags.
The bones of our pure brothers are flutes . . .
with them others are making strange music.
But don't shudder unknown sister,
or brother of fate.
As you study the stars
take heart, go on.
The law of life stays the same . . .
human beings can't understand each other.

And this evening before sunset
all of you will go back to your houses,
whether they are mud or marble,
and calmly close the treacherous
shutters of your windows.
Shut them from the wicked Capital,
shut them to the face of humanity,
and to the face of your god . . .
Even the lamp on your table
will be extinguished
by your soul's clear whispers.

    TR. PETER BALAKIAN AND NEVART YAGHLIAN

≈ The Dance

In the town of Bardez where Armenians
were still dying,
a German woman, trying not to cry
told me the horror she witnessed:

"This incomprehensible thing I'm telling you about,
I saw with my own eyes.
Behind my window of hell
I clenched my teeth
and watched with my pitiless eyes:

the town on Bardez turned
into a heap of ashes.
Corpses piled high as trees.
From the waters, from the springs,
from the streams and the road,
the stubborn murmur of your blood
still revenges my ear.

Don't be afraid. I must tell you what I saw,
so people will understand
the crimes men do to men.
For two days, by the road to the graveyard . . .
Let the hearts of the whole world understand.
It was Sunday morning,
the first useless Sunday dawning on the corpses.
From dusk to dawn in my room,
with a stabbed woman,
my tears wetting her death.
Suddenly I heard from afar
a dark crowd standing in a vineyard
lashing twenty brides
and singing dirty songs.

Leaving the half-dead girl on the straw mattress,
I went to the balcony on my window
and the crowd seemed to thicken like a clump of trees.
An animal of a man shouted, "you must dance,
dance when our drum beats."
With fury whips cracked
on the flesh of these women.
Hand in hand the brides began their circle dance.
Now, I envied my wounded neighbor
because with a calm snore
she cursed the universe
and gave her soul up to the stars . . .

In vain I shook my fists at the crowd.
'Dance,' they raved,
'dance till you die, infidel beauties.
With your flapping tits, dance!
Smile for us.

You're abandoned now, you're naked slaves,
so dance like a bunch of fuckin' sluts.
We're hot for you all.'
Twenty graceful brides collapsed.
'Get up,' the crowd roared,
brandishing their swords.
Then someone brought a jug of kerosene.
Human justice, I spit in your face.
The brides were anointed.
'Dance,' they thundered—
here's a fragrance you can't get in Arabia.'
With a torch, they set
the naked brides on fire.
And the charred bodies rolled
and tumbled to their deaths . . .
I slammed the shutters
of my windows,
and went over to the dead girl
and asked: 'How can I dig out my eyes?'

TR. PETER BALAKIAN AND NEVART YAGHLIAN

VAHAN TEKEYAN (1878–1945)

Unlike his fellow poets Siamanto and Daniel Varoujan, Vahan Tekeyan
survived the Turkish execution of 1.5 million Armenians in 1915, be-
cause he was in Jerusalem on business. When news of the genocide
reached him, he left Jerusalem for Cairo, where he lived in exile until his
death in 1945.

≈ Forgetting

Forgetting. Yes, I will forget it all.
        One after the other. The roads I crossed.
The roads I did not. Everything that happened.
        And everything that did not.

I am not going to transport anymore,
          nor drag the silent past, or that "me"
who was more beautiful and bigger
          than I could ever be.

I will shake off the weights
          thickening my mind and sight,
and let my heart see the sun as it dies.

Let a new morning's light open my closed eyes.
          Death, is that you here? Good Morning.
Or should I say Good Dark?

1940

TR. DIANA DER HOVANESSIAN AND MARZBED MARGOSSIAN

≈ Prayer on the Threshold of Tomorrow

Look. New sprouts push through the fields.
But which are thorns and which wheat
I do not know. Perhaps to the appetite
that is sated, all is chaff,
while to the hungry all is wheat.

Undistinguishable sounds, blows, footfalls
thud in the distance, an agonizing attack,
where the oppressed plant red
flames with their blood.
And the rains sweat and expand
into floods that shake the walls
of the oldest dams.

Lord, now is the time to send
your wisdom and kindness
to the tortured who, although
they have forgotten, need you as they hurl
themselves closer to the precipice.

Oh, God, who trimmed the wick of the mind
and poured the oil of life, do not let

your lamps be overturned.
Let them illuminate paths to your truth.

Plant love in the eyes of today's
and tomorrow's mighty. Do not let
their hearts close.

And do not let the hearts of the child
and the aged be strangers
to tenderness and hope.

Let the struggle of our time be short.
Let it be settled with justice.

Let the fortress of egos,
that huge barricade,
crumble. And let every treasure
go to every man. Let every garden
gate be open. But let no flower be crushed.
No single branch fall.

1930

TR. DIANA DER HOVANESSIAN AND MARZBED MARGOSSIAN

≈ Dream

I dreamed the heavy sky suddenly opened a gate.
The leaden heavens, sinking with weight
almost flattening us, by pressing down,
loosened, like a lid, so I could see in

that place (no longer dim). Sitting beside
clear running water and green fields: lively children,
shy brides, and virgin girls with downcast eyes
and smiles carefree and bright.

Happy mothers nearby, tears of tenderness,
old men, haloed with silver hair, on rocks,
brave men, blessing the peace. And grazing

around them, their centuries-old flocks
of lambs. In the distance, muzzle bent,
a wolf slinking off, surprised, to see his victims again.

1917

TR. DIANA DER HOVANESSIAN AND MARZBED MARGOSSIAN

≈ The Country of Dust

Small. Miniaturized, yet you insist
on shaking your canyons and cliffs with huge
spasms as if you were the center of the earth
and the magnet that draws out and fills every sea.

So small. A corner. Not even a corner.
Scattered points, dispersed and dispersing lines
of fallen walls, walls you imagine the palace
you once raised from this mantle of dust.

How can you dream of old architecture
today when every edifice caves in
to make way for new shapes?

Any shock can erase you forever and no eye
will even blink. Yours alone the concern. But hope
rises like the sun. Accumulate. Dust consolidates into stone.

1933

TR. DIANA DER HOVANESSIAN AND MARZBED MARGOSSIAN

World War I

(1914-1918)

World War I, sometimes known as "the Great War," followed forty years of relative peace on the European continent. From the end of the Franco-Prussian War, the great powers in Europe (France, Germany, Russia, England, and Austria-Hungary) did not confront each other directly; rather, they formed protective alliances and argued over colonial possessions and the proper division of the declining Ottoman Empire. There were frictions: the Austrians and the Russians were constantly in conflict, the French and the Germans were beset by mutual distrust, and although France was Britain's historical enemy, the British were more alarmed by the growth of the German navy. World War I began, however, over the status of Serbia: when Archduke Franz Ferdinand was assassinated in Sarajevo in the summer of 1914, Austria declared war on the Serbians, and Russia came to the aid of its Slavic client state. The Germans declared war on the Russians and set across Belgium to attack the French, who were allied with Russia. By ignoring Belgian neutrality, the Germans antagonized the English. Japan and the Ottoman Empire were soon involved. Italy joined England and France in 1915, and by 1917, Bulgaria, Romania, Greece, Portugal, and the United States had entered the war.

War technology had advanced; the perceived military glories of the cavalry charge and the infantry assault were rendered archaic by the invention of magazine rifles and machine guns. Soldiers endured both the violence and the tedium of trench warfare; Paul Fussell has claimed that one could have walked from the North Sea to the Swiss border underground, through a vast network of such trenches, and the troops confined to them were often hungry, and plagued as well by pestilence, dysentery, dawn attacks, and bombardments. The carnage was unprecedented: at Verdun, 315,000 French and 280,000 German soldiers died. At the Somme, the British and the Germans together suffered more than 800,000 dead. In the face of such destruction and the deadly parity in the trenches, even newer technologies were advanced: tanks, poison gas, and aerial warfare and bombing were all developed during World War I.

This was a new kind of conflict, one in which whole nations were mobilized in the war effort, and whole nations starved by blockades. Finally, after close to four years of bloodshed, the prospect of revolutionary collapse at home and the inevitability of defeat on the field led the German leaders to sue for peace. Armistice was declared in November 1918. The war claimed more than ten million lives. It also led to the destruction of the German, Austro-Hungarian, and Russian empires.

Of the soldier poets of the Great War, more than fifty were British. Poets on both sides of the conflict turned away from patriotic, romantic views of war toward a cynical, clear-eyed, and elegiac portrayal of war's actual conditions.

EDWARD THOMAS (1878–1917)

Welsh writer Thomas saw publication of his first book when he was nineteen, but did not write poetry until he was thirty-six, at the encouragement of Robert Frost. When World War I broke out, Thomas was initially reluctant to join the army, but he enlisted in 1915 and was commissioned the following year. He was killed on Easter Sunday 1917. Thomas's collected poems were not published until 1920. In "The Owl," written in 1915, the war intrudes upon the peaceful reverie of a traveler.

≈ The Owl

Downhill I came, hungry, and yet not starved;
Cold, yet had heat within me that was proof
Against the North wind; tired, yet so that rest
Had seemed the sweetest thing under a roof.

Then at the inn I had food, fire, and rest,
Knowing how hungry, cold, and tired was I.
All of the night was quite barred out except
An owl's cry, a most melancholy cry.

Shaken out long and clear upon the hill,
No merry note, nor cause of merriment,
But one telling me plain what I escaped
And others could not, that night, as in I went.

And salted was my food, and my repose,
Salted and sobered, too, by the bird's voice
Speaking for all who lay under the stars,
Soldiers and poor, unable to rejoice.

GUILLAUME APOLLINAIRE   (1880–1918)

Brought up in the south of France, son of a Polish noblewoman and an Italian officer, Apollinaire came to Paris at the turn of the century and quickly established himself as a leading avant-garde poet and defender of progressive art. He is credited with having coined the term "surrealism" (later the name of a complex movement whose practitioners advocated synthesizing the unconscious and conscious minds). Having become a French citizen in order to enlist for service in World War I, he was seriously wounded in March 1916. In the poem "Shadow," he addresses his dead comrades; "The Little Car" evokes his sudden return to Paris on the eve of war. Apollinaire died in the influenza epidemic of 1918.

≈ Shadow

Here you are near me once more
Memories of my comrades in battle
Olive of time
Memories composing now a single memory
As a hundred furs make only one coat
As those thousands of wounds make only one newspaper article
Impalpable dark appearance you have assumed
The changing form of my shadow
An Indian hiding in wait throughout eternity
Shadow you creep near me
But you no longer hear me
You will no longer know the divine poems I sing
But I hear you I see you still
Destinies
Multiple shadow may the sun watch over you

You who love me so much you will never leave me
You who dance in the sun without stirring the dust
Shadow solar ink
Handwriting of my light
Caisson of regrets
A god humbling himself

TR. ANNE GREET

≈ Post Card

(Sent to André Rouveyre, 20 August 1915)

I write to you beneath this tent
While summer day becomes a shade
And startling magnificent
Flowers of the cannonade
Stud the pale blue firmament
And before existing fade

TR. OLIVER BERNARD

≈ The Little Car

On the 31st day of August in the year 1914
I left Deauville shortly before midnight
in Rouveyre's little car

Including his chauffeur there were three of us

We said goodbye to a whole epoch
Furious giants were looming over Europe
The eagles were leaving their eyries expecting the sun
Voracious fishes were swimming up from the abysses
Nations were rushing together to know each other through and
     through
The dead were trembling with fear in their dark dwellings

The dogs were barking in the direction of the frontiers
As I went I carried within me all the armies that were fighting

I felt them rising within me and spreading out over the regions
    through which their columns wound
With the forests the happy villages of Belgium
Francorchamps and Eau Rouge and the *pouhons*
A region through which invasions are always taking place
And the railway arteries along which those who were going away to
    die
Saluted one more time a life full of colours
The deep oceans where monsters were stirring
In old carcasses of wrecks
The unimaginable heights where men fight
Higher than the eagle soars
Man fights there against man
And falls suddenly like a shooting star
I felt within me new beings full of dexterity
Building a new universe and running it as well
A merchant of unheard-of opulence and of prodigious stature
Was setting out an extraordinary display of stock
And gigantic shepherds were driving forward
Great dumb flocks grazing on words as they went
And at them barked all the dogs along the road

I shall never forget this journey by night during which none of us said a word

O   h   r
dark   O   u
departure   tender   O   which d   r
when our 3   night of   vil towards   e   i
headlights failed before the war lages
B L A C K S M I T H S   R E C A L L E D   *MORNING*

BETWEEN MIDNIGHT AND ONE IN T H E
      n   V
  e   a   r   e   r   s   a
L i s i e u x   or else   i l l e s the
  the very   g o l d
    blue   en

and 3 times we had to stop to change a burst tyre

And when having passed through Fontainebleau
During the afternoon
We got to Paris
At the moment at which the mobilization posters were going up
We understood my comrade and I

That the little car had brought us into a
New age
And that although we were both already fully grown men
We had nevertheless just been born

TR. OLIVER BERNARD

≈ **Stanzas Against Forgetting**

You asked neither for glory nor tears
Nor an organ nor prayers for the dying
Eleven years now already eleven years
All you did was simply take up arms
Death does not blind the eyes of partisans

On the walls of our towns your faces
Blackbearded, wild and menacing
Were spattered like bloodstains to frighten passersby
And moreover your names were foreign and difficult to pronounce

No one seemed to see you, you who were French by choice
People averted their eyes from you all day
But during blackout, wandering hands
Wrote DIED FOR FRANCE under your photographs
And thanks to that the mornings were less bleak

By the end of February when your last hour arrived
Everything was the uniform color of frost
It was then that one of you calmly said
Bless you all, bless you all who will survive
I die without hatred for the German people

Adieu to sorrow and to pleasure Adieu to the roses
Adieu to life and to light and to the wind
Get married, be happy and think of me often
You who will remain in the beauty of things
When it's all over in Erivan

A full winter sun lights the hills
How beautiful nature is, how broken my heart

But justice will soon follow in our triumphant steps
My beloved, o my darling, my orphaned love
I implore you to live and bear a child

They numbered twenty-three when the guns flowered
Twenty-three who gave their hearts before their time
Twenty-three foreigners who were our brothers
Twenty-three who loved life unto death
Twenty-three who called out *La France* as they fell

TR. CAROLYN FORCHÉ

GOTTFRIED BENN (1886–1956)

Already a well-known German expressionist poet when war broke out in August 1914, Benn was called to the front, where he received the Iron Cross. A committed anti-socialist, he saluted the Nazi takeover in 1933 and served as an active apologist for the new regime until 1934, when he withdrew his support and went into the army as a way of avoiding persecution. In spite of his overt politics, the Nazis distrusted his "decadent" modernism. Forbidden to write or publish in 1943, he continued to do so. The poems of this time include "Monologue." After the war Benn was recognized as the most important poet in German since Bertolt Brecht.

≈ Monologue

Their colons fed with mucus, brains with lies
these chosen races, coxcombs of a clown,
in pranks, astrology and flight of birds
construing their own ordure! Slaves—
from icy and from burning territories,
gross with vermin more and more slaves come,
hungry and whiplash-driven hordes of them:
Then all that's personal, the downy cheek,
with scruf and scab, swells to a prophet's beard!

Ah, Alexander and Olympia's offspring,
that least of all! They wink whole Hellesponts,
and skim all Asia! Puffed up, pustules
with vanguard, covert squadrons and with minions
that none may prick them! Minions; the best seats
for wrestling and in court! Let no man prick them!
Minions, joyriders, bandages, broad streamers—
broad streamers fluttering from dream and world:
the clubfoot sees the stadiums destroyed,
skunks trample under foot the lupin fields

because the scent makes them suspect their own:
Nothing but excrement! The obese
course after the gazelle,
the windswift one, the lovely animal!
Inverse proportion enters everything:
The puddle plumbs the source, the worm the ell,
toad squirts his liquid in the violet's mouth,
and—hallelujah!—whets his pot on stones:
The reptile horde as history's monument!
The Ptolemaic line as tic-tac language,
the rat arrives as balm against the plague.
Most foul sings murder. Gossips wheedle
obscenity from psalms.

And this earth whispers discourse with the moon,
then round its hips it hangs a Mayday feast
then lets the rose pass, then stews the corn,
forbids Vesuvius erupt, won't let the cloud
become a caustic that would prick and shrivel
the beasts' base form whose fraud contrived this state—
oh, all the play on earth of fruit and rose
is given up to evil's usury,
brain-fungus, and the gorge's speckling lies
of the above-named sort, proportion inverse!

To die means leaving all these things unsolved,
the images unsure, and hungry dreams
abandoned in the rifts between the worlds—
but action means: to serve vulgarity,

aid and abet iniquity, means loneliness
and dropping furtively the great solution
that visions are and the desire of dreams,
for gain, for gold, promotion, posthumous fame,
while giddily like a moth, indifferent
as a petard the end is near and bodes
a meaning that is different—

A sound, a curve, a chink of blue almost,
reverberated through the park one night
as I stood there—: a song,
only an outline, casual, three notes heard,
and occupied all space and made the night
so full, the garden full of apparitions,
created so the world and bedded me
prostrate within the stream of things, the sad
sublime infirmity of being's birth—:
a sound, only a curve—: but being's birth—
only a curve, proportion it restored
and comprehended all things, act and dreaming . . .

A garland intertwined of scarlet brains
whose flowers grown from scattered fever-seed
shut to each other, keeping separate:
'the coloration form' and 'edges frayed,
the last thread snapping' and 'a hard cold contour,'
these spicy pickles of the protoplasm,
Here transformation starts: the beasts' base form
shall so decay the very word corruption
will smell for it too much of heaven—the vultures
are gathering now and famished hawks are poised!

TR. CHRISTOPHER MIDDLETON

≈ Fragments

Fragments,
Refuse of the soul,
Coagulations of blood of the twentieth century:

Scars—interrupted cycle of early creation,
The historic religions of five centuries pulverized.
Science: cracks in the Parthenon,
Planck with his quantum theory merging
In the new confusion with Kepler and Kierkegaard—

Yet there were evenings that went in the colors
Of the Father of all, dissolute, far-gathering,
Inviolate in their silence
Of coursing blue,
Color of the introvert:
Then one relaxed
With the hands caught up round the knee
Peasant-wise, simple,
And resigned to the quiet drink
And the sound of the servants' concertina—

And others
Provoked by inner scrolls of paper,
Vaulted pressures,
Constrictions in the building of style
Or pursuits of love.

Crises of expression and bouts of eroticism,
That is the man of today,
His inwardness a vacuum;
The survival of personality
Is preserved by the clothing
Which, where material is good, may last ten years.

The rest fragments,
Half tones,
Snatches of melody from neighbors' houses,
Negro spirituals
Or Ave Marias.

TR. VERNON WATKINS

SIEGFRIED SASSOON (1886–1967)

Sassoon, born in London, enlisted in 1914 and served in France as a lieutenant in the infantry. Originally supportive of the war, he became increasingly disenchanted, and when he was wounded in 1917, he attempted to have himself court-martialed. He was deemed "temporarily insane" and thus denied his day in court. In spite of this experience, Sassoon returned to the front and was wounded a second time. He published two books of poetry during the war and later toured the United States, giving readings and advocating pacifism.

≈ A Working Party

Three hours ago he blundered up the trench,
Sliding and poising, groping with his boots;
Sometimes he tripped and lurched against the walls
With hands that pawed the sodden bags of chalk.
He couldn't see the man who walked in front;
Only he heard the drum and rattle of feet
Stepping along barred trench boards, often splashing
Wretchedly where the sludge was ankle-deep.

Voices would grunt 'Keep to your right—make way!'
When squeezing past some men from the front-line:
White faces peered, puffing a point of red;
Candles and braziers glinted through the chinks
And curtain-flaps of dug-outs; then the gloom
Swallowed his sense of sight; he stooped and swore
Because a sagging wire had caught his neck.

A flare went up; the shining whiteness spread
And flickered upward, showing nimble rats
And mounds of glimmering sand-bags, bleached with rain;
Then the slow silver moment died in dark.
The wind came posting by with chilly gusts
And buffeting at corners, piping thin.

And dreary through the crannies; rifle-shots
Would split and crack and sing along the night,
And shells came calmly through the drizzling air
To burst with hollow bang below the hill.

Three hours ago he stumbled up the trench;
Now he will never walk that road again:
He must be carried back, a jolting lump
Beyond all need of tenderness and care.

He was a young man with a meagre wife
And two small children in a Midland town;
He showed their photographs to all his mates,
And they considered him a decent chap
Who did his work and hadn't much to say,
And always laughed at other people's jokes
Because he hadn't any of his own.

That night when he was busy at his job
Of piling bags along the parapet,
He thought how slow time went, stamping his feet
And blowing on his fingers, pinched with cold.
He thought of getting back by half-past twelve,
And tot of rum to send him warm to sleep
In draughty dug-out frowsty with the fumes
Of coke, and full of snoring weary men.

He pushed another bag along the top,
Craning his body outward; then a flare
Gave one white glimpse of No Man's Land and wire;
And as he dropped his head the instant split
His startled life with lead, and all went out

≈ The Death-Bed

He drowsed and was aware of silence heaped
Round him, unshaken as the steadfast walls;
Aqueous like floating rays of amber light,

Soaring and quivering in the wings of sleep.
Silence and safety; and his mortal shore
Lipped by the inward, moonless waves of death.

Someone was holding water to his mouth.
He swallowed, unresisting; moaned and dropped
Through crimson gloom to darkness; and forgot
The opiate throb and ache that was his wound.
    Water—calm, sliding green above the weir.
    Water—a sky-lit alley for his boat,
    Bird-voiced, and bordered with reflected flowers
    And shaken hues of summer; drifting down,
    He dipped contented oars, and sighed, and slept.

Night, with a gust of wind, was in the ward,
Blowing the curtain to a glimmering curve.
Night. He was blind; he could not see the stars
Glinting among the wraiths of wandering cloud;
Queer blots of colour, purple, scarlet, green,
Flickered and faded in his drowning eyes.

Rain—he could hear it rustling through the dark;
Fragrance and passionless music woven as one;
Warm rain on drooping roses; pattering showers
That soak the woods; not the harsh rain that sweeps
Behind the thunder, but a trickling peace,
Gently and slowly washing life away.

He stirred, shifting his body; then the pain
Leapt like a prowling beast, and gripped and tore
His groping dreams with grinding claws and fangs.
    But someone was beside him; soon he lay
    Shuddering because that evil thing had passed.
    And death, who'd stepped toward him, paused and stared.

Light many lamps and gather round his bed.
Lend him your eyes, warm blood, and will to live.
Speak to him; rouse him; you may save him yet.
He's young; he hated War; how should he die
When cruel old campaigners win safe through?

But death replied: 'I choose him.' So he went,
And there was silence in the summer night;
Silence and safety; and the veils of sleep.
Then, far away, the thudding of the guns.

≈ **Repression of War Experience**

Now light the candles; one; two; there's a moth;
What silly beggars they are to blunder in
And scorch their wings with glory, liquid flame—
No, no, not that,—it's bad to think of war,
When thoughts you've gagged all day come back to scare you;
And it's been proved that soldiers don't go mad
Unless they lose control of ugly thoughts
That drive them out to jabber among the trees.

Now light your pipe; look, what a steady hand,
Draw a deep breath; stop thinking, count fifteen,
And you're as right as rain . . .
                              Why won't it rain? . . .
I wish there'd be a thunder-storm to-night,
With bucketsful of water to sluice the dark,
And make the roses hang their dripping heads.
Books; what a jolly company they are,
Standing so quiet and patient on their shelves,
Dressed in dim brown, and black, and white, and green,
And every kind of colour. Which will you read?
Come on; O *do* read something; they're so wise.
I tell you all the wisdom of the world
Is waiting for you on those shelves; and yet
You sit and gnaw your nails, and let your pipe out,
And listen to the silence: on the ceiling
There's one big, dizzy moth that bumps and flutters;
And in the breathless air outside the house
The garden waits for something that delays.
There must be crowds of ghosts among the trees,—
Not people killed in battle,—they're in France,—
But horrible shapes in shrouds—old men who died
Slow, natural deaths,—old men with ugly souls,
Who wore their bodies out with nasty sins.

You're quiet and peaceful, summering safe at home;
You'd never think there was a bloody war on! . . .
O yes, you would . . . why, you can hear the guns.
Hark! Thud, thud, thud,—quite soft . . . they never cease—
Those whispering guns—O Christ, I want to go out
And screech at them to stop—I'm going crazy;
I'm going stark, staring mad because of the guns.

GEORG TRAKL (1887–1914)

Recognized as a leading avant-garde poet before the war, Trakl received (along with Rainer Maria Rilke) a large anonymous stipend from the philosopher Ludwig Wittgenstein. He enlisted as a dispensing chemist in the Austrian army in 1914, and after the Austrian defeat at Grodek in Galicia, a region of eastern Europe, he was left to care for ninety wounded men. Some committed suicide in his presence. After attempting suicide himself, Trakl was placed under observation in a psychiatric ward, where he died from a self-administered overdose of cocaine. "In the East" and "Grodek" (his last poem) were written while Trakl was at the front in Galicia.

≈ A Romance to Night

Under a tent of stars a lonely man
Walks through the silence of midnight.
A boy wakes, bewildered by his dreams,
His gray face wasting away into the moon.

At a barred window
A half-witted woman with loose hair is weeping.
Lovers float by on the pond
Continuing their sweet journey.

The murderer laughs until he grows pale in the wine,
Horror of death consumes the afflicted.
Naked and wounded, a nun prays
Before the Savior's agony on the cross.

A mother sings softly in her sleep.
Content, her child
Gazes into the night.
Laughter fades in from the whorehouse.

Below, in the alley next to the tavern, by lamplight,
The dead paint silence on the walls
With their white hands.
The one sleeping continues to whisper.

TR. DANIEL SIMKO

≈ Downfall

Above the white pond
Wild birds have flown away.
In the evening an icy wind blows from our stars.

Above our graves
Night leans down with its shattered forehead.
Under the oaks, we rock in a silver skiff.

The town's white walls keep ringing.
Beneath the arches of thorns,
O my brother, we are the blind hands climbing toward midnight.

TR. DANIEL SIMKO

≈ In the East

The dark wrath of people
Is the wild organ music of a winter storm,
A purple wave of battle,
Leafless stars.

With broken eyebrows and silver arms,
The night beckons to dying soldiers.
Ghosts of those killed moan
In the shade of the autumn ash tree.

A thorny wilderness surrounds the city.
From bloody doorsteps the moon
Hunts terrified women.
Wild wolves have broken through the gates.

TR. DANIEL SIMKO

≈ Grodek

In the evening the autumn woods ring
With deadly weapons, the sun rolls somberly
Over the golden plains and blue lakes,
And night embraces
The dying warriors, the wild lament
Of their broken mouths.
Red clouds gather silently over the meadow,
Where an angry God, which is spilled blood itself, lives. A cold moon.
All roads end in black decay.
Under the golden branches of night and stars,
A sister's shadow staggers through the silent grove
To greet the ghosts of heroes, the bloodied heads,
And the dark flutes of autumn keep playing softly in the reeds.
O prouder grief! You, brass altars,
Today the hot flame of the spirit is fed by a more violent pain—
The grandsons still unborn.

TR. DANIEL SIMKO

WILFRED OWEN (1893–1918)

Owen was wounded in France in the summer of 1917, after spending
seven months at the front. Sent back to England, he was befriended
and encouraged by Siegfried Sassoon. In spite of efforts to keep him in
England, Owen was returned to military service in France, where he
was conspicuous for his bravery. He was killed on November 4, 1918,
exactly one week before the Armistice. He is considered the foremost
antiwar poet of World War I.

≈ Dulce et Decorum Est

Bent double, like old beggars under sacks,
Knock-kneed, coughing like hags, we cursed through sludge,
Till on the haunting flares we turned our backs
And towards our distant rest began to trudge.
Men marched asleep. Many had lost their boots
But limped on, blood-shod. All went lame; all blind;
Drunk with fatigue; deaf even to the hoots
Of tired, outstripped Five-Nines that dropped behind.

Gas! Gas! Quick, boys!—An ecstasy of fumbling,
Fitting the clumsy helmets just in time;
But someone still was yelling out and stumbling,
And flound'ring like a man in fire or lime . . .
Dim, through the misty panes and thick green light,
As under a green sea, I saw him drowning.

In all my dreams, before my helpless sight,
He plunges at me, guttering, choking, drowning.

If in some smothering dreams you too could pace
Behind the wagon that we flung him in,
And watch the white eyes writhing in his face,
His hanging face, like a devil's sick of sin;
If you could hear, at every jolt, the blood
Come gargling from the froth-corrupted lungs,
Obscene as cancer, bitter as the cud
Of vile, incurable sores on innocent tongues,—
My friend, you would not tell with such high zest
To children ardent for some desperate glory,
The old Lie: Dulce et decorum est
Pro patria mori.

October 1917

≈ Anthem for Doomed Youth

What passing-bells for these who die as cattle?
—Only the monstrous anger of the guns.

Only the stuttering rifles' rapid rattle
Can patter out their hasty orisons.
No mockeries now for them; no prayers nor bells;
Nor any voice of mourning save the choirs,—
The shrill, demented choirs of wailing shells;
And bugles calling for them from sad shires.

What candles may be held to speed them all?
Not in the hands of boys but in their eyes
Shall shine the holy glimmers of goodbyes.
The pallor of girls' brows shall be their pall;
Their flowers the tenderness of patient minds,
And each slow dusk a drawing-down of blinds.

September–October 1917

≈ Exposure

Our brains ache, in the merciless iced east winds that knive us . . .
Wearied we keep awake because the night is silent . . .
Low, drooping flares confuse our memory of the salient . . .
Worried by silence, sentries whisper, curious, nervous,
        But nothing happens.

Watching, we hear the mad gusts tugging on the wire,
Like twitching agonies of men among its brambles.
Northward, incessantly, the flickering gunnery rumbles,
Far off, like a dull rumour of some other war.
        What are we doing here?

The poignant misery of dawn begins to grow . . .
We only know war lasts, rain soaks, and clouds sag stormy.
Dawn massing in the east her melancholy army
Attacks once more in ranks on shivering ranks of grey,
        But nothing happens.

Sudden successive flights of bullets streak the silence.
Less deathly than the air that shudders black with snow,
With sidelong flowing flakes that flock, pause, and renew;

We watch them wandering up and down the wind's nonchalance,
    But nothing happens.

Pale flakes with fingering stealth come feeling for our faces—
We cringe in holes, back on forgotten dreams, and stare, snow-dozed,
Littered with blossoms trickling where the blackbird fusses,
    —Is it that we are dying?

Slowly our ghosts drag home; glimpsing the sunk fires, glozed
With crusted dark-red jewels; crickets jingle there;
For hours the innocent mice rejoice: the house is theirs;
Shutters and doors, all closed: on us the doors are closed,—
    We turn back to our dying.

Since we believe not otherwise can kind fires burn;
Nor even suns smile true on child, or field, or fruit.
For God's invincible spring our love is made afraid;
Therefore, not loath, we lie out here; therefore were born,
    For love of Good seems dying.

Tonight, this frost will fasten on this mud and us,
Shrivelling many hands, puckering foreheads crisp.
The burying-party, picks and shovels in shaking grasp,
Pause over half-known faces. All their eyes are ice,
    But nothing happens.

December 1917; September 1918

E.E. CUMMINGS (1894–1962)

Cummings, born in Cambridge, Massachusetts, was educated at Harvard. He volunteered for the Ambulance Corps in World War I and served in France. Cummings's pacifist leanings led to his imprisonment in a French detention center on suspicion that he was a spy. He was released, and became known as one of the leading and most accessible American modernists, a poet whose work was strongly influenced by cubist painting and imagist verse, as well as experimentation with typography.

≈ (i sing of Olaf glad and big)

i sing of Olaf glad and big
whose warmest heart recoiled at war:
a conscientious object-or
his wellbeloved colonel (trig
westpointer most succinctly bred)
took erring Olaf soon in hand;
but—though an host of overjoyed
noncoms (first knocking on the head
him)do through icy waters roll
that helplessness which others stroke
with brushes recently employed
anent this muddy toiletbowl,
while kindred intellects evoke
allegiance per blunt instruments—
Olaf(being to all intents
a corpse and wanting any rag
upon what God unto him gave)
responds, without getting annoyed
"I will not kiss your f.ing flag"

straightway the silver bird looked grave
(departing hurriedly to shave)

but—though all kinds of officers
(a yearning nation's blueeyed pride)
their passive prey did kick and curse
until for wear their clarion
voices and boots were much the worse,
and egged the firstclassprivates on
his rectum wickedly to tease
by means of skilfully applied
bayonets roasted hot with heat—
Olaf(upon what were once knees)
does almost ceaselessly repeat
"there is some s. I will not eat"

our president, being of which
assertions duly notified

threw the yellowsonofabitch
into a dungeon, where he died

Christ(of His mercy infinite)
i pray to see; and Olaf, too

preponderatingly because
unless statistics lie he was
more brave then me:more blond than you.

≈ am was.   are leaves few this.   is these a or

am was.   are leaves few this.   is these a or
scratchily over which of earth dragged once
-ful leaf. & were who skies clutch an of poor
how colding hereless. air theres what immense
live without every dancing. singless on-
ly a child's eyes float silently down
more than two those that and that noing our
gone snow gone
                    yours mine
                        . We're
alive and shall be: cities may overflow (am
was) assassinating whole grassblades, five
ideas can swallow a man;three words im
-prison a woman for all her now: but we've
such freedom such intense digestion so
much greenness only dying makes us grow

ROBERT GRAVES (1895–1985)

Graves graduated from the Charterhouse School in London just before
World War I, and signed up as an officer in the Royal Welsh Fusiliers.
His conclusion that the war was a continuation of the indifferent brutal-
ity of English private education was recorded in his beautiful memoir
of those years, *Goodbye to All That*. After the Armistice, Graves attended
Oxford University, taught at the University in Cairo, and finally settled

in Majorca, where he wrote poetry, novels, essays, travel books, and plays, and completed his study of poetic myth, *The White Goddess.*

≈ Recalling War

Entrance and exit wounds are silvered clean,
The track aches only when the rain reminds.
The one-legged man forgets his leg of wood,
The one-armed man his jointed wooden arm.
The blinded man sees with his ears and hands
As much or more than once with both his eyes.
Their war was fought these twenty years ago
And now assumes the nature-look of time,
As when the morning traveller turns and views
His wild night-stumbling carved into a hill.

What, then, was war? No mere discord of flags
But an infection of the common sky
That sagged ominously upon the earth
Even when the season was the airiest May.
Down pressed the sky, and we, oppressed, thrust out
Boastful tongue, clenched fist and valiant yard.
Natural infirmities were out of mode,
For Death was young again: patron alone
Of healthy dying, premature fate-spasm.

Fear made fine bed-fellows. Sick with delight
At life's discovered transitoriness,
Our youth became all-flesh and waived the mind.
Never was such antiqueness of romance,
Such tasty honey oozing from the heart.
And old importances came swimming back—
Wine, meat, log-fires, a roof over the head,
A weapon at the thigh, surgeons at call.
Even there was a use again for God—
A word of rage in lack of meat, wine, fire,
In ache of wounds beyond all surgeoning.

War was return of earth to ugly earth,
War was foundering of sublimities,

Extinction of each happy art and faith
By which the world has still kept head in air,
Protesting logic or protesting love,
Until the unendurable moment struck—
The inward scream, the duty to run mad.

And we recall the merry ways of guns—
Nibbling the walls of factory and church
Like a child, piecrust; felling groves of trees
Like a child, dandelions with a switch.
Machine-guns rattle toy-like from a hill,
Down in a row the brave tin-soldiers fall:
A sight to be recalled in elder days
When learnedly the future we devote
To yet more boastful visions of despair.

c. 1938

EUGENIO MONTALE (1896–1981)

Montale's formative experience came as an officer in the Italian infantry
during World War I. Marked by the cultural pessimism that pervaded
postwar culture, Montale was an early opponent of Fascism. During
World War II, when he was a director of a library in Florence, he joined
the "hermetic" movement of poets; their highly subjective, difficult
verse has been described by Joseph Brodsky as "an act of cultural
self-defense—linguistic self-defense, in the case of poetry—against
Fascism." Montale was awarded the Nobel Prize for Literature in 1975.

≈ The Storm

> *Les princes n'ont point d'yeux pour voir ces grand's merveilles,*
> *Leurs mains ne servent plus qu'à nous persécuter . . .*
> —Agrippa d'Aubigné: *À Dieu*

The storm splattering the tough magnolia
leaves, with the long rolling March thunder
and hail,

(tinklings of crystal in your nocturnal
nest startle you, out of gold gone
from the mahoganies, on the edging
of bound books, a grain of sugar
still burns in the shell
of your eyelids)

the lightning blanching
wall and trees, freezing them in that
forever of an instant—marble manna
and destruction—which you carry sculpted
inside you for your damnation, and that binds you
to me, strange sister, more than love—
then the hard crack, the castanets, the shaking
of tambourines over the thieving ditch,
the stamp of the fandango, and overhead,
some gesture, groping . . .
As when you turned around and, with your hand, the cloud of hair
clearing from your forehead,

you waved to me—and stepped into darkness.

TR. WILLIAM ARROWSMITH

≈ The Fan

Ut pictura . . . The disconcerting lips,
the glances, signals, the days now gone—
I try to fix them as through a telescopic lens
inverted, mute, unchanging, but more
alive. It was a tournament
of men and armor routed in that smoke
battered by the east wind, and now dawn, a tremor,
crimsons the smoke, shatters the haze.
The mother-of-pearl light, the dizzily plunging
ravine, swallow their victims still,
but all at once the plumes upon your cheek begin to whiten,
perhaps the day is saved! Oh hammerblows

of your revelation, raw lightnings, thunderings
on the hordes! (Is he who knows you doomed to die?)

TR. WILLIAM ARROWSMITH

≈ Personae Separatae

Like the golden scale that emerges
from the somber background, then melts away
in the corridor of skeletal
carob trees, are even we "separated persons"
in the eyes of others? Speech is a little thing;
in these raw and clouded new moons, space
is little too; what's missing,
what wrenches the heart and makes me linger here
among the trees, waiting for you, is a lost
sense, or fire, if you prefer, to print the ground
with parallel figures, reconciled shadows,
shafts of sunlight framing the fresh-cut trunks
in the clearings, and fill the hollow stumps
where the ants nest. The human forest
is too mutilated and torn, that everlasting
voice too deaf, too fretful
the gash melting over the snowy
peaks of Lunigiana. Your form
passed this way, paused by the ditch
among the eel-pots piled on the ground, then dissolved
like a sigh, all around—no gurgling horror
was in it, in you light still found
light, today no longer, now that at day-
break, it's already almost night.

TR. WILLIAM ARROWSMITH

≈ Day and Night

Even a feather in flight can sketch
your form, or the sunbeam playing hide-and-seek
among the furniture, rebounding from the roofs,
from a child's mirror. Around the walls

trailing wisps of steam lengthen the poplars'
spires, while the knife-grinder's parrot on his trestle
ruffles his feathers. Then the hot, stifling night
over the little square, and the footsteps, and always this bitter
exhaustion of sinking only to rise the same,
from centuries, from seconds; of nightmares that can't
recover the light of your eyes in the incandescent
cave—and still the same proclamations and the long wail
of grief on the veranda
if suddenly the shot rings out, your throat
reddens, your wings shatter, O parlous
harbinger of dawn,
and cloisters and clinics waken
to a rending blare of trumpets . . .

TR. WILLIAM ARROWSMITH

ANDRÉ BRETON (1896–1966)

Breton served in the medical corps in World War I, even though he deplored the nationalism that accompanied that conflict. He fought during the 1930s against the totalitarians of the right and protested injustices in the Soviet Union. One of the founders of surrealism, Breton was fascinated by the junction where dream and reality meet. He influenced poets (including Philippe Souppault) and painters (Salvador Dalí and Max Ernst). His own work was a fusion of the lyricism of poetry and prose. Breton, called a "permanent exile" by Jean-Paul Sartre, was forced to flee France when the Germans invaded. He lived in the United States from 1941 to 1946, but in 1947 returned to France, where he continued to espouse surrealism.

≈ **More than Suspect**

The oaks are stricken by a serious illness
They dry up after having let go
Into the glow of a sump at sunset
A whole throng of generals' heads

TR. MARY ANN CAWS AND JEAN-PIERRE CAUVIN

≈ War

I watch the Beast as it licks itself
The better to blend into all of its surroundings
Its eyes the color of heavy seas
Unexpectedly are the pond drawing unto itself the dirty linen the
    garbage
The one that always stops man
The pond with its little Place de l'Opéra in its belly
Because phosphorescence is the key to the eyes of the Beast
That licks itself
And its tongue
Darting one never knows in advance in what direction
Is a plexus of furnaces
From underneath I gaze at its plate
Made of lamps in bags
And under the royal blue vault
Of ungilded arches arrayed in perspective one within the other
While the breath runs rampant being made of the infinite
        generalization of one of those bare-chested wretches who appear
        in the public square swallowing kerosene torches in an acrid
        shower of coins
The Beast's pustules are resplendent owing to the immolations of
        young men on which the Number gorges
Its flanks protected by the shimmering scales that armies are
Convex scales each one of which turns perfectly on its pivot
Although they depend on each other no less than roosters that jeer at
        each other at dawn from dungheap to dungheap
The default of consciousness is at hand yet some persistently maintain
        that the day will dawn
The door I meant the Beast licks itself under the wing
And some thieves can be seen convulsed is it with laughter in the back
        of a tavern
The mirage alleged to have been goodness is rationalized
It's a lode of quicksilver
Such as could be lapped up in one gulp
I thought the Beast was turning toward me I saw the filth of the
        lightning once again
How white it is in its membranes in the nimbleness of its birch groves
        where a lookout is being posted

In the riggings of its ships at whose prow a woman is plunging whom
    the exertions of lovemaking have adorned with a green mask
False alarm the Beast holds its claws in an erectile crown around the
    breasts
I try not to falter too much when it wags its tail
Which is at the same time the beveled coach and the whiplash
In the suffocating smell of the tiger-beetle
From its litter fouled with black blood and gold it sharpens one of its
    horns moonward on the enthusiastic tree of wrongs
By coiling itself with fearsome lasciviousness
Flattered
The Beast licks its sex I've said nothing

TR. MARY ANN CAWS AND JEAN-PIERRE CAUVIN

Revolution and Repression in the Soviet Union

(1917–1991)

Czarist Russia suffered greatly during World War I: the failure of the Russian army, the corruption of the bureaucracy, and the malevolent influence of the holy man and politician Rasputin on the Czarina all led to a crisis of confidence in the old system, which had been deteriorating since Russia's terrible defeat in 1905 at the hands of the Japanese. The abdication of the Czar in the early months of 1917 led to a series of rather weak provisional governments of an increasingly leftist tendency. The Bolshevik wing of the Social Democrats, led by Vladimir I. Lenin and Leon Trotsky, came to power in the autumn of that year and instituted the first Communist government of the newly named Soviet Union.

The Communists faced a difficult task: asserting military control over the vast territory of the old Czarist empire (sections of which had become independent with the German defeat in 1918), quelling insurrections from opposing groups (few of whom were Czarists), and withstanding foreign expeditionary forces landing in the Soviet Union, mainly from Japan, Great Britain, France, and the United States, ostensibly to protect national interests but also, perhaps more important, to defeat Communism in its first victorious manifestation. The civil war lasted three years and was brutal; it established the ability of the Communists to maintain power.

After consolidating their victory in 1920, the Communists had to decide on goals and policies: should they aim for creation of a world revolution, or should they modernize the Soviet Union? The ensuing debate formed the basis of the power struggle between Trotsky and Stalin after Lenin's death in 1924. Joseph Stalin, an efficient and cold-blooded administrator, was able to use the party apparatus (and its ancillaries, such as the political police) to win control.

Stalin's drive to propel the Soviet Union into the twentieth century was brutal. It began in 1928 with the collectivization of all farms, entailing the forced removal and frequent execution of the landowning peasantry; millions died and many millions more suffered the damaging effects of this decisive move toward planned economics of scale. The industrialization of the Soviet Union was accelerated as rigid controls were imposed on all aspects of life. The coercive powers of the state—from the foreman on the factory floor to the secret police and the courts—were summoned to implement Stalin's plans, including the forced assimilation of ethnic minorities. Art was subject to extreme strictures and censorship; the experimentation that marked the first years of the revolution gave way to the aridities of "socialist realism."

The decade of the 1930s was particularly grim. Between 1934 and 1938, rapid and painful industrialization was accompanied by the "Great Purges," during which elements within the Communist Party attempted to silence all possible dissent: arrest, torture, execution, and the "gulag" (a system of prisons and labor camps) were used to ensure a strict adherence to Party discipline. After the Nazi invasion of 1941, Stalinist terror was succeeded by the terrors of a world war. It took the Soviets two years to expel the Germans from their borders (hence in the USSR, World War II came to be known as "the Great Patriotic War"). In the end, the Soviet Union lost twenty million people.

Peace brought no relief with the dawn of the era known as the Cold War. Stalin's death brought relative liberalization to the Soviet Union, but the "thaw" was short-lived. Furthermore, the Soviets made it clear (in East Germany in 1953, Hungary in 1956, and Czechoslovakia in 1968) that no dissent would be tolerated within their sphere of domination. Nikita Khrushchev's forced removal in 1964 ended the brief period of reformist energy; for two more decades the Soviet Union pursued repressive tendencies abroad and at home.

Mikhail Gorbachev came to power in 1985 with broad plans for economic and social reform and a dual commitment to *perestroika* (reconstruction) and *glasnost* (openness). During his first years, the economy faltered, but there was greater freedom. In the summer of 1991, an attempted *coup d'état* by Communist hardliners, opposed by Russian President Boris Yeltsin, fell apart within three days, ushering in momentous changes: the Communist Party was banned, and the Soviet Union was reconfigured and renamed the Union of Sovereign States. Since then, eleven former Soviet states (Russia, Kazakhstan, Kirghizia, Tadzhikistan, Uzbekistan, Turkmenistan, Azerbaijan, Armenia, Ukraine, Moldova, and Byelorussia) have formed the Commonwealth of Independent States, and the Baltic republics of Estonia, Latvia, and Lithuania have become independent. The Republic of Georgia remains undecided about its future status.

VELIMIR KHLEBNIKOV (1885–1922)

Khlebnikov was one of the founders of futurism, whose adherents wanted to shock the bourgeois and advocated a cultural purge. He was imprisoned while a university student for participating in riots. He wandered through prerevolutionary Russia with virtually no belongings, writing poetry and prose. Khlebnikov actively supported the revolution, seeing the possibilities for a Slavic utopia. During the civil war, he continued his wanderings, although he was often desperately ill and was at various times imprisoned by both Bolsheviks and anti-Bolshevik "Whites." In 1921 he traveled with the Red Army, to Persia, where he contracted the typhus which killed him at the age of thirty-seven.

≈ It has the unassuming face of a burnt-out candle

It has the unassuming face of a burnt-out candle.
Fire-eye, lacking its lashes
of downpour and rain.
It burned our fields, our land,
whole populations of stalks of grain
shaken like straw.
The fields grew smokey and the grain turned
yellow as death and fell.
The grain shriveled and mice ate it.
Is the sky sick? Does the sky hurt?
Where are its watery lashes?
What became of wet weather, and pounding rain?
Furious fire-eye, burning our hayfields,
our grasses and gardens,
constantly burning, its cloud brows gone.
People sat down in a daze
to wait for a miracle, and
there wasn't one. They were waiting to die.
This was sky-blue disaster.
This was drought. After a run of caring years,
this changeling.
Now everything is different—grain and rain—
and denies the farmer's labor.
Didn't the plowman's sweating hand
scatter good seed that spring?
Didn't the farmer stand all spring
looking up, hoping for rain?
Fire-eye. Naked
golden glare,
burning the fields

of the Volga plain.
The fires of heaven were merciless.
They burned four regions beginning with S.

TR. PAUL SCHMIDT

≈ Suppose I make a timepiece of humanity

Suppose I make a timepiece of humanity,
Demonstrate the movement of the century hand—
Will war not wither like an unused letter, drop
From your alphabet, vanish from our little gap
Of time? Humanity has piles, got by rocking
In armchairs forever and ever, compressing
The mainspring of war. I tell you, the future is
Coming, and upon it my superhuman dreams.
I know you are true believing wolves—
I squeeze my shots into the bull's-eye like yours—
But can't you hear fate's needle, rustling
In her wonderworking seams?
The force of my thoughts will inundate
The structures of existing states—
I'll reveal to the serfs of old stupidity
The magic city of Kitezh, risen from its lake.
When the band of Presidents of Planet Earth
Will feed our appalling hunger with a new crust,
Then the rough lug nuts of existing states
Will yield easily to the turn of our wrench.
And when the bearded lady
Throws the long-awaited stone,
That, you will say,
Is what we've been wanting
For centuries. Ticking timepiece of humanity!
Move like the arrow of my thoughts!
Grow as governments destroy themselves, grow
Through this book, let Planet Earth
Be sovereignless at last! PRESPLANEARTH alone
Will be our sovereign song.
I tell you, the universe is the scratch

Of a match on the face of the calculus,
And my thoughts are a picklock at work
On a door, and behind it someone is dying . . .

January 28, 1922

TR. PAUL SCHMIDT

ANNA AKHMATOVA (1889–1966)

Born near St. Petersburg, Akhmatova gained a reputation as a poet in the years before the revolution, opposing symbolism while advocating a poetry of tangible experience. She was married three times: her first husband, the poet Nikolai Gumilyov, was executed for anti-Bolshevik activities in 1921; her second marriage, to Tamara Shileiko, lasted only three years; and her third husband, Nikolai Punin, died in prison. The poem "Requiem" arises out of her experience of her son's confinement. Her work was unofficially banned in the USSR from 1925 until 1940, and then again for a decade after World War II. Only in the late 1950s did she once again gain recognition; in 1964, she was elected president of the Writers' Union, from which she had earlier been expelled.

≈ Requiem

1935–1940

No foreign sky protected me,
no stranger's wing shielded my face.
I stand as witness to the common lot,
survivor of that time, that place.

1961

Instead of a Preface

In the terrible years of the Yezhov terror I spent seventeen months waiting in line outside the prison in Leningrad. One day somebody in the crowd identified me. Standing behind me was a woman, with lips

blue from the cold, who had, of course, never heard me called by name
before. Now she started out of the torpor common to us all and asked
me in a whisper (everyone whispered there):

"Can you describe this?"

And I said: "I can."

Then something like a smile passed fleetingly over what had once
been her face.

Leningrad, 1 April 1957

Dedication

Such grief might make the mountains stoop,
reverse the waters where they flow,
but cannot burst these ponderous bolts
that block us from the prison cells
crowded with mortal woe. . . .
For some the wind can freshly blow,
for some the sunlight fade at ease,
but we, made partners in our dread,
hear but the grating of the keys,
and heavy-booted soldiers' tread.
As if for early mass, we rose
and each day walked the wilderness,
trudging through silent street and square,
to congregate, less live than dead.
The sun declined, the Neva blurred,
and hope sang always from afar.
Whose sentence is decreed? . . . That moan,
that sudden spurt of woman's tears,
shows one distinguished from the rest,
as if they'd knocked her to the ground
and wrenched the heart out of her breast,
then let her go, reeling, alone.
Where are they now, my nameless friends
from those two years I spent in hell?
What specters mock them now, amid
the fury of Siberian snows,
or in the blighted circle of the moon?
To them I cry, Hail and Farewell!

March 1940

Prologue

That was a time when only the dead
could smile, delivered from their wars,
and the sign, the soul, of Leningrad
dangled outside its prison-house;
and the regiments of the condemned,
herded in the railroad-yards,
shrank from the engine's whistle-song
whose burden went, "Away, pariahs!"
The stars of death stood over us.
And Russia, guiltless, beloved, writhed
under the crunch of bloodstained boots,
under the wheels of Black Marias.

I

At dawn they came and took you away.
You were my dead: I walked behind.
In the dark room children cried,
the holy candle gasped for air.
Your lips were chill from the ikon's kiss,
sweat bloomed on your brow—those deathly flowers!
Like the wives of Peter's troopers in Red Square
I'll stand and howl under the Kremlin towers.

1935

II

Quietly flows the quiet Don;
into my house slips the yellow moon.

It leaps the sill, with its cap askew,
and balks at a shadow, that yellow moon.

This woman is sick to her marrow-bone,
this woman is utterly alone,

with husband dead, with son away
in jail. Pray for me. Pray.

III

Not, not mine: it's somebody else's wound.
I could never have borne it. So take the thing
that happened, hide it, stick it in the ground.
Whisk the lamps away . . .

                  Night.

IV

They should have shown you—mocker,
delight of your friends, hearts' thief,
naughtiest girl of Pushkin's town—
this picture of your fated years,
as under the glowering wall you stand,
shabby, three hundredth in the line,
clutching a parcel in your hand,
and the New Year's ice scorched by your tears.
See there the prison poplar bending!
No sound. No sound. Yet how many
innocent lives are ending . . .

V

For seventeen months I have cried aloud,
calling you back to your lair.
I hurled myself at the hangman's foot.
You are my son, changed into nightmare.
Confusion occupies the world,
and I am powerless to tell
somebody brute from something human,
or on what day the word spells, "Kill!"
Nothing is left but dusty flowers,
the tinkling thurible, and tracks
that lead to nowhere. Night of stone,
whose bright enormous star
stares me straight in the eyes,
promising death, ah soon!

VI

The weeks fly out of mind,
I doubt that it occurred:
how into your prison, child,

the white nights, blazing, stared;
and still, as I draw breath,
they fix their buzzard eyes
on what the high cross shows,
this body of your death.

VII

The Sentence

The word dropped like a stone
on my still living breast.
Confess: I was prepared,
am somehow ready for the test.

So much to do today:
kill memory, kill pain,
turn heart into a stone,
and yet prepare to live again.

Not quite. Hot summer's feast
brings rumors of carouse.
How long have I foreseen
this brilliant day, this empty house?

Summer 1939

VIII

To Death

You will come in any case—so why not now?
How long I wait and wait. The bad times fall.
I have put out the light and opened the door
for you, because you are simple and magical.
Assume, then, any form that suits your wish,
take aim, and blast at me with poisoned shot,
or strangle me like an efficient mugger,
or else infect me—typhus be my lot—
or spring out of the fairytale you wrote,
the one we're sick of hearing, day and night,
where the blue hatband marches up the stairs,
led by the janitor, pale with fright.
It's all the same to me. The Yenisei swirls,

the North Star shines, as it will shine forever;
and the blue lustre of my loved one's eyes
is clouded over by the final horror.

The House on the Fontanka,
19 August 1939

IX

Already madness lifts its wing
to cover half my soul.
That taste of opiate wine!
Lure of the dark valley!

Now everything is clear.
I admit my defeat. The tongue
of my ravings in my ear
is the tongue of a stranger.

No use to fall down on my knees
and beg for mercy's sake.
Nothing I counted mine, out of my life,
is mine to take:

not my son's terrible eyes,
not the elaborate stone flower
of grief, not the day of the storm,
not the trial of the visiting hour,

not the dear coolness of his hands,
not the lime trees' agitated shade,
not the thin cricket-sound
of consolation's parting word.

4 May 1940

X

Crucifixion

"Do not weep for me, Mother, when I am in my grave."

I

A choir of angels glorified the hour,
the vault of heaven was dissolved in fire.

"Father, why hast Thou forsaken me?
Mother, I beg you, do not weep for me. . . ."

II

Mary Magdalene beat her breasts and sobbed,
His dear disciple, stone-faced, stared.
His mother stood apart. No other looked
into her secret eyes. Nobody dared.

1940–1943

Epilogue

I

I have learned how faces fall to bone,
how under the eyelids terror lurks
how suffering inscribes on cheeks
the hard lines of its cuneiform texts,
how glossy black or ash-fair locks
turn overnight to tarnished silver,
how smiles fade on submissive lips,
and fear quavers in a dry titter.
And I pray not for myself alone . . .
for all who stood outside the jail,
in bitter cold or summer's blaze,
with me under that blind red wall.

II

Remembrance hour returns with the turning year.
I see, I hear, I touch you drawing near:

the one we tried to help to the sentry's booth,
and who no longer walks this precious earth,

and that one who would toss her pretty mane
and say, "It's just like coming home again."

I want to name the names of all that host,
but they snatched up the list, and now it's lost.

I've woven them a garment that's prepared
out of poor words, those that I overheard,

and will hold fast to every word and glance
all of my days, even in new mischance,

and if a gag should blind my tortured mouth,
through which a hundred million people shout,

then let them pray for me, as I do pray
for them, this eve of my remembrance day.

And if my country ever should assent
to casting in my name a monument,

I should be proud to have my memory graced,
but only if the monument be placed

not near the seas on which my eyes first opened—
my last link with the sea has long been broken—

nor in the Tsar's garden near the sacred stump,
where a grieved shadow hunts my body's warmth,

but here, where I endured three hundred hours
in line before the implacable iron bars.

Because even in blissful death I fear
to lose the clangor of the Black Marias,

to lose the banging of that odious gate
and the old crone howling like a wounded beast.

And from my motionless bronze-lidded sockets
may the melting snow, like teardrops, slowly trickle,

and a prison dove coo somewhere, over and over,
as the ships sail softly down the flowing Neva.

March 1940

TR. STANLEY KUNITZ AND MAX HAYWARD

BORIS PASTERNAK (1890–1960)

Pasternak published his first book of poetry in 1914. An early supporter of the revolution (whose praise he incorporated in his longer works of the 1920s), he fell out of favor with the Party and survived the 1930s as a translator. A brief period of publication during World War II came to a halt in 1946, when he was forced back into silence. His most famous work, *Dr. Zhivago,* could not be published in the Soviet Union; it appeared in Italy in 1957. Pasternak was forced by the authorities to decline the Nobel Prize, awarded for his poetry in 1958. He was threatened with expulsion, deprived of his livelihood, and forbidden to publish. The banned poem "Hamlet" was read at his funeral.

≈ Hamlet

The buzz subsides. I have come on stage.
Leaning in an open door
I try to detect from the echo
What the future has in store.

A thousand opera-glasses level
The dark, point-blank, at me.
Abba, Father, if it be possible
Let this cup pass from me.

I love your preordained design
And am ready to play this role.
But the play being acted is not mine.
For this once let me go.

But the order of the acts is planned,
The end of the road already revealed.
Alone among the Pharisees I stand.
Life is not a stroll across a field.

1946

TR. JON STALLWORTHY AND PETER FRANCE

≈ **Fresco Come to Life**

Again the shells were falling.
As on board ship, the cloud
And night sky over Stalingrad
Rocked in a plaster shroud.

Earth droned, as if in prayer
To ward off the shrieking shell,
And with its censer threw up smoke
And rubble where it fell.

Whenever, between fighting he
Went round his company under fire,
A sense of strange familiarity
Haunted him like desire.

These hedgehog buildings, where could he
Have seen their bottomless holes before?
The evidence of past bombardments
Seemed fabulous and familiar.

What did it mean, the four-armed sign,
Enclosed in the pitch-black frame?
Of whom did they remind him,
The smashed floors and the flame?

And suddenly he saw his childhood,
His childhood, and the monastery; heard
The penitents, and in the garden
The nightingale and mocking-bird.

He gripped his mother with a son's hand,
And devils, fearing the archangel's spear,
Leaped from the chapel's sombre frescoes
Into just such pits as here.

And the boy saw himself in armour.
Defending his mother in shining mail,

And fell upon the evil one
With its swastika-tipped tail.

And nearby in a mounted duel
Saint George shone down on the dragon,
And water-lilies studded the pond
And birds sang crazily on and on.

The fatherland, like the forest's voice,
A call in the wood and the wood's echo,
Beckoned with an alluring music
And smelt of budding birch and willow.

How he remembers those clearings
Now, when in pursuit he impales
And tramples enemy tanks
For all their fearful dragon scales.

He has crossed the frontiers of the world,
And the future, like the firmament,
Already rages, not a dream,
Approaching, and magnificent.

1944

TR. JON STALLWORTHY AND PETER FRANCE

≈ **Mary Magdalene (I)**

As soon as night descends, we meet.
Remorse my memories releases.
The demons of the past compete,
And draw and tear my heart to pieces,
Sin, vice and madness and deceit,
When I was slave of men's caprices
And when my dwelling was the street.

The deathly silence is not far;
A few more moments only matter,
Which the Inevitable bar.

But at the edge, before they scatter,
In front of thee my life I shatter,
As though an alabaster jar.

O what might not have been my fate
By now, my teacher and my saviour,
Did not eternity await
Me at the table, as a late
New victim of my past behaviour!

But what can sin now mean to me,
And death, and hell, and sulphur burning,
When, like a graft onto a tree,
I have—for everyone to see—
Grown into being part of thee
In my immeasurable yearning?

When pressed against my knees I place
Thy precious feet, and weep, despairing,
Perhaps I'm learning to embrace
The cross's rough four-sided face;
And, fainting, all my being sways
Towards thee, thy burial preparing.

TR. LYDIA PASTERNAK SLATER

VICTOR SERGE   (Victor Lvovich Kibalchich)   (1890–1947)

Born in Belgium, the son of émigrés from Czarist Russia, Serge endured detentions and exile throughout his life. As an anarchist in Paris, he was arrested for terrorism in 1912, and, although innocent of violent crimes, he served five years in prison. As a "Bolshevik agent" he was interned in France again in 1917, and in the early 1930s, when he became critical of Stalin, was arrested for sending his literary works abroad and sent into internal exile. He was expelled from Russia in 1936 and settled in Paris, but left when the Nazis invaded. Unable to enter the United States because of his Communist past, he lived in extreme poverty in Mexico until his death. His work includes twenty books of fiction, poetry, and historical writings. The first three poems that follow were written during his internal exile; "Hands" was one of his last poems.

≈ The Asphyxiated Man

Green bushes are bursting with giant flowers,
on the doorstep of the small hospital made of gray boards
there are these sleeping flowers
that smell of chloroform.

A nurse dressed in white is seated on the steps,
she's a brunette with the wide eyes of the plains,
she cracks sunflower seeds between her teeth.

The patient, squatting on the ground in an oversize shirt, where his
      uncelebrated martyr's body totters,
stretches his bony neck; his face has a strange gray color,
he looks like a drowned man badly drowned, badly fished out, and
      sent on his way,
it is the face of asphyxiation, of the terror
of the last days,
pierced by eyes anterior to any possible resurrection.
His hoarse breathing shoos the buzzing flies,
I see the veins throb in his neck.
His other-worldly eyes cry out to me that there is no more air:
"Citizen! What have they done with all the air?"

Two high-breasted girls stop in front of this asphyxiated man.
The one in a sailor's jacket and with an anchor and a lover's name
      tattooed on her bare arm
and who has her hair cut short and sensual pink nostrils
says to her friend:
"He's done for, dear. Oh my, what an ugly death's head!"
She puts her arm around her friend's frail shoulders.
"Let's go, Charlotte!" she says.

The flier who fell at dawn from seventh heaven, in a parachute,
and who knows that there's air to drown in, to break up in, air, air to
      fall in,

kilometers of air and fear to cross without flinching
to die or to obtain the certificate, first-class rations, and that
    knowledge of the sky that is no more than a new ignorance of
    the heavens—
the flier's eyes follow the young women.
"There's nothing anyone can do for the poor old guy now. There's no
    point in even looking at him. Let's go, girls."

He would like to dance tonight in Linden Gardens with the tattooed
    girl of the sensual pink nostrils,
he would suddenly take her breasts in his hands—
"You're a great kid and I could buy you some silk stockings, y'know,
we're the happy youth of the birth of socialism."

Believers say that Christ died on the cross for you,
it hardly shows.
The Savior botched your salvation.

The lecturers at the Atheists Club say that revolutions are made to
    save you and people like you.
You'd hardly know that, either,
and yet all those important people are very positive,
all those healthy people.

Your papers prove that you fought to save yourself
with Chapaev, with Furmanov, with my friend Mitia, the deported
    wino,
down the Ural River stripped by dawns—
but even that didn't do you any good.

And your blood burning from the civil wars, your partisan's seething
    rage,
all that would be lost, poor folk, if there weren't good authors,
servile glory hounds, good money makers
to get memorable books and scenarios out of it.

The nurse has finished munching her seeds, she has gone away.
The asphyxiated man remains alone among the green bushes
in the dazzling light, colors, and pain,
alone in the universe,

alone in the pure, inaccessible, unbreathable azure,
where his black mouth vainly begs for air.

Luminous disks descend, ascend, explode there
and I am here, dressed in white, eye sockets framed in gold, useless,
I, the only person conscious of his suffering and death,
I, the last, impotent human face he'll ever see,
I who have nothing for him but this absurd remorse.

Orenberg, summer 1935

TR. JAMES BROOK

≈ Dialectic

I

We were born
in the time of the first perfected machine guns;
They were waiting for us, these excellent perforators
of armor plate and brains haunted by spirituality . . .

Have no doubt, ever since we began to ply the trade of most unwilling
      victim
—almost since time began—
we've known how to quaff every bitter drink,
gall, hemlock (now out of fashion), the little glass of rum
before the guillotine . . .

Jamaica rum, tropical sap,
be gentle on the palate of the deathly pale guy
who's paying for the crime of others
and for ours,
and place in our mouths a little of the bitterness
that his mouth distills for the peace of the best men.

We know how to carry all the crosses, wooden crosses,
swastikas,
climbing a little calvary really isn't anything
for the thieves and christs that we all are.

We have courage.
Ecce homo proletarians
and intellectuals "of all trades."

And if it's necessary once more to go up against the wall
of the desperate Communards,
we'll be there!

No doubt somewhat despite ourselves, once the wine is poured, we'll
drink it.
Long live the Commune, here's to everybody, long live man!
Cream of the assassins, brass hats, Versaillais!
Watch out, Signor Capitan, on the last step
of the last cellar:
my check is cashed at the Cheka.

II

These are leaders of armies, big capitalists, great executioners?
Heroes of the battles of Polesye, Voluyy, and the Carpathians?
These are generals, these trembling old men on all fours, crying, with
     moist eyes
and clouded hearts?
These are Knights of St. George and St. Andrew?
Go ahead, then, St. Capitalist the Assassinated,
it's now your turn.
As for me, I couldn't care less if you don't know what the Marquis de
     Gallifet did.
I don't know anything, either; me, I'm just a foreman from Gorlovka
and I haven't read books.
But there is someone greater than us who's forgotten nothing.

III

By order of the Rev. Comm.
they perish in a ditch in Chernavka
under the sabres of metal-workers from Taganka,
miners from Kashtanka,
and an anarchist bleeding from the death of his dream.
They perish exactly like—on September 2, 1792,
at the Abbaye Prison—Messieurs Montmorin,
Sombreuil, and Rulhière, gentlemen of the king's chamber.

Throat-slitting makes a muffled sound, a mad, disgusting sound,
crowd noise, delirious and sinister sound of waves.
Bailiff Maillart consulted a big register.
"To the La Force Prison!" He wiped his face with the back of his gray
    hand,
oh, a firm hand is needed to serve the first republic!
At dusk Citizen Billaud came to harangue the killers:
"*Sans culottes*! Brutus, Cinna, the glory of Rome,
the revolution will live in centuries of centuries to come,
the Commune sends you a barrel of good wine."

IV

"See," said the young, freckle-faced propagandist,
"see how materialist history repeats itself."

V

You've taught us so well the dirty trade practiced by the strongest
that in the end we will become masters at it.
We will have pounding hearts, pulsing brows,
eyes full of horrible images like remorse . . .
And then let them bury us and forget us
let nothing begin again and let the earth flourish . . .

Let's go, let's go, let's go!

Orenburg, 1935

TR. JAMES BROOK

≈ Constellation of Dead Brothers

André who was killed in Riga,
Dario who was killed in Spain,
Boris whose wounds I dressed,
Boris whose eyes I closed.

David, my bunk mate,
dead without knowing why
in a quiet orchard in France—

David, your astonished suffering
—six bullets for a 20-year-old heart . . .

Karl, whose nails I recognized
when you had already turned to earth,
you, with your high brow and lofty thoughts,
what was death doing with you!
Dark, tough human vine.

The North, the waves, the ocean
capsize the boat, the Four, now pallid,
drink deeply of anguish,
farewell to Paris, farewell to you all,
farewell to life, God damn it!

Vassili, throughout our sleepless midnights
you had the soul of a combatant
from Shanghai,
and the wind effaces your tomb
in the cornfields of Armavir.

Hong Kong lights up, hour of tall buildings,
the palm resembles the scimitar,
the square resembles the cemetery,
the evening is sweltering and you are dying,
Nguyên, in your prison bed.

And you, my decapitated brothers,
the lost ones, the unforgiven,
the massacred, René, Raymond,
guilty but not denied.

O rain of stars in the darkness,
constellation of dead brothers!

I owe you my blackest silence,
my resolve, my indulgence
for all these empty-seeming days,
and whatever is left me of pride
for a blaze in the desert.

But let there be silence
on these lofty figureheads!
The ardent voyage continues,
the course is set on hope.

When will it be your turn, when mine?

The course is set on hope.

1935

TR. JAMES BROOK

≈ Hands

*Terra-cotta by a 16th-century Italian artist, sometimes attributed to Michelangelo.
London Museum.*

What astonishing contact, old man, your hands establish with our
    own!
How vain the centuries of death before your hands . . .

The artist, nameless like you, surprised them in the act of grasping
—who knows if the gesture still vibrates or has just ended?
The veins pulse, they are old veins toughened by the song of the
    blood,
Oh, what are they grasping, your hands of fading strength,
do they cling to earth, do they cling to flesh
for the last or the next-to-last time,
are they gathering the crystal containing purity,
are they caressing the living darkness containing fertility,
are they patient,
are they determined, ardent, resistant,
are they secretly weak?
What is certain is their pride.

The veins of your hands, old man, express prayer,
the prayer of your blood, old man, the next-to-last
prayer,
neither verbal prayer nor clerical prayer,

but the prayer of conscious ardor,
potent—impotent.
Their presence confronts the world with itself,
questions it as one questions what one loves
definitively
without any possible response.

Am I alone, I deaf, I so separated from you,
I so detached from myself,
Am I as alone in knowing as you are,
I alone at this moment and reaching out to you
through time?

Or are we alone together
among all those who in the course of time are alone with us,
forming the one choir that murmurs in our shared veins,
our singing veins?

I wanted to tell you, old man, something moving,
moved,
fraternal,
to find for you, in the name of all others, a naked word
in the northern lights
in the glow on the glaciers,
a simple, intimate, and loyal word.

You, you didn't know
that the veins in the temples of the electrocuted
boil like knots of rebellious blood
under the skin glistening with sweat more horrible than the sweat of
    Christ on the cross.
Someone told me the sight recalled
a fly stalked by a strange spider,
and the fly a soul that had been saved.

Oh, what could I do, oh what could I do to soothe your veins,
I who know torture, you who know torture,
we must yet be capable, for each other,
from one end of time to the other,
of throwing into the inexorable balance of the universe
at least the fragility of a thought, a sign, a line of verse

that perhaps has neither substance nor radiance yet exists,
as real as the imploring veins of your hand,
as real as my veins, so little different . . .

May the final glow of the final dawn,
may the final intermittent star,
may the final distress in the final waiting,
may the final smile of the serene mask
be on the veins of your hand, old man I've found.

A drop of blood falls from one sky to another,
dazzling.

Our hands are unconscious, tough, ascendant, conscious,
plainsong, delighted suffering,
nailed to rainbows.
Together, together, joined,
they have here seized
the unexpected.

And we didn't know
that together we held
this dazzling thing.

A drop of blood—
a single ray of light falls from one hand to the other,
dazzling.

Mexico, November 1947

TR. JAMES BROOK

OSIP MANDELSTAM (1891–1938)

The Warsaw-born Russian poet Mandelstam began writing in boyhood.
His early work was symbolist, but his devotion to classicism led him to
join Akhmatova's circle, which rejected the mysticism and imprecision
of the symbolists in favor of a poetry of concrete reality. Mandelstam

spent World War I in the Crimea and returned to Moscow in 1918, nostalgic for the Russian Empire. He was arrested in 1934, after reading aloud "The Stalin Epigram" to a group of friends, one of whom must have been an informer. Exiled for three years, then rearrested in Moscow in 1938, he was sentenced to five years in a labor camp. It is likely that he died in a transit camp near Vladivostok. That we have any of his poetry is a tribute to his wife, Nadezhda Mandelstam, who preserved much of his work by committing it to memory.

≈ The Stalin Epigram

Our lives no longer feel ground under them.
At ten paces you can't hear our words.

But whenever there's a snatch of talk
it turns to the Kremlin mountaineer,

the ten thick worms his fingers,
his words like measures of weight,

the huge laughing cockroaches on his top lip,
the glitter of his boot-rims.

Ringed with a scum of chicken-necked bosses
he toys with the tributes of half-men.

One whistles, another meows, a third snivels.
He pokes out his finger and he alone goes boom.

He forges decrees in a line like horseshoes,
One for the groin, one the forehead, temple, eye.

He rolls the executions on his tongue like berries.
He wishes he could hug them like big friends from home.

TR. W. S. MERWIN AND CLARENCE BROWN

≈ **Mounds of human heads are wandering into the distance**

Mounds of human heads are wandering into the distance.
I dwindle among them. Nobody sees me. But in books
much loved, and in children's games I shall rise
from the dead to say the sun is shining.

TR. W. S. MERWIN AND CLARENCE BROWN

≈ **Leningrad**

I've come back to my city. These are my own old tears,
my own little veins, the swollen glands of my childhood.

So you're back. Open wide. Swallow
the fish-oil from the river lamps of Leningrad.

Open your eyes. Do you know this December day,
the egg-yolk with the deadly tar beaten into it?

Petersburg! I don't want to die yet!
You know my telephone numbers.

Petersburg! I've still got the addresses:
I can look up dead voices.

I live on back stairs, and the bell,
torn out nerves and all, jangles in my temples.

And I wait till morning for guests that I love,
and rattle the door in its chains.

Leningrad, December 1930

TR. W. S. MERWIN AND CLARENCE BROWN

≈ I was washing outside in the darkness

I was washing outside in the darkness,
the sky burning with rough stars,
and the starlight, salt on an axe-blade.
The cold overflows the barrel.

The gate's locked,
the land's grim as its conscience.
I don't think they'll find the new weaving,
finer than truth, anywhere.

Star-salt is melting in the barrel,
icy water is turning blacker,
death's growing purer, misfortune saltier,
the earth's moving nearer to truth and to dread.

1921

TR. W. S. MERWIN AND CLARENCE BROWN

MARINA TSVETAYEVA (1892–1941)

Considered one of the greatest poets of the twentieth century, Tsvetayeva was a friend of both Anna Akhmatova and Osip Mandelstam. After the revolution, her husband fought in the civil war with the White Russians, and upon their defeat, she fled to Prague and Paris. She lived in exile until 1939, but was estranged from other exiles, partly because her admiration for the poetry of Vladimir Mayakovsky was considered pro-Soviet. Disaffected, she returned to the Soviet Union, in spite of official hostility toward her; during the 1930s, her daughter was twice imprisoned, and her husband was jailed and murdered by the secret police. Evacuated from Moscow with her son in 1941, impoverished and unable to write or publish, she committed suicide, and was buried in an unmarked grave. "Poems to Czechoslovakia," a late sequence, was written in protest over the Nazi occupation of that country.

≈ A white low sun . . .

A white low sun, low thunderclouds; and back
behind the kitchen-garden's white wall, graves.
On the sand, serried ranks of straw-stuffed forms
as large as men, hang from some cross-beam.

Through the staked fence, moving about, I see
a scattering: of soldiers, trees, and roads;
and an old woman standing by her gate
who chews on a black hunk of bread with salt.

What have these grey huts done to anger you,
my God? and why must so many be killed?
A train passed, wailing, and the soldiers wailed
as its retreating path got trailed with dust.

Better to die, or not to have been born,
than hear that plaining, piteous convict wail
about these beautiful dark eyebrowed women.
It's soldiers who sing these days. O Lord God.

TR. DAVID McDUFF AND JON SILKIN

≈ *from* Poems to Czechoslovakia

VI

They took   quickly, they took   hugely,
    took the mountains and their entrails.
They took our coal, and took our steel
    from us, lead they took also and crystal.

They took the sugar, and they took the clover
    they took the North and took the West.
They took the hive, and took the haystack
    they took the South from us, and took the East.

Vary   they took and Tatras   they took,
    they took the near at hand and far away.
But   worse than taking paradise on earth from us
    they won the battle for our native land.

Bullets they took from us, they took our rifles
   minerals they took, and comrades too:
But while our mouths have spittle in them
   The whole country   is still armed.

VIII

What tears in eyes now
weeping with anger and love
Czechoslovakia's tears
Spain in its own blood

and what a black mountain
has blocked the world   from the light.
It's time—It's time—It's time
to give back to God   his ticket.

I refuse to be. In
the madhouse of the inhuman
I refuse   to live.
With the wolves of the market place

I refuse   to howl,
Among the sharks of the plain
I refuse to swim   down
where moving backs make a current.

I have no need of holes
for ears, nor prophetic eyes:
to your mad world there is
one answer: to refuse!

1938

tr. Elaine Feinstein

≈ You, walking past me

You, walking past me,
not toward my dubious witchcraft—
if you only knew how much fire,
how much life, was wasted

and what heroic passion there was
in a chance shadow, a rustle . . .
and how my heart was incinerated,
expended for nothing.

O train flying in the night,
carrying away sleep at the station . . .
though I know that even then
you wouldn't know—if you knew—

that's why my speeches are abrupt
in the perpetual smoke of my cigarettes—
in my lighthaired head—
how much dark and menacing need!

TR. MARY MADDOCK

≈ *from the cycle* Akhmatova

I

. . . In my melodious city cupolas burn,
and a vagrant poet sings of the bright cathedral
I give you my chiming city,
Akhmatova! and my heart.

II

I hold my head and think
—what conspiracies—
I hold my head and sing
in this late hour, at daybreak.

The furious wave
that hurtled me into its spindrift!
I sing of you, you—alone
like the moon in the sky!

You swoop down like a crow into my heart,
hooknosed, piercing
clouds. Your anger is deadly,
like your approval.

Over my pure gold Kremlin
your night expands.
The bliss of song
tightens around my throat like a belt.

I'm happy! Dawn
never burned cleaner!
I'm happy! I give you my gift
and leave like a beggar.

Your voice—its depth! its darkness!—
stops my breathing.
For the very first time I name you
muse of Tsarskoye Selo.

VI

You won't fall behind. I'm the convict,
you're the guard. One fate.
One in that void,
we order fresh horses.

Now I'm calm!
My eyes are clear!
Free me, my companion,
let me walk to the pine tree!

XI

You block the zenith sun
and hold stars in your palm!
If only the doors were thrown open—
and I could come to you like wind

stutter, blush
and cast down my eyes.
Calm, I sob
as in childhood when I am forgiven.

TR. MARY MADDOCK

VLADIMIR MAYAKOVSKY   (1893–1930)

Son of a Georgian forester, Mayakovsky became an active revolution-
ary and was arrested three times during his adolescence. A founder of
Russian futurism, he opposed symbolism, mysticism, and the cult of
beauty and advocated a new language "beyond sense." He supported
the Bolshevik revolution in 1917, wrote propaganda, and founded jour-
nals. The revolution, he felt, demanded a new art, but the Communist
Party considered avant-garde art too dangerous. Frustrated by ever-
increasing pressure from Stalinist authorities, he committed suicide in
Moscow in 1930. The unfinished poem "At the Top of My Voice"
was conceived as a monument to a doomed man—himself. "Past one
o'clock" was his last poem, and may be read as his suicide note.

≈ *from* At the Top of My Voice

First Prelude to the Poem

My most respected
                    comrades of posterity!
Rummaging among
                    these days'
                                petrified crap,
exploring the twilight of our times,
you,
     possibly,
            will inquire about me too.
And, possibly, your scholars
                    will declare,
with their erudition overwhelming
                    a swarm of problems;
once there lived
            a certain champion of boiled water,
and inveterate enemy of raw water.
Professor,
        take off your bicycle glasses!

I myself will expound
          those times
               and myself.
I, a latrine cleaner
        and water carrier,
by the revolution
          mobilized and drafted,
went off to the front
           from the aristocratic gardens
of poetry—
        the capricious wench.
She planted a delicious garden,
the daughter,
        cottage,
          pond
           and meadow.
Myself a garden I did plant,
myself with water sprinkled it.
Some pour their verse from water cans;
others spit water
        from their mouth—
the curly Macks,
        the clever Jacks—
but what the hell's it all about!
There's no damming all this up—
beneath the walls they mandoline:
"Tara-tina, tara-tine,
tw-a-n-g . . ."
It's no great honor, then,
          for my monuments
to rise from such roses
above the public squares,
           where consumption coughs,
where whores, hooligans, and syphilis
          walk.
Agitprop
     sticks
       in my teeth too,
and I'd rather
       compose
         romances for you—

more profit in it
         and more charm.
But I
    subdued
        myself,
            setting my heel
on the throat
        of my own song.
Listen,
    comrades of posterity,
to the agitator,
        the rabble-rouser.
Stifling
      the torrents of poetry,
I'll skip
      the volumes of lyrics;
as one alive,
        I'll address the living.
I'll join you
       in the far communist future,
I, who am
      no Esenin super-hero.
My verse will reach you
         across the peaks of ages,
over the heads
      of governments and poets.
My verse
    will reach you
not as an arrow
      in a cupid-lyred chase,
not as worn penny
      reaches a numismatist,
not as the light of dead stars reaches you.
My verse
    by labor
       will break the mountain chain of years,
and will present itself
      ponderous,
        crude,
          tangible,
as an aqueduct,

by slaves of Rome
constructed,
enters into our days.
When in mounds of books,
where verse lies buried,
you discover by chance the iron filings of lines,
touch them
with respect,
as you would
some antique
yet awesome weapon.
It's no habit of mine
to caress
the ear
with words;
a maiden's ear
curly-ringed
will not crimson
when flicked by smut.
In parade deploying
the armies of my pages,
I shall inspect
the regiments in line.
Heavy as lead,
my verses at attention stand,
ready for death
and for immortal fame.
The poems are rigid,
pressing muzzle
to muzzle their gaping
pointed titles.
The favorite
of all the armed forces,
the cavalry of witticisms,
ready
to launch a wild hallooing charge,
reins its chargers still,
raising
the pointed lances of the rhymes.
And all
these troops armed to the teeth,

which have flashed by
                    victoriously for twenty years,
all these,
          to their very last page,
I present to you,
                    the planet's proletarian.
The enemy
          of the massed working class
is my enemy too,
                    inveterate and of long standing.
Years of trial
              and days of hunger
                              ordered us
to march
          under the red flag.
We opened
          each volume
                    of Marx
as we would open
                    the shutters
                              in our own house;
but we did not have to read
                    to make up our minds
which side to join,
                    which side to fight on.
Our dialectics
              were not learned
                              from Hegel.
In the roar of battle
                    it erupted into verse,
when,
      under fire,
                    the bourgeois decamped
as once we ourselves
                    had fled
                              from them.
Let fame
          trudge
                    after genius
like an inconsolable widow
                    to a funeral march—

die then, my verse,
                  die like a common soldier,
like our men
                who nameless died attacking!
I don't care a spit
               for tons of bronze;
I don't care a spit
               for slimy marble.
We're men of a kind,
                  we'll come to terms about our fame;
let our
      common monument be
socialism
            built
                in battle.
Men of posterity
              examine the flotsam of dictionaries:
out of Lethe
          will bob up
                the debris of such words
as "prostitution,"
            "tuberculosis,"
                "blockade."
For you,
          who are now
                healthy and agile,
the poet,
        with the rough tongue
                of his posters,
has licked away consumptives' spittle.
With the tail of my years behind me,
                  I begin to resemble
those monsters,
          excavated dinosaurs.

TR. GEORGE REAVEY

≈ Past one o'clock. . . .

Past one o'clock. You must have gone to bed.
The Milky Way streams silver through the night.
I'm in no hurry; with lightning telegrams
I have no cause to wake or trouble you.
And, as they say, the incident is closed.
Love's boat has smashed against the daily grind.
Now you and I are quits. Why bother then
to balance mutual sorrows, pains, and hurts.
Behold what quiet settles on the world.
Night wraps the sky in tribute from the stars.
In hours like these, one rises to address
The ages, history, and all creation.

TR. GEORGE REAVEY

DANIIL KHARMS (1905–1942)

Kharms was the leader of the postrevolutionary avant-garde literary
group known as Oberiu (an acronym for the Russian words for "Asso-
ciation for Real Art"). His writings were fantastic and absurdist, and as
black humor became increasingly dangerous in the early years of Stalin-
ism, Kharms was forced to retreat from his literary experiments. Dur-
ing the 1930s he wrote children's fiction. He was arrested in August
1941 and was murdered in February of the following year. In "An
Event on the Street," Kharms parodies the rationale of traditional nar-
ratives of hero worship.

≈ Symphony No. 2

Anton Mikhailovich spat, said "Ugh," spat again, said "Ugh" again, spat
again, said "Ugh" again, and went out. The hell with him. I'd better tell
you about Ilya Pavlovich.

Ilya Pavlovich was born in 1893 in Constantinople. When he was still
a small boy, they moved to Petersburg, and there he graduated from the
German School on Kirochnaya Street. Then he had a job in some kind

of store; then he did something else; and when the Revolution started, he emigrated. Well, the hell with him. I'd better tell you about Anna Ignatievna.

But it is not so easy to tell you about Anna Ignatievna. First of all, I know almost nothing about her, and secondly, I have just fallen off my chair and forget what I was going to say. So I'd better tell you about myself.

I am tall, fairly intelligent; I dress meticulously and in good taste; I don't drink, I don't go to the races, but I like ladies. And ladies don't dislike me. They like it when I go out with them. Serafima Izmaylovna invited me to her place more than once, and Zinaida Yakovlevna also said that she was always glad to see me. But a funny thing happened to me with Marina Petrovna that I want to tell you about. An absolutely ordinary thing, but an amusing one. Becuase of me, Marina Petrovna lost all her hair—bald as the palm of your hand. It happened this way: once I went to see Marina Petrovna, and bang! she lost all her hair. That was all.

TR. GEORGE GIBIAN

≈ The Beginning of a Beautiful Day (A Symphony)

The rooster had hardly crowed when Timofey jumped out of the window onto the roof and frightened all the passers-by who were on the street at that hour. The peasant Khariton stopped, picked up a stone, and threw it at Timoefy. Timofey disappeared somewhere. "That is a clever one!" the herd of people shouted, and Zubov ran full speed and rammed his head into a wall. "Oh!" a woman with a swollen cheek shouted. But Komarov beat up the woman, and the woman ran howling through the doorway. Fetelyushin walked past and laughed at them. Komarov walked up to him and said, "Hey, you greaseball," and hit Fetelyushin in the stomach. Fetelyushin leaned against the wall and started to hiccup. Romashkin spat from the top-story window, trying to hit Fetelyushin. At that moment, not far from there, a big-nosed woman was beating up her kid with a trough. A fattish young mother rubbed a pretty little girl's face against the brick wall. A little dog broke its thin leg and rolled around on the pavement. A little boy ate some kind of loathsome thing out of a spittoon. At the grocery store there was a long line for sugar. The women swore loudly and pushed one another with bags. The peasant Khariton got drunk on denatured alcohol and stood in front of the women with unbuttoned trousers and said bad words.

Thus began a beautiful summer day.

TR. GEORGE GIBIAN

≈ An Event on the Street

Once a man jumped out of a streetcar, but so clumsily that he fell under an automobile.

Traffic on the street stopped, and a policeman tried to find out how the accident had happened.

The driver was explaining something for a long time, pointing with his finger at the front wheels of the automobile. The policeman felt the wheels with his hand and wrote the name of the street in his little book.

A fairly large crowd gathered round.

A man with dim eyes kept falling off the policeman's stand all the time.

A woman kept looking around all the time at another woman, who in her turn kept looking around all the time at the first woman.

Then the crowd dispersed and traffic started moving again.

The citizen with the dim eyes kept on falling off the stand for a long time, but in the end he, too, clearly despairing of getting himself securely seated on the policeman's stand, simply lay down on the sidewalk. At that moment a man who was carrying a chair fell down hard, under the streetcar.

A policeman came again; again a crowd gathered, and traffic stopped. The man with the dim eyes again started falling off the policeman's stand. Well, and then everything became all right, and even Ivan Semyonovich Karpov went into a restaurant.

NATALYA GORBANEVSKAYA (1936–)

Gorbanevskaya was expelled from Moscow University in her second year there, partly because of the "decadence" and "pessimism" of her poetry. After traveling around the Soviet Union, she worked as a translator and editor in Leningrad. In January 1968 she was a signatory of a letter condemning the arrest of two intellectuals and joined protests against their trial. In August of that same year, she and six friends demonstrated against the Soviet invasion of Czechoslovakia and were beaten up and arrested. She chronicled her experience in underground publications and in newspapers in the West. Early in 1969, she was a founder of a civil rights group in the USSR. She was arrested for her publications in December 1969 and sent to a psychiatric hospital "of special type," where she was forcibly given drug therapy. She left the Soviet Union in 1975 for Austria.

≈ Sukhanovo

Leafless buoyancy
of bare groves in April,
green moss, transparent
stream, cold horse-tail.

Oblivious buoyancy
like a dream of eroded words,
transparent day, green aspen grove
of a hundred trunks.

Cold bend of the river
and in the far distance
the transparent wind is whistling
in the rosy osier bed.

*

Here, as in a painting, noon burns yellow,
and the very air, like grief, is disembodied,
and in the utter silence, like a winged army,
the crows in Crow Park hang overhead.

But the mouldering leaves of years past
cling to my elbows, to my hands reeking
of cigarette smoke, and the bare shrubbery thrusts
its arms among my tangled curls.

I have left home so far behind me,
like a plane that in dense fog wanders
from the aerodrome into the darkness . . .
Am I living or dead, am I leaves or grass?

*

Wipe the bliss of half-sleep from your cheeks
and open your eyes wide until the lids ache,
the filth and whiteness of the ward
is like the voluntary flag of your bondage.

The emptiness and narrowness of the ward—
close your eyes tightly until your cheeks ache.
Wipe the smile off your chapped lips,
but swallow the ineffectual scream.

The half-dark, half-light of the ward—
and your neighbour, with closed eyes,
insensibly cursing the white light,
soundlessly dissolves in tears.

*

In my own twentieth century
where there are more dead than graves
to put them in, my miserable,
forever unshared love

among these Goya images
is nervous, faint, absurd,
as, after the screaming of jets,
the trump of Jericho.

*

In the bird scream and whistle,
I open the window, open myself.
Before the grand presence passing by
I hide, like a farmyard fowl.

The white flame of flight
fades. The transcendental howl
subsides. In the empty sky
a magpie wags its tail.

*

But day clings to the tree shadow
and does not depart;
it moves like a rusted engine,
and the faint echo of its last
sobbing rays hangs over the wood
like a sun in the sky.

*

Goodbye!—and I am myself amazed
how bright and cold it grows,
how the rain stops drizzling.
Goodbye!—like a little ladleful I spill
into the broad clear river,
into the deep gentle Lethe.

*

You howl, you weep copiously
on the green grass
and again return to your slavery,
your mind numbed.

You howl, you weep, you swallow
bitter tears,
down steep hill slopes you roll
into the nettles.

And again you return. How long will you
continue thus?
Your palms tingle all over with the burs.
Sharpen a pencil,

seated at your desk, scrawl a line, scribble it
on your wrist;
spot a blade of grass with
a drop of blood.

*

Make appointments in December,
when even the lips freeze in the cold,
but how may one descend from poetry to prose
and overcome the craving of the body?

I circle the cold columns,
catarrhal parking lots,
offend the passing traffic of men and cars
and find no place in the world.

It's quicker by the underpass, but
you can't get far from yourself;
sleep, swallow, morsel of transmigration,
like a piece of ice on the rock of asphalt.

*

Now I am sick, and feverish, and in a sweat.
I ramble on of you in my delirium,
of the long wished for, of the unloved,
of that which is dear to me and which is not.
I fall through into a nether world of oblivion,
where only the body wags its heavy tongue,
while the soul, poor creature,
lies in a dungeon under lock and key.

And there, in the depths, the dark, the gorge,
you loom, like a desert mirage
and my low voice calls out, cries.
. . . The pillow is hot against my cheek,
the cannon booms towards dense noon,
and deafness fills the throat, a bitter taste the eyes.

TR. DANIEL WEISSBORT

JOSEPH BRODSKY (1940–   )

In February 1964, Brodsky, who had left school at fifteen, was tried in
Leningrad as a "social parasite" who had corrupted young people with
his "pornographic" and anti-Soviet verse. In response to the judge's
questions about where he had received the authority to write poems, he
answered, "From God." Although a number of defense witnesses
claimed he was indeed a poet, Brodsky was sentenced to five years of
hard labor in the Archangelsk region of the USSR. Through the inter-
vention of Anna Akhmatova, Dmitri Shostakovich, and others, he was
freed after eighteen months. For the next seven years he made a meager
living as a translator in Leningrad, writing poems he couldn't publish.
In 1972, he went into exile, settling in the United States, where his
formal, metered verse has influenced young American poets. He has
received the highest honors, including the Nobel Prize for Literature,
and has been named Poet Laureate of the United States.

≈ The Berlin Wall Tune

To Peter Viereck

This is the house destroyed by Jack.
   This is the spot where the rumpled buck
stops, and where Hans gets killed.
   This is the wall that Ivan built.

This is the wall that Ivan built.
   Yet trying to quell his sense of guilt,
he built it with modest gray concrete,
   and the booby traps look discreet.

Under this wall that (a) bores, (b) scares,
   barbed-wire meshes lie flat like skeins
of your granny's darnings (her chair still rocks!).
   But the voltage's too high for socks.

Beyond this wall throbs a local flag
   against whose yellow, red, and black
Compass and Hammer proclaim the true
   Masonic dream's breakthrough.

The border guards patiently in their nest
   through binoculars scan the West
and the East; and they like both views
   devoid, as it were, of Jews.

Those who are seen here, thought of, felt,
   are kept on a leash by the sense of Geld
or by a stronger Marxist urge.
   The wall won't let them merge.

Come to this wall if you hate your place
   and face a sample of cosmic space
where no life forms can exist at all
   and objects may only fall.

Come to this scornful of peace and war,
   petrified version of either/or

meandering through these bleak parts which act
  like your mirror, cracked.

Dull is the day here. In the night
  searchlights illuminate the blight
making sure that if someone screams,
  it's not due to bad dreams.

For dreams here aren't bad: just wet with blood
  of one of your like who's left his pad
to ramble at will; and in his head
  dreams are replaced with lead.

Given that, it's only time
  who has guts enough to commit the crime
of passing this place back and forth on foot:
  at pendulums they don't shoot.

That's why this site will see many moons
  while couples lie in their beds like spoons,
while the rich are wondering what they wish
  and single girls eat quiche.

Come to this wall that beats other walls:
  Roman, Chinese, whose worn-down, false
molars envy steel fangs that flash,
  scrubbed of thy neighbor's flesh.

A bird may twitter a better song.
  But should you consider abortion wrong
or that the quacks ask too high a fee,
  come to this wall, and see.

  TR. JOSEPH BRODSKY

≈ **To Urania**

To I.K.

Everything has its limit, including sorrow.
A windowpane stalls a stare. Nor does a grill abandon

a leaf. One may rattle the keys, gurgle down a swallow.
Loneliness cubes a man at random.
A camel sniffs at the rail with a resentful nostril;
a perspective cuts emptiness deep and even.
And what is space anyway if not the
body's absence at every given
point? That's why Urania's older than sister Clio!
In daylight or with the soot-rich lantern,
you see the globe's pate free of any bio,
you see she hides nothing, unlike the latter.
There they are, blueberry-laden forests,
rivers where the folk with bare hands catch sturgeon
or the towns in whose soggy phone books
you are starring no longer; farther eastward surge on
brown mountain ranges; wild mares carousing
in tall sedge; the cheekbones get yellower
as they turn numerous. And still farther east, steam dreadnoughts
or cruisers,
and the expanse grows blue like lace underwear.

TR. JOSEPH BRODSKY

≈ Elegy

About a year has passed. I've returned to the place of battle,
to its birds that have learned their unfolding of wings from a subtle
lift of a surprised eyebrow, or perhaps from a razor blade
—wings, now the shade of early twilight, now of stale bad blood.

Now the place is abuzz with trading in your ankles' remnants, bronzes
of sunburnt breastplates, dying laughter, bruises,
rumors of fresh reserves, memories of high treason,
laundered banners with imprints of the many who since have risen.

All's overgrown with people. A ruin's a rather stubborn
architectural style. And the heart's distinction
from a pitch-black cavern
isn't that great; not great enough to fear
that we may collide again like blind eggs somewhere.

At sunrise, when nobody stares at one's face, I often
set out on foot to a monument cast in molten
lengthy bad dreams. And it says on the plinth "Commander
in chief." But it reads "in grief," or "in brief," or "in going under."

TR. JOSEPH BRODSKY

IRINA RATUSHINSKAYA (1954–   )

Ratushinskaya's first brush with the Soviet authorities came in 1977
when she protested the overtly anti-Semitic policies of the Odessa
Pedagogical Institute, where she taught, and when a play she had co-
written was banned after one performance. After a period of official
harassment for her human rights activities, she was arrested in 1981 for
"disturbing the peace," then arrested again the next year for her "anti-
Soviet" writings and affiliations. She was sentenced to seven years in a
harsh labor camp, where she was beaten and force-fed. Her work from
this period, published in *samizdat* journals and smuggled out of the
country, has been translated into several languages. She was released in
1986 and emigrated to the West.

≈ 'Try to cover your shivering shoulders'

Try to cover your shivering shoulders in rags of the oldest,
Though your dress has great holes in, hugging it close to your breast
With that useless adjustment, knowing there's no pin to hold it,
All the fever of freedom degrading to evenings of coldness
And how many such evenings to live through can only be guessed.
And what is it for?
For the sake of what vision inviting?
Surely not for that country where hands are for hiding behind,
Where from tomb-tops they watch whether everyone finds it exciting?
But rebellious children keep exercise books for their writing,
Know how to hide them from dads who from birth have been blind.
Discard what is past then,
Those booklets and songs need suppressing,

Do not fear to grow wings since you're destined for life after all!
But a boat sails the Lethe, a paper boat bearing a blessing
And these words you unpick:
'You must die'—but is that so distressing?
You just feel slightly sick,
As you enter the stain on the wall.

Shizo, November 1984

TR. DAVID McDUFF

≈ 'But only not to think'

. . . But only not to think about the journey
On roads hot, dusty, to be walked all day.
Preserve me, my uncompromising reason,
Don't let the reins go now, only half-way.

A long time yet we must fight off together
The suffocating nights, the prison airs,
The prison dreams—hallucinations, almost,
The senseless gibes of executioners,

The treachery of the wearied, and their kisses'
Poison . . . Die, but afterwards fight on—
Not knowing how long the term, and not possessing
The right yet to declare our strength is done.

Don't let us weaken; punish with refusal
Each childish 'Can't take any more, I'm through . . .'
Preserve me in this midnight age, my reason.
Keep me from harm—and I'll watch over you.

Small Zone, November 1984

TR. DAVID McDUFF

The Spanish Civil War

(1936–1939)

The Spanish Civil War remains an important and still deeply traumatic event, for it seemed at the time to be a struggle over the future of all mankind.

Spain had become a constitutional monarchy in the 1870s; it became a military dictatorship in the 1920s and a republic in 1931. The new state was reformist, incurring the wrath of the left, which considered the reforms too weak, and the right, which considered them too extensive. The leftist tradition in Spain was not Leninist; it was marked by anarcho-syndicalism, that is, a belief in absolute equality, minimal government, and strong trade unionism. The anarchists wanted a complete transformation of their society, the abolition of the church, and the elimination of private property. They called for democracy and the collectivization of all aspects of life. The Nationalists, conversely, stood for a strong church, a strong army, the sanctity of private property, and the maintenance of a strict social hierarchy.

The Republic survived five years of strikes, assassinations, and terrorism. The election of a leftist government in 1936 alarmed the right. Francisco Franco, a general exiled to the Canary Islands, led troops from Spanish Morocco across the Mediterranean to attack the Republic. The army was supported by the church and the petty bourgeoisie; it also received extensive assistance from Adolf Hitler and Benito Mussolini. France and England remained officially neutral, although the French sent some clandestine assistance to the Republicans. Only Stalin came to the Republic's aid, and his aims were markedly contradictory: he wanted to stop Fascism but he was unhappy with the prospect of unruly Spanish leftists remaining in power. The Russians organized the so-called International Brigades: forty thousand foreigners from more than fifty countries came to the aid of the Republicans. In what became a particularly vicious war, the Nationalists used terror as a method of control, and the Republicans were given to violent reprisals.

In the end, the Republic's downfall was hastened by Stalin's rapid reversal in the face of the Munich Agreement of 1938: fearing a German attack on the Soviet Union, the Russian leader withdrew all support from the Republican cause. The Republicans fell to the strong Nationalist war machine, the bravery of their militias no match for German and Italian firepower. In the end, the fighting claimed one million lives.

After the war, 250,000 people were imprisoned, and 340,000 went into exile. The war showed how effective *Blitzkrieg* was going to be: in just over three hours on a warm market day in 1937 in the Basque city of Guernica, German planes were able to demolish the center of town and kill many civilians, some of whom were machine-gunned as they tried to flee into the hills. The Spanish Civil War, though fueled by ethnic rage, was also the first international fight over purely ideological principles, and served as a harbinger of the philosophical conflicts of the next half century.

ANTONIO MACHADO (1875–1939)

A descendant of freethinking Spanish intellectuals, Machado had already published two books of poetry by the time of his marriage in 1909. His youthful wife (only fifteen years old at her wedding) died two years later. He resisted the impulse toward suicide, and arranged the transfer of his teaching position from Soria to Baeza, then to Segovia. In 1932, a year after the Spanish monarchy fell and the Second Spanish Republic was proclaimed, Machado returned to Madrid, and in spite of his conviction that poetry should be apolitical, became a committed spokesman for the Republican cause. While his early work was richly introspective, his later poems are marked by his experience of the war. "Today's Meditation" was written after he was forced to leave the fallen capital of Madrid for Valencia. A short time later, he joined the exodus from Spain into France, where he died in exile.

≈ Rainbow at Night

For Don Ramon del Valle-Inclán

The train moves through the Guadarrama
one night on the way to Madrid.
The moon and the fog create
high up a rainbow.
Oh April moon, so calm,
driving the white clouds!

The mother holds her boy
sleeping on her lap.

The boy sleeps, and nevertheless
sees the green fields outside,
and trees lit up by sun,
and the golden butterflies.

The mother, her forehead dark
between a day gone and a day to come,
sees a fire nearly out
and an oven with spiders.

There's a traveler mad with grief,
no doubt seeing odd things;
he talks to himself, and when he looks
wipes us out with his look.

I remember fields under snow,
and pine trees of other mountains.

And you, Lord, through whom we all
have eyes, and who sees souls,
tell us if we all one
day will see your face.

TR. ROBERT BLY

≈ Coplas

In the high wilderness
I see some cold poplars
and a white road.

In that stony place—
(landscape of the moon!)
does no one remember it?

The gusts of February
rip through the lemon trees.
I don't sleep so I won't dream.

TR. ROBERT BLY

≈ **Today's Meditation**

The fiery palm tree in front of me,
that the setting sun is just now leaving,
this late and silent afternoon,
inside our peaceful garden,
while flowery old Valencia
drinks the Guadalaviar waters—
Valencia of delicate towers,
in the joyful sky of Ausias March,
her river turns entirely into roses
before it arrives at the sea—
I think of the war. The war
is like a tornado moving
through the bleak foothills of the Duero,
through the plains of standing wheat,
from the farmlands of Extremadura
to these gardens with private lemons,
from the grey skies of the north
to these salty marshes full of light.
I think of Spain, all of it sold out,
river by river, mountain by mountain, sea to sea.

TR. ROBERT BLY

FEDERICO GARCÍA LORCA (1898–1936)

Poet and playwright, pianist, actor and director, García Lorca was per-
haps the most vital artistic force of twentieth-century Spain. Part of the
group of Spanish poets known as the Generation of '27, he was in-
fluenced by surrealism, the Gypsy *cante jondo* (traditional Andalusian
lyrics), and the rich cultural life of his adopted city, Granada. His is an
elegiac poetry, intensely lyrical and charged with *duende*—the force of a
passionate, dark spirit. Always a poet of the people, he was moved by
the events of the Spanish Civil War, and in a letter to Rafael Martínez
Nadal wrote: "The idea of art for art's sake is something that would be
cruel if it weren't, fortunately, so ridiculous. . . . Rafael, there will be
bodies all over these fields. I've made up my mind, I'm going to

Granada. God's will be done." In the summer of 1936, he was abducted
by right-wing forces and summarily executed on the orders of one of
Franco's generals. "Casida of Sobbing" was among his last poems, and
was published posthumously.

≈ Little Infinite Poem

To take the wrong road
is to arrive at the snow
and to arrive at the snow
is to get down on all fours for twenty centuries and eat the grasses of
    the cemeteries.

To take the wrong road
is to arrive at woman,
woman who isn't afraid of light,
woman who kills two roosters in one second,
light which isn't afraid of roosters,
and roosters who don't know how to sing on top of the snow.

But if the snow took the wrong heart
the southern wind could very well arrive,
and since the air cares nothing for groans
we will have to get down on all fours again and eat the grasses of the
    cemeteries.

I saw two mournful wheat heads made of wax
burying a countryside of volcanoes;
and I saw two insane little boys who wept as they leaned on a
    murderer's eyeballs.

But two, that is not a number!
All it is is an agony and its shadow,
it's only the guitar where love feels its discouragement,
it's only the demonstration of something else's infinity
a castle raised around a dead man,
and the scourging of the new resurrection that will never end.

Dead people hate the number two,
but the number two makes women drop off to sleep,

and since women are afraid of light
light shudders when it has to face the roosters,
and since all roosters know is how to fly over the snow
we will have to get down on all fours and eat the grasses of the
     cemeteries forever.

TR. ROBERT BLY

≈ **Rundown Church**

(Ballad of the First World War)

I had a son and his name was John.
I had a son.
He disappeared into the vaulted darkness one Friday of All Souls.
I saw him playing on the highest steps of the Mass
throwing a little tin pail at the heart of the priest.
I knocked on the coffins. My son! My son! My son!
I drew out a chicken foot from behind the moon and then
I understood that my daughter was a fish
down which the carts vanish.
I had a daughter.
I had a fish dead under the ashes of the incense burner.
I had an ocean. Of what? Good Lord! An ocean!
I went up to ring the bells but the fruit was all wormy
and the blackened match-ends
were eating the spring wheat.
I saw the stork of alcohol you could see through
shaving the black heads of the dying soldiers
and I saw the rubber booths
where the goblets full of tears were whirling.
In the anemones of the offertory I will find you, my love!
when the priest with his strong arms raises up the mule and the ox
to scare the nighttime toads that roam in the icy landscapes of the
     chalice.
I had a son who was a giant,
but the dead are stronger and know how to gobble down pieces of the
     sky.
If my son had only been a bear,
I wouldn't fear the secrecy of the crocodiles
and I wouldn't have seen the ocean roped to the trees

to be raped and wounded by the mobs from the regiment.
If my son had only been a bear!
I'll roll myself in this rough canvas so as not to feel the chill of the
     mosses.
I know very well they will give me a sleeve or a necktie,
but in the innermost part of the Mass I'll smash the rudder and then
the insanity of the penguins and seagulls will come to the rock
and will make the people sleeping and the people singing on the
     street-corners say:
he had a son.
A son! A son! A son
and it was no one else's, because it was his son!
His son! His son! His son!

TR. ROBERT BLY

≈ The Quarrel

For Rafael Méndez

     The Albacete knives, magnificent
with stranger-blood,
flash like fishes
on the gully slope.
Light crisp as a playing
card snips out of bitter
green the profiles of riders
and maddened horses.
Two old women in an olive
tree are sobbing.
The bull of the quarrel
is rising up the walls.
Black angels arrived
with handkerchiefs and snow water.
Angels with immense wings
like Albacete knives.
Juan Antonio from Montilla
rolls dead down the hill,
his body covered with lilies,
a pomegranate on his temples.

He is riding now on the cross of fire,
on the highway of death.

    The State Police and the judge
come along through the olive grove.
From the earth loosed blood moans
the silent folksong of the snake.
"Well, your honor, you see,
it's the same old business—
four Romans are dead
and five Carthaginians."

    Dusk that the fig trees and the
hot whispers have made hysterical
faints and falls on the bloody
thighs of the riders,
and black angels went on flying
through the failing light,
angels with long hair,
and hearts of olive-oil.

    TR. ROBERT BLY

≈ Casida of Sobbing

    I have shut my balcony door
because I don't want to hear the sobbing,
but from behind the grayish walls
nothing else comes out but sobbing.

    Very few angels are singing,
very few dogs are barking,
a thousand violins fit into the palm of my hand.

    But the sobbing is a gigantic dog,
the sobbing is a gigantic angel,
the sobbing is a gigantic violin,
tears close the wind's jaws,
all there is to hear is sobbing.

    TR. ROBERT BLY

RAFAEL ALBERTI (1902–   )

Alberti had already achieved recognition as a cubist painter in Madrid by 1915, when he contracted tuberculosis and was forced to seek treatment in a sanitarium. When he later met Salvador Dalí, García Lorca, and Luis Bunuel, he began writing poetry seriously, and his first book of poems won Spain's National Prize for Literature. He espoused Communism in the late 1920s, edited a revolutionary journal, and fought actively on the Republican side during the Spanish Civil War. Forced into exile, he emigrated to Argentina in 1940 and to Rome in 1964; he was not allowed to return to his beloved Spain until 1977, after thirty-eight years. Considered a worthy member of the so-called Generation of '27, Alberti was awarded the Lenin Prize in 1965. These selections, from *Sobre los angeles,* are poems of exile.

≈ The Warlike Angels

North, South

Wind at war with wind.
I, the tower in no man's land.

Whirlwind cities in a rout
down the mountain passes streaming.
Cities of the southern wind,
that did see me.

Down the snowy slopes, there roll
towns.
Towns and people I don't know,
cities of the northern wind,
that never saw.

Hordes of sea and hordes of land,
names and questions, memories,
face to face.

Heaps and bundles of cold hate,
hand to hand.

I, the no man's tower between,
livid tower all hung about
with dead souls that once had seen,
that never saw me.

Wind and wind that fight it out.

TR. GEOFFREY CONNELL

≈ Punishments

It is when gulfs and bays of blood,
clotted with dead and vengeful stars,
flood into my dreams.
When gulfs and bays of blood
capsize the beds that were sailing,
and, on the world's right, an angel dies forgotten.
When the winds reek of brimstone
and mouths by night taste of bone, glass, and wire.
Hear me.

I did not know that doors moved from place to place,
that souls could blush for their bodies,
nor that at the end of a tunnel, the light would bring death.
Hear me yet.

The sleepers want to run away.
But those graves of the sea are not still,
those graves which open through neglect and weariness of the sky are
        not stable,
and the dawns stumble upon disfigured faces.
Hear me yet. There's still more.

There are nights when the hours turn to stone in space,
when veins do not flow
and when the silences raise up centuries and gods to come.
A thunderbolt shuffles tongues and jumbles words.

Think of the shattered spheres,
of the dry orbits of the uninhabited men,
of the dumb millennia.
More, more yet. Hear me.

You can see that bodies are not where they were,
that the moon is growing cold through being stared at,
and that a child's crying deforms the constellations.
Mildewed skies corrode our desert brows,
where each minute buries its nameless corpse.
Hear me, hear me for the last time.

For there's always a last time that follows the fall of the high
        wasteland,
the advent of the cold in forgetful dreams,
and death's headlong stoops upon the skeleton of nothingness.

TR. GEOFFREY CONNELL

≈ The Angels of the Ruins

But at last there came the day, the hour of shovels and buckets.
The light didn't expect the minutes to topple
because in the sea it was distracting the land-nostalgia of the drowned.
No one expected an esparto daybreak from the skies,
or that angels would chase down verdigris stars upon mankind.

Suits didn't expect that their bodies would emigrate so soon.
The aridity of beds fled down a navigable dawn.

You hear talk of benzine,
of catastrophes caused by unexplained lapses of memory.
They're grumbling in heaven about the treachery of the rose.
I gossip with my soul about gunpowder smuggling
to the left of the corpse of a nightingale friend of mine.
Don't come close.

You never thought that your shadows would return to the shade
when a revolver bullet shattered my silence.
But at last that second arrived,

disguised as night awaiting an epitaph.
Quicklime is the screen stirred by the projections of the dead.

I've told you not to come close.
I've asked you for a little breathing space:
just sufficient for understanding a dream
and for an aimless nausea to explode flowers and boilers.

The moon was very tender before the traffic accidents
and used to come down to the furnaces by way of the factory
    chimneys.
Now she is dying, sullied, on an unforeseen petrol map,
attended by an angel who hastens her death agony.
Men of zinc, pitch, and lead forget it all.

Men of tar and slime forget
that their ships and their trains
in bird's-eye view
are just an oil stain in the midst of the world,
hedged in by crosses on every side.
They have forgotten.
As I have, we all have.

And now no one expects the arrival of the express,
the official visit of the light to underprivileged seas,
the resurrection of voices in charring echoes.

    TR. GEOFFREY CONNELL

W. H. AUDEN (1907–1973)

Auden, born in York, England, drove an ambulance for the Loyalists in
Spain in 1937, an experience that led to the selection included here. He
emigrated to the United States before the outbreak of World War II
and became an American citizen in 1946—the poem "September 1,
1939" is a poetic response to the criticism he received for abandoning
his country in a time of war. In the 1940s Auden began to move away

from the emphasis on politics and psychoanalysis that marked his early work toward the Christian theology that informs his later poetry and plays. (It is worth noting that he later chose to exclude both "Spain 1937" and "September 1, 1939" from the canon of his work.) Auden was a noted critic as well as a poet and playwright. He died in Austria in 1973.

≈ Spain 1937

Yesterday all the past. The language of size
Spreading to China along the trade-routes; the diffusion
            Of the counting-frame and the cromlech;
Yesterday the shadow-reckoning in the sunny climates.

Yesterday the assessment of insurance by cards,
The divination of water; yesterday the invention
            Of cart-wheels and clocks, the taming of
Horses; yesterday the bustling world of the navigators.

Yesterday the abolition of fairies and giants;
The fortress like a motionless eagle eyeing the valley,
            The chapel built in the forest;
Yesterday the carving of angels and of frightening gargoyles;

The trial of heretics among the columns of stone;
Yesterday the theological feuds in the taverns
            And the miraculous cure at the fountain;
Yesterday the Sabbath of Witches. But to-day the struggle.

Yesterday the installation of dynamos and turbines;
The construction of railways in the colonial desert;
            Yesterday the classic lecture
On the origin of Mankind. But to-day the struggle.

Yesterday the belief in the absolute value of Greek;
The fall of the curtain upon the death of a hero;
            Yesterday the prayer to the sunset,
And the adoration of madmen. But to-day the struggle.

As the poet whispers, startling among the pines
Or, where the loose waterfall sings, compact, or upright
        On the crag by the leaning tower:
'O my vision. O send me the luck of the sailor.'

And the investigator peers through his instruments
At the inhuman provinces, the virile bacillus
        Or enormous Jupiter finished:
'But the lives of my friends. I inquire, I inquire.'

And the poor in their fireless lodgings dropping the sheets
Of the evening paper: 'Our day is our loss. O show us
        History the operator, the
Organizer, Time the refreshing river.'

And the nations combine each cry, invoking the life
That shapes the individual belly and orders
        The private nocturnal terror:
'Did you not found once the city state of the sponge,

'Raise the vast military empires of the shark
And the tiger, establish the robin's plucky canton?
        Intervene. O descend as a dove or
A furious papa or a mild engineer: but descend.'

And the life, if it answers at all, replies from the heart
And the eyes and the lungs, from the shops and squares of the city:
        'O no, I am not the Mover,
Not to-day, not to you. To you I'm the

'Yes-man, the bar-companion, the easily-duped:
I am whatever you do; I am your vow to be
        Good, your humourous story;
I am your business voice; I am your marriage.

'What's your proposal? To build the Just City? I will.
I agree. Or is it the suicide pact, the romantic
        Death? Very well, I accept, for
I am your choice, your decision: yes, I am Spain.'

Many have heard it on remote peninsulas,
On sleepy plains, in the aberrant fishermen's islands,
      In the corrupt heart of the city;
Have heard and migrated like gulls or the seeds of a flower.

They clung like burrs to the long expresses that lurch
Through the unjust lands, through the night, through the alpine
    tunnel;
      They floated over the oceans;
They walked the passes: They came to present their lives.

On that arid square, that fragment nipped off from hot
Africa, soldered so crudely to inventive Europe,
      On that tableland scored by rivers,
Our fever's menacing shapes are precise and alive.

To-morrow, perhaps, the future: the research on fatigue
And the movements of packers; the gradual exploring of all the
      Octaves of radiation;
To-morrow the enlarging of consciousness by diet and breathing.

To-morrow the rediscovery of romantic love;
The photographing of ravens; all the fun under
      Liberty's masterful shadow;
To-morrow the hour of the pageant-master and the musician.

To-morrow for the young the poets exploding like bombs,
The walks by the lake, the winter of perfect communion;
      To-morrow the bicycle races
Through the suburbs on summer evenings: but to-day the struggle.

To-day the inevitable increase in the chances of death;
The conscious acceptance of guilt in the fact of murder;
      To-day the expending of powers
On the flat ephemeral pamphlet and the boring meeting.

To-day the makeshift consolations; the shared cigarette;
The cards in the candle-lit barn and the scraping concert;
      The masculine jokes; to-day the
Fumbled and unsatisfactory embrace before hurting.

The stars are dead; the animals will not look:
We are left alone with our day, and the time is short and
        History to the defeated
May say Alas but cannot help or pardon.

≈ September 1, 1939

I sit in one of the dives
On Fifty-Second Street
Uncertain and afraid
As the clever hopes expire
Of a low dishonest decade:
Waves of anger and fear
Circulate over the bright
And darkened lands of the earth,
Obsessing our private lives;
The unmentionable odour of death
Offends the September night.

Accurate scholarship can
Unearth the whole offence
From Luther until now
That has driven a culture mad,
Find what occurred at Linz,
What huge imago made
A psychopathic god:
I and the public know
What all schoolchildren learn,
Those to whom evil is done
Do evil in return.

Exiled Thucydides knew
All that a speech can say
About Democracy,
And what dictators do,
The elderly rubbish they talk
To an apathetic grave;
Analysed all in his book,
the enlightenment driven away,
The habit-forming pain,

Mismanagement and grief:
We must suffer them all again.

Into this neutral air
Where blind skyscrapers use
Their full height to proclaim
The strength of Collective Man,
Each language pours its vain
Competitive excuse:
But who can live for long
In an euphoric dream;
Out of the mirror they stare,
Imperialism's face
And the international wrong.

Faces along the bar
Cling to their average day:
The lights must never go out,
The music must always play,
All the conventions conspire
To make this fort assume
The furniture of home;
Lest we should see where we are,
Lost in a haunted wood,
Children afraid of the night
Who have never been happy or good.

The windiest militant rash
Important Persons shout
Is not so crude as our wish:
What mad Nijinsky wrote
About Diaghilev
Is true of the normal heart;
For the error bred in the bone
Of each woman and each man
Craves what it cannot have,
Not universal love
But to be loved alone.

From the conservative dark
Into the ethical life

The dense commuters come,
Repeating their morning vow,
'I *will* be true to the wife,
I'll concentrate more on my work',
And helpless governors wake
To resume their compulsory game:
Who can release them now,
Who can reach the deaf,
Who can speak for the dumb?

All I have is a voice
To undo the folded lie,
The romantic lie in the brain
Of the sensual man-in-the-street
And the lie of Authority
Whose buildings grope the sky:
There is no such thing as the State
And no one exists alone;
Hunger allows no choice
To the citizen or the police;
We must love one another or die.

Defenceless under the night
Our world in stupor lies;
Yet, dotted everywhere,
Ironic points of light
Flash out wherever the Just
Exchange their messages:
May I, composed like them
Of Eros and of dust,
Beleaguered by the same
Negation and despair,
Show an affirming flame.

September 1939

≈ Epitaph on a Tyrant

Perfection, of a kind, was what he was after,
And the poetry he invented was easy to understand;

He knew human folly like the back of his hand,
And was greatly interested in armies and fleets;
When he laughed, respectable senators burst with laughter,
And when he cried the little children died in the streets.

January 1939

MIGUEL HERNANDEZ (1910–1942)

Born into a peasant family, Hernandez received only two years of formal education and was a goatherd as a boy. Settling in Madrid in 1933, the year his first book of poems appeared, he fought for the Loyalists during the Spanish Civil War and wrote poems in honor of the cause. He was arrested by Franco's troops in 1939 and sent to a concentration camp, from which he escaped. Captured again and sentenced to death, he was saved from execution by an international protest and freed, but then arrested a third time. Sentenced to life imprisonment, then to thirty years, Hernandez died—dressed in rags he had sewn together—at thirty-one of tuberculosis contracted in prison.

≈ I go on in the dark, lit from within . . .

I go on in the dark, lit from within; does day exist?
Is this my grave, or the womb of my mother?
Something beats against my skin like a cold
stone that starts to grow warm, scarlet, tender.

Maybe I'm still waiting to be born,
or maybe I've been dead all the time. Darkness rules me.
If life is this, I wonder what death would be,
or what I'm getting out of an anxiety this eternal.

Held in chains by these clothes, it looks as if I want
to go naked, to get rid of what can't ever
be me, and makes eyes look troubled and far away.

But the black cloth of mourning, far off, walks with me,
shadow for shadow, toward the darkness, until it rolls
down to the naked life blossoming out of pure nothing.

TR. TIMOTHY BALAND

≈ War

Old age in the towns.
The heart without an owner.
Love without any object.
Grass, dust, crow.
And the young ones?

In the coffins.

The tree alone and dry.
Woman like a stick
of widowhood across the bed.
Hatred there is no cure for.
And the young ones?

In the coffins.

TR. HARDIE ST. MARTIN

≈ Waltz Poem of Those in Love and Inseparable Forever

They never left
the walled garden of their arms.
They wound in circles
about the red rosebush of the lips.
Storms tried to part them
out of pure spite;
so did hard-bitten axes
and bony lightning.

They added something good
to a land of pale hands.

Their bodies measured cliffs
being shoved along by wind
between crumbling mouths.
They rummaged through shipwreck after shipwreck,
their arms each time
growing deeper into their bodies.

Hunted down, crushed,
left alone and abandoned
by moons and memories,
Marches and Novembers,
they saw themselves whirled
like dust that counts for nothing:
they saw themselves whirled,
but they have each other's arms forever.

Written in Count of Toreno Prison at the end of 1939, in the album of a friend

TR. TIMOTHY BALAND

≈ July 18, 1936–July 18, 1938

It is blood. It is not hail, battering my temples.
It is two years of blood; two enormous bloods.
Blood that acts like the sun, you come devouring,
till all the balconies are left drowned and empty.

Blood that is the best of all riches.
Blood that stored up its gifts for love.
See it stirring up seas, surprising trains,
breaking bulls' spirits as it heartens lions.

Time is blood. Time circulates through my veins.
In the presence of the clock and daybreak, I am more than wounded,
and I hear blood colliding, of every shape and size.

Blood where even death could hardly bathe:
moving brilliance of blood that has not grown pale,
because my eyes, a thousand years old, have given it shelter.

TR. TIMOTHY BALAND

≈ **Tomb of the Imagination**

A stonemason wanted . . . he dared to want. . . .
A stonemason wanted, stone upon stone,
wall after wall, to raise an image to the wind,
to the unchaining wind of the future.

He wanted a structure capable of the ethereal.
He dared to want. How deeply he wanted!
An imagination lifted stones made of feathers,
walls made of birds, toward the south wind.

He laughed. He worked. He sang. Walls
like wingbeats flew from his arms
with a force greater than the wing of thunder.
But wingbeats don't last so long.

Finally, stone was his agent. And a mountain
that never rests has the power to fly.
Stone by stone it weighs down and crushes
all it encloses, even a world of living desire.

A stonemason wanted. . . . But stone recovers
its grim brutal density in an instant.
That man worked on his own prison. And in his work
he and the wind were driven headlong.

TR. TOM JONES

≈ **Lullaby of the Onion**

*Lines for his son, after receiving a letter from his wife in which she said that all she
had to eat was bread and onions.*

An onion is frost
shut in and poor.
Frost of your days
and of my nights.
Hunger and onion,

black ice and frost
huge and round.

My son is lying now
in the cradle of hunger.
The blood of an onion
is what he lives on.
But it is your blood,
with sugar on it like frost,
onion and hunger.

A dark woman
turned into moonlight
pours herself down thread
by thread over your cradle.
My son, laugh,
because you can swallow the moon
when you want to.

Lark of my house,
laugh often.
Your laugh is in your eyes
the light of the world.
Laugh so much
that my soul, hearing you,
will beat wildly in space.

Your laugh unlocks doors for me,
it gives me wings.
It drives my solitudes off,
pulls away my jail.
Mouth that can fly,
heart that turns to
lightning on your lips.

Your laugh is the sword
that won all the wars,
it defeats the flowers
and the larks,
challenges the sun.

Future of my bones
and of my love.

The body with wings beating,
the eyelash so quick,
life is full of color
as it never was.
How many linnets
climb with wings beating
out of your body!

I woke up and was an adult:
don't wake up.
My mouth is sad:
you go on laughing.
In your cradle, forever,
defending your laughter
feather by feather.

Your being has a flying range
so high and so wide
that your body is a newly
born sky.
I wish I could climb
back to the starting point
of your travel!

Your laugh, eight months old,
with five orange blossoms.
You have five tiny
ferocities.
You have five teeth
like five new
jasmine blossoms.

They will be the frontier
of kisses tomorrow,
when you feel your rows
of teeth are a weapon.
You will feel a flame

run along under your teeth
looking for the center.

My son, fly away, into the
two moons of the breast:
the breast, onion-
sad, but you, content.
Stay on your feet.
Stay ignorant of what's happening,
and what is going on.

TR. ROBERT BLY

World War II

(1939–1945)

World War II involved all the nations of Europe, the United States, and a vast swath of land along the Pacific rim to the border of India and the islands of the South Pacific; it was fought during the Russian winter, in the deserts of North Africa, and in the jungles of New Guinea. Its cost was remarkable: more than seventy-eight million people were either killed or wounded, with the Soviet Union alone losing twenty million. The combatants numbered some fifty million young men and women.

It is difficult to say precisely when the war began, for the two decades that separated the Treaty of Versailles and the invasion of Poland in 1939 were a preparation for conflict. This was particularly true for Germany, where the wounds caused by a humiliating defeat in 1918 made aggressive militarism more appealing. One can claim that the war began with the Japanese incursions into China in 1931 or with the outbreak of the Spanish Civil War, in which the German air force experimented with *Blitzkrieg* against forces armed by the Russians. We can be sure, however, that the Nazi rise to power in Germany in 1933 made war a terrifying probability which the other European powers tried for six years to avert. The first major crisis came when, in direct contravention of its commitments at Versailles, Germany militarized the Rhineland in 1936. By 1939, when the Nazis annexed part of Czechoslovakia and forced a union with Austria (called the Anschluss), war became inevitable. When the Nazis took Poland on September 1, 1939, the French and the English gave up their policy of appeasement and on September 3 declared war. France was overrun in spring 1940.

The British thus were vulnerable; their primary ally had fallen to the enemy, and the United States, although more than willing to lend material aid, was unwilling to commit to a war. The Germans prepared to invade Britain by following tactics that had worked well in the Netherlands: terror bombing and the achievement of air superiority, followed by a land war. The strategy did not work. Although the Luftwaffe wrought havoc on London and cities like Coventry, the Royal Air Force (RAF) was successful in holding back the enemy. During the summer of 1940, the "Battle of Britain" left the British undefeated.

Denmark and Norway fell to the Nazis in 1940; Bulgaria, Hungary, and Romania joined the Germans and their allies the Italians in 1941. Yugoslavia and Greece were overcome the same year. So by 1941, most of Europe was either conquered by or allied with Germany.

The course of the war began to change in 1941. In the summer of 1941, the Germans broke their pact with the Russians and invaded the

Soviet Union. On December 7 of that year, the Japanese, who had annexed French Indochina and whose goal was to proceed through the South Pacific, bombed the American naval base at Pearl Harbor. The United States and Britain declared war on Japan on December 8; Germany then declared war on the United States.

At first, neither the invasion of the Soviet Union nor the American entry into the war seemed disastrous for the Axis powers of Germany, Italy, and Japan. The Japanese were able to overrun Indonesia, Malaysia, and Burma. The Germans had invaded the Caucasus in the Soviet Union and were almost in Egypt. But the Russians stopped the Nazis at Stalingrad, the British under General Bernard L. Montgomery launched a campaign in North Africa, and the Allies were victorious at the battles of the Coral Sea and Midway. It took close to three years to drive the Japanese—island by island and country by country—back toward Japan; the war against the Japanese did not end until summer 1945, after the United States dropped nuclear bombs on the Japanese cities of Hiroshima and Nagasaki.

The war in Europe was no less bloody than the struggle in the Pacific: it took the Allied forces close to a year to fight their way from Sicily to Rome. France was invaded in 1944 and the Germans were finally defeated in May of 1945.

At the end of World War II, the Russian army stood in possession of vast areas of Eastern Europe. The British and the Americans had liberated most of Western Europe and Greece. There, at the final stages of the conflict, the long-simmering tensions between the Allies became apparent: the Allied firebombing of Dresden and the nuclear bombing of Hiroshima and Nagasaki were as much warnings to the Soviets as they were attacks on the Germans and Japanese. The struggle against Fascism shaded over into the ideological and military struggle between Communism and capitalism that came to be known as the Cold War.

Because of the new emphasis on air warfare during World War II, there ceased to be a clear distinction between soldier and civilian. In many countries, civilians went underground; irregular partisan resistance movements were formed, fighting from ghettoes, farms and cities. Members of the resistance were treated, when captured, like bandits— they were summarily executed and their bodies were left as warnings to others. The bombing of civilians, the resistance movements, and the organized atrocities such as the Holocaust made World War II a truly global war, affecting all sectors of society. Only sub-Saharan Africa and South America were not directly involved in the struggle.

GERTRUDE STEIN (1874–1946)

By the time of World War II, Stein, an American, had become a cultural force in France. Her circle included Picasso and Matisse, she ran a salon for expatriate writers at her apartment on the Rue de Fleurus in Paris, and she wrote difficult, experimental works which explored the possibilities of syntax and repetition. She spent the war in Bilignin, in occupied France, and wrote about life under the Nazis in *Wars I Have Seen* and *Winners and Losers: A Picture of Occupied France*—cannon fire, blown bridges, aerial bombing, and rationing. After the liberation, her apartment in Paris became a tourist attraction for American soldiers. She died after a futile operation in July 1946. Just before she died, she was able to ask, "What is the answer?" She got no response. Her last words were "In that case, what is the question?"

≈ Scenes from the Door

The Ford

It is earnest.
Aunt Pauline is earnest.
We are earnest.
We are united.
Then we see.

Red Faces

Red flags the reason for pretty flags.
And ribbons.
Ribbons of flags
And wearing material
Reason for wearing material.
Give pleasure.
Can you give me the regions.
The regions and the land.
The regions and wheels.

All wheels are perfect.
Enthusiasm.

What Is This

You can't say it's war.
I love conversation.

Do you like it printed.
I like it descriptive.
Not very descriptive.
Not very descriptive.
I like it to come easily
Naturally
And then.
Crystal and cross.
Does not lie on moss.
The three ships.
You mean washing the ships.
One was a lady.
A nun.
She begged meat
Two were husband and wife.
They had a rich father-in-law to the husband.
He did dry cleaning.
And the third one.
A woman.
She washed.
Clothes.
Then this is the way we were helped.
Not interested
We are very much interested.

Daughter

Why is the world at peace.
This may astonish you a little but when you realise how easily Mrs. Charles Bianco sells the work of American painters to American millionaires you will recognise that authorities are constrained to be relieved. Let me tell you a story. A painter loved a woman. A musician did not sing. A South African loved books. An American was a woman and

needed help. Are Americans the same as incubators. But this is the rest of the story. He became an authority.

A Radical Expert

Can you please by asking what is expert. And then we met one another. I do not think it right. Marksman. Expert. Loaf. Potato bread. Sugar Card. Leaf. And mortar. What is the meaning of white wash. The upper wall.
That sounds well.
And then we sinned.
A great many jews say so.

America

Once in English they said America. Was it English to them.
Once they said Belgian.
We like a fog.
Do you for weather.
Are we brave.
Are we true.
Have we the national colour.
Can we stand ditches.
Can we mean well.
Do we talk together.
Have we red cross.
A great many people speak of feet.
And socks.

MAX JACOB (1876–1944)

A painter and a poet, friend of Apollinaire and Picasso, Max Jacob was an innovative writer of prose poems combining humor and deep mysticism. Born a Jew, Jacob converted to Catholicism after having a vision of Christ in the Paris apartment he shared with Picasso, and he later entered the Benedictine Abbey in Saint-Benoît-sur-Loire. His origins, however, made him vulnerable during World War II: he was deported and died of pneumonia in Drancy, a transit camp in France.

≈ War

At night the suburban boulevards are full of snow; the bandits are soldiers. I am attacked with swords and laughter and stripped clean: I save myself only to fall into another square. Is this the courtyard of a barracks, or of an inn? So many swords! So many lancers! It's snowing! I'm being pricked by a poisoned syringe: they want to kill me; a skeleton's head veiled with crepe bites my finger. Dim streetlamps cast the light of my death in the snow.

TR. MICHAEL BROWNSTEIN

≈ In Search of the Traitor

The hotel again! My friend Paul is a prisoner of the Germans. My God, where is he? Lautenbourg, a rooming house on the Rue Saint-Sulpice, but I don't know his room number! The office in the lobby is a pulpit that's too tall for me to see—I would like—is there a Miss Cypriani here? . . . It must be Room 21 or 26 or 28, and of course I begin thinking about the cabalistic significance of these numbers. And it's Paul who is a German prisoner for having betrayed his colonel: what kind of an age are we living in? 21, 26, 28—they are numbers painted in white on a black background with three keys. Who is Miss Cypriani? Another spy.

TR. MICHAEL BROWNSTEIN

≈ Moon Poem

Sometime during the night there are three mushrooms which are the moon. They change position each month at midnight, as abruptly as a cuckoo appears singing from a clock. In the garden there are rare flowers that are small sleeping men, a hundred of them—it's the reflection from the mirror. In my darkened room a luminous censer is prowling, then two . . . and phosphorescent balloons, it's the reflection from a mirror. In my head a bee is speaking.

TR. MICHAEL BROWNSTEIN

≈ **The Horrible Today**

It was nothing more than a Neapolitan Christmas creche. The light fell on the cape of a doll with a fox's head wearing a policeman's hat. This fox was questioning Oedipus in a condescending tone. "You won't answer, Oedipus?" "Have you paid me for that?"

TR. RON PADGETT

EZRA POUND (1885–1972)

In 1920, Pound left the United States, first for Paris and then Italy. He became enamored of Fascism, which he espoused in a number of notorious radio broadcasts during World War II. He was indicted for treason in 1943, arrested in 1944, and sent to a stockade in Pisa, where he wrote the *Pisan Cantos,* excerpted here. Flown to the United States to stand trial in 1945, he was instead sent to St. Elizabeths, a mental hospital in Washington, D.C. The indictment for treason was not dismissed until 1958. On his release from the hospital, he returned to Italy, where he lived until his death. Pound was considered one of the most influential poets of the twentieth century; he worked closely with T. S. Eliot and William Carlos Williams, among others.

≈ *from* **Pisan Canto LXXIV**

The enormous tragedy of the dream in the peasant's bent
        shoulders
        Manes! Manes was tanned and stuffed,
        Thus Ben and la Clara *a Milano*
            by the heels at Milano
That maggots shd/ eat the dead bullock
DIGENES, διγενές, but the twice crucified
            where in history will you find it?
yet say this to the Possum: a bang, not a whimper,
        with a bang not with a whimper,
To build the city of Dioce whose terraces are the colour of stars.

The suave eyes, quiet, not scornful,
                    rain also is of the process.
What you depart from is not the way
and olive tree blown white in the wind
washed in the Kiang and Han
what whiteness will you add to this whiteness,
                              what candor?
"the great periplum brings in the stars to our shore."
You who have passed the pillars and outward from Herakles
when Lucifer fell in N. Carolina.
if the suave air give way to sirocco
'OY TIΣ, 'OY TIΣ? Odysseus
                the name of my family.
the wind also is of the process,
                          sorella la luna
Fear god and the stupidity of the populace,
but a precise definition
        transmitted thus Sigismundo
        thus Duccio, Thus Zuan Bellin, or trastevere with La Sposa
Sponsa Cristi in mosaic till our time / deification of emperors
but a snotty barbarian ignorant of T'ang history need not deceive one
        nor Charlie Sung's money on loan from anonimo
that is, we suppose Charlie had some
and in India the rate down to 18 per hundred
but the local loan lice provided from imported bankers
so the total interest sweated out of the Indian farmers
        rose in Churchillian grandeur
as when, and plus when, he returned to the putrid gold standard
as was about 1925   Oh my England
that free speech without free radio speech is as zero
        and but one point needed for Stalin
you need not, i.e. need not take over the means of production;
money to signify work done, inside a system
        and measured and wanted
"I have not done unnecessary manual labour"
says the R. C. chaplain's field book
            (preparation before confession)
squawky as larks over the death cells
            militarism progressing westward
im Westen nichts neues

and the Constitution in jeopardy
and that state of things not very new either

"of sapphire, for this stone giveth sleep"
not words whereto to be faithful
        nor deeds that they be resolute
            only that bird-hearted equity make timber
                and lay hold of the earth
and Rouse found they spoke of Elias
in telling the tales of Odysseus   'OY TIΣ
                    'OY TIΣ
"I am noman, my name is noman"
but Wanjina is, shall we say, Ouan Jin
or the man with an education
and whose mouth was removed by his father
        because he made too many *things*
whereby cluttered the bushman's baggage
vide the expedition of Frobenius' pupils about 1938
                to Auss'ralia
Ouan Jin spoke and thereby created the named
                    thereby making clutter
the bane of men moving
and so his mouth was removed
as you will find it removed in his pictures
                in principio verbum
            paraclete or the verbum perfectum: sinceritas
from the death cells in sight of Mt. Taishan @ Pisa
as Fujiyama at Gardone
when the cat walked the top bar of the railing
and the water was still on the West side
flowing toward the Villa Catullo
where with sound ever moving
                in diminutive poluphloisboios
in the stillness outlasting all wars
"La Donna" said Nicoletti
            "la donna,
                la donna!"
"Cosa deve continuare?"
"Se casco" said Bianca Capello
"non casco in ginnocchion"

and with one day's reading a man may have the key in his hands
Lute of Gassir. Hooo Fasa
came a lion-coloured pup bringing fleas
and a bird with white markings, a stepper
     under *les six potences*
Absouldre, que tous nous vueil absoudre
lay there Barabbas and two thieves lay beside him
infantile synthesis in Barabbas
minus Hemingway, minus Antheil, ebullient
and by name Thos. Wilson
Mr. K. said nothing foolish, the whole month nothing foolish;
"if we weren't dumb, we wouldn't be here"
     and the Lane gang.
Butterflies, mint and Lesbia's sparrows,
the voiceless with bumm drum and banners,
     and the ideogram of the guard roosts
el triste pensier si volge
   ad Ussel. A Ventadour
     va il consire, el tempo rivolge
and at Limoges the young salesman
bowed with such french politeness "No that is impossible."
I have forgotten which city
But the caverns are less enchanting to the unskilled explorer
   than the Urochs as shown on the postals,
we will see those old roads again, question,
     possibly
but nothing appears much less likely,
     Mme Pujol,
and there was a smell of mint under the tent flaps
especially after the rain
     and a white ox on the road toward Pisa
     as if facing the tower,
dark sheep in the drill field and on wet days were clouds
in the mountains if under the guard roosts.
   A lizard upheld me
   the wild birds wd not eat the white bread
   from Mt Taishan to the sunset
From Carrara stone to the tower
   and this day the air was made open
     for Kuanon of all delights,

Linus, Cletus, Clement
whose prayers,
the great scarab is bowed at the altar
the green light gleams in his shell
plowed in the sacred field and unwound the silk worms early
in tensile
in the light of light is the *virtù*
"sunt lumina" said Erigena Scotus
as of Shun on Mt Taishan
and in the hall of the forebears
as from the beginning of wonders
the paraclete that was present in Yao, the precision
in Shun the compassionate
in Yu the guider of waters

顯

4 giants at the 4 corners
three young men at the door
and they digged a ditch round about me
lest the damp gnaw thru my bones
to redeem Zion with justice
sd/ Isaiah. Not out on interest said David rex
the prime s.o.b.
Light tensile immaculata
the sun's cord unspotted
"sunt lumina" said the Oirishman to King Carolus,
"OMNIA,
all things that are are lights"
and they dug him up out of sepulture
soi disantly looking for Manichaeans.
Les Albigeois, a problem of history,
and the fleet at Salamis made with money lent by the state to the
shipwrights
Tempus tacendi, tempus loquendi.
Never inside the country to raise the standard of living
but always abroad to increase the profits of usurers,
dixit Lenin,
and gun sales lead to more gun sales
they do not clutter the market for gunnery
there is no saturation
Pisa, in the 23rd year of the effort in sight of the tower

and Till was hung yesterday
for murder and rape with trimmings   plus Cholkis
   plus mythology, thought he was Zeus ram or another one
        Hey Snag wots in the bibl'?
        wot are the books ov the bible?
        Name 'em, don't bullshit ME.

H.D. (Hilda Doolittle) (1886–1961)

Daughter of a professor of astronomy, H.D. attended Bryn Mawr College and was a lifelong friend (and onetime fiancée) of Ezra Pound. One of the founders of Anglo-American poetic modernism, she is best known for her work as an imagist. Married to the English poet Richard Aldington, she lived in London from 1911 on, and after their divorce spent the rest of her life traveling and writing in the companionship of Bryher, a novelist and wealthy daughter of a shipping magnate, who was able to secure for H.D. both the stimulation and the solitude necessary to her work. The two women spent the war years in England, enduring the London Blitz of 1940, which is the occasion for the allusive selection excerpted here.

≈ *from* The Walls Do Not Fall

To Bryher

for Karnak 1923
from London 1942

I

An incident here and there,
and rails gone (for guns)
from your (and my) old town square:

mist and mist-grey, no colour,
still the Luxor bee, chick and hare
pursue unalterable purpose

in green, rose-red, lapis;
they continue to prophesy
from the stone papyrus:

there, as here, ruin opens
the tomb, the temple; enter,
there as here, there are no doors:

the shrine lies open to the sky,
the rain falls, here, there
sand drifts; eternity endures:

ruin everywhere, yet as the fallen roof
leaves the sealed room
open to the air,

so, through our desolation,
thoughts stir, inspiration stalks us
through gloom:

unaware, Spirit announces the Presence;
shivering overtakes us,
as of old, Samuel:

trembling at a known street-corner,
we know not nor are known;
the Pythian pronounces—we pass on

to another cellar, to another sliced wall
where poor utensils show
like rare objects in a museum:

Pompeii has nothing to teach us,
we know crack of volcanic fissure,
slow flow of terrible lava,

pressure on heart, lungs, the brain
about to burst its brittle case
(what the skull can endure!):

over us, Apocryphal fire,
under us, the earth sway, dip of a floor,
slope of a pavement

where men roll, drunk
with a new bewilderment,
sorcery, bedevilment:

the bone-frame was made for
no such shock knit within terror,
yet the skeleton stood up to it:

the flesh? it was melted away
the heart burnt out, dead ember,
tendons, muscles shattered, outer husk dismembered,

yet the frame held:
we passed the flame: we wonder
what saved us? what for?

II

Evil was active in the land,
Good was impoverished and sad;

Ill promised adventure,
Good was smug and fat;

Dev-ill was after us,
tricked up like Jehovah;

Good was the tasteless pod,
stripped from the manna-beans, pulse, lentils:

they were angry when we were so hungry
for the nourishment, God;

they snatched off our amulets,
charms are not, they said, grace;

but gods always face two-ways,
so let us search the old highways

for the true-rune, the right-spell,
recover old values;

nor listen if they shout out,
your beauty, Isis, Aset or Astarte,

is a harlot; you are retrogresive,
zealot, hankering after old flesh-pots;

your heart, moreover,
is a dead canker,

they continue, and
your rhythm is the devil's hymn,

your stylus is dipped in corrosive sublimate,
how can you scratch out

indelible ink of the palimpsest
of past misadventures?

VI

In me (the worm) clearly
is no righteousness, but this—

persistence; I escaped spider-snare,
bird-claw, scavenger bird-beak,

clung to grass-blade,
the back of a leaf

when storm-wind
tore it from its stem;

I escaped, I explored
rose-thorn forest,

was rain-swept
down the valley of a leaf;

was deposited on grass,
where mast by jewelled mast

bore separate ravellings
of encrusted gem-stuff

of the mist
from each banner-staff:

unintimidated by multiplicity
of magnified beauty,

such as your gorgon-great
dull eye can not focus

nor compass, I profit
by every calamity;

I eat my way out of it;
gorged on vine-leaf and mulberry,

parasite, I find nourishment:
when you cry in disgust,

a worm on the leaf,
a worm in the dust,

a worm on the ear-of-wheat,
I am yet unrepentant,

for I know how the Lord God
is about to manifest, when I,

the industrious worm,
spin my own shroud.

IX

Thoth, Hermes, the stylus,
the palette, the pen, the quill endure,

though our books are a floor
of smouldering ash under our feet;

though the burning of the books remains
the most perverse gesture

and the meanest
of man's mean nature,

yet give us, they still cry,
give us books,

folio, manuscript, old parchment
will do for cartridge cases;

irony is bitter truth
wrapped up in a little joke,

and Hatshepsut's name is still circled
with what they call the *cartouche.*

X

But we fight for life,
we fight, they say, for breath.

so what good are your scribblings?
this—we take them with us

beyond death; Mercury, Hermes, Thoth
invented the script, letters, palette;

the indicated flute or lyre-notes
on papyrus or parchment

are magic, indelibly stamped
on the atmosphere somewhere,

forever; remember, O Sword,
you are the younger brother, the latter-born,

your Triumph, however exultant,
must one day be over,

in the beginning
was the Word.

SAINT-JOHN PERSE (ALEXIS SAINT-LÉGER LÉGER) (1887–1975)

Saint-John Perse was born on the Caribbean island of Guadeloupe. He entered the French foreign service, served as an ambassador between 1916 and 1921, and became secretary-general of the French Ministry of Foreign Affairs. Exiled from France after the Nazi occupation, he was deprived of his French citizenship by the Vichy government. For almost twenty years he lived in the United States, where he worked at the Library of Congress and taught at Harvard. His poetry is epic, metaphysical, and richly infused with images. Circumspect and private about his poetry, Perse nonetheless gained a wide reputation, and he was awarded the Nobel Prize for Literature in 1960. The poem excerpted here is a reflection of his despair at the fate of France during World War II.

≈ *from* Exile

To Archibald MacLeish

I

Doors open on the sands, doors open on exile,
   The keys with the lighthouse keepers, and sun beaten out on the threshold stone:
   Leave me, dear host, your house of glass on the sands . . .
   Summer, all gypsum, whets its lance-heads in our wounds,
   I have chosen a place glaring and null as the bone-heap of the seasons,

And, on all the shores of the world, the ghost of the god in smoke abandons his bed of asbestos.

The spasms of lightning are for the delight of Princes in Taurida.

II

Dedicated to no shores, imparted to no pages, the pure beginning of this song . . .

Others in temples seize on the painted altar horns:

My fame is on the sands! my fame is on the sands! . . . And it is no error, O Peregrine,

To desire the barest place for assembling on the wastes of exile a great poem born of nothing, a great poem made from nothing . . .

Whistle, O slings about the world, sing, O conches on the waters!

I have built upon the abyss and the spindrift and the sand-smoke. I shall lie down in cistern and hollow vessel,

In all stale and empty places where lies the taste of greatness.

". . . There were fewer breezes to flatter the Julii; fewer alliances to assist the great priestly castes.

Where the sands go to their song, there go the Princes of exile,

Where there were high taut sails, there goes the wreck more silken than a lute-maker's dream,

Where there were great military actions, there lies whitening now the jawbone of an ass,

And the rounding sea rolls her noise of skulls on the shores,

And all things in the world to her are in vain, so we heard one night at the world's edge

From the wind's militias in the sands of exile . . ."

Wisdom in the foam, O plagues of the mind in the creptation of salt and the milk of quicklime!

I learn a science from the soul's insurrections . . . The wind tells us its piracies, the wind tells us its errors!

Like the Rider, lariat in hand, at the gate of the desert,

I watch in this vast arena signs of good omen soaring.

And morning, for our sake, moves her prophetic finger through sacred writings.

Exile is not of yesterday! exile is not of yesterday! . . . "O vestiges, O premises,"

Says the stranger on the sands, "the whole world is new to me . . ."
And the birth of his song is no less alien to him.

III

". . . There has always been this clamour, there has always been this splendour,

And like a great feat of arms on the march across the world, like a census of peoples in exodus, like a foundation of empires in praetorian tumult, ah! like an animation of lips over the birth of great Books,

The huge muffled thing loose in the world, and suddenly growing huger like drunkenness . . .

". . . There has always been this clamour, there has always been this grandeur,

This thing wandering about the world, this high trance about the world, and on all the shores of the world, by the same breath uttered, the same wave uttering

One long phrase without pause forever unintelligible . . .

". . . There has always been this clamour, there has always been this furor,

And this tall surf at the pitch of passion, always, at the peak of desire, the same gull on the wing, the same gull under way, rallying with spread wings the stanzas of exile, and on all the shores of the world, by the same breath uttered, the same measureless lamentation

Pursuing across the sands my Numidian soul . . ."

I know you, monster-head! Once more face to face. We take up the long debate where we left off.

And you may urge your arguments like snouts low over the water: I will leave you no rest and no respite.

On too many frequented shores have my footsteps been washed away before the day, on too many deserted beds has my soul been delivered up to the cancer of silence.

What more do you want of me, O breath of origin? And you, what more would you drag from my living lips,

O power wandering about my threshold, O Beggarwoman on our roads and on the trail of the Prodigal?

The wind tells us its age, the wind tells us its youth . . . Honour thine exile, O Prince!

And all at once all is power and presence for me, here where the theme of nothingness rises still in smoke.

". . . Higher, night by night, this silent clamour upon my sill, higher, night by night, this ring of the ages in their bristling scales,

And on all the shores of the world a fiercer iambic verse to be fed from my being! . . .

So great an altitude can never annul the sheer fall from thy sill, O Seizer of swords at dawn,

O Handler of eagles by their angles, Feeder of women shrill in their iron plumes!

All things at birth bristle to the east of the world, all flesh at birth exults in the first fires of day!

And here, a greater murmur is rising around the world, like an insurrection of the soul . . .

You shall not cease, O clamour, until, upon the sands, I shall have sloughed off every human allegiance. (Who knows his birthplace still?)"

TR. DENIS DEVLIN

YVAN GOLL (1891–1950)

Born on the border between France and Germany, Goll wrote in both French and German and was known as a leading expressionist poet of highly personal, nonrepresentational poetry. He was educated in Berlin before World War I and at its outbreak fled to Switzerland and then to Paris, where he became one of the founders of surrealism. With the advent of World War II, he was forced into exile again, moving to New York. He remained there until 1945, when he returned to Paris. He died of leukemia in 1950. "Lackawanna Elegy" was written during his exile in New York.

≈ **Your Sleep**

Your sleep is a closed almond
The almond of strength, of growth,
There is nothing that does not happen inside this fruit!
You are the earth of a great dream
From your heart small rose-colored almond trees are growing
Oh happy Umbrian countryside!
But on the hill the huts of men are burning

And their sons will die before Easter
Cracked bells beat at your ear
I hear them as if they were in sea-shells
Death-candles shine through your temples
Blood runs from your closed eyes
Alas, when you open them,
What color will they be?

TR. PAUL ZWEIG

≈ The Last River

The last river leaves for desolation
It doesn't even carry a last boat
It is not made of water or blood
It surged from the earth in thick vomit

It is dead like the rivers of the moon
And yet the logical moon keeps her distance
More antiseptic than iodine or chlorine
She refuses to touch this river of men

The exhaustion of a continent flows down
The torn caps of socialism swirl in eddies
The ripped cupboards of the holy family
And the carcasses of the watch-dogs of God

Shadows set out their watches run down
They will never again learn the exact time
Adrift on a current of lead
They even leave behind their tombstones already paid for.

TR. GALWAY KINNELL

≈ Lackawanna Elegy

America
    The tongues of your rivers burn with thirst
America
    The coal in your mountains goes mad with sunlight

America
   The arms of your sequoias ask pity of the storms
America America

      Your heart's drum
      Eats its own bones
      The eyes of your clocks
      Turn counter-clockwise seeking the past

And on her crumbling headland the Indian woman
Turns toward you eyes weighed down with asphalt
Her mercury and orange head shrinks just slightly
Her small breasts bared to the gnawing white ants

      She paints on the sand
      The oracle which a night effaces
      A rattlesnake gripped in her teeth
      She exorcises the white ghost
      Locked in the Kiva of hate

A shiver of feathers down the reed of the spine
Stirs your ash body America
A thorn is stuck in your twilight brow
A thorn is sown in the fields of hemp
A thorn is screwed into the heel of your dancers

America beware of your past
Of the Katchinas filled with menace
For wrath ripens its fiery apple
In the orchards of the Appalachians
In the desert colored by witches

In the rose-garden of your sick soul
The holocaust waits to begin.

    TR. GALWAY KINNELL

PAUL ÉLUARD   (1895–1952)

A Parisian by birth, Éluard served in World War I and returned to the French capital in time to be influenced by the dadaists, an early-twen-tieth-century avant-garde movement which advocated freedom and disdained tradition. With André Breton, he helped found surrealism, but broke with his friend over the Spanish Civil War, because he re-fused to remain neutral. Éluard joined the intellectual opposition to Hitler in 1939 and went on to fight with the resistance. After the war, he traveled extensively in the service of the Communist Party. A *poète engagé,* he is known for his poignant love poems. "November 1936" was written out of his concern for the Republican cause during the Spanish Civil War; the other selections were written in occupied France.

≈ November 1936

Look the builders of ruins are working
They are rich patient tidy dark and ugly
But they do their best to stay alone on earth
Detached from man they heap the dirt upon him
Without a mind they fold up mansions flat.

One gets used to everything
Except these leaden birds
Except their hatred of shining things
Except making way for them.

Speak of the sky the sky empties
Autumn does not matter much
Our masters stamped their feet
We forgot autumn
And we shall forget our masters.

A city declining an ocean made of a drop of water spared
Made of a single diamond cut in broad daylight

Madrid a city familiar to those who suffered
From this frightful blessing that denies example
Who suffered
From the torment that the lustre of this blessing needs.

Let the mouth return towards its truth
Whisper rare smile like a broken chain
Let man delivered of his senseless past
Rise before his brother a friendly face

And give to reason roving wings.

TR. GILBERT BOWEN

≈ Meetings

To Germaine and Georges Hugnet

I

Sweet monster you hold death in your beak
Sweet monster the good milk pearls at your breasts
In your happy eyes my wretched eyes
Go to cut the wheat dry up the fountains
And turn the human roads away from you.

II

The cruel ravishing bears
Born the same day as the war
Pronounce innocent wishes.

III

The prisoner's cell
Which was not too large for a spider.

IV

Blindworm beam of the balance
Between two transparent hatreds.

V

Look out your feathers overflow
You tremble at not flying.

VI

Here I am born what a mistake
Says friend dog for always

VII

The fields pink green yellow
Are brilliant insects
Gone
From my infinite field of May.

VIII

Houses and streets extinguished in my ears
I dream of you crows who sing the silence

Crows with encrusted beaks
So old
That they know themselves no longer in the world.

IX

Here a thousand magpies dispute
A thousand little diurnal moons.

X

To make us forget the cold
On the snow a finger traced
The blonde silhouette of a lion.

XI

Be careful of your paws
Man has his feet in blood.

TR. LLOYD ALEXANDER

≈ Nazi Song

The mad flight of a butterfly
The window the escape
The interminable sun
The inexhaustible promise
Which makes sport of bullets
Circles the eyes with a shudder

The tree is new the tree is bleeding
My children it is springtime
The last of the seasons
Hasten and enjoy it
It is the death-camp or the prison
The rifle-shot or the front

This is the last mothers' festival
The heart surrenders let us do homage
Everywhere to death and misery
And Germany enslaved
And Germany cowering
In the blood in the pus
In the open wounds she has dug
Our task is finished

So sing and sing well
The good master assassins.

TR. LLOYD ALEXANDER

≈ Dawn Dissolves the Monsters

They did not know
That the beauty of man is greater than man

They lived to think they thought to keep silent
They lived to die and they were useless
They recovered their innocence in death

They had put in order
In the name of riches
Their misery their beloved

They gnawed away the flowers and the smiles
They found a heart only at the end of their rifles

They did not understand the curses of the poor
Of the poor carefree tomorrow

Sunless dreams made them eternal
But to change the cloud to mud
They went down they looked no longer at the sky

All their night their death their fine shadow misery
Misery for the others

We shall forget these indifferent enemies

Soon masses
Will repeat the bright flame in a very gentle voice
The flame for us two for us alone patience
For us two in every place the kiss of the living.

TR. LLOYD ALEXANDER

≈ To Her of Whom They Dream

Nine hundred thousand prisoners of war
Five hundred thousand political prisoners
One million forced workers

Mistress of their slumber
Give them the strength of men
The happiness of being on earth
In the immense shadow give them
The lips of a sweet love
Like the oblivion of suffering

Mistress of their slumber
Daughter wife sister and mother

With breasts swollen with kisses
Give them our country
Such as they have always loved it
A country mad with life

A country where the wine sings
Where the harvests have a good heart
Where the children are clever
Where the old men are finer
Than fruit trees white with blossoms
Where one may speak to women

Nine hundred thousand prisoners of war
Five hundred thousand political prisoners
One million forced workers

Mistress of their slumber
Black snow of white sleepless nights
Across a bloodless fire
Sainte Aube with the blindman's cane
Show them a new road
Out of their wooden prisons

They are paid to know
The worst forces of evil
Still they have held good
They are riddled with virtues
As many as they have wounds
For they must survive

Mistress of their repose
Mistress of their awakenings
Give them liberty
But keep with us our shame
For having been able to believe in shame
Even to stifle it.

TR. LLOYD ALEXANDER

Tristan Tzara (Sami Rosenstock) (1896–1963)

Born in Romania, Tzara was one of the founders of Dada in Zurich in 1916. After World War I he moved to Paris and led French dadaism until he declared it dead in 1924. After a seven-year quarrel with André Breton was patched up in 1929, he joined the surrealists, but left them in the mid-1930s to become a member of the Communist Party. He served the Party during the Spanish Civil War as a delegate to Spain for the "Association for the Defense of Culture." Returning to France during World War II, he fought with the resistance. "Waking" is an example of his surrealist work, and the second selection is an homage to fellow surrealist poet and member of the resistance Robert Desnos.

≈ **Waking**

Hasten toward immense and earthly joy, the eyelids blinking as they dance against the wall of night. Enough of explicit death, light-hearted death used down to the nail polish, youth lost in the apostrophes of hypocrisy! Enough of the lifeless breath of hearts woven into salubrious baskets. Hasten toward the human joy inscribed on your forehead like an indelible debt!

A new form of summer vegetable is falling on the world's mist in tufts of slow grass, covering it with a thin layer of expected joy, of a glorious future foreshadowed in the steel. Hurry up, it is a brilliant human joy waiting for you at the turn-off point of this dismembered world, spoken in tongue of asphalt! There are reverses, springs sealed off, lips on tambourines and eyes without indifference. Salt and fire await you on the mineral hill of the incandescence of living.

TR. Mary Ann Caws

≈ **For Robert Desnos**

in the white of my thought
a blackbird shrieks the grass sings

over the decapitated town
whistles the sudden air of blood
shaking the ripe tree
beggar of light

milady will you
and death displays his wrist watch
empty teeth on the band
and the bones of a thousand witnesses
milady will you
the dead wood of strong jaws
quietly closes the workings

one single hope in your head
in your head a forest
by the breaking of stars
I have known the melody
from which memory rises
there is no more resounding voice
in Paris paved with leaves
a summer does not respond when it is called
I am alone in knowing it

forget your sons your mothers
youth springtimes
lovers' kisses
the gold of time
a naked name is still flying about

in the nights around the lamps
and the clenched fist of towns
lifts to the heart of day
this light this revolt
which you offer to passersby
in the palm of your hand
that of the world

in your arms which a wave could sweep away
one bird nothing more except anger
a face at my window

a joy is floating
my secret my reason for being
and the world

TR. MARY ANN CAWS

PHILIPPE SOUPAULT (1897–1990)

An active translator and journalist as well as a poet, Soupault was an early collaborator with André Breton and a founder of surrealism. The organizer of Radio Tunisia, he was arrested by the Vichy government and imprisoned in Vichy, where he was tortured by the Nazis and held for six months before escaping to Algeria, where he set up Radio Algeria. One of his early novels was translated by William Carlos Williams, and he himself worked with James Joyce on a translation of part of *Finnegans Wake*. His poetry is musical, highly associative, and linguistically playful.

≈ Poems from Saint Pelagia Prison

I

Wednesday on a barge
and you Saturday like a flag
the days have crowns
like kings and dead men
lissome as a kiss my hand
rests on chained foreheads
A child cries for her doll
and we'll have to start over again
Monday and Tuesday cold-blooded
four Thursdays off from work

II

a thread unravels
a shadow falls
a butterfly explodes
chrysalis or glow worm

III

Who mounts
the storm
a balloon
honey or silver moon
Four by four
Let's look for the children
the parents of children
the children of children
the bells of springtime
the beginnings of summer
the regrets of autumn
the silence of winter
an elephant in his bathtub
and the three sleeping children
singular singular tale
tale of the setting sun

TR. PAULETTE SCHMIDT

≈ One o'Clock

Here are the brains here the hearts
here the bloody packets
and the vain tears and cries
of hands turned inside out
Here is all the rest pell-mell
Everything the death throe mourns
The wind can just as well blow wild
gesturing
or whistle low like a crafty animal
and time collapses
like a large gray bird
on this heap where bubbles are born
Nothing remains after all
but this ash on the lips
this taste of ash in the mouth
forever

TR. PAULETTE SCHMIDT

≈ Condemned

Warm night fallen night
Lost time
Farther than the night
the last hour
the only one that matters
Scattered forces secret night
when the time is near
when finally and again
I must lean into this conquering
shadow
lean into this ending into this fire
into what is fading away
Sighs silences sufferings
A little courage a second
only
and already this slowness ends
a faint light lost
Winds from heaven, wait
for a word a gesture
once and for all
I raise my hand
you'd think the battle
begins and is
deep down
farther perhaps
the sound of the gallop
of a bell
forgotten
forgotten

TR. PAULETTE SCHMIDT

≈ You Who Sleep

In the west you're still asleep
But already in the east
dawn comes on
like pain

It is the hour
of those who are no more
of those who wait
who hold their tongues
to die
like all the rest
the ones who came before them
Is that the sea betraying silence
Is it hunger howling with the wind
Listen listen
all of you who sleep
and you who suffer more
each day
who no longer hope
but are still watching

TR. PAULETTE SCHMIDT

BERTOLT BRECHT (1898–1956)

Brecht was born in Augsburg, the capital of Bavarian Swabia. His early plays are fine examples of expressionist drama and exhibit the radical staging techniques that were his trademark. One of the most important poets and playwrights of the twentieth century, he is most famous in the United States for *The Threepenny Opera,* a scathing attack on the corruption of the Weimar Republic (and on capitalism in general). Brecht was a committed Marxist (the Nazi Party had marked him for execution as early as 1923) and in 1933 was forced to flee Germany. His sixteen-year exile brought him to Denmark, Sweden, Finland, and the United States, where he was called before the House Committee for Un-American Activities. He returned to East Berlin in 1949, where he founded a theater company and remained an independent voice in spite of official pressure. "From a German War Primer" was written against the prewar German leadership, particularly the "house-painter," Adolf Hitler.

≈ The God of War

I saw the old god of war stand in a bog between chasm and rockface.

He smelled of free beer and carbolic and showed his testicles to adolescents, for he had been rejuvenated by several professors. In a hoarse wolfish voice he declared his love for everything young. Nearby stood a pregnant woman, trembling.

And without shame he talked on and presented himself as a great one for order. And he described how everywhere he put barns in order, by emptying them.

And as one throws crumbs to sparrows, he fed poor people with crusts of bread which he had taken away from poor people.

His voice was now loud, now soft, but always hoarse.

In a loud voice he spoke of great times to come, and in a soft voice he taught the women how to cook crows and seagulls. Meanwhile his back was unquiet, and he kept looking round, as though afraid of being stabbed.

And every five minutes he assured his public that he would take up very little of their time.

TR. MICHAEL HAMBURGER

≈ When Evil-Doing Comes Like Falling Rain

Like one who brings an important letter to the counter after office
    hours: the counter is already closed.
Like one who seeks to warn the city of an impending flood, but speaks
    another language. They do not understand him.
Like a beggar who knocks for the fifth time at a door where he has four
    times been given something: the fifth time he is hungry.
Like one whose blood flows from a wound and who awaits the doctor:
    his blood goes on flowing.
So do we come forward and report that evil has been done us.

The first time it was reported that our friends were being butchered
    there was a cry of horror. Then a hundred were butchered. But
    when a thousand were butchered and there was no end to the
    butchery, a blanket of silence spread.

When evil-doing comes like falling rain, nobody calls out 'stop!'

When crimes begin to pile up they become invisible. When sufferings
become unendurable the cries are no longer heard. The cries, too,
fall like rain in summer.

TR. JOHN WILLETT

≈ From a German War Primer

AMONGST THE HIGHLY PLACED
It is considered low to talk about food.
The fact is: they have
Already eaten.

The lowly must leave this earth
Without having tasted
Any good meat.

For wondering where they come from and
Where they are going
The fine evenings find them
Too exhausted.

They have not yet seen
The mountains and the great sea
When their time is already up.

If the lowly do not
Think about what's low
They will never rise.

THE BREAD OF THE HUNGRY HAS
ALL BEEN EATEN
Meat has become unknown. Useless
The pouring out of the people's sweat.
The laurel groves have been
Lopped down.
From the chimneys of the arms factories
Rises smoke.

THE HOUSE-PAINTER SPEAKS OF
GREAT TIMES TO COME
The forests still grow.
The fields still bear
The cities still stand.
The people still breathe.

ON THE CALENDAR THE DAY IS NOT
YET SHOWN
Every month, every day
Lies open still. One of those days
Is going to be marked with a cross.

THE WORKERS CRY OUT FOR BREAD
The merchants cry out for markets.
The unemployed were hungry. The employed
Are hungry now.
The hands that lay folded are busy again.
They are making shells.

THOSE WHO TAKE THE MEAT FROM THE TABLE
Teach contentment.
Those for whom the contribution is destined
Demand sacrifice.
Those who eat their fill speak to the hungry
Of wonderful times to come.
Those who lead the country into the abyss
Call ruling too difficult
For ordinary men.

WHEN THE LEADERS SPEAK OF PEACE
The common folk know
That war is coming.
When the leaders curse war
The mobilisation order is already written out.

THOSE AT THE TOP SAY: PEACE
AND WAR
Are of different substance.
But their peace and their war
Are like wind and storm.

War grows from their peace
Like son from his mother
He bears
Her frightful features.

Their war kills
Whatever their peace
Has left over.

ON THE WALL WAS CHALKED:
They want war.
The man who wrote it
Has already fallen.

THOSE AT THE TOP SAY:
This way to glory.
Those down below say:
This way to the grave.

THE WAR WHICH IS COMING
Is not the first one. There were
Other wars before it.
When the last one came to an end
There were conquerors and conquered.
Among the conquered the common people
Starved. Among the conquerors
The common people starved too.

THOSE AT THE TOP SAY COMRADESHIP
Reigns in the army.
The truth of this is seen
In the cookhouse.
In their hearts should be
The selfsame courage. But
On their plates
Are two kinds of rations.

WHEN IT COMES TO MARCHING MANY DO NOT
KNOW
That their enemy is marching at their head.
The voice which gives them their orders

Is their enemy's voice and
The man who speaks of the enemy
Is the enemy himself.

IT IS NIGHT
The married couples
Lie in their beds. The young women
Will bear orphans.

GENERAL, YOUR TANK IS A POWERFUL VEHICLE
It smashes down forests and crushes a hundred men.
But it has one defect:
It needs a driver.

General, your bomber is powerful.
It flies faster than a storm and carries more than an elephant.
But it has one defect:
It needs a mechanic.

General, man is very useful.
He can fly and he can kill.
But he has one defect:
He can think.

TR. JOHN WILLETT, RALPH MANHEIM, AND ERICH FRIED

≋ **To Those Born Later**

I

Truly, I live in dark times!
The guileless word is folly. A smooth forehead
Suggests insensitivity. The man who laughs
Has simply not yet had
The terrible news.

What kind of times are they, when
A talk about trees is almost a crime
Because it implies silence about so many horrors?
That man there calmly crossing the street

Is already perhaps beyond the reach of his friends
Who are in need?

It is true I still earn my keep
But, believe me, that is only an accident. Nothing
I do gives me the right to eat my fill.
By chance I've been spared. (If my luck breaks, I am lost.)

They say to me: Eat and drink! Be glad you have it!
But how can I eat and drink if I snatch what I eat
From the starving, and
My glass of water belongs to one dying of thirst?
And yet I eat and drink.

I would also like to be wise.
In the old books it says what wisdom is:
To shun the strife of the world and to live out
Your brief time without fear
Also to get along without violence
To return good for evil
Not to fulfil your desires but to forget them
Is accounted wise.
All this I cannot do:
Truly, I live in dark times.

II

I came to the cities in a time of disorder
When hunger reigned there.
I came among men in a time of revolt
And I rebelled with them.
So passed my time
Which had been given to me on earth.

My food I ate between battles
To sleep I lay down among murderers
Love I practised carelessly
And nature I looked at without patience.
So passed my time
Which had been given to me on earth.

All roads led into the mire in my time.
My tongue betrayed me to the butchers.
There was little I could do. But those in power
Sat safer without me: that was my hope.
So passed my time
Which had been given to me on earth.

Our forces were slight. Our goal
Lay far in the distance
It was clearly visible, though I myself
Was unlikely to reach it.
So passed my time
Which had been given to me on earth.

III

You who will emerge from the flood
In which we have gone under
Remember
When you speak of our failings
The dark time too
Which you have escaped.

TR. JOHN WILLETT, RALPH MANHEIM, AND ERICH FRIED

≈ The World's One Hope

1 Is oppression as old as the moss around ponds?
The moss around ponds is not avoidable.
Perhaps everything I see is natural, and I am sick and want to remove
what cannot be removed?
I have read songs of the Egyptians, of their men who built the pyra-
mids. They complained of their loads and asked when oppression
would cease. That's four thousand years ago.
Oppression, it would seem, is like the moss and unavoidable.

2 When a child is about to be run down by a car one pulls it on to the
pavement.
Not the kindly man does that, to whom they put up monuments.
Anyone pulls the child away from the car.

But here many have been run down, and many pass by and do nothing of the sort.
Is that because it's so many who are suffering? Should one not help them all the more because they are many? One helps them less. Even the kindly walk past and after that are as kindly as ever they were before walking past.

3 The more there are suffering, then, the more natural their sufferings appear. Who wants to prevent the fishes in the sea from getting wet?
And the suffering themselves share this callousness towards themselves and are lacking kindness towards themselves.
It is terrible that human beings so easily put up with existing conditions, not only with the sufferings of strangers but also with their own.
All those who have thought about the bad state of things refuse to appeal to the compassion of one group of people for another. But the compassion of the oppressed for the oppressed is indispensable.
It is the world's one hope.

TR. JOHN WILLETT, RALPH MANHEIM, AND ERICH FRIED

BENJAMIN PÉRET (1899–1959)

A close friend of André Breton and an active surrealist from the start of the movement, the French-born Péret wrote poetry, novels, and polemics. He joined the Communist Party in 1926, worked as an organizer for the Trotskyist Fourth International in Brazil in the early 1930s, and was expelled from Brazil for his political activities. On his return to Europe, he participated in the Spanish Civil War, fighting on the side of the Trotskyists in Catalonia, then became disaffected with the Communists and joined the anarchists in 1937. When World War II began, he was arrested by the Nazis, imprisoned, and ransomed. Unable to enter the United States because of his past affiliations, he fled to Mexico, where he struggled to support himself. He returned to France after the war and lived in Paris until his death.

≈ Hymn of the Patriotic War Veterans

Look how handsome I am
I hunted for moles in the Ardennes
fished for sardines on the Belgian coast
I'm an old war veteran

If the Marne flows into the Seine
it's because I won back the Marne
If there's wine in the Champagne region
it's because I pissed there

Even though I threw down my rifle butt
the Tauben still spit in my eye
that's how I got decorated
Long live the republic

I got rabbit punches in the ass
I was blinded by goat turds
asphyxiated by my horse's dung
then they gave me the Cross of Honor

But now I'm out of the army
pomegrenades explode in my face
and lemons burst in my hand
And yet I'm an old war veteran

To remind everyone of my ribbon
I've painted my nose red
and I've got parsley sticking out of it
for the Cross of War

I'm an old war veteran
look how handsome I am

TR. KEITH HOLLAMAN

≈ Nungesser und Coli Sind Verreckt

They took off
and tricolor flags came out of their assholes
In the sewer of the French sky
they were more at ease than toads
but when they had sailed past their spit
the sharks came to meet them
and caught up with them somewhere between two waves
capped with top hats
like patriotic pallbearers
But they had already decomposed
and in their eyes the worms pretended to be question marks
The waves spit in disgust as they came nearer
and swallowed them with a single hiccup
Soak in the big urinal you old croutons
Not even a lecherous maniac with crumbling fingers
would dare touch your wretched putridness
You've kicked the bucket Nungesser and Coli
you still missed the unjust war
and those you assassinated come up to you now
They have executioners' eyes and garrote hands
but they smile knowing that they are finally avenged
Today the beautiful sea monsters
come to sniff the sponges of your bodies
and say
Ugh they're French stinking of holy water
leave them for their country's priests
who will make their skulls into communion chalices
and use their bones for candlesticks
As for us we will have huffing bankers
generals covered with vomit
and the usual complete idiots found in every country

TR. KEITH HOLLAMAN

FRANCIS PONGE (1899–1988)

Ponge, an early surrealist, became a militant Communist in 1936 and did not break with the Party until 1947. He was active in the resistance during World War II and organized journalists to the cause. He lived in Algeria for two years and returned to Paris in 1949 to teach. His precise explorations of the world of objects won him the support and friendship of Jean-Paul Sartre, and his attempt to abandon traditional poetic practices and found a "new rhetoric" has become the subject of numerous philosophical meditations.

≈ The Sun as a Spinning Top (I)

It is perfectly natural for the Sun to shine initially in the upper lefthand corner of the first page of this book.

Brilliant Sun! At first, an exclamation of joy and in response the acclamation of the world (even through tears, but it makes them shine).

There is every reason to believe (curious expression) that we are inside the sun; or at least inside the system of its power and its love.

The day is the pulp of a fruit, the sun is the pit. And we, drowned in this pulp like its imperfections, its spots, its *defects*. We are symmetrical in relationship to its center. Its rays envelop us, run past us, and then go on to play far ahead.

Night is the spectacle, the consideration; but the day is a prison, the forced labor of the sky.
This star is pride itself. The only instance where pride is justified.
Satisfied by what? Satisfied with itself, dominating everything.
Everything created is lit by it, warmed by it, recreated by it.

"The sun dispels the clouds, recreates them, and then goes through the rider, without even using all its strength . . ." (La Fontaine, Phoebe and Boreas).

Brusquely, the flashes of light and heat together blanch the outside of the sails.

But in the long run, cold currents of water in the bath always win out.

The sun animates a world which it had first damned to extinction: it is then only a feverish or agonizing animation.

In the last stages of its rule, it creates human beings capable of contemplating it; then they die, altogether, and yet they remain as spectators (or escorts).

The sun, animating, lighting what contemplates it, plays a psycho-complicated game with it, flirts with it.

At times, its nozzle inundates us, at times, only the roof or a large window.

In the great barrel of the sky, it is the radiant bung, often enveloped in a rag of dull clouds, but always humid, so powerful is the interior pressure of the fluid, so impregnating its nature.

At the moment of his death, Goethe saw the bung give way and the fluid (pure and dangerous) spurt out, and he said: "More light." That may indeed be *death*.

Dazzling sea-urchin. Clew. Dented wheel. A blow of the fist. Tomahawk. Bludgeon.

Here, the *first* and *last* are all mixed up.
Drums and drumbeat.
Every object finds its place between two rolls of the drum.

TR. SERGE GAVRONSKY

≈ The Silent World Is Our Only Homeland

Addressing the readers of a well-run newspaper, that is, one abounding in "capital" pronouncements of the "greatest" world-wide publicists, I need hardly inform them that we are doubtless running ahead on the prodromes of a new civilization, while for centuries the decay of the preceding one has been following along. Indications of the new era can be seen primarily in the painting of the Paris school since Cézanne, and in the French poetry of the 1870's. Only it seems that poetry has not quite caught up with painting in that it has produced fewer constructed works, works that make their impact by form alone (but we are seeing to that).

Since World War I everything has been dominated by the great schism in the declining civilization, which hastens evolution. Only the geniuses in painting, Braque in the lead, have been supporting the new spirit. And it is only as of the last few years (almost everyone having previously thought the contrary) that we can afford to congratulate ourselves for staying on *that side,* since the delightful anarchy prevailing there at least lets the seeds live, take root (more often than not in misery), survive in any event, and sometimes reach the surface.

In short, we know, only lately—and this is what is essentially MOD-ERN—how civilizations are born, live and die. We know that after a period of discovering new values (always taken directly from the cosmos, but magnified and unrealistic), what follows is their elaboration, elucidation, dogmatization and refinement; we know above all, because in Europe we have been living with it since the Reformation, that as soon as values are dogmatized schisms arise, followed sooner or later by catastrophe.

Yes. That is what we cannot forget, and what many poets have understood. That, if it is anywhere, is the GREATNESS of modern man and, for the first time perhaps, PROGRESS (?). We know that we must necessarily go through the whole cycle I have just described, for such is the nature of man. At least we can try not to linger in either of these periods, and above all to get out of the dangerous classical period as fast as possible, that period of perfect mythology and dogmatization. So that, rather than end INEVITABLY in catastrophe, LET US IMMEDI-ATELY ABOLISH VALUES, in every work (and in every method), AT THE VERY MOMENT WE DISCOVER, ELABORATE, ELUCIDATE, REFINE THEM. This, in poetry for example, is the lesson learned from Mallarmé. This, moreover, is the point of all great masterworks and what makes them eternally valid; nothing can prevent the MEANINGS, which have been LOCKED into the humblest OBJECT OR PERSON, from always *striking the hour,* the serial hour (of Hell or Paradise).

In these terms, one will surely understand what I consider to be the function of poetry. It is to nourish the spirit of man by giving him the cosmos to suckle. We have only to lower our standard of dominating nature and to raise our standard of participating in it in order to make the reconciliation take place. When man becomes proud to be not just the site where ideas and feelings are produced, but also the crossroad where they divide and mingle, he will be ready to be saved. Hope therefore lies in a poetry through which the world so invades the spirit of man that he becomes almost speechless, and later reinvents a language. Poets should in no way concern themselves with human relationships, but should get to the very bottom. Society, furthermore, takes good care of putting them there, and the love of things keeps them there; they are the ambassadors of the silent world. As such, they stammer, they murmur, they sink into the darkness of logos—until at last they reach the level of ROOTS, where things and formulas are one.

This is why, whatever one says, poetry is much more important then any other art, any other science. This is also why poetry has nothing in common with what appears in the poetry anthologies of today. True poetry is what does not pretend to be poetry. It is in the dogged drafts of a few maniacs seeking the new encounter.

It could well be that the very beauty of the world is what makes life so difficult for us. Did I say difficult? Beauty is the impossible which lasts. We have everything to say . . . and can say nothing; that is why we begin anew each day, on the widest variety of subjects and in the greatest number of imaginable procedures. We do not set out to write a BEAUTIFUL text, a beautiful page, a beautiful book. Absolutely not! We simply refuse to be DEFEATED: 1) by the beauty or fascination of Nature, or even the humblest object; nor do we recognize any hierarchy among the things to be said; 2) by language; we will continue to try; 3) we have lost all desire for relative success and all taste for admitting it. We couldn't care less about the usual criteria. Only lassitude stops us. The monopolization of these criteria by a few hucksters has thoroughly disinclined us from any further sermonizing on MEASURE or EXCESS. We know that we successively reinvent the WORST mistakes of every stylistic school of every period. So much the better! We don't want to say what we think, which is probably of no interest (as is evident here). We want to be UNSETTLED in our thinking. (Have I said it often enough? I'll say it again).

The silent world is our only homeland. We make use of its possibilities according to the needs of the times.

1952

TR. BETH ARCHER

≈ The Water of Tears

To cry or see one cry is rather embarrassing to see: between crying and
seeing too many charms are interspersed . . . But between seeing and
crying are so many connections that between crying and seeing we
cannot watch the tears.

(He takes the woman's head in his hands.)

Dearest head! What's going on in there?

Clinging to the cranial rock, the nicest little octopus ever would
remain there quietly—serving, for each batting of the lashes, merely as
a burette—if some sudden surge of sentimental tide, some violent
seizure (regrettable or welcome) did not at times press it (harder) to
express itself (better).

(He leans over.)

Dearest face! And what happens then?

A little globule pearls in the corner of the eye. Tepid, salty . . . Clear,
convincing . . .

(She smiles.)

This is how at times a face glows!

This is how at times one can gather from man's head something that
reaches him from the deepest realities—the marine world . . .

The brain, by the way, smells of fish! Contains a good bit of phos-
phorus . . .

(She starts to cry again.)

Ah, if between seeing and knowing there is some connection, then
from knowing to crying there must be still others!

To cry or see one cry is rather embarrassing to see . . . But I do think
about it . . .

(He collects a tear from the edge of his lashes.)

From the eye to the slide of a microscope, is it not, conversely, a
teardrop that is appropriate?

"Oh, pearls of Amphitrite! SUCCESSFUL EXPRESSIONS!

"Between the water of tears and the water of the sea there can only
be a slight difference, if—in that difference, all of man perhaps . . ."

Laboratory comrades, please verify.

1944

TR. BETH ARCHER

≈ **The Prairie**

When Nature, at our awaking, sometimes proposes to us
Precisely what we were intending,
Praise at once swells in our throats.
We think we are in paradise.

So it was with the prairie I wish to tell of,
And which provides my subject for today.

Since this has more to do with a way of being
Than with a platter set before our eyes,
The word is more fitting than paint
Which would not do at all.

Taking a tube of green and spreading it on the page
Does not make a prairie.
They are born in another way.

They surge up from the page.
And the page should furthermore be brown.

Let us then prepare the page on which today may be born
A verdant verity.

Sometimes then—we might also say in some places—
Sometimes, our nature—
I mean by that Nature on our planet
And what we are each day on awaking—
Sometimes, our nature has prepared us (for) a prairie.

But what is it that blocks our way?
In this little underbrush half-shade half-sun,
Who sets these spokes in our wheels?
Why, as soon as we emerge over the page,
In this single paragraph, so many scruples?

Why then, seen from here, this limited fragment of space,
Stretched between four rocks or four hawthorn hedges,
Barely larger than a handkerchief,
Moraine of the forests, downpour of adverse signs,
This prairie, gentle surface, halo of springs

And of the original storm sweet sequel
In unanimous anonymous call or reply to the rain,
Why does it suddenly seem more precious to us
Than the finest of Persian rugs?

Fragile but not frangible,
The soil at times reconquers the surface,
Marked by the little hooves of the foal that galloped there,
Trampled by the cattle that pushed slowly toward the watering
  place . . .
While a long procession of Sunday strollers, without
Soiling their white shoes, moves ahead
Following the little stream, swollen by drowning or perdition,
Why then, from the start, does it prohibit us?

Could we then already have reached the naos,
That sacred place for a repast of reasons?
Here we are, in any case, at the heart of pleonasms
And at the only logical level that befits us.
Here the prayer wheel is already turning,
Yet without the slightest idea of prostration,
For that would be contrary to the verticalities of the place.

Crasis of *paratus,* according to Latin etymologists,
Close [*pres*] to rock and rill,
Ready [*pret*] to be mown or grazed,
Prepared for us by nature,
Pré, paré, pres, pret.

The prairie [*pré*] lying here like the ideal past participle
Is equally rever(d) end as our prefix of prefixes,
Pre-fix within prefix, pre-sent within present.

No way out of our original onomatopeias.
In that case, back into them.

No need, furthermore, to get out,
Their variations being adequate to account
For the marvelously tedious
Monotony and Variety of the world.
For its perpetuity, in short.

Yet must they be pronounced.
Spoken. And perhaps parabolized.
All of them, told.

(Here a long passage should intervene—somewhat like the intermi-
nable harpischord solo of the 5th Brandenburg Concerto, that is, tedi-
ous and mechanical, yet at the same time mechanizing, not so much
because of the music as the logic, reasoning from the lips, not the chest
or the heart—in which I shall try to explain, and I mean explain, two or
three things: to begin with, if *pré*, in French, represents one of the most
important and primordial of logical notions, it holds equally true for the
physical (geophysical), since what is involved is a metamorphosis of
water which, instead of evaporating, at the summons of heat, directly
into clouds, chooses here—by clinging to the earth and passing
through it, that is, through the kneaded remains of the past of the three
kingdoms and particularly through the finest granulations of the min-
eral kingdom, ultimately reimpregnating the universal ashtray—to
renew life in its most elementary form, grass: element-aliment. This
chapter, which is *also* to be the music for the prairies, will sound thin
and elaborate, with numerous appoggiaturas, so as to end (if it ends)
both accelerando and rinforzando, in a kind of thunderclap which
makes us seek refuge in the woods. The perfecting of this passage could
easily take me a few more years. However it turns out . . .)

The original storm spoke at length.

Did the original storm not thunder so long within us
Precisely so that
                    —for it rolls away, only
                    partially filling the lower
                    horizon where it lightens still—
Readying for the most urgent, rushing to the most pressing,
We would leave these woods,
Would pass between these trees and our remaining scruples,
And, leaving behind all portals and colonnades,
Transported suddenly by a quiet enthusiasm
For a verity that might today be verdant,
Would soon find ourselves stretched out on this prairie,
Long ago prepared for us by nature
                    —where nothing matters any
                    more but the blue sky.

The bird flying over it in the opposite direction to writing
Reminds us of the concrete; and its contradiction,
Marking the differential note of *pré*,
Whether *pres* or *pret*, or the *prai* of prairie,
Sounds short and sharp like the tearing
Of meaning in the all too clear sky.
For the place of long discussion can just as well
Become the place of decision.

Of two equals standing on arrival, one at least,
After a crossed assault with oblique weapons,
Will remain lying,
First above, then below.

Here then, on this prairie, is the occasion, as befits,
To come to an end, prematurely.

Gentlemen typesetters,
Place here, I beg you, the final dot.

Then, beneath, with no spacing added, lay my name,
In lower case, naturally,
        Except the initials, of course,
        Since they are also the initials
        Of Fennel and Parsnip which
        <u>Tomorrow will be growing up on top.</u>
            Francis Ponge

TR. BETH ARCHER

ROBERT DESNOS (1900–1945)

Though André Breton praised Desnos as "the poet who has gone further than any of us into the unknown," Desnos parted company with Breton. He refused to join the Communist Party, and was intent on pursuing a career in journalism. He became active in the French resistance and wrote anti-Nazi poems, then was arrested by the Gestapo in 1944, interrogated under torture, and sent to the concentration

camps at Compeigne, then Buchenwald and Floha. He died of typhus
at Terezin two days after the liberation. "The Night Watchman of
Pont-au-Change" chronicles his activities in the resistance, and "Letter
to Youki" is a poetic missive to his lover, written during his internment.

≈ Ars Poetica

Across the snout
Picked up in the mud and slime
Spit out, vomited, rejected—
I am the verse witness of my master's breath—
Left over, cast off, garbage
Like the diamond, the flame, and the blue of sky
Not pure, not virgin
But fucked to the core
fucked, pricked, sucked, ass fucked, raped
I am the verse witness of my master's breath
Fucker and violator
Not a maiden
There's nothing dirtier than virginity
Ouf! Here today gone tomorrow
Good muddy earth where I set my foot
I ride the wind, the great wind and the sea
I am the verse witness of my master's breath
That cracks farts sings snores
Great storm-wind heart of the world
there is no longer a foul weather
I love all the weathers I love the time
I love the high wind
The great wind the rain the screams the snow the sun the fire and
all that is earth muddy or dry
And let it collapse!
And let it rot!
Rot old flesh old bones
Across the snout
And let it break your teeth and make your gums bleed
I am the verse witness of my master's breath
The water is running with its absurd hummingbird song
of nightingale and alcohol burning in a saucepan
running down my body

A mushroom rots in the corner of a dark forest
    where an incredibly beautiful woman is lost, sloshing in bare feet
There's something rotting at the oak roots
A gold medal couldn't resist it
It's mushy
It's deep
It gives in
There's something rotting at the oak roots
A moon from long ago
Is reflected in this rot
Smell of death smell of life of embrace
Comical shadow-creatures must be rolling
struggling and kissing here   ·
There's something rotting at the oak roots
And it blows even worse at the summit
Nests shaken and the famous hummingbird from before
Rushed
Hoarse nightingales
Foliage of the immense and fluttering forests
Soiled and crumbled like shit-house paper
Hellish and high tides from the summit
of the forests your waves draw toward the sky
The fleshy hills in a foam
of clearings and pastures veined by
rivers and minerals
At last here he comes out of his cave
The skinned-alive one who sings with his throat slit
No nails at the end of his fingers
Orpheus is his name
Cold-blooded fucker, confidant of the Sibyls
A Bacchus eunuch delirious and clairvoyant
A man once of good earth and come from a good seed by good wind
Speaks, bleeds, and keels over
Broken teeth split kidneys knotted arteries
Worthless heart
While the river flows rolls and makes
the grotesque wreckage of houseboats drunk
coal flowing from them
Reaches the plain and reaches the sea
froths rolls and soaks into
the sand the salt and the coral

I will come into your waves
After the worn-out river
Watch out for your fleet
Watch out for your coral, your sand, your salt for your feasts
Come out of the walls with passwords
Out of snouts
Across teeth
Good weather
For the men worthy of this name
Good weather for rivers and trees
Good weather for the sea
The froth and the mud remain
And the joy of living
And one hand in mine
And the joy of living
I am the verse witness of my master's breath.

TR. CAROLYN FORCHÉ

≈ The Night Watchman of Pont-au-Change

I am the night watchman of rue de Flandre.
I keep watch while Paris sleeps.
To the north a faraway fire ruddles the sky.
I know the passage of bombers over the city.

I am the night watchman of Point du Jour.
The Seine bathes itself in darkness behind the viaduct of Auteuil.

Beneath twenty-three bridges crossing Paris.
To the west I hear bombs going off.

I am the night watchman of Port Dorée.
Around the castle-keep forest of Vincennes,
the darkness that has never known light grows darker.

I have heard the cries in the direction of Creteil
And of trains rolling east on revolutionary song-tracks.

I am the night watchman of Poterne des Peupliers.
The south wind carries its acrid smoke to me,
Its unreliable rumors and the death rattles

Of those who give themselves up, somewhere, in Plaisance or
    Vaugirard.

To the south, to the north, the east, the west,
There is nothing but the thunder of war approaching Paris.

I am the night watchman of Pont-au-Change
Keeping watch at the heart of Paris in her wildest rumor
Where I recognize the panicked nightmares of the enemy,
The victory shouts of our friends and those of the French.
The suffering cries of our brothers tortured by Hitler's Germans

I am the night watchman of Pont-au-Change
Watching not only this night over Paris
This stormy night over Paris in her fever and collapse
But over the whole world that surrounds and crushes us.
In the cold air all the columns of war
March toward this place where, after so long a time, men still live.

Cries, songs, sounds of the dying, war, it comes from everywhere.
Victory, suffering and death, sky the color of white wine and tea,
From the four corners of earth, across all the world's impediments
With the scent of vanilla, damp earth and blood,
Of salt water, dust and the woodpile,
Of kisses from an unknown giantess on every step of earth slick with
    human flesh.

I am the night watchman of Pont-au-Change
And I salute you at the threshold of a day to come,
All you comrades of the rue de Flandre at the Poterne des Peupliers,
Of the Point du Jour at the Port Dorée.

I salute you who sleep
After hard secret work,
Printers, bomb carriers, unriveters of rails, fire starters
Distributors of tracts, smugglers, message bearers,
I salute you, all of you who resist, children of twenty
And men more enduring than bridges, sturdy men of all seasons.
I salute you at the threshold of a new day.

I salute you over the edge of the Tamise,
Comrades of all countries here at this meeting,

In the old English capital,
In old London and old Brittany,

Americans of all races and colors,
Beyond the Atlantic expanse,
From Canada to Mexico, from Brazil to Cuba,
Comrades of Rio, of Tehuantepec, of New York and San Francisco.

I have met with the whole world on the Pont-au-Change,
Watchman and fighters like you. See you soon.
Having been warned by his footsteps ringing the pavement,
I, too, have slaughtered the enemy.

He is dead in the gutter, Hitler's man,
His anonymous face smeared with mud, his memory rotting.
While I heard your voices from the four seasons.
Friends, friends and brothers of friendly nations.
I have heard your voices in the scent of African orange trees.
In the slow moving scent of the Pacific,
White squadrons of hands outstretched in the darkness,
Men of Algeria, Honolulu, Chungking,
Men of Fez, of Dakar and Ajaccio.

Drunken and terrible cries, the beating of lungs and hearts,
Of the cheek of Russian flaming in snow
Of Lake Illmen at Kiev, of the Dnieper at Pripet
You reach me, born of millions of breasts.

I have listened to you and understood you, Norwegians, Danes,
    Dutchmen,
Belgians, Czechs, Poles, Greeks, Luxembourgians,
Albanians and Yugoslavs, comrades in the fight.
I listen to your voices and I call you,
I call you in my language known to all
The language that has only one word:
Liberty

And I tell you that I am watching and I have killed Hitler's man.
He is dead in the deserted street.
In the heart of the unmoved city I have avenged my brothers

At the fort of Romainville and at Mont Valerien
In the fleeting echoes of a reborn world, the city and its seasons.

And others like me watch and kill
Like me they listen for steps on deserted streets
Like me they listen to rumors and the fighting on earth.

At Port Dorée, at Point du Jour,
Rue de Flandre and Poterne des Puepliers,
Across all of France, in the cities and fields,
My friends listen for songs in the night
And are lulled to their solitude by rumours and battles for land.

For the earth is a camp lit by thousands of spiritual fires.
At the vigil of battle one bivouacs all over the world.
And perhaps, comrades, you hear the voices
That come from here when night falls,
Tearing at lips hungry for kisses
And soaring long over open country
Like migratory birds blind to the light of beacons
Who hurl themselves against the burning glass.

That my voice managed to reach you ever
Warm and joyful and resolute,
Without dread and without remorse
That my voice reached you with those of my comrades,
Voices of ambush and the French vanguard.

Listen to us in your turn, sailors, pilots, soldiers.
We wish you good morning.
We do not speak to you of our suffering but of our hope,
On the threshold of a new day we say good morning,
To you who are near also to you
Who will receive our morning prayer
At the moment when twilight, in straw boots, enters your houses.

And good morning just the same and good morning for tomorrow
And good morning of good heart and all our kin
Good morning, good morning, the sun will rise over Paris

Even if hidden by clouds it will still be there
Good morning, good morning, with all of my heart bonjour.

Valentin Guillois
Europe

TR. CAROLYN FORCHÉ

≈ Letter to Youki

15 July 1944

My love,

Our suffering would be unbearable if we couldn't regard it as a passing and sentimental illness. Our reunion will make our life beautiful for at least thirty years. For my part, I'm taking a deep swig of youth, and I will return filled with love and strength. During work a birthday, my birthday, was the occasion for a long meditation on you. Will this letter reach you in time for your birthday? I would have liked to give you a hundred thousand American cigarettes, a dozen couture dresses, an apartment on the rue de Seine, an automobile, a little house in the Compiègne forest, the one on Belle Isle and a little four-penny bouquet. In my absence, you can go ahead and buy the flowers. I will repay you for them. The rest I promise you for later.

But before all else, drink a bottle of good wine and think of me. I hope our friends won't leave you alone on this day. I thank them for their devotion and their courage. I received a package from Jean-Louis Barrault about a week ago. Kiss him on the cheek for me as well as Madeleine Renaud, as the package is a proof that my letter did arrive. I have not received a reply, but I'm waiting for one every day. Kiss the whole family for me, Lucienne, Tante Juliette, Georges. If you meet Passeur's brother, give him my regards and ask him if he knows anyone who can come and help you. What's new with my books at the press? I have many ideas for poems and novels. I'm sorry that I have neither the freedom nor the time to write them. You can, however, tell Gallimard that within three months of my return they will receive the manuscript for a love story in an entirely new genre. I am closing for today.

Today, the 15th of July, I receive four letters, from Barrault, Julia, Dr. Benet, and Daniel. Thank them and excuse me for not having replied. I have the right to only one letter a month. Still nothing from

your hand, but they do give me news of you; this will be for next time. I
hope that this letter is as our life to come. My love, I kiss you as tenderly
as honorability permits in a letter which must be passed by the censor.
A thousand kisses. And have you received the little hope chest that I
sent to the hotel in Compiègne?

Robert

TR. CAROLYN FORCHÉ

JACQUES PRÉVERT (1900–1977)

Prévert left school at the age of fifteen and worked at various jobs
before entering the military service at twenty. He was posted to Lor-
raine, and later to Turkey during its occupation by the French. In 1925
he joined the French surrealists in Paris and published his first works in
the surrealist magazine *Commerce*. His poetry collection *Paroles* appeared
in 1946 to overnight popular acclaim, particularly among the French
working class. These two selections were written during his military
service in World War II.

≈ Song in the Blood

There are great puddles of blood on the world
where's it going all this spilled blood
is it the earth that drinks it and gets drunk
funny kind of drunkography then
so wise . . . so monotonous . . .
No the earth doesn't get drunk
the earth doesn't turn askew
it pushes its little car regularly its four seasons
rain . . . snow
hail . . . fair weather . . .
never is it drunk
it's with difficulty it permits itself from time to time
an unhappy little volcano
It turns, the earth

it turns with its trees . . . its gardens . . . its houses
it turns with its great pools of blood
and all living things turn with it and bleed . . .
It doesn't give a damn
the earth
it turns and all living things set up a howl
it doesn't give a damn
it turns
it doesn't stop turning
and the blood doesn't stop running . . .
Where's it going all this spilled blood
murder's blood . . . war's blood . . .
misery's blood . . .
and the blood of men tortured in prisons . . .
the blood of children calmly tortured by their papa and their
      mama . . .
and the blood of men whose heads bleed in padded cells
and the roofer's blood
when the roofer slips and falls from the roof
And the blood that comes and flows in great gushes
with the newborn . . . with the new baby . . .
the mother cries . . . the baby cries . . .
the blood flows . . . the earth turns
the earth doesn't stop turning
the blood doesn't stop flowing
Where's it going all this spilled blood
blood of the blackjacked . . . of the humiliated . . .
of suicides . . . of firing squad victims . . . of the condemned . . .
and the blood of those that die just like that . . . by accident
In the street a living being goes by
with all his blood inside
suddenly there he is dead
and all his blood outside
and other living beings make the blood disappear
they carry the body away
but it's stubborn the blood
and there where the dead one was
much later all black
a little blood still stretches . . .
coagulated blood

life's rust body's rust
blood curdled like milk
like milk when it turns
when it turns like the earth
like the earth that turns
with its milk . . . with its cows . . .
with its living . . . with its dead . . .
the earth that turns with its trees . . . with its living beings . . . its
    houses . . .
the earth that turns with marriages . . .
burials . . .
shells . . .
regiments . . .
the earth that turns and turns and turns
with its great streams of blood.

TR. LAWRENCE FERLINGHETTI

≈ Barbara

Remember Barbara
It rained without letup in Brest that day
And you walked smiling
Glowing ravishing drenched
Under the rain
Remember Barbara
It rained without letup in Brest
And I passed you on the Rue de Siam
You smiled
And I smiled too
Remember Barbara
You whom I did not know
You who did not know me
Remember
Remember that day just the same
Do not forget
A man was taking shelter in a doorway
And he called out your name
Barbara
And you ran toward him under the rain

Drenched ravishing glowing
And you threw yourself into his arms
Remember that Barbara
And do not be angry with me if I call you by your first name
I call all those I love by their first names
Even if I have met them only once
I call all who love by their first names
Even if I do not know them
Remember Barbara
Do not forget
That gentle, happy rain
On your happy face
On that happy town
That rain on the sea
On the arsenal
On the boat of Ouessant
Oh Barbara
What shit war is
What has become of you now
Under the rain of iron
Of fire of steel of blood
And he who held you in his arms
Lovingly
Is he dead missing or still living
Oh Barbara
It rains without letup in Brest
As it rained before
But it is not the same everything is ruined
It is a rain of mourning terrible and desolate
No longer even a storm
Of iron of steel of blood
Only of clouds
That burst
And disappear like dogs
Down the streams of Brest
Like dogs that will rot far away
Far away very far from Brest
Of which there is nothing left

TR. HARRIET ZINNES

SALVATORE QUASIMODO (1901–1968)

Born in Sicily, Quasimodo was associated during the 1930s with the "hermetic" poets, the difficulty of whose work was meant to serve as a firm but quiet opposition to Fascism. The advent of World War II, however, changed Quasimodo's poetic: in order to bear witness to the sufferings of his countrymen, he began to write with greater clarity and directness. He was imprisoned for his anti-Fascist activities during World War II. Quasimodo was awarded the Nobel Prize for Literature in 1959.

≈ 19 January 1944

I read you the soft verses of antiquity
and the words, born of the vineyards
and tents on the banks of eastern
rivers—how mournful they fall
and desolate in this profoundest night
of war where no one flies
the sky of the angels of death,
and we hear the wind thunder with ruin
shaking the metal sheets that up here
divide the balconies, and gloom rises
from the dogs howling in gardens
at the rifle shots of patrols
on the empty streets. Someone is alive.
Someone, perhaps, is alive. But we, here,
absorbed in listening to the ancient voice
seek for a sign that outreaches life,
earth's dark sorcery
where even among the tombs of rubble
the malign grass rears up its flower.

TR. JACK BEVAN

≈ Man of My Time

You are still the one with stone and sling,
man of my time. You were there in the cockpit,
with evil wings, the sundials of death,
—I have seen you—in the fire-chariot, at the gallows,
at the torture wheels. I have seen you: it was you
with your knowledge precisely extermination-guided,
loveless, Christless. You have killed again
as before, as your fathers killed, as the beasts
killed when first they saw you.
And this blood smells as it did on the day
when the brother said to the other brother:
Let us go into the fields. And that chill, clinging echo
has reached down even to you, within your day.
Forget, O sons, the blood clouds
risen from earth, forget the fathers:
their tombs sink down in the ashes,
the black birds, the wind, cover over their hearts.

TR. JACK BEVAN

≈ To the Fifteen of Piazzale Loreto

Esposito, Fiorani, Fogagnolo,
Casiraghi, you names, who are you? Ghosts?
Soncini, Principato, you, Del Riccio,
Temolo, Vertemati, Gasparini,
dead inscriptions? Galimberti, Ragni,
you, Bravin, Mastrodomenico, Poletti,
leaves of a tree of blood?
Dear blood of ours that does not soil the earth,
blood that initiates the earth
in the hour of rifle fire.
We are shamed by the lead wounds in your backs;
too long has passed. Death falls again
from funeral mouths; the foreign
flags still hanging over your houses
are asking death. Believing they are alive
they fear death at your hands.

The watch we keep is no mourning,
no vigil of tears at your tombs;
death that is life can cast no shadow.

TR. JACK BEVAN

≈ **Auschwitz**

Far from the Vistula, along the northern plain,
love, in a death-camp there at Auschwitz:
on the pole's rust and tangled fencing, rain
funeral cold.
No tree, no birds in the grey air
or above our thought, but limp
pain that memory leaves
to its silence without irony or anger.
You ask no elegies or idylls: only
the meaning of our destiny, you, here,
hurt by the mind's war,
uncertain at the clear
presence of life. For life is here
in every No that seems a certainty:
here we shall hear the angel weep, the monster, hear
our future time
beating the hereafter that is here, forever
in motion, not an image
of dreams, of possible pity.
Here are the myths, the metamorphoses.
Lacking the name of symbols or a god,
they are history, earth places,
they are Auschwitz, love. How suddenly
the dear forms of Alpheus and Arethusa
changed into shadow-smoke!

Out of that hell hung with a white
inscription 'work will make you free'
there came the endless smoke
of many thousand women thrust at dawn
out of the kennels up to the firing-wall,
or, screaming for mercy to water, choked,

their skeleton mouths under the jets of gas.
You, soldier, will find them in your annals
taking the forms of animals and rivers,
or are you too, now, ash of Auschwitz,
medal of silence?
Long tresses in glass urns can still be seen
bound up with charms, and an infinity
of ghostly little shoes and shawls of Jews:
relics of a time of wisdom,
of man whose knowledge takes the shape of arms,
they are the myths, our metamorphoses.

Over the plains where love and sorrow
and pity rotted, there in the rain
a No inside us beat;
a No to death that died at Auschwitz
never from the pit of ashes
to show itself again.

TR. JACK BEVAN

STANLEY KUNITZ (1905–)

Kunitz published his first book in 1930 and his second in 1944, while serving in the United States Army. He had won several awards for his poetry by the time he produced his *Selected Poems,* which won him a 1959 Pulitzer Prize. Kunitz has edited dictionaries of literary biography, has taught at a number of universities, and has been a translator of Anna Akhmatova. He was judge of the Yale Series of Younger Poets Award, and many young American poets revere him as mentor.

≈ Father and Son

Now in the suburbs and the falling light
I followed him, and now down sandy road
Whiter than bone-dust, through the sweet
Curdle of fields, where the plums

Dropped with their load of ripeness, one by one.
Mile after mile I followed, with skimming feet,
After the secret master of my blood,
Him, steeped in the odor of ponds, whose indomitable love
Kept me in chains. Strode years; stretched into bird;
Raced through the sleeping country where I was young,
The silence unrolling before me as I came,
The night nailed like an orange to my brow.

How should I tell him my fable and the fears,
How bridge the chasm in a casual tone,
Saying, "The house, the stucco one you built,
We lost. Sister married and went from home,
And nothing comes back, it's strange, from where she goes.
I lived on a hill that had too many rooms:
Light we could make, but not enough of warmth,
And when the light failed, I climbed under the hill.
The papers are delivered every day;
I am alone and never shed a tear."

At the water's edge, where the smothering ferns lifted
Their arms, "Father!" I cried, "Return! You know
The way. I'll wipe the mudstains from your clothes;
No trace, I promise, will remain. Instruct
Your son, whirling between two wars,
In the Gemara of your gentleness,
For I would be a child to those who mourn
And brother to the foundlings of the field
And friend of innocence and all bright eyes.
O teach me how to work and keep me kind."

Among the turtles and the lilies he turned to me
The white ignorant hollow of his face.

≈ **Night Letter**

The urgent letter that I try to write
Night after night to you to whom I turn,
The staunchless word, my language of the wound,

Begins to stain the page. Here in my room
With my unkenneled need, the Faustian dog
That chews my penitential bones, I hope
And do not hope, I pray and mock my prayer,
Twisting my coils, this dangling life of mine,
Now twelve years come of age, and me unpleased
With all my ways, my very littlest ones,
My part, my lines, unless you hold them dear.
Where is your ministry? I thought I heard
A piece of laughter break upon the stair
Like glass, but when I wheeled around I saw
Disorder, in a tall magician's hat,
Keeping his rabbit-madness crouched inside,
Sit at my desk and scramble all the news.
The strangest things are happening. Christ! the dead,
Pushing the membrane from their face, salute
The dead and scribble slogans on the walls;
Phantoms and phobias mobilize, thronging
The roads; and in the Bitch's streets the men
Are lying down, great crowds with fractured wills
Dumping the shapeless burden of their lives
Into the rivers where the motors flowed.

Of those that stood in the doorway, self-accused,
Besmeared with failure in the swamps of trade,
One put a gun in his examiner's hand,
Making the judgment loud; another squats
Upon the asylum floor and plays with toys,
Like the spiral of a soul balanced on a stone,
Of a new gadget for slicing off the thumb;
The rest whirl in the torment of our time.
What have we done to them that what they are
Shrinks from the touch of what they hoped to be?
"Pardon," I plead, clutching the fragile sleeve
Of my poor father's ghost returned to howl
His wrongs. I suffer the twentieth century,
The nerves of commerce wither in my arm;
Violence shakes my dreams; I am so cold,
Chilled by the persecuting wind abroad,
The oratory of the rodent's tooth,

The slaughter of the blue-eyed open towns,
And principle disgraced, and art denied.
My dear is it too late for peace, too late
For men to gather at the wells to drink
The sweet water; too late for fellowship
And laughter at the forge; too late for us
To say, "Let us be good each to the other"?
The lamps go singly out; the valley sleeps;
I tend the last light shining on the farms
And keep for you the thought of love alive,
As scholars dungeoned in an ignorant age
Tended the embers of the Trojan fire.
Cities shall suffer siege and some shall fall,
But man's not taken. What the deep heart means,
Its message of the big, round, childish hand,
Its wonder, its simple lonely cry,
The bloodied envelope addressed to you,
Is history, that wide and mortal pang.

≈ The Last Picnic

The guests in their summer colors have fled
Through field and hedgerow. Come, let's pick
The bones and feathers of our fun
And kill the fire with a savage stick.

The figures of our country play,
The mocking dancers, in a swirl
Of laughter waved from the evening's edge,
Wrote finis to a pastoral.

Now the tongue of the military man,
Summoning the violent,
Calls the wild dogs out of their holes
And the deep Indian from his tent,

Not to be tamed, not to be stamped
Under. Earth-faced, behind this grove,
Our failures creep with soldier hearts,
Pointing their guns at what we love.

When they shall paint our sockets gray
And light us like a stinking fuse,
Remember that we once could say,
Yesterday we had a world to lose.

Louis MacNeice (1907–1963)

The son of an Anglican minister in Northern Ireland, educated in England, MacNeice was a lecturer in classics when his second book of poems came out in 1935, establishing his reputation. He traveled to Spain in the waning days of the Spanish Republic ("The New Year comes with bombs," he wrote). After trips to Iceland, Ireland, and the United States, MacNeice returned to Britain in 1940, where he was deemed ineligible for active service because of bad eyesight; he lived in London during the Blitz. He worked for the BBC and wrote plays, criticism, and autobiography. He died of pneumonia in 1963. Mac-Neice's poetry is expressive, sensuously immediate, and strongly situated in the modern, "impure" world. These selections arise out of MacNeice's experience of the bombing of London.

≈ Prayer Before Birth

I am not yet born; O hear me.
Let not the bloodsucking bat or the rat or the stoat or the
    club-footed ghoul come near me.

I am not yet born; console me.
I fear that the human race may with tall walls wall me,
    with strong drugs dope me, with wise lies lure me,
        on black racks rack me, in blood-baths roll me.

I am not yet born; provide me
With water to dandle me, grass to grow for me, trees to talk
    to me, sky to sing to me, birds and a white light
        in the back of my mind to guide me.

I am not yet born; forgive me
For the sins that in me the world shall commit, my words
   when they speak me, my thoughts when they think me,
      my treason engendered by traitors beyond me,
        my life when they murder by means of my
          hands, my death when they live me.

I am not yet born; rehearse me
In the parts I must play and the cues I must take when
   old men lecture me, bureaucrats hector me, mountains
      frown at me, lovers laugh at me, the white
        waves call me to folly and the desert calls
          me to doom and the beggar refuses
            my gift and my children curse me.

I am not yet born; O hear me,
Let not the man who is best or who thinks he is God
   come near me.

I am not yet born; O fill me
With strength against those who would freeze my
   humanity, would dragoon me into a lethal automaton,
      would make me a cog in a machine, a thing with
        one face, a thing, and against all those
          who would dissipate my entirety, would
            blow me like thistledown hither and
              hither or hither and thither
                like water held in the
                  hands would spill me.

Let them not make me a stone and let them not spill me.
Otherwise kill me.

≈ Brother Fire

When our brother Fire was having his dog's day
Jumping the London streets with millions of tin cans
Clanking at his tail, we heard some shadow say
'Give the dog a bone'—and so we gave him ours;

Night after night we watched him slaver and crunch away
The beams of human life, the tops of topless towers.

Which gluttony of his for us was Lenten fare
Who mother-naked, suckled with sparks, were chill
Though cotted in a grill of sizzling air
Striped like a convict—black, yellow and red;
Thus were we weaned to knowledge of the Will
That wills the natural world but wills us dead.

O delicate walker, babbler, dialectician Fire,
O enemy and image of ourselves,
Did we not on those mornings after the All Clear,
When you were looting shops in elemental joy
And singing as you swarmed up city block and spire,
Echo your thought in ours? 'Destroy! Destroy!'

≈ Troll's Courtship

(Written after an air raid, April 1941)

I

In the misty night humming to themselves like morons
They ramble and rumble over the roof-tops, stumble and shamble
     from pile to pillar,
In clodhopping boots that crunch the stars
And a blank smirk on their faces:
     Pretty Polly won't die yet.

Skittle-alley horseplay, congurgitation . . . they don't know what they
     are doing,
All they can do is stutter and lurch, riding their hobby, grinding
Their hobnails into our bodies, into our brains, into the domed
Head where the organ music lingers:
     Pretty Polly won't die yet.

Here they come—I thought we had lost them—
Here they come once more and once too many with their rough and

Tumble antics, here they
Are, they are, they ARE:
> *Pretty Polly won't die yet,*
> *Oh, won't she?*

II

Than which not any could be found other
And outside which is less than nothing—
This, as they call it, life.
But such as it is, gurgling and tramping, locking their thumbs before
    they
Turn the pages over, tear them out, they
Wish it away, they
Puff with enormous cheeks, put paid to
Hours and minutes—thistledown in the void.

III

Death has a look of finality;
We think we lose something but if it were not for
Death we should have nothing to lose, existence
Because unlimited would merely be existence
Without incarnate value. The trolls can occasion
Our death but they are not able
To use it as we can use it.
Fumbling and mumbling they try to
Spell out Death correctly; they are not able.

IV

Than which not any. Time
Swings on the poles of death
And the latitude and the longitude of life
Are fixed by death, and the value
Of every organism, act and moment
Is, thanks to death, unique.

V

This then is our answer under
The crawl of lava, a last

Shake of the fist at the vanishing sky, at the hulking
Halfwit demons who rape and slobber, who assume
That when we are killed no more will be heard of us—
Silence of men and trolls' triumph.
A wrong—in the end—assumption.
Barging and lunging out of the clouds, a daft
Descent of no-good gods, they think to
Be rid for ever of the voice of men but they happen
To be trying what even trolls
Can never accomplish, they happen
To be—for all their kudos—
Wrong, wrong in the end.

RENÉ CHAR (1907–1988)

Considered by Albert Camus the greatest French poet of this century, Char was born in the south of France, and joined the surrealists in 1930. He supported the Republicans during the Spanish Civil War, was mobilized into the French army in 1939, and narrowly escaped arrest by the Vichy government as a suspected Communist. Char became a leader in the French resistance and was decorated for bravery at the end of the war. According to Char, the poet "is that part of a man stubbornly opposed to calculated projects." *Leaves of Hypnos* is a journal Char kept during his days in the resistance.

≈ Argument

How can we live without the unknown in front of us?

Men of today want the poem to be in the image of their lives, composed of such little consideration, of such little space, and burned with intolerance.

Because it is no longer given to them to act supremely, in this fatal preoccupation of self-destruction at the hands of their fellow-men, because their inert wealth holds them back and enslaves them, men of today, their instinct weakened, lose—still keeping alive—even the dust of their names.

Born from the summons of becoming and from the anguish of retention, the poem, rising from its well of mud and of stars, will bear witness, almost silently, that it contained nothing which did not truly exist elsewhere, in this rebellious and solitary world of contradictions.

TR. MARY ANN CAWS

≈ Unbending Prayer

Preserve for us rebellion, lightning, the illusory agreement, a laugh for the trophy slipped from our hands, even the whole lengthy burden that follows, whose difficulty leads us to a new rebellion. Preserve for us fate and the primrose.

TR. MARY ANN CAWS

≈ Man flees suffocation

Man flees suffocation.

Man, whose appetite beyond imagination becomes airtight still laying in supplies, will find freedom by his hands, rivers suddenly swollen.

Man who grows blunt through premonitions, who deforests his inner silence and divides it into stages, the latter one is the maker of bread.

To the former, prison and death. To the latter, the repasturing of the Word.

To exceed the economy of creation, to increase the blood of gestures, task of all light.

We hold the ring where the devilish nightingale and the angelic key are chained together, side by side.

Over the ridge of our bitterness, the dawn of conscience advances and lays down its loam.

August ripening. One dimension traverses the fruit of the other. Warring dimensions. Deported from the yoke and from the nuptials, I strike the iron of invisible hinges.

TR. MARY ANN CAWS

≈ Leaves of Hypnos No. 128

The baker hadn't yet unfastened the iron shutters of his shop when the village was besieged, gagged, hypnotized, completely brought to a standstill. Two companies of SS and a detachment of militia held it under the muzzle of their machineguns and mortars. Then began the ordeal.

The inhabitants were tossed out of their houses and summoned to assemble in the central square. Keys in the doors. An old man, hard of hearing, who didn't respond to the order quickly enough, saw the four walls and roof of his barn blown to pieces by a bomb. Since four o'clock I'd been alerted. Marcelle had come to my shutter to whisper the word to me. I'd realized immediately the uselessness of trying to get past the cordon of surveillance and out into the countryside. I quickly changed lodgings. The uninhabited house where I took refuge allowed, in the last extremity, an effective armed resistance. I could follow from the window, behind the yellowed curtains, the nervous comings and goings of the occupying forces. Not one of my men was in the village. That thought reassured me. Some kilometers away, they would follow my instructions and remain under cover. Blows reached me, punctuated by curses. The SS had surprised a young mason who was coming back from retrieving some traps. His fright set him up for their tortures. A voice bent over the swollen body shouting: "Where is he? Show us," followed by silence. And kicks and riflebutts raining. An insensate rage possessed me, chased my anguish away. My hands communicated to my gun their clenched sweat, exalted its contained power. I calculated that the poor devil would hold his tongue for five minutes yet, then, inevitably, he *would talk*. I was ashamed to wish him dead before this happened. Then there appeared rushing from each street a flood of women, children, old men, going to the place of assembly, according to a *concerted plan*. They hurried without haste, literally streaming over the SS, paralyzing them "in all good faith." The mason was left for dead. Furious, the patrol ploughed its way through the crowd and made further off. With an infinite prudence now, some anxious and kindly eyes looked in my direction, passed like a flashing lamp on my window. I half revealed myself and a smile broke from my pallor. I held to these people by a thousand confidant threads of which not one would break.

I loved my kind wildly that day, well beyond sacrifice.*

*Wasn't it chance that had chosen me as prince that day rather than this village's heart being ripe for me? (1945)

TR. CID CORMAN

≈ Disdained Apparitions

Civilizations are viscous. History shipwrecks, Gold slips from God no longer straddling our suspicious walls, man batters at the ear of man, Time misleads itself, fission is on its way. What next?

Science can only furnish to devastated man a blind beacon, a weapon of distress, tools without legend. For the most demented: the drill whistle.

Those who have installed this eternal compensator, as a final victory over the temporal, were themselves only temporary jailers. They hadn't violated the tragic nature—interloper, pillager, as if in abeyance—of human beings.

Putrescent light, obscurity wouldn't be the worst condition.

There was only a half-freedom. It was all that was granted. Half-freedom for the man in motion. Half-freedom for the insect that sleeps and waits in its chrysalis. Phantom, barest memory, freedom in uprising.

Freedom was at the summit of a mass of covert obediences and accepted conventions disguised by an irreproachable deceit.
Freedom is found in the heart of one who has not ceased to wish for it, to dream of it, who has won it in the face of crime.

TR. PAUL MANN

GÜNTER EICH (1907–1972)

Eich served in the Wehrmacht during World War II and was taken prisoner by the Americans. He was released in 1946. His "Inventory," first published in 1948, which takes stock of a prisoner's belongings, is one of the most familiar German poems since the war. One of the founders of Gruppe 47 (a group of left-wing German writers which included Paul Celan, Günter Grass, and Erich Fried), Eich was also a playwright. He married the poet Ilse Aichinger. He believed that writers should oppose political power and "controlled language," and felt that in his own poems he was investigating the unknown.

≈ Inventory

This is my cap,
this is my coat,
here's my shaving gear
in a linen sack.

A can of rations:
my plate, my cup,
I've scratched my name
in the tin.

Scratched it with this
valuable nail
which I hide
from avid eyes.

In the foodsack is
a pair of wool socks
and something else that I
show to no one,

it all serves as a pillow
for my head at night.
The cardboard here lies
between me and the earth.

The lead in my pencil
I love most of all:
in the daytime it writes down
the verses I make at night.

This is my notebook,
this is my tarpaulin,
this is my towel,
this is my thread.

TR. DAVID YOUNG

≈ **Old Postcards**

I

Here's where I wanted to put the streetcars
and swing
on the chain around the war memorial.
A sign for the deaf and dumb.
A sermon for the bakers
lolling about in the morning wind.

II

The view, gradually
colored by glue,
leaf cover and road
all cut
by the same knife.
The asphalting planned
like dying.

III

Two kinds of handwriting—
a bicycle trip
to the castle ruins.
But we're okay.
Playing in the black sand.
Chewing bread
for the holes in the wallpaper.

IV

Blowtube on Sedan Day,
three zero four,
it's red in the lime trees.
Tomorrow tomorrow tomorrow.

V

Hold tight
to the tanners' ropes
till the angels come

with their huge caps and shoulder cloth,
according to evidence of the stones,
the print in the smoke
you can trust.

VI

Tell me something
from the catalogues,
and where you've been so long,
about the stamps in the beehive,
our grandfathers' professions
and the smell of hooves.
I'll count the drops for you
on the sugar,
a prime number,
and I'll eat with you.

VII

Paris,
which reminds me of
Mexican hats,
ribbons
with the steps of lovers,
information booths and mustard seeds.

VIII

There are
no cranes here.
But there are women
and races and
a laugh to keep you pondering,
old as
Renaissance staircases,
the steps of the prisoners
going down.

IX

We're among the last.
To our left someone who

knew caves left yesterday.
Our preserves are all gone.
I was thinking, even yesterday,
of the oil jugs of the crusaders,
handed over to their besiegers,
honorably,
of the rain.

X

Why the coffee
wasn't drunk?
Well we were sitting okay
right down in the flooded parts,
our rented boats
between the boulevard trees.
Why the sugar
wouldn't dissolve?
Nothing ever ended.
Here's what still needs
telling: the cups, a
Charlotte who was taking our money, her
sad ruffles wet through and through.

XI

Fine,
fine.
But when the war is over
we'll go to Minsk
and pick up Grandmother.

TR. STUART FRIEBERT

≈ Geometrical Place

We have sold our shadow,
it hangs on a wall in Hiroshima,
a transaction we knew nothing of,
from which, embarrassed, we rake in interest.

And, dear friends, drink my whiskey,
I won't be able to find the tavern any more,
where my bottle stands
with its monogram,
old proof of a clear conscience.

I didn't put my penny in the bank
when Christ was born
but I've seen the grandchildren
of dogs trained to herd people
on the hills near the Danube School,
and they stared at me.

And I want, like the people of Hiroshima,
to see no more burnt skin,
I want to drink and sing songs,
to sing for whiskey,
and to stroke the dogs, whose grandfathers
sprang at people
in quarries and barbed wire.

You, my shadow,
on the bank at Hiroshima,
I want to visit you with all the dogs
now and then
and drink to you
to the prosperity of our accounts.

The museum is being demolished,
in front of it
I will slip to you
behind your railing,
behind your smile—our cry for help—
and we'll suit each other again,
your shoes into mine
precise
to the second.

TR. DAVID YOUNG

≈ Seminar for Backward Pupils

I

While the dead
cool quickly
a slow waltz
for the S.P.D.

Enough of rose bouquets
for the proper occasion,
speak finally of
crumpled print
and the goulash
foolishly spilled
on striped trousers.

We need a
patriotic stay-at-home zither
for five places
in a realistically designed
government bunker.

II

Then came
mustard-skilled men,
turnip counters,
delegates of welfare.

Wooden eye, be watchful!

They scoured us clean
with sandpaper,
factual accounts
and politeness.

Wooden eye, be watchful!

Now we know everything:
the sun lies always before us.
We define freedom anew:

soon
we'll be rid of it.

Wooden eye.

III

We crossed
the frontier of a hundred boots
and my memory went into action,
the letters from A to Z
occurred to me
and the numbers almost to one hundred,
my abilities
boot, heel and toe.
And I decided
to take service
in the dungeons of justice.

TR. DAVID YOUNG

CESARE PAVESE (1908–1950)

Born in the Italian Piedmont, Pavese, novelist and poet, was arrested
for anti-Fascist activities in 1935 and imprisoned for a year in Calabria,
where he wrote many of the poems of his first book, *Lavorare Stanca*
(*Hard Labor*), from which these selections come. His poetry shows the
influence of his American models, among them Walt Whitman, Herman Melville, and Gertrude Stein: he eschews the introspection and
hermeticism of his contemporaries for a more straightforward, almost
muscular diction. Soon after winning the prestigious Strega Prize in
1950 for his last novel, *The Beautiful Summer,* Pavese committed suicide
over an unhappy love affair.

≈ August Moon

There's the sea, far beyond the yellow hills,
far beyond the clouds. But between the sea and here

are long terrible days, hills rippling and cresting
in the sky. Here on the hill is the olive tree,
and the pond of water so small a man can't see his face,
and the stubble: mile after mile of stubble.

And the moon, rising. Her husband lies stretched out
in a field, his skull cracked open by the sun.
A woman can't drag a corpse around as if it were
a sack. The moon rises, casting a little shadow
under the gnarled branches. The woman in shadow looks up,
grinning in terror at that huge face, all blood,
clotting and soaking every crease in the hills.
The corpse stretched out in the fields doesn't move,
or the woman in the shadow. Only the eye of blood
seems to be winking at someone, pointing the way.

Slow shudders crawl across the naked hills
in the distance, and the woman feels them at her back,
like when they were running through that sea of wheat.
And the branches of the olive, lost in that sea
of moonlight, move in—even the tree's shadow
starts to darken and thicken and swallow her up.

She runs out into the moonlight and its horror,
and the breeze comes after her rustling over the rocks
and a thin fine shape gnawing at her bare feet,
and the pain in her womb. Doubled over, she hides in the shadow,
crumpling on the rocks and gnawing at her lips.
The ground beneath her dark, drenched with blood.

TR. WILLIAM ARROWSMITH

≈ Words from Confinement

Bright and early we went down to the fishmarket
to wash stale eyes alive. The fish were
scarlet, green, silver, color of the sea.
The sea was shining, all scales of silver,
but the fish were brighter. We thought of home.

Beautiful too the women, with jars on their heads,
olive green, and molded like their hips,
softly rounded. We thought of our women,
how they talk and laugh and walk down the street.
We all laughed. Out at sea, it was raining.

In vineyards, along ravines, grapes and leaves
glisten with rain. The sky is ruddy
with scattered clouds, colored with sun
and pleasure. On earth, smells; in the sky,
colors. We were on our own; unguarded.

We thought of home, the way a man thinks
of morning after a sleepless night. The sea
smelled musty, and we reveled in freshness,
in the moistness of the fruit and the colors of the fish.
We were drunk on the news: we were going home!

TR. WILLIAM ARROWSMITH

GEORGE OPPEN (1908–1984)

Oppen, an American, moved in 1929 to France, where he and his wife, Mary, published Ezra Pound, William Carlos Williams, and Louis Zukovsky's *The "Objectivists" Anthology*. Returning to New York in 1935, they joined the Communist Party, and Oppen effectively gave up writing poetry for the next two decades. He served in the U.S. Army during World War II and was wounded just before V-E Day. Early in the Cold War, Oppen was harassed by the FBI, and he and his family fled to Mexico rather than inform on their friends and colleagues. They returned to the United States in 1958. Oppen started writing again in 1964 and won the Pulitzer Prize for poetry in 1969.

≈ Route

'the void eternally generative'
    the *Wen Fu* of Lu Chi

I

Tell the beads of the chromosomes like a rosary,
Love in the genes, if it fails

We will produce no sane man again

I have seen too many young people become adults, young
       friends become old people, all that is not ours,

The sources
And the crude bone

        —we say

Took place

Like the mass of the hills.

'The sun is a molten mass.' Therefore

Fall into oneself—?

reality, blind eye
Which has taught us to stare—

Your elbow on a car-edge
Incognito as summer,

I wrote. Not you but a girl
At least

Clarity, clarity, surely clarity is the most beautiful
       thing in the world,
A limited, limiting clarity

I have not and never did have any motive of poetry
But to achieve clarity

II

Troubled that you are not, as they say,
Working—
I think we try rather to understand,
We try also to remain together

There is a force of clarity, it is
Of what is not autonomous in us,
We suffer a certain fear

Things alter, surrounded by a depth
And width

The unreality of our house in moonlight
Is that if the moonlight strikes it
It is truly there tho it is ours

III

Not to reduce the thing to nothing—

I might at the top of my ability stand at a window
and say, look out; out there is the world.

Not the desire for approval nor even for love—O,
that trap! From which escaped, barely—if it fails

we will produce no sane man again

IV

Words cannot be wholly transparent. And that is the
        'heartlessness' of words.

Neither friends nor lovers are coeval . . .

as for a long time we have abandoned those in
        extremity and we find it unbearable that we should
        do so . . .

The sea anemone dreamed of something, filtering the sea
      water thru its body,

Nothing more real than boredom—dreamlessness, the
      experience of time, never felt by the new arrival,
      never at the doors, the thresholds, it is the native

Native in native time . . .

the purity of the materials, not theology, but to present
      the circumstances

V

In Alsace, during the war, we found ourselves on the edge of the
Battle of the Bulge. The front was inactive, but we were spread so thin
that the situation was eerily precarious. We hardly knew where the next
squad was, and it was not in sight—a quiet and deserted hill in front of
us. We dug in near a farmhouse. Pierre Adam, tho he was a journeyman
mason, lived with his wife and his children in that farmhouse.

During the occupation the Germans had declared Alsace a part of
Greater Germany. Therefore they had drafted Alsatian men into the
German army. Many men, learning in their own way that they were to
be called, dug a hole. The word became a part of the language: faire un
trou. Some men were in those holes as long as two and three years. It
was necessary that someone should know where those holes were; in
winter it was impossible for a man to come out of his hole without
leaving footprints in the snow. While snow was actually falling, how-
ever, a friend could come to the hole with food and other help. Pierre,
whom many people trusted, knew where some two dozen of those
holes were.

The Germans became aware that men were going into hiding, and
they began to make reprisals. If the man was young and unmarried, they
killed his parents. If the man was married, they took his wife into
Germany to the army brothels, it was said. They took the children into
Germany, and it was not certain whether those children would remem-
ber where they came from. Pierre told me this story:

Men would come to Pierre and they would say: I am thinking of making a hole. Pierre would say: yes. They would say then: but if I do they will kill my parents; or: they will take my wife and my children. Then Pierre would say, he told me: *if* you dig a hole, I will help you.

He knew, of course, what he was telling me. You must try to put yourself into those times. If one thought he knew anything, it was that a man should not join the Nazi army. Pierre himself learned, shortly before the Americans arrived, that he was about to be drafted. He and his wife discussed the children. They thought of tattooing the children's names and addresses on their chests so that perhaps they could be found after the war. But they thought that perhaps the tattooing would be cut out of the children. . . . They did not, finally, have to make that decision, as it turned out. But what a conversation between a man and his wife—

There was an escape from that dilemma, as, in a way, there always is. Pierre told me of a man who, receiving the notification that he was to report to the German army, called a celebration and farewell at this home. Nothing was said at that party that was not jovial. They drank and sang. At the proper time, the host got his bicycle and waved good-bye. The house stood at the top of a hill and, still waving and calling farewells, he rode with great energy and as fast as he could down the hill, and, at the bottom, drove into a tree.

It must be hard to do. Probably easier in an automobile. There is, in an automobile, a considerable time during which you cannot change your mind. Riding a bicycle, since in those woods it is impossible that the tree should be a redwood, it must be necessary to continue aiming at the tree right up to the moment of impact. Undoubtedly difficult to do. And, of course, the children had no father. Thereafter.

VI

Wars that are just? A simpler question: In the event, will you or will you not want to kill a German. Because, in the event, if you do not want to, you won't.

. . . and my wife reading letters she knew were two weeks late and did not prove I was not dead while she read. Why did I play all that, what was I doing there?

We are brothers, we are brothers?—these things are composed of a moral substance only if they are untrue. If these things are true they are perfectly simple, perfectly impenetrable, those primary elements which can only be named.

A man will give his life for his friend provided he wants to.

In all probability a man will give his life for his child provided his child is an infant.

. . . One man could not understand me because I was saying simple things; it seemed to him that nothing was being said. I was saying: there is a mountain, there is a lake

A picture seen from within. The picture is unstable, a moving picture, unlimited drift.
Still, the picture exists.

The circumstances:

VII

And if at 80

He says what has been commonly said
It is for the sake of old times, a cozy game

He wishes to join again, an unreasonable speech
Out of context

VIII

Cars on the highway filled with speech,
People talk, they talk to each other;

Imagine a man in the ditch,
The wheels of the overturned wreck
Still spinning—

I don't mean he despairs, I mean if he does not
He sees in the manner of poetry

IX

The cars run in a void of utensils
—the powerful tires—beyond
Happiness

Tough rubbery gear of invaders, of the descendents
Of invaders, I begin to be aware of a countryside
And the exposed weeds of a ditch

The context is history
Moving toward the light of the conscious

And beyond, culvert, blind curb, there are also names
For these things, language in the appalling fields

I remember my father as a younger man than I am now,
My mother was a tragic girl
Long ago, the autonomous figures are gone,
The context is the thousands of days

X

Not the symbol but the scene this pavement leads
To roadsides—the finite

Losing its purposes
Is estranged

All this is reportage.

If having come so far we shall have
Song

Let it be small enough.

Virgin
what was there to be thought

comes by the road

XI

Tell the life of the mind, the mind creates the finite.

All punishes him. I stumble over these stories—
Progeny, the possibility of progeny, continuity

Or love that tempted him

He is punished by place, by scene, by all that holds
all he has found, this pavement, the silent symbols

Of it, the word it, never more powerful than in this
moment. Well, hardly an epiphany, but there the thing
is all the same

All this is reportage

XII

To insist that what is true is good, no matter, no matter,
     a definition—?

That tree
    whose fruit . . .

The weight of air
Measured by the barometer in the parlor,
Time remains what it was

Oddly, oddly insistent

haunting the people in the automobiles,

shining on the sheetmetal,

open and present, unmarred by indifference,

wheeled traffic, indifference,
the hard edge of concrete continually crumbling

into gravel in the gravel of the shoulders,
Ditches of our own country

Whom shall I speak to

XIII

Department of Plants and Structures—obsolete, the old name
In this city, of the public works

Tho we meant to entangle ourselves in the roots of the world

An unexpected and forgotten spoor, all but indestructible
      shards

To owe nothing to fortune, to chance, nor by the power of
      his heart
Or her heart to have made these things sing
But the benevolence of the real

Tho there is no longer shelter in the earth, round helpless belly
Or hope among the pipes and broken works

'Substance itself which is the subject of all our planning'

And by this we are carried into the incalculable

XIV

There was no other guarantee

Ours aren't the only madmen tho they have burned thousands
of men and women alive, perhaps no madder than most

Strange to be here, strange for them also, insane and criminal,
who hasn't noticed that, strange to be man, we have come
rather far

We are at the beginning of a radical depopulation of the earth

Cataclysm . . . cataclysm of the plains, jungles, the cities

Something in the soil exposed between two oceans

As Cabeza de Vaca found a continent of spiritual despair
in campsites

His miracles among the Indians heralding cataclysm

Even Cortés greeted as revelation . . . No I'd not emigrate,
I'd not live in a ship's bar wherever we may be headed

These things at the limits of reason, nothing at the limits
of dream, the dream merely ends, by this we know it is the
real

That we confront

Anna Swir (Anna Swirszczynska) (1909–1984)

The daughter of a painter, Anna Swir was born in Warsaw, and grew up
in her father's atelier. In 1939, when her city was taken over by the
Nazis, she served as a military nurse in a makeshift hospital during the
sixty-three-day Warsaw Uprising. She escaped execution and survived
the war but was unable to write of her experiences until 1974. A femi-
nist, known also as the author of books for children, Swir died of
cancer in 1984.

≈ I Am Afraid of Fire

Why am I so afraid
running in the street
that is burning.

After all, there are no people here
only fire buzzing up to the sky
and that crash is not a bomb,
it's only three floors collapsed.

Naked liberated flames dance,
they wave their arms
through the holes of windows.
It's sinful
to spy on
naked flames,
it's sinful to eavesdrop
on the speech of free fire.

I run away from that speech
which resounded on the earth
earlier than the speech of man.

TR. CZESLAW MILOSZ

≈ A Conversation Through the Door

At five in the morning
I knock on his door.
I say through the door:
In the hospital at Sliska Street
your son, a soldier, is dying.

He half-opens the door,
does not remove the chain.
Behind him his wife
shakes.

I say: your son asks his mother
to come.
He says: the mother won't come.
Behind him the wife
shakes.

I say: the doctor allowed us
to give him wine.
He says: please wait.

He hands me a bottle through the door,
locks the door,
locks it with a second key.

Behind the door his wife
begins to scream as if she were in labor.

TR. CZESLAW MILOSZ

≈ We Survived Them

For a solemn opening
of his post-mortem exhibit
he will arrive and stand by me
in his old grey sweater.
Stooping,
strong.

Nobody will see him
only I will look at him.
He will say:
—We survived them.

TR. CZESLAW MILOSZ

≈ White Wedding Slippers

At night
my mother opened a chest and took out
her white silk wedding slippers.
Then she daubed them
a long time with ink.

Early in the morning
she went in those slippers
to the street
to line up for bread.
It was ten degrees,
she stood
for three hours in the street.

They were handing out
one quarter of a loaf per person.

TR. CZESLAW MILOSZ

Stephen Spender (1909–)

An Oxford-educated Englishman of German Jewish descent, Spender was living in Germany when the Nazis rose to power. His first important book of verse was published in the year of Hitler's accession to power. Spender was briefly a Communist and worked in Spain for the Loyalists; this experience served as the basis for the poem "Ultima Ratio Regum." After returning to England, he served in the Auxiliary Fire Service during the London Blitz, about which he wrote a number of poems. He was knighted in 1983.

≈ Ultima Ratio Regum

The guns spell money's ultimate reason
In letters of lead on the Spring hillside.
But the boy lying dead under the olive trees
Was too young and too silly
To have been notable to their important eye.
He was a better target for a kiss.

When he lived, tall factory hooters never summoned him
Nor did restaurant plate glass windows revolve to wave him in.

His name never appeared in the papers.
The world maintained its traditional wall
Round the dead with their gold sunk deep as a well
Whilst his life, intangible as a Stock Exchange rumour, drifted outside.

O too lightly he threw down his cap
One day when the breeze threw petals from the trees.
The unflowering wall sprouted with guns
Machine gun anger quickly scythed the grasses;
Flags and leaves fell from hands and branches;
The tweed cap rotted in the nettles.

Consider his life which was valueless
In terms of employment, hotel ledgers, news files.
Consider. One bullet in ten thousand kills a man.
Ask. Was so much expenditure justified
On the death of one so young, and so silly,
Lying under the olive trees, O world, O death?

≈ Air Raid Across the Bay at Plymouth

I

Above the whispering sea
And waiting rocks of the black coast,
Across the bay, the searchlight beams
Swing and swing back across the sky.

Their ends fuse in a cone of light
Held for a bright instant up
Until they break away again
Smashing that image like a cup.

II

Delicate aluminium girders
Project phantom aerial masts
Swaying crane and derrick
Above the sea's just surging deck.

III

Triangles, parallels, parallelograms,
Experiment with hypotheses
On the blackboard sky,
Seeking that X
Where the raider is met
Two beams cross
To chalk his loss.

IV

A buzz, felt as ragged but unseen
Is chased by two Excaliburs of light

A thud. An instant gleams
Gold sequins shaken from a black-silk screen.

V

Round the coast, the waves
Chuckle between rocks.
In the fields, the corn
Rustles with metallic clicks.

≈ **Rejoice in the Abyss**

The great pulsation passed. Glass lay around me
Resurrected from the end. I walked
Along streets of slate-jabbering houses,

Against an acrid cloud of dust, I saw
The houses kneel, revealed each in its abject
Prayer, my prayer as well: 'Oh God,
Spare me the lot that is my neighbour's.'

Then, in the upper sky, indifferent to our
Sulphurous nether hell, I saw
The dead of the bombed graveyard, a calm tide
Under the foam of stars above the town.

And on the roof-tops there stood London prophets
Saints of Covent Garden, Parliament Hill Fields,
Hampstead, Hyde Park Corner, Saint John's Wood,
Crying aloud in cockney fanatic voices:
'In the midst of Life is Death!' They kneeled
And prayed against the misery manufactured
In mines and ships and mills, against
The greed of merchants, vanity of priests.
They sang: 'We souls from the abyss
To whom the stars are fields of flowers,
Tell you: Rejoice in the abyss!
For hollow is the skull, the vacuum
In the gold ball, St. Paul's gold cross.
Unless you will accept the emptiness

Within the bells of foxgloves and cathedrals,
Each life must feed upon the deaths of others,
The shamelessly entreating prayer
Of every house will be that it is spared
Calamity that strikes its neighbour.'

≈ Epilogue to a Human Drama

When pavements were blown up, exposing wires,
And the gas mains burned blue and gold,
And brick and stucco were pulverized—a cloud
Pungent with smells of mice, corpses, anxiety.
When the reverberant emptied facades
Of West End theatres, shops and churches,
Isolated in a vacuum of silence, suddenly
Cracked and blazed and fell with the seven-maned
Lions of Wrath, licking the stony fragments—

Then the sole voice heard through deserted streets
Was the Cassandra bell which rang, released
To quench those fires that ran through city walls.
London burned with unsentimental dignity,
Of resigned kingship. Banks and palaces
Stood near the throne of domed St. Paul's
Like courtiers round the royal sainted martyr.
August shadows of night
And flares of concentrated light
Dropped from the sky to paint a final scene
Illuminated agony of bursting stone.

Who can wonder then that every word
In burning London, stepped out of a play?
On the stage there were heroes, maidens, fools,
Victims, a Chorus. The heroes won medals,
The fools spat quips into the skull of death,
The wounded waited with the humble patience
Of animals trapped within a cellar
For the pickaxes to break with light water.
The Chorus assisted, bringing cups of tea.

DYLAN THOMAS (1914–1953)

A Welshman, Thomas served as a fire watchman during the London Blitz, an experience that left its mark on the two poems included here. Thomas was also a prose writer and a playwright, but he is most famous for his intensely lyrical, syntactically complex, and tightly compressed poetry, and for the power of his acclaimed poetry readings. At his death in New York in 1953, he was mourned internationally.

≈ A Refusal to Mourn the Death, by Fire, of a Child in London

Never until the mankind making
Bird beast and flower
Fathering and all humbling darkness
Tells with silence the last light breaking
And the still hour
Is come of the sea tumbling in harness

And I must enter again the round
Zion of the water bead
And the synagogue of the ear of corn
Shall I let pray the shadow of a sound
Or sow my salt seed
In the least valley of sackcloth to mourn

The majesty and burning of the child's death.
I shall not murder
The mankind of her going with a grave truth
Nor blaspheme down the stations of the breath
With any further
Elegy of innocence and youth.

Deep with the first dead lies London's daughter,
Robed in the long friends,
The grains beyond age, the dark veins of her mother,

Secret by the unmourning water
Of the riding Thames.
After the first death, there is no other.

≈ Ceremony after a Fire Raid

I

Myselves
The grievers
Grieve
Among the street burned to tireless death
A child of a few hours
With its kneading mouth
Charred on the black breast of the grave
The mother dug, and its arms full of fires.

Begin
With singing
Sing
Darkness kindled back into beginning
When the caught tongue nodded blind,
A star was broken
Into the centuries of the child
Myselves grieve now, and miracles cannot atone.

Forgive
Us forgive
Us your death that myselves the believers
May hold it in a great flood
Till the blood shall spurt,
And the dust shall sing like a bird
As the grains blow, as your death grows, through our heart.

Crying
Your dying
Cry,
Child beyond cockcrow, by the fire-dwarfed
Street we chant the flying sea
In the body bereft.

Love is the last light spoken. Oh
Seed of sons in the loin of the black husk left.

II

I know not whether
Adam or Eve, the adorned holy bullock
Or the white ewe lamb
Or the chosen virgin
Laid in her snow
On the altar of London,
Was the first to die
In the cinder of the little skull,
O bride and bride groom
O Adam and Eve together
Lying in the lull
Under the sad breast of the head stone
White as the skeleton
Of the garden of Eden.

I know the legend
Of Adam and Eve is never for a second
Silent in my service
Over the dead infants
Over the one
Child who was priest and servants,
Word, singers, and tongue
In the cinder of the little skull,
Who was the serpent's
Night fall and the fruit like a sun,
Man and woman undone,
Beginning crumbled back to darkness
Bare as the nurseries
Of the garden of wilderness.

III

Into the organpipes and steeples
Of the luminous cathedrals,
Into the weathercocks' molten mouths
Rippling in twelve-winded circles,
Into the dead clock burning the hour

Over the urn of sabbaths
Over the whirling ditch of daybreak
Over the sun's hovel and the slum of fire
And the golden pavements laid in requiems,
Into the bread in a wheatfield of flames,
Into the wine burning like brandy,
The masses of the sea
The masses of the sea under
The masses of the infant-bearing sea
Erupt, fountain, and enter to utter for ever
Glory glory glory
The sundering ultimate kingdom of genesis' thunder.

ROBERT LOWELL (1917–1977)

Lowell, born to one of Boston's most illustrious families, was initially supportive of the war, but, became disillusioned; when his induction notice arrived in 1943, he refused to go. In a letter to President Roosevelt, Lowell argued that a war against civilians and geared toward unconditional surrender was an atrocity, and that it was incumbent upon free citizens of a democratic nation to take moral stands against injustice. He was sentenced to a year and a day in prison. At West Street Jail in New York City, his cell adjoined that of the condemned gangster Meyer Lepke, who said to Lowell, "I'm in for killing. What are you in for?" Lowell's reply: "I'm in for refusing to kill." Lowell was released in 1944, and went on to become the preeminent poet of his generation.

≈ Memories of West Street and Lepke

Only teaching on Tuesdays, book-worming
in pajamas fresh from the washer each morning,
I hog a whole house on Boston's
"hardly passionate Marlborough Street,"
where even the man
scavenging filth in the back alley trash cans,
has two children, a beach wagon, a helpmate,
and is a "young Republican."

I have a nine months' daughter,
young enough to be my granddaughter.
Like the sun she rises in her flame-flamingo infants' wear.

These are the tranquilized Fifties,
and I am forty. Ought I to regret my seedtime?
I was a fire-breathing Catholic C.O.,
and made my manic statement,
telling off the state and president, and then
sat waiting sentence in the bull pen
beside a Negro boy with curlicues
of marijuana in his hair.

Given a year,
I walked on the roof of the West Street Jail, a short
enclosure like my school soccer court,
and saw the Hudson River once a day
through sooty clothesline entanglements
and bleaching khaki tenements.
Strolling, I yammered metaphysics with Abramowitz,
a jaundice-yellow ("it's really tan")
and fly-weight pacifist,
so vegetarian,
he wore rope shoes and preferred fallen fruit.
He tried to convert Bioff and Brown,
the Hollywood pimps, to his diet.
Hairy, muscular, suburban,
wearing chocolate double-breasted suits,
they blew their tops and beat him black and blue.

I was so out of things, I'd never heard
of the Jehovah's Witnesses.
"Are you a C.O.?" I asked a fellow jailbird.
"No," he answered, "I'm a J.W."
He taught me the "hospital tuck,"
and pointed out the T-shirted back
of *Murder Incorporated's* Czar Lepke,
there piling towels on a rack,
or dawdling off to his little segregated cell full
of things forbidden the common man:
a portable radio, a dresser, two toy American

flags tied together with a ribbon of Easter palm.
Flabby, bald, lobotomized,
he drifted in a sheepish calm,
where no agonizing reappraisal
jarred his concentration on the electric chair—
hanging like an oasis in his air
of lost connections. . . .

HOWARD NEMEROV (1920–1991)

Born in New York City, Nemerov enlisted in the Canadian air force in 1941 before the United States entered the war. As a pilot, he flew combat missions against German shipping in the North Sea, then joined the U.S. Army Air Forces in 1943. A fiction writer as well as a poet, Nemerov taught at a number of universities in the United States, received numerous prizes for his work, and in 1990 was named Poet Laureate of the United States. His poem "Ultima Ratio Reagan" (referring to the former President) may be read as a play on Stephen Spender's poem "Ultima Ratio Regum," which is also included in this volume.

≈ Night Operations, Coastal Command RAF

Remembering that war, I'd near believe
We didn't need the enemy, with whom
Our dark encounters were confused and few
And quickly done, so many of our lot
Did for themselves in folly and misfortune.

Some hit our own barrage balloons, and some
Tripped over power lines, coming in low;
Some swung on takeoff, others overshot,
And two or three forgot to lower the wheels.

There were those that flew the bearing for the course
And flew away forever; and the happy few

That homed on Venus sinking beyond the sea
In fading certitude. For all the skill,
For all the time of training, you might take
The hundred steps in darkness, not the next.

≈ Models

I

The boy of twelve, shaping a fuselage
Of balsa wood so easy to be sliced
Along the grain but likely to get crushed
Under the razor when it was cut across;

Sanding the parts, glueing and lacquering
And pasting on the crosses and the rings
The brave identities of Fokker and Spad
That fought, only a little before his birth,

That primitive, original war in the air
He made in miniature and flew by hand
In clumsy combat, simulated buzz:
A decade away from being there himself.

II

The fuselage in the factory was aligned on North
So that the molecules lay along the axis,
Or so they said, to make the compass read
A right magnetic course; and after an attack

You headed the aircraft to what you hoped was North
And fired one more burst at the empty night
To set the shaken compass true again:
It straightened the molecules, or so they said.

The broken circle with the centered cross
Projecting the image at infinity
Quivered before him in the vacant air
Till it lay on the target like a haloing light.

III

And memory, that makes things miniature
And far away, and fit size for the mind,
Returned him in the form of images
The size of flies, his doings in those days

With theirs, the heroes that came out of the sun
To invent the avant-garde war of the air—
Richthofen, Rickenbacker, and the rest—
Where if you were shot it would be in the back,

Where the survivors, by their likenesses
Before and after, aged decades in a year,
Cruel-mouthed and harsh, and thought the young recruit
Not worth their welcome, as unlike to last.

≈ Ultima Ratio Reagan

The reason we do not learn from history is
Because we are not the people who learned last time.

Because we are not the same people as them
That fed our sons and honor to Vietnam
And dropped the burning money on their trees,

We know that we know better than they knew,
And history will not blame us if once again
The light at the end of the tunnel is the train.

Erich Fried (1921–1988)

Born to a family of Austrian Jews, Fried became a socialist in the 1930s. After his father perished in a concentration camp, Fried and his mother emigrated to England, where he helped save more than seventy Jews from occupied Europe. Although he remained in Britain for the rest of his life, in part working for the BBC, Fried wrote in German, and although his exile occurred during World War II, he continued to turn his attention to political problems and social concerns. The poem "What Things Are Called," for example, is a meditation on the language of the Vietnam War.

≈ One Kind of Freedom Speaks

Those who loved freedom
got me with their sweat
in the sleepless nights
of their dungeons and dingy rooms

Those who loved freedom
fed me with their blood
taught me to stand and walk
on their bones

Those who loved freedom
called me to the capital
bore me into the palace
placed me on the throne

Now I am free
to rule in their spirit
I stick very closely
to what they taught me

I still tread their bones
underfoot
I still drink the blood
of those who loved freedom

TR. GEORG RAPP

≈ Exile

He took
flight

and let
his homeland
go

What did he take
flight
with?
With wife
and child

And where
did his homeland
go?
Of course
to the devil

His flight
was genuinely
taken
with this
experience

nobody else
was taken
only
his flight

TR. GEORG RAPP

≈ My Girlfriends

Slowly in three to four weeks
or suddenly over night
my girls turn into
my aunts and elderly cousins

I see them anxiously
chewing their false teeth
and with arthritic fingers
wipe their spat-at faces

They arrive at Theresienstadt
with suitcases and bundles
They fall out of the window
still groping for their glasses

When they stretch in my bed
they are trying to stand to attention
in order to be spared
when the sick are picked out

I see them discoloured blue
when I kiss them in the morning
stacked in sixes
—the shit and vomited bile

washed off with garden hoses—
ready for transfer
from the gas chamber
to the incinerators

TR. GEORG RAPP

≈ What Things Are Called

Why were you not like the tree Trung Quan?
a girl says

That means
her lover is one of those burnt

The leaves of the tree Trung Quan do not catch fire
like bamboo poles or like human skin

II

Lazy Dog
is the name for an iron cross
between aerial bomb and dum-dum bullet
Safety Detonator
is a peasant tied to a rope
and driven ahead across a minefield

Tug of War
is dragging a prisoner
on a rope
behind a tank
through a village
by way of warning

Bundle
is a corpse
in a plaited mat
Harvest
a row of Bundles
in a field

III

Some things mean as much
as the mood of
a high official or senior officer

And some mean as little
as the life of
a handful of peasants father mother three children

IV

Pacifying a village
means not only beheading
peasants who were suspect or had been denounced

Pacifying also means
cutting out their liver
and throwing it into the air
The liver is the seat of courage

V

Wearing black jackets and trousers
means
being a peasant

Being killed
means afterwards
having been a Vietcong

TR. GEORG RAPP

JÁNOS PILINSZKY (1921–1981)

Pilinszky was conscripted into the Hungarian army in 1944, and his unit was sent to Germany in early 1945. There he saw concentration camps for the first time, an experience that marked him spiritually and as a poet. These poems are from that period. He returned to Hungary at the close of 1945, working in radio and as an editor, but his active literary life was interrupted by the Communist takeover in 1948 and he did not return to editing until 1956. Pilinszky wrote poetry, plays, fiction, and literary criticism; he is among the best-known contemporary Hungarian poets.

≈ Harbach 1944

At all times I see them.
The moon brilliant. A black shaft looms up.
Beneath it, harnessed men
haul an immense cart.

Dragging that giant wagon
which grows bigger as the night grows
their bodies are divided among
the dust, their hunger and their trembling.

They are carrying the road, they are carrying the land,
the bleak potato fields,
and all they know is the weight of everything,
the burden of the skylines

and the falling bodies of their companions
which almost grow into their own

as they lurch, living layers,
treading each other's footsteps.

The villagers stay clear of them,
the gateways withdraw.
The distance, that has come to meet them,
reels away back.

Staggering, they wade knee deep
in the low, darkly-muffled clatter
of their wooden clogs
as through invisible leaf litter.

Already their bodies belong to silence.
And they thrust their faces towards the height
as if they strained for a scent
of the faraway celestial troughs

because, prepared for their coming
like an opened cattle-yard,
its gates flung savagely back,
death gapes to its hinges.

TR. TED HUGHES AND JANOS CSOKITS

≈ Passion of Ravensbrück

He steps out from the others.
He stands in the square silence.
The prison garb, the convict's skull
blink like a projection.

He is horribly alone.
His pores are visible.
Everything about him is so gigantic,
everything is so tiny.

And this is all.
       The rest—
the rest was simply

that he forgot to cry out
before he collapsed.

TR. TED HUGHES AND JANOS CSOKITS

≈ On the Wall of a KZ-Lager

Where you have fallen, you stay.
In the whole universe, this is your place.
Just this single spot.
But you have made this yours absolutely.

The countryside evades you.
House, mill, poplar,
each thing strives to be free of you
as if it were mutating in nothingness.

But now it is you who stay.
Did we blind you? You continue to watch us.
Did we rob you? You enriched yourself.
Speechless, speechless, you testify against us.

TR. TED HUGHES AND JANOS CSOKITS

≈ Frankfurt 1945

In the river bank, an empty sandpit—
all that summer we took the refuse there.
Gliding among villas and gardens
we came to a bridge. Then a dip of the road
and the wooden fence of the racetrack.
A few jolts, and the truck began to slow down.
But even before the brakes could tighten
the first surge of hunger overwhelmed us.

Among the spilling buckets and the bursting sacks—
horror of the spines, stooping into position!
Then among those toppled crates began
the pitiless pre-censorship,
interrogating the gristle of the offal.

And there, on all fours, hunger
could not stomach its own fury,
but revolted and surrendered.

They were lost in the dust and filth.
The whole truck shook, howling.
The swill clogged their hearts
and swamped their consciousness.
They burrowed to the bottoms of the filled cans
till their mouths and eyes were caked.
They drowned in that living sludge
and there they were resurrected with heads buried.

And they brought back, scrap by scrap,
what had been utterly lost with them,
wringing their salvation, drunkenly,
out of the gouged mush—
but before their joy could properly be seized
the poison of comprehension stirred.
First, only the bitterness in their mouths,
then their hearts tasted the full sadness.

TR. TED HUGHES AND JANOS CSOKITS

ILSE AICHINGER (1921–   )

Aichinger spent World War II in her native city of Vienna, in danger of
discovery and deportation for being part Jewish. Her Jewish grand-
mother died at Auschwitz. In her poetry, Aichinger tries to reclaim
what she can of a German language debased by Nazism. She lives in
Germany and was married to the late Gunter Eich, whose work is also
represented here. "In Which Names" is a poem infused with her expe-
rience of mixed ancestry. Aichinger is also noted for her novels and
short stories.

≈ Glimpse from the Past

I've gotten used to this window
and to the snow falling through my eyes,
but who has followed the lost ones
through the open garden gate,
who left his seal upon what was there,
the rain barrel
and the moon as moon,
every frozen blade of grass?
Who rocked before dawn,
and made the ropes crack,
who lays his wax hand on the kitchen window,
lay down in whiteness
and accepted me myself?

TR. ALLEN H. CHAPPEL

≈ In Which Names

The name Alissa,
the name Inverness,
when and
dragged up
from what edges of desolation,
through which orders
monastic, conventual orders
lengthwise or diagonal
and whence, whence not,
how durable,
how wasteful
with wall rings,
under winter suns
into opened ditches,
embankments, cradles
with fires, ringlets,
oh names, names,
at least with
neither of you two am I christened
and bear no guilt.

TR. ALLEN H. CHAPPEL

≈ Enumeration

The day on which you
came into the ice without shoes,
the day on which
the two calves
were driven to slaughter,
the day on which I
pierced my left eye,
but no longer,
the day on which
the butcher's newspaper read,
life goes on,
the day on which it continued.

TR. ALLEN H. CHAPPEL

LOUIS SIMPSON (1923–   )

While a student at Columbia University, Simpson entered military service in 1943, serving in the tank corps and then as an infantryman in the Battle of the Bulge. After an illness late in the war, he returned to New York, where he completed graduate work. He was awarded a Pulitzer Prize in 1964. In the preface to his *Collected Poems,* Simpson writes: "During the war I felt there was an intelligence watching and listening. Or were we listening to one another? When I came upon an old trench of the First World War I remembered . . . lines by Wilfred Owen. . . . Weeks later, in the snow around Bastogne, I could apply [his] words to myself and my companions."

≈ The Runner

This is the story of a soldier of the 101st Airborne Division of the Army of the United States.

The Runner is fiction; the episodes and characters are imaginary. But the fiction is based on the following history.

On September 17, 1944, parachute and glider infantry of the First British Air-borne Division, the American 82nd and 101st Airborne Divisions, and a Polish brigade, descended in eastern Holland, at Eindhoven, Grave, Nijmegen, and Arn-hem. Their object was to make a bridgehead across the Lower Rhine at Arnhem. The British Second Army would join them and advance from Arnhem into the plains of northern Germany.

At Arnhem the British airborne troops were attacked by enemy units in over-whelming strength, and forced back across the river. The more fortunate Americans defended a corridor from Eindhoven to Nijmegen. The fighting, bitter at first, settled into a stalemate, and, with the coming of the rainy season, petered out entirely.

In mid-November the 82nd and 101st were drawn back to Rheims, to re-equip and get the drizzle out of their bones.

On December 17, they were alerted for combat. A German attack was developing in Belgium. The divisions were hurried by truck into the Ardennes, and on the night of December 19, the 101st were digging in around Bastogne.

This poem is for Donald Hall who encouraged me to write it.

I

"And the condemned man ate a hearty meal,"
The runner said. He took his mess kit over
To the garbage can. He scraped his mess kit out,
Then dipped it in the can of soapy water,
And swished it in the can of clean, hot water,
And came back to his place.

                The company
Was spread along one edge of the airfield,
Finishing lunch. Those with the appetite
Were going through the chow line once again.
They looked all pockets, pockets and baggy pants.
They held their mess kits out to the sweating cooks,
Who filled them up; then bore their precious load
Apart.

      The runner felt in his breast pocket
For cigarettes. He lit one and inhaled.
Leaning back on his pack, his feet sprawled out,
He stared at the ranks of gliders and towplanes
And said, "I wonder if . . ."

      "Agh!" said a voice,
"Why don't you dry up, Dodd!"

       He looked around
And met the eyes of Kass, the radioman,
Glaring beneath the rim of his steel helmet.

"What?" said the runner.

      "Who needs your remarks?
First, the condemned men eat a hearty meal,
And then you wonder . . ."

      "When we're coming back."

"What's it to you?"

      The runner didn't answer.
Sometimes it seemed that anything he said
Rubbed someone the wrong way. He'd only meant
He hoped the outfit would come back to England.
He liked the village where they had been quartered,
And London, where he'd gone on two-day passes.
He liked the pubs, the mugs of mild-and-bitter,
And country lanes. Some day, when they came back,
He'd go off on his own. Rent a bicycle.
He'd see some of the country by himself.
And if he got to London . . .

      With a roar
An engine started. Other engines followed.
A gale from the propellers swept around him.

"Fall in!" said the First Sergeant.

      Dodd got up
And hoisted on his pack.

      "Get a move on!"
That's how it was: you always had to wait,
And then you had to hurry. He closed his belt,

And slung his rifle over his right shoulder.
The section formed.

              "Where's Wheeler?" said the sergeant.
And here came Wheeler at a run. "You, Wheeler . . ."
The sergeant followed him with imprecations
As Wheeler ducked in place at Dodd's right hand.
Out of the side of his mouth: "Look what I got,"
Said Wheeler, and he showed in his clenched fist
A bundle of the new invasion money.
"Over in F Company," he whispered.
"The dice was really hot."

            " Ten-*hut*! For-*ard*
Arch!" said the sergeant, and they started off
Across the concrete runway. It seemed long.
Dodd's mouth was dry; his legs were weak. At last
They came up to the glider, their box kite—
High wings and rudder, little wheels that hardly
Lifted it off the ground—a canvas coffin.
Ungainly as a duck, it wouldn't fly
Unless it had to.

          Through the open door
Under the wing, they climbed up one by one,
Toppling with their burdens. Found their seats.
And sat in two rows, looking at each other.
Dodd fastened his safety belt and clasped his gun
Between his knees. The Captain entered last.
They waited. The glider trembled in the blast
Of wind from the towplane. The pilots entered,
Leaping up lightly, and made their way forward
To the controls.

         The runner could see nothing
Beyond the glider's high, transparent nose;
But now, he thought, the towplane would be turning
Into the wind. Two men would run the cable
Back from the plane and hook it to the glider.
Then, with a louder blast of the propellers,
The plane would start to roll.

                    The glider jerked
Forward, and rolled, creaking, and gathered speed.
The bumping stopped, and with a sudden lightness
They were airborne. Constricted where he sat,
Dodd prayed to nothing in particular:
Let the rope hold; no current whirl us down
Smashing on concrete.

                    They were well away.
He stared at the slender pilots in their pinks
And sporty caps and glasses; at their hands
On the half-wheel. His life was in those hands.
He thought of shell bursts, the green canvas torn,
Men writhing in their belts, the pilots' hands
Fallen from the controls, a sickening drop.
And then he thought of fields with pointed stakes
That would shear through the sides. Of plunging out
Into machine-gun fire.

II

                    "We're almost there,"
The next man said.

                  The pilots were peering down.
One nodded, and the other raised his hand
And grasped the lever that released the cable,
And pulled it down.

                  The glider soared, then fell
Slanting away. The wing rose up again.
They glided down on silence and the wind.

The fields were rushing at them, tilted steep.
Dodd braced himself. The glider leveled, lightly
Bumped on the ground, and rolled to a dead stop.

The door was open. They were climbing through.
And now were standing in an open field
Flat as a pancake. Gliders strewed the scene.

Others were skimming down; and still the sky
Was filled with gliders.

                  From their lifted bows
The gliders were disgorging jeeps and cannon.
Riflemen formed their files and marched away.
Dodd's section took its place in the company.
The Captain raised his arm; he swept it down,
And they were marching.

                  On the bright horizon
A windmill stood. The land was crossed with dykes.
It looked like a Dutch painting. To their left
A wood began. They marched in that direction.

The day was hot, and Dodd began to sweat.
Then to his ears came the familiar sound
Of guns, the battle-roll, continuous.
Then all his other days were like a dream.
This was reality: the heat, the load
Strapping his shoulder, and the sound of guns.

The war, after Normandy, had seemed remote.
He had been there; his courage had been proved
To his own satisfaction. He had listened
To talk about the fighting, and he'd talked
And lost the sense of truth. He had forgotten
The smell of apples and the fear of death.
Now he remembered. And it seemed unjust
That he should be required to survive
Again. The sound increased. The battleground
Looked ominous. Visions of a huge mistake
Struck at his heart.

III

The company was entering the woods.

"Dodd," said the sergeant, "take this message up
To Lieutenant Farr."

He stepped out of the file
And hastened to the front. The lead platoon
Was walking slowly, with the scouts ahead.
He gave the message.

"Right," said the lieutenant.
The runner started back. As he went by
Faces stared into his inquiringly.
He seemed possessed of an important secret.

Shots went off behind him. He crouched and swung
Out of the path, and lay in the scrub, face down.
The firing stopped. A voice was calling "Medic!"

Fisher, a sergeant of the third platoon,
Came up the path, bent low. He shook Dodd's shoulder:
"Who's doing all the shooting?"

"*I* don't know,"
Dodd said. The sergeant, with a grim expression,
Stared at him, and went on.

The runner waited.
Why didn't they get it over with!

"Move out!"

He got to his feet. The path filled up with men.
He made his way back, past the sweating faces
Now streaked with dust. He fell in with his section,
Turned round, and traveled up the path again
He'd just traversed.

The files ahead were parting.
The men looked down, as into a precipice.
There was a body lying in the way.
It was Santelli, of the first platoon.
Dodd had just seen him going out in front;
He walked like a dancer, with a short, neat step,
Rifle held crosswise.

He lay huddled up
On his left side; his helmet had rolled off;
His head was seeping blood out in the dirt.

The files ahead were lagging; then they hurried.
"Keep your intervals!" the Captain shouted.
They hated him together.

              At the break
They sprawled out of the path, in the underbrush.
Santelli's death had made them strangely silent.
Their helmets bowed their heads down on their chests.
Under the distant thudding of the guns,
The weight of all their burdens and the sky,
They couldn't speak, or stir themselves, or lift
A cigarette.

              Dodd thought about Santelli.
One of the afternoons it seemed forever
All they would do was practice for the war
With marches, tactics, and map exercises,
He lay beneath the wall of an English garden,
Sucking a stalk of grass, and watched the clouds,
And far above the clouds, a fleet of bombers
Trailing long plumes of white across the blue.
Close by, Santelli sat, paring his nails
With a pocketknife

                "Hey, runner-boy," he said
In the familiar and sneering tone
That Dodd despised. "What're we doin, hey?
You've been to college, right?" His little eyes
Were sharp with mockery—a little man
Of pocketknives and combs. "You ought to know.
What's it all about?"

IV

A plane flew glittering out of the sun—
A *Thunderbolt*. It swooped and disappeared

Behind a screen of trees. Then a staccato
Sound began. Machine guns. The plane rose
And flew away. They watched it till it vanished.

"On your feet," the sergeant said.

                              "My aching back!"
Someone said; but the gripe lacked conviction.
They stood and crumbled out their cigarettes,
And rolled the paper into little balls,
As though they'd like to keep the battlefield
Clean as a barracks.

                         As Dodd marched, the weight
Sawed at his shoulders: pack and ammunition,
Gas mask and trench tool, bayonet, grenades.
He plodded with clenched jaws, his eyes cast down
On the dusty path, the heels moving ahead.
He stayed, it seemed, in a fixed position;
It was the scene that moved.

                              The path reeled in
Another corpse. It came to him boot-first:
A German soldier on his back, spread-eagle,
A big, fresh-blooded, blond, jack-booted man
In dusty gray. Stepping around the fingers,
Around the bucket helmet, Dodd stared down.
A fly lit on the teeth. He looked away
And to the front, where other attitudes
Of death were waiting. He assumed them all,
One by one, in his imagination,
In order to prevent them.

                         Small-arms fire
Was crackling through the wood. Platoons spread out
In arrow-shaped formations.

                    "Dig in!"

                         He dug.
The shovel sank in sand; he hacked at roots.

Overhead shells were whispering, and smoke
Came drifting back.

        Two planes went whistling over.
They darted searching on the front.
They dived, and from their wings plunged rockets down
In smoking streaks. The ground shook with concussions.

"We're moving out!"

        Dodd climbed out of the hole
That he had dug. The company moved in silence
Through the burning wood.

V

Beyond the wood there stretched an open road.
They filed out on it. In a field of hay
A plane perched on its nose, a *Messerschmitt,*
The black cross glaring.

        Houses stood here and there.
In front of one, a mattress had been laid,
and on the mattress, a German officer.
He was puffed up with air like a balloon,
Belly and limbs swelling as if to split
His uniform. The grass was stuck with feathers.

Night was falling; the light had left the fields.
The road approached a village. At the entrance
A German half-track had been blown apart,
Its mustard-yellow metal torn and scorched;
Out of it spilled the crew, burned black as rubber.
The street, as they passed through, was strewn with dead,
A presentation of boot soles and teeth,
Letters, cigars, the contents of their lives.

The cannonading was more loud, and flashes
Lit the darkening sky. A company
Of paratroopers passed them, coming back
With somber faces.

VI

Night. And the fields were still. The cannonade
Was flickering and grumbling through the sky.
Red flashes lined the clouds. No breath of wind
Was moving. In the holes that they had dug
The tired troops were sleeping on their arms.

"Dodd, get up!"

                  He struggled out of his bag.

The First Sergeant leaned over: "Take this message
Back to Battalion."

              Dodd took the paper,
His helmet and his M-1, and set off,
Still half asleep.

            Darkness without a moon
Surrounded him. He made his lonely way
Over a road that skirted trees and dykes.
The guns were rumbling; shells went fluttering over;
Machine-gun tracers sparkled distantly.
A flare popped in the sky and glimmered down;
He waited in the shadow of a tree
Till it went out. And took the road again.

A deepening of black, a looming wall,
Was Battalion C.P. The guard called out:
"Halt! Who's there?"

               The runner spoke the password:
"Kansas!" and was admitted by the guard
Into the courtyard. There he gave his message
To a tech-sergeant; sat down on a bench,
And waited, looking at the pulsing sky.

"Runner!"

        He answered.

"Take this message back."

That was his job. Now all I need, he thought,
Is one of those Philip Morris uniforms
The bellboys wear.

        The road was long and dark.
And it was weird to be alone in Holland
At midnight on this road. As he went on
He felt he had no weight. The landscape seemed
To have more things to think of than his journey.
These errands gave him little satisfaction.
Some men might think he led the life of Riley,
Safe and warm and dry, around Headquarters.
A man could be a runner all his life
And never be shot at. That's what they thought.
But how about the shelling? He'd been shelled
As much as anyone. And back in France,
At Carentan, he had been shot at—plenty!
It wasn't his fault he never had a chance
To fire back. Now, right here on this road,
He might be killed by accident. But still,
That wouldn't be the same as being brave.
He had no chance to be thought so, no part
In the society of riflemen.
So, as he went, he reasoned with himself.

VII

Next day the company went up on line
Near Veghel. They were digging round a church,
In the cemetery, and were just knee-deep
When hell broke loose.

        The screaming and flat crack
Of eighty-eights.

      Airbursts.

        The metal slashed
The trees and ricocheted. Bit in the ground.

The runner on his belly lay contracting
Under the edge of metal. From a tree
A yard away, leaves flew.

A voice cried "Medic!"

His belly and his buttocks clenched each time
A shell came in. And they kept coming in.
He felt a sting between his shoulder blades.
I'm wounded! he thought, with a rush of joy.

"Dodd!" someone called.

He went on hands and knees

Toward the voice.

"Over here," it urged him.

It was his sergeant, with a dozen cases
Of mortar shells.

"Take them up to the mortars,"
The sergeant said. "They're out of ammunition."

He took two cases, one beneath each arm,
And ran off, dodging among the trees and graves.
He found the mortars and came running back
To get another load. The crack and hum
Of the artillery was all around him.
He felt the sting of the place where he'd been hit.
He knew that he was brave.

On the last trip,
Kneeling above a mortar, as he lowered
The cases gently, one of the mortar crew
Said, "You're a good man, Dodd."

That night he lay
Smiling, without a care, beneath the sky.
He had done all that could be expected.

VIII

October, and the sky was turning gray.
The battle line had settled. Every night
The bombers flew, going to Germany
At a great height. And back the other way
The V-1's came. The soldiers in their holes
Heard them droning and saw the rhythmic flames
Carrying woe to Antwerp and to England.

They dozed or watched. Then it began to rain,
And always rained. It seemed they were never dry.
Winter was in the air. Paths turned to mud.
By day and night the shells came shrieking in;
They got so they could tell a dying fall
And pay the rest no mind. They lived with mud.
They cooked and ate their rations in the can,
And tried to dry their socks between two rains.
Cold and sullen, under a raincoat roof,
They shivered in their holes.

              One moonlit night
Dodd was returning on his way alone.
There was a wind; the haunted shadows stirred,
And rainpools glimmered in the moonlit fields.

There was a field the runner loathed to cross.
A place of horrors. Here, on the first day,
There's been fierce charges, combats at close range,
And the dead were mixed as they had fallen.
Here crouched the German soldier with his *schmeisser*
Close to the parachutist in his rage—
Putrid things, never to be forgotten.
The field was swelling, shining with an aura
Of pale corruption.

           To avoid it, Dodd
Went by another path he did not know,
Leading, it seemed, back to the company.
But in a while a fearful premonition
Stopped him. In a shadow, cold with dread,

He stood listening. The branches stirred,
And all at once there was a clash of arms,
The sounds of footsteps. Stealthily he turned
To slip away.

>   *"Were geht da?"*

>   He ran.
He plunged into the darkness, blind with panic.
A storm of shots erupted at his back.
Brambles tore at his legs. He climbed a bank,
Clawing, and stumbled down the other side.
Then, as he ran, he shouted out the password:
"Ohio!" like a dog drenched with hot water.
His rifle fell. He left it where it was.
"Ohio!" He collided with a branch
And staggered. At his back the storm increased.
Red tracers streaked the air. Across a ditch
He leaped. And ran across the road beyond.
A hole was in his way; he cleared it with
A stride, and the dark figure starting up
Out of the hole. He kept on running, shouting
"Ohio!" A shape standing in the path
Snatched at him; he swerved out of its grasp.
There was a maze of holes. He stumbled, reeled,
And fell. His helmet flew off with a clang.

Feet were approaching. He lay still as death.
"It's Dodd," said a voice.

>   At last, he looked up
Into the faces of the third platoon.
Fisher. Others. They looked down in wonder.

IX

The regiment was bivouacked near Rheims
In tents on the bare plain. Wind-driven clouds
Streamed over, and the land in chilly streaks
Heaved like a sea. The wind hummed on the ropes
And whipped the tent flaps.

Dodd, stretched on his cot,
Could see and hear the third platoon at drill.
They turned to the flank and to the flank again;
They marched to the rear.

"Count cadence . . . cadence count!"

"Hup . . . two . . . three . . . four!" they answered on the wind.
The sun flashed from the slanting rifle butts.

The corporal shouted: "When I say Ohio,
To the rear march, and double-time like hell!"
There was a burst of laughter, then: "Ohio!
Run!" the corporal said, "Hup . . . two . . . three . . . four!
Halt! Now we'll try that movement once again.
When I give the word Ohio, turn around
And double-time as if your name is Dodd.
Make it look good. All right now—forward, 'arch!
Ohio!"

Dodd rolled over on his face.
He saw himself once more before the Captain:
"Screaming the password . . . throwing away your gun . . .
Keep out of my sight, Dodd. You make me sick."

And then, the jokes, from reveille to sleep:
"That is Ohio, one of the midwest boys."
Replacements would be sent to see Ohio
To draw their running shoes. "I'm from Cleveland,"
One of them told him. "What part are you from?"

He turned upon his back. Right overhead
His jacket hung, with regimental ribbons,
The bronze star, and his shameful purple heart.
He stared at it. If he could only sleep
The time between, until the sergeant came
To put him on another hard detail!
That was his punishment: to dig latrines,
Pick cigarette butts up, scrub greasy pots—
Or to do nothing for a live-long day
But think and try to read, in a cold tent.

When the men came in, they would ignore him—

"You going in to town?"

                    "You said it, man!"

Polishing up their paratrooper boots
Until the toes reflected a lit match;
Blousing the trousers in their boot tops; brushing
Their jackets; tucking ties between two buttons;
Cocking their caps—

                    "Let's go!"

                              He fell asleep,
And dreamed that he was climbing. On the crest
A dummy stood, with stiff, ballooning arms
And painted face, in Prussian uniform.
He reached the arms and swung them. It went "B-r-r-r-m!"
Like a machine gun. "B-r-r-m!" the sound came out
The dummy's painted lips and barrel belly.
Then he was walking over a green field.
It was a country he had never seen,
With haystacks, a warm wind, and distant barns.
Shadows were walking with him, and a voice
Spoke with the measure of a travelogue:
"*Vingtième Division* . . . fifty per cent . . ."
Another voice inquired: "Casualties?"
"No," said the first voice, "all of them are dead."
And it continued: "*Douzième Infanterie* . . .
Fifty per cent . . ." As the first voice was speaking,
Over the field, as on a movie screen,
Hands were imposed; they held a scarlet cloth
And folded it. "René de Gaumartin,"
The voice continued, "Cardinal of France."
Again the hands were folding a red robe.
"Marcel Gaumartin, Cardinal of France."
And as the voice and the hands continued
Their meditative play, Dodd came upon
A girl in black. She had fair hair and skin,
Plain features, almost ugly, but her eyes

Were large, they shot out tender rays of light.
The voice said, "Mademoiselle de Maintenon."
In his dream, Dodd laughed. *De Maintenon!* She said,
In a voice remote with sadness, "Yes," and smiled,
"I try not to think of them too much."

                    He woke,
And his heart was light. It was a vision,
He thought. What does it mean? What eyes she had!
That field, with the wind blowing, and the clouds!
And yet, it was absurd. The words were nonsense.

He went out of his tent.

                The third platoon
Were sitting down, taking a smoking break.
"Ohio!" someone shouted. "Where you running?"

He walked the other way, toward a rise
With trees, the only trees in all the plain,
Leaving the tents behind.

                He climbed the slope
And sat beneath a tree. On the horizon
Rheims, with the cathedral, like a ship
Traveled the plain. Clouds were streaming over
The spire; their swift shadows ran like waves.
He lit a cigarette. Then, near at hand,
He saw the earth was trenched. A long depression,
No more than a foot deep, with rotten posts
And scraps of wire, wound across the slope.
He stood, and walked along it. The earth gave
Under his boots. He picked up a small scrap
Of wire, and it crumbled. He surmised
This was a trench dug in the first Great War.
Who knew? Perhaps an older war than that.
He faced the East, to Germany and Russia.
Shadows were standing with him. It was cold.
They watched, wrapped in old overcoats, forgotten.
They stamped their feet. The whole world was deserted
Except for them; there was nobody left.

On the imagined parapet, a cross
Howled in the wind; and there were photographs
Of girls and children; bunches of cut flowers.
Then, on the pitted, gaunt escarp, the night,
The melancholy night, swept with grandeur.
Far in the dark, star shells were blossoming.
They stamped their feet. It was too cold. Too much
To expect of them. Their boots sank in the mud.
Their veins seemed ice; their jaws creaked with the cold.
They spoke; their words were carried on the wind,
Mingled, and lost.

                But now, an actual sound
Arrived distinctly. When he turned to look,
The camp was stirring; men ran to and fro.
He saw the third platoon halt in their drill,
Fall out, and run toward their tents. He moved;
He ground his cigarette out underfoot,
And hastened down the slope.

                      "Where have you been?"

Said the First Sergeant.

                  "I've been for a walk.

What's going on?"

                "Full field. Ready to move
In half an hour."

                Dodd's tent was in confusion.
The men were cramming rations in their packs,
Rolling their sleeping bags, cleaning their weapons.
He labored with stiff fingers.

                Trucks drew up.
Outside.

        "Get a move on!" a corporal shouted.

Dodd hitched on his pack.

                    The company
Fell in and shuffled, straightening their ranks,
Eyes to the right.

            "Let's go!"

                    Dodd took his place
In the line of olive drab, the overcoats,
Helmets, packs, the gloved hands holding weapons.
The roll was called; he answered to his name.

They marched up to the trucks.

                "Mount up!"

                        He climbed
Into a truck, and was packed in. The gate
Clanged shut behind him.

X

Day turned to dusk; the truck went jolting on;
The wind was drumming on the canvas hood
And prying coldly down the runner's back.
Dusk turned to evening, and the trucks behind
Were hidden. He dozed off. Monotony
Had numbed his senses like an anesthetic.
When the gears shifted he would nearly wake.
Sometimes the truck would stop for no clear reason,
And faces, blinking in their woolen caps,
Lifted and muttered; someone tried to stretch,
And this set off a ripple of complaints.
Then the truck moved again.

                    Once they dismounted,
And Dodd saw that the road wound through a forest.
There was a hill on one side; on the other,
The trees descended into a ravine.
Against that bank, a group of people stood:
Women and children dressed in country black,

With kerchiefs round their heads, and an old man
Close by a cart. The cart was piled with things:
A mattress, pots and pans. They stood in silence
Watching the soldiers. Then the trucks re-loaded,
And the onlookers vanished.

                They were driving
More slowly now. The men were all awake.
Another stop. Again the tailgate opened,
And they dismounted.

              This, then, was the place.
Colliding in the dark, they formed platoons,
And marched away.

            A signpost read *Bastogne.*
They marched through a dark village with locked doors,
And were led off the road, into the woods.
The path was very dark, the march confused,
With frequent halts.

            They halted in one place
Endlessly; they reclined, propped on their packs.
His helmet dragged Dodd's head back on his neck;
His feet got cold; under his woolen shirt
The sweat was trickling, then began to chill.

Then they were roused, pressed on without a pause,
Till, on a ridge commanding a black slope,
They halted. And the order came: "Dig in!"

Dodd unhitched his pack, laid it on the ground,
And leaned his rifle on it. From his belt
He took his trench tool out, and opened it.
He stuck the shovel blade into the ground
And levered it. He'd barely circumscribed
A foxhole, when a cold chill touched his cheek—
Snow!

      That's all we needed, the runner said
To the malignant sky.

From branch to branch
Snow glimmered down and speckled the dim ground.
Dodd dragged a fallen branch across his hole
And made a roof.

              "Pack up," the sergeant said.
"We're moving out."

                God help them, they were led
By officers and morons, who had orders
For wearing leather out and breaking spades,
To give employment to the men at home
Who, on this freezing night, were warm in bed
With soldiers' wives!

              Having said so, they walked
On in the stumbling dark, till once again
They halted, in a place just like the first.

"Dig in!"

          And it was useless, but they dug
With the energy of a supreme contempt
Marvelous holes—each clammy wedge of earth
An accusation flung in heaven's face.

Then, like a sound engendered by their mood,
An angry muttering rose on the night.
It faded, and again came to their ears—
The sound of guns.

             At last, Dodd's hole was finished.
He lowered himself, rolled out his sleeping bag,
And pushed into it. Flickerings of light
Twitched overhead; the guns were coming closer.
Here, it was still. The snow came drifting down.

"Dodd, you're on guard."

               He climbed out of his hole.

"There, by the trees."

He walked across the snow,
And as he went he looked around, astonished—
The sky was lit with spots of burning red
In a great circle.

As he stood on guard,
Surveying the black slope, the distant fires,
A man approached. Dodd challenged him. He spoke
The password, and came slogging through the trees.
A runner from Battalion. Brushing snow
Out of his neck, he asked for the C.P.
Dodd pointed: "Over there. Close to the barn.
What's happening now?"

"We're up a creek, that's what!
They're coming—panzers from the Russians front,
Under Von Runstedt. Panzers and SS.
I was just talking to a man who said
The line at St. Vith has been overrun
By tanks. It was a total massacre.
They're dropping paratroopers too," he said,
And turned away. He paused again to add:
"Everyone else is pulling out but us,"
And trudged away, leaving Dodd to his thoughts.

XI

The night was long. And day seemed less to rise
Then darkness to withdraw. Dodd, in his hole,
Could hear the fire of small arms, that seems
More threatening to the solitary man
Than does artillery.

One hole away
A helmet like a turtle shell was stirring.
A puffy face with whiskers turned around;
It was the mailman, Lopez. He arranged
Twigs on the snow. On these, his drinking mug.

He struck a match, applied it to the twigs,
and nursed the flame with cupped hands, bending over.

Under the hanging sky, congealed with clouds,
Fog trailed and clung to the earth; and the Ardennes,
The spectral firs, their branches cloaked with snow,
Stood stark against the foggy atmosphere.

Dodd stamped his feet. He stooped, and from his pack
Took a K-ration box. He tore it open,
Shook out the can of egg, the pack of biscuits,
The packet of coffee. He removed a glove
And with that hand put snow into his mug.
Poured coffee in, and mixed it with his spoon.
He scooped a hollow in the snow, and piled
Some twigs in it, and strips of the ration box.
And then put the mug on, and lit the pile.

Voices came floating up—loud gutturals;
A whine and clanking of machinery.
He picked his gun up.

                              At the foot of the slope
The trees were shaking, parting. There emerged
A cannon barrel with a muzzle brake.
It slid out like a snake's head, slowly swinging.
It paused. A flash of light came from its head;
A thunder clap exploded to Dodd's left;
Metal whanged on the slope, a spume of black
Hung in the air.

                              Then, endlessly it seemed,
The barrel slid out. With a thrash of branches
A tank appeared. It lurched, seemed to consider,
And then came on, at an appalling rate.
The engine whined; the tracks jingled and squeaked.
And imperceptibly, out of the trees
Stood men, like apparitions in the snow.

And now it was a swarm of walking men
In field-gray and in white, with capes and hoods.

Dodd placed his elbows on the snow, took aim—
There was another thunder clap. He ducked
And came upright again. To left and right
Rifles were firing. Hastily he pointed
The muzzle at a running, hooded shape,
And pressed the trigger. As in a nightmare
Nothing happened. A bullet cracked by his head.
The safety catch was on. He pressed it forward,
And aimed the gun again, and squeezed the trigger.
The butt kicked in his shoulder, the brass jumped
Into the snow.

          The tank was growing large.
The cannon flashed. Machine-gun tracers curved
Toward it, and played sparkling on the steel.
Still it came on, glittering in return
From its machine guns. Then, a crashing flame
Struck it, leaving a trail of smoke in air.
The tank shuddered. It slewed broadside around.
Inside the plates, as on an anvil, hammers
Were laboring. It trembled with explosions,
And smoke poured out of it.

              The slope was still,
Sprawling with hooded figures—and the rest
Gone back into the trees. Then there began
The sound of the wounded.

          Dodd stood up
And looked around. In the next hole, a helmet
Moved cautiously.

        "Lopez," he inquired,
"Are you all right?"

        "Jesus!" the mailman said.

With a shaking hand, Dodd felt for cigarettes.
He breathed tobacco deep into his lungs.
On the twigs where he had left it balanced
His mug was hissing and—he held it—warm.

XII

Sometimes the snow came drifting down again.
And when it ceased, eddies and gusts of wind
Would lift it in long skirts that swept across
The dead. It packed into the stiffened folds
Of clothing. When night fell, a freezing wind
Encased the tree trunks in bright sheaths of ice
And hung bright icicles on every branch,
And clamped the dead in rigid attitudes.

A shell came whistling down. The runner clenched
His fists. It crashed. Another shell came in.
The crashes jarred the ground. Then, from the rear,
A battery replied; shells fluttered back.

"Dodd!"

      He unzipped his bag, put on his helmet,
And stood.

      "Where are you?"

      It was the First Sergeant.

"Here," the runner answered.

      "Take this message
Back to Battalion. Are you listening?"

"Yes," he said.

      "To Colonel Jesserman.
The Captain says we need a fifty-seven
Or tank-destroyer. Tell him that it's urgent.
Now you repeat the message."

      Dodd did so.
He slung his rifle over his right shoulder
And climbed out of his hole.

                    "Keep out of trouble,"
The sergeant said. "Don't stop for anything."
Dodd started to move off. The sergeant grasped
His arm: "Watch out! They may have got patrols
Between us and Battalion. Good luck!"

Dodd waved his hand, although it was too dark
For the other to see him. And set off
In what seemed to be the right direction.

Rome, December 2, 1957

RICHARD HUGO (1923–1982)

Born in Seattle, Hugo was educated at the University of Washington. During World War II, he served in the U.S. Army Air Forces and was awarded both the Distinguished Flying Cross and the Air Medal. Two decades later, he made a pilgrimage back to the Italy of his war years and wrote the poems included here. He worked for the Boeing Company until 1963, and taught at the University of Montana from 1964 until his death. Sometimes misread as a "regional" poet, Hugo was notable for the breadth of his concerns, the harshness of his landscapes, and his strong epistolary poems, which influenced a generation of American poets.

≈ Napoli Again

Long before I hear it, Naples bright
with buildings trumpets from the hill.
A tugboat toots "*paisan*" and I am back.
That dock I sailed from eighteen years ago.
This bay had a fleet of half-sunk ships.
Where those dapper men are drinking wine,
a soldier beat an urchin with a belt.
Fountains didn't work. I remember stink.
Streets and buildings all seemed brown.

Romans hate such recent ruins,
bombed-out houses you do not repair.
Better pillars one must work to date.
Forget the innocent cut down,
cats gone crazy from the bombs
waiting down those alleys for delicious eyes.
Here, the glass replaced in *galleria* roofs,
cappuccino too high priced, it's hard
to go back years and feed the whores for free.

I'll never think of virgin angels here.
Did I walk this street before,
protesting: I am kind. You switch the menu,
gyp me on the bill. Remember me? My wings?
The silver target and the silver bomb?
Take the extra coin. I only came
to see you living and the fountains run.

≈ A View from Cortona

Land breaks yellow south below, pale squares
of green about to yellow. One long road
splits the summer on its way to Rome.
Twenty years ago today, the G.I.'s came.
Did bells ring then? Were the natives glad?
The liberators, loud and oddly young,
ignored this view, the lovely dome
of the cathedral halfway down the hill,
the yellow tile igniting summer
spreading to that wide south out of war.

Remember? No view? Long nights at home,
Nothing to do. Radio down so the old
could sleep. Staring at walls and trying
to write. Brown sugar on bread
and your life that might go on forever.
Only the garden dying each fall
or rain sudden on windows, breaking the void.
Nothing older than photos. Not one thing new

in the room. The 1880 valentine
kept flaking under the glass.

They think I'm German here. My passport
makes me friend. High in this hotel
I watch clouds play their shade across the miles
the G.I.'s came, loving wine so loud
Italians couldn't understand. Why stop here?
I was going to Perugia when this stark town
of medieval stone rode high above me,
at me out of sky. I turned up the hill
certain I'd vanish, someday, gone
in a moment, up a thousand-year-old street,
fat and silly from behind, curving out of sight
into a past weak as the future of stone.

≈ The Yards of Sarajevo

Time of day: a dim dream, probably
late afternoon. Children watch our train
pull into the yard. Other late dark
afternoons and porches seem remote.
These people, tracks and cars were what
we came to bomb nineteen years ago
and missed six miles through blinding clouds.

One war started here. The coal smoke
of our dirty train compounds the gloom.
The past is always dim. A plot. A gun.
The Archduke falling. A world gone
back to mud. Our long day from Dubrovnik
grates to a stop. Air is getting black.
I was five miles up there sighting
on this spot. I can't speak Serb or read
Cyrillic listings of departure times.

Even long wars end. Dukes and Kings
tell peasants old jokes underground.
This was small and foreign five miles down.
Why am I at home? The tongue is odd,

the station loud. All rebuilt
and modern. Only the lighting bad.

ANTHONY HECHT (1923–   )

After graduating from Bard College in 1944, Hecht served in the U.S.
Army, both in Europe and in the Pacific. He has said that his "cumula-
tive sense of these experiences is grotesque beyond anything I could
possibly write." These poems, among his best-known, are an attempt to
give voice to that horror. After the war he received an M.A. from
Columbia University, and he has taught at a number of universities. His
second book, *The Hard Hours,* won the Pulitzer Prize for poetry in 1968.

≈ More Light! More Light!

For Heinrich Blücher and Hannah Arendt

Composed in the Tower before his execution
These moving verses, and being brought at that time
Painfully to the stake, submitted, declaring thus:
"I implore my God to witness that I have made no crime."

Nor was he forsaken of courage, but the death was horrible,
The sack of gunpowder failing to ignite.
His legs were blistered sticks on which the black sap
Bubbled and burst as he howled for the Kindly Light.

And that was but one, and by no means one of the worst;
Permitted at least his pitiful dignity;
And such as were by made prayers in the name of Christ,
That shall judge all men, for his soul's tranquillity.

We move now to outside a German wood.
Three men are there commanded to dig a hole
In which the two Jews are ordered to lie down
And be buried alive by the third, who is a Pole.

Not light from the shrine at Weimar beyond the hill
Nor light from heaven appeared. But he did refuse.
A Luger settled back deeply in its glove.
He was ordered to change places with the Jews.

Much casual death had drained away their souls.
The thick dirt mounted toward the quivering chin.
When only the head was exposed the order came
To dig him out again and to get back in.

No light, no light in the blue Polish eye.
When he finished a riding boot packed down the earth.
The Luger hovered lightly in its glove.
He was shot in the belly and in three hours bled to death.

No prayers or incense rose up in those hours
Which grew to be years, and every day came mute
Ghosts from the ovens, sifting through crisp air,
And settled upon his eyes in a black soot.

≈ It Out-Herods Herod. Pray You, Avoid It.

Tonight my children hunch
Toward their Western, and are glad
As, with a Sunday punch,
The Good casts out the Bad.

And in their fairy tales
The warty giant and witch
Get sealed in doorless jails
And the match-girl strikes it rich.

I've made myself a drink.
the giant and witch are set
To bust out of the clink
When my children have gone to bed.

All frequencies are loud
With signals of despair;

In flash and morse they crowd
The rondure of the air.

For the wicked have grown strong,
Their numbers mock at death,
Their cow brings forth its young,
Their bull engendereth.

Their very fund of strength,
Satan, bestrides the globe;
He stalks its breadth and length
And finds out even Job.

Yet by quite other laws
My children make their case;
Half God, half Santa Claus,
But with my voice and face,

A hero comes to save
The poorman, beggarman, thief,
And make the world behave
And put an end to grief.

And that their sleep be sound
I say this childermas
Who could not, at one time,
Have saved them from the gas.

DENISE LEVERTOV (1923–   )

Levertov, born in England, served as a nurse during World War II, and later emigrated to the United States, where she became an American citizen. Influenced by the work of William Carlos Williams and associated with the poets of the Black Mountain school, Levertov eventually distanced herself from all poetic schools and movements. "Christmas 1944" arises out of her experience of World War II. Committed to feminism and antiwar activism, in 1965 she declared, "The poem has a social effect of some kind whether or not the poet wills it to have. It has kinetic force, it sets in motion . . . elements in the reader that would otherwise be stagnant." She traveled to Hanoi in 1972; the last three poems reflect that experience.

≈ Christmas 1944

Bright cards above the fire bring no friends near,
fire cannot keep the cold from seeping in.
Spindrift sparkle and candles on the tree
make brave pretence of light; but look out of doors:
Evening already surrounds the curtained house,
draws near, watches;
gardens are blue with frost, and every carol
bears a burden of exile, a song of slaves.
Come in, then, poverty, and come in, death:
this year too many lie cold, or die in cold
for any small room's warmth to keep you out.
You sit in empty chairs, gleam in unseeing eyes;
having no home now, you cast your shadow
over the atlas, and rest in the restlessness
of our long nights as we lie, dreaming of Europe.

A painted bird or boat above the fire,
a fire in the hearth, a candle in the dark,
a dark excited tree, fresh from the forest,
are all that stand between us and the wind.
The wind has tales to tell of sea and city,
a plague on many houses, fear knocking on the doors;
how venom trickles from the open mouth of death,
and trees are white with rage of alien battles.
Who can be happy while the wind recounts
its long sagas of sorrow? Though we are safe
in a flickering circle of winter festival
we dare not laugh; or if we laugh, we lie,
hearing hatred crackle in the coal,
the voice of treason, the voice of love.

≈ **Fragrance of Life, Odor of Death**

All the while among
the rubble even, and in
the hospitals, among the wounded,
                    not only beneath
                    lofty clouds

                        in temples
                    by the shores of lotus-dreaming
                    lakes

a fragrance:
flowers, incense, the earth-mist rising
of mild daybreak in the delta—good smell
of life.

It's in America
where no bombs ever
have screamed down smashing
the buildings, shredding the people's bodies,
tossing the fields of Kansas or Vermont or Maryland into
                                        the air
to land wrong way up, a gash of earth-guts . . .
it's in America, everywhere, a faint seepage,
I smell death.

Hanoi-Boston-Maine, November 1972

≈ **In Thai Binh (Peace) Province**

For Muriel and Jane

I've used up all my film on bombed hospitals,
bombed village schools, the scattered
lemon-yellow cocoons at the bombed silk-factory,

and for the moment all my tears too
are used up, having seen today
yet another child with its feet blown off,
            a girl, this one, eleven years old,

patient and bewildered in her home, a fragile
small house of mud bricks among rice fields.

So I'll use my dry burning eyes
to photograph within me
dark sails of the river boats,
warm slant of afternoon light
apricot on the brown, swift, wide river,
village towers—church and pagoda—on the far shore,

and a boy and small bird both
perched, relaxed, on a quietly grazing
buffalo.   Peace within the
            long war.

It is that life, unhurried, sure, persistent,
I must bring home when I try to bring
the war home.
            Child, river, light.

Here the future, fabled bird
that has migrated away from America,
nests, and breeds, and sings,

common as any sparrow.

≈ Weeping Woman

She is weeping for her lost right arm.
She cannot write the alphabet any more
on the kindergarten blackboard.

She is weeping for her lost right arm.
She cannot hold her baby and caress it at the same time
ever again.

She is weeping for her lost right arm.
The stump aches, and her side.

She is weeping for her lost right arm.
The left alone cannot use a rifle
to help shoot down the attacking plane.

In the wide skies over the Delta
her right hand that is not there
writes indelibly,
            'Cruel America,
when you mutilate our land and bodies,
it is your own soul you destroy,
not ours.'

TAMURA RYUICHI (1923–   )

Ryuichi discovered poetry as a high school student in Tokyo, where he first read Auden and Spender. No supporter of Japanese militarism, he entered Meiji University to avoid the draft, but was forced to join the service in 1943. At war's end, he returned to Tokyo, where the family home had been destroyed by bombing, obtained a job as an editor, and became a founding member of the "Waste Land," a group of Japanese modernists inspired by T. S. Eliot. Ryuichi resolutely addresses public issues in his work (war, imperialism, exile), but at the same time his voice is intensely private. He has become one of Japan's leading writers.

≈ My Imperialism

I sink into bed
on the first Monday after Pentecost
and bless myself
since I'm not a Christian

Yet my ears still wander the sky
my eyes keep hunting for underground water
and my hands hold a small book
describing the grotesqueness of modern white society
when looked down at from the nonwhite world

in my fingers there's a thin cigarette—
I wish it were hallucinogenic
though I'm tired of indiscriminate ecstasy

Through a window in the northern hemisphere
the light moves slowly past morning to afternoon
before I can place the red flare, it's gone:
darkness

Was it this morning that my acupuncturist came?
a graduate student in Marxist economics, he says he changed
to medicine to help humanity, the animal of animals, drag itself
    peacefully to its deathbeds
forty years of Scotch whiskey's roasted my liver and put me
into the hands of a Marxist economist
I want to ask him about Imperialism, A Study—
what Hobson saw in South Africa at the end of the nineteenth century
may yet push me out of bed
even if you wanted to praise imperialism
there aren't enough kings and natives left
the overproduced slaves had to become white

Only the nails grow
the nails of the dead grow too
so, like cats, we must constantly
sharpen ours to stay alive
Only The Nails Grow—not a bad epitaph
when K died his wife buried him in Fuji Cemetery
and had To One Woman carved on his gravestone
true, it was the title of one of his books
but the way she tried to have him only
to herself almost made me cry
even N, who founded the modernist magazine Luna
while Japan prepared to invade China
got sentimental after he went on his pension;
F, depressed
S, manic, builds house after house
A has abdominal imperialism: his stomach's colonized his legs
M's deaf, he can endure the loudest sounds;
some people have only their shadows grow

others become smaller than they really are
our old manifesto had it wrong: we only looked upward
if we'd really wanted to write poems
we should have crawled on the ground on all fours—
when William Irish, who wrote The Phantom Lady, died
the only mourners were stock brokers
Mozart's wife was not at his funeral

My feet grow warmer as I read
Kotoku Shusui's Imperialism, Monster of the Twentieth Century,
    written back in 1901
when he was young N wrote "I say strange things"
was it the monster that pumped tears from his older eyes?

Poems are commodities without exchange value
but we're forced to invade new territory
by crises of poetic overproduction

We must enslave the natives with our poems
all the ignorant savages under sixty
plagued by a surplus of clothes and food—
when you're past sixty
you're neither a commodity
nor human

    TR. CHRISTOPHER DRAKE

≈ October Poem

In crisis you may know me
beneath my smooth skin
emotions break like hard rain
corpse after corpse is thrown up
on deserted October shores

    October is my empire
    my gentle hands rule what is being lost
    my small eyes watch what is disappearing
    my soft ears hear the silence of what is dying

Through fear you may know me
in my plentiful blood
flows a time of total murder
fresh hunger shivers
in October's cold sky

    October is my empire
    my dead troops occupy all the wet cities
    my dead pilots circle above missing minds
    my dead populace signs documents for those still dying

TR. CHRISTOPHER DRAKE

≈ Standing Coffin

I

Don't touch my corpse
your hands can't touch death
mix my corpse with the masses
ram it into the rain

    We have no hands
    no hands to touch death with

I know city windows
windows in front of no one;
you've never been in any room
in any city, anywhere:
marriage, work,
desire, sleep, even death
have been evicted from your rooms
and become, like you, unemployed

    We have no work
    no work to touch death with

I know city rain
streetless crowds of umbrellas;
you've never been under a roof
in any city, anywhere:

values, beliefs,
revolution, hope, even life
have been evicted from under your roofs
and become, like you, unemployed

> We have no work
> no work to touch life with

II

Don't load me in the ground
your death can never be laid in the ground
shove my corpse in a standing coffin
jam it straight up

> We have no graves on earth
> no graves that can hold our corpses

I know death on earth
know the meaning of death on earth;
your death has never been in a grave
in any country, anywhere;
girlbody floating down the river,
bird's blood, broken voices
have been evicted from your earth
and become, like you, exiles

> We have no country on earth
> no country on earth worth our deaths

I know the values of the earth
values lost from the face of the earth;
your lives have never held anything large
in any country, anywhere:
wheat stacked for the future,
animals in traps, little sisters
have been evicted from your lives
and become, like you, exiles

> We have no country on earth
> no country on earth worth our lives

III

Don't burn my corpse
fire can't burn your death
hang my corpse in civilization
hang it till it rots

> We have no fire
> no fire to burn corpses

I know your civilization
civilization without love or death;
you've never been in a family
in any home, anywhere:
a father's single tear,
a mother's cries in labor, hauntings of the heart
have been evicted from your homes
and become, like you, invalids

> We have no love
> but the sick love of patients

I know your hospital rooms
your dreams that nick bed after bed;
you've never really been to sleep
in any sickroom, anywhere:
hands hanging from beds,
eyes finding major things, thirsting souls
have been evicted from your hospitals
and become, like you, invalids

> We have no poison
> no poison to cure ourselves with

TR. CHRISTOPHER DRAKE

≈ Spiral Cliff

In the photo a deer
is falling off a cliff
chased by

a lion? a tiger? a human?
only the deer is shown
you can't see what's after it,
a wild animal
God or big capital

Our century ends without decadence
after the night and fog of Nazi gas chambers
after Soviet forced labor camps
after two U.S. atomic bombs on Japan
there's no thrill left in killing,
no fear of the soul, no crime in adultery
there aren't even any more scenes
for Namboku's Kabuki ghosts to appear in
since ghosts are always individuals;
if you want to find any spooks now
you have to look in the boardrooms
of huge corporations, but even they
may not scare you the way a roller coaster will,
crime and evil disconnected into
rising   falling   centrifugal
centripetal force without decadence,
children, their bodies pure delight,
adults screaming and fainting
our century ends on pure speed

The only thing that terrifies me
is blank paper
what dreams will live and die there?
I'm afraid of high places
the cliff in me
am I the hunter
or the prey?

My cliff juts between dreams
spiraling
humans can't fall like the deer
to fall straight down we must
leap off the cliffs of Saipan
the New Guinea front, enter trapped
soldiers jumping on the Burma front,

to know the deer's fear and joy
we must live straight down

Winterdawn
I pat on wooden clogs, shatter some frost,
bring in the paper, lie horizontally
across my bed, turn to
the political and economic advertisements
of a large massacre, a civil war
and then the stock columns

Vanishing
cliff dream
vertical dream
elementally

Gone

TR. CHRISTOPHER DRAKE

ALAN DUGAN (1923–)

After attending Queens College in Flushing, New York, Dugan served
in the U.S. Army Air Forces during World War II as an aircraft engine
repairman in the Pacific theater. He was awarded the Pulitzer Prize for
poetry in 1962, and has also received a National Book Award and a Prix
de Rome. Dugan married artist Judith Shahn, and now serves as a staff
member for poetry at the Fine Arts Work Center in Provincetown,
Massachusetts.

≈ Memorial Service for the Invasion Beach Where the Vacation in the Flesh Is Over

I see that there it is on the beach. It is
ahead of me and I walk toward it: its
following vultures and contemptible dogs
are with it, and I walk toward it. If,

in the approach to it, I turn my back
to it, then I walk backwards: I
approach it as a limit. Even if I fall
to hands and knees, I crawl to it.
Backwards or forwards I approach it.

There is the land on one hand, rising, and
the ocean on the other, falling away;
what the sky does, I can not look to see,
but it's around, as ever, all around.
The courteous vultures move away in groups
like functionaries. The dogs circle and stare
like working police. One wants a heel
and gets it. I approach it, concentrating so
on not approaching it, going so far away
that when I get there I am sideways like
the crab, too limited by carapace to say:

"Oh here I am arrived, all; yours today."
No: kneeling and facing away, I will
fall over backwards in intensity of life
and lie convulsed, downed struggling,
sideways even, and should as vulture ask
an eye as its aperitif, I grant it,
glad for the moment wrestling by a horse
whose belly has been hollowed from the rear,
who's eyeless. The wild dog trapped in its ribs
grins as it eats its way to freedom. Not
conquered outwardly, and after rising once,
I fall away inside, and see the sky around
rush out away in the vulture's craw
and barely can not hear them calling, "Here's one."

≈ On an East Wind from the Wars

The wind came in for several thousand miles all night
and changed the close lie of your hair this morning. It
has brought well-travelled sea-birds who forget
their passage, singing. Old songs from the old
battle- and burial-grounds seem new in new lands.

They have to do with spring as new in seeming as
the old air idling in your hair in fact. So new,
so ignorant of any weather not your own,
you like it, breathing in a wind that swept
the battlefields of their worst smells, and took the dead
unburied to the potter's field of air. For miles
they sweetened on the sea-spray, the foul washed off,
and what is left is spring to you, love, sweet,
the salt blown past your shoulder luckily. No
wonder your laugh rings like a chisel as it cuts
your children's new names in the tombstone of thin air.

≈ Portrait from the Infantry

He smelled bad and was red-eyed with the miseries
of being scared while sleepless when he said
this: "I want a private woman, peace and quiet,
and some green stuff in my pocket. Fuck
the rest." Pity the underwear and socks,
long burnt, of an accomplished murderer,
oh God, of germans and replacements, who
refused three stripes to keep his B.A.R.,
who fought, fought not to fight some days
like any good small businessman of war,
and dug more holes than an outside dog
to modify some Freudian's thesis: "No
man can stand three hundred days
of fear and mutilation and death." What he
theorized was a joke: "To keep a tight
asshole, dry socks and a you-deep hole
with you at all times." Afterwards,
met in a sports shirt with a round wife, he was
the clean slave of a daughter, a power brake
and beer. To me, he seemed diminished
in his dream, or else enlarged, who knows?,
by its accomplishment: personal life
wrung from mass issues in a bloody time
and lived out hiddenly. Aside from sound
baseball talk, his only interesting remark
was, in pointing to his wife's belly, "If

he comes out left foot first" (the way
you Forward March!), "I am going to stuff
him back up." "Isn't he awful?" she said.

INGEBORG BACHMANN (1926–1973)

Bachmann spent World War II in Austria, during its annexation by
Nazi Germany. A student of philosophy, she wrote a dissertation on
Heidegger and published an influential essay on Wittgenstein. She be-
came famous for her first book of poetry, which was published in 1953.
After 1964, she stopped writing poetry altogether as a political protest.
She did, however, continue to write stories, librettos, and novels as well
as radio plays. She was at work on a trilogy of novels when she died of
burns sustained in a fire in her apartment in Rome in 1973. "Early
Noon" and "In the Storm of Roses" date from World War II. "A Kind
of Loss" is a late poem of her self-imposed exile.

≈ Early Noon

Softly the linden grows green in the opening summer.
Far from cities the dull gleaming moon
of day flickers. Already it is noon:
already the rays of light stir in the fountain,
already the battered wing of the fairytale bird
lifts itself from broken glass,
and the hand, deformed from throwing stones,
sinks into awakening corn.

Where Germany's sky blackens the earth
its beheaded angel seeks a grave for its hate
and hands you the bowl of its heart.

A handful of pain is lost over the hill.

Seven years later
you realize once more,

by the fountain in front of the gate:
don't look in too deep
for your eyes will swell with tears.

Seven years later,
in a house of death,
yesterday's hangmen drink
the golden goblet dry.
Your eyes would sink to the floor.

Already it is noon: the iron
grows crooked in the ashes, the flag
is raised on a thorn, and in the rocks
of an ancient dream the eagle
shall remain wrought.

Only hope cowers blinded in the light.

Take off hope's chains, lead her down
the slope, put your
hand over her eyes—
let no shadow scorch her!

Where Germany's earth blackens the sky,
a cloud looks for words and fills the crater with silence,
before summer hears it call through the thin rain.

The unspeakable, said softly, steals over the land:
already it is noon.

TR. MARK ANDERSON

≈ **In the Storm of Roses**

Wherever we turn in the storm of roses,
thorns illuminate the night. And the thunder
of a thousand leaves, once so quiet on the bushes,
is right at our heels.

TR. MARK ANDERSON

≈ A Kind of Loss

Used together: seasons, books, a piece of music.
The keys, teacups, bread basket, sheets and a bed.
A hope chest of words, of gestures, brought back, used, used up.
A household order maintained. Said. Done. And always a hand was
    there.

I've fallen in love with winter, with a Viennese septet, with summer.
With village maps, a mountain nest, a beach and a bed.
Kept a calendar cult, declared promises irrevocable,
bowed before something, was pious to a nothing

(—to a folded newspaper, cold ashes, the scribbled piece of paper),
fearless in religion, for our bed was the church.

From my lake view arose my inexhaustible painting.
From my balcony I greeted entire peoples, my neighbors.
By the chimney fire, in safety, my hair took on its deepest hue.
The ringing at the door was the alarm for my joy.

It's not you I've lost,
but   the   world.

    TR. MARK ANDERSON

GÜNTER GRASS (1927–)

Best known as Germany's foremost postwar novelist, Grass was born a
Kashubian in what was then Danzig, now the Polish city of Gdansk.
He welcomed the German invasion in 1939 and served in the Luftwaffe
from 1944 to 1945, when he was wounded and captured by the Amer-
icans. His convalescence took place in a hospital in Marienbad, adja-
cent to the Dachau concentration camp. Upon his return to Danzig,
he found the city destroyed. Salman Rushdie has written: "The practi-
tioners of 'rubble literature'—Grass himself being one of the most
prominent of these—took upon themselves the Herculean task of rein-
venting the German language, of tearing it apart, ripping out the poi-

soned parts, and putting it back together." Grass's most famous work is the novel *The Tin Drum*. His poetry explores the fragmented postwar consciousness.

≈ Music for Brass

Those days we slept in a trumpet.
It was very quiet in there,
we never dreamed it would sound,
lay, as if to prove it,
open-mouthed in the gorge—
those days, before we were blown out.

Was it a child, on his head
a helmet of studied newspaper,
was it a scatty hussar
who walked at a command out of the picture,
was it even those days death
who breathed that way on his rubber stamp?

Today, I don't know who woke us,
disguised as flowers in vases,
or else in sugar bowls,
threatened by anyone who drinks coffee
and questions his conscience:
one lump or two, or even three.

Now we're on the run and our luggage with us.
All half-empty paper bags, every crater in our beer,
cast-off coats, clocks that have stopped,
graves paid for by other people,
and women very short of time,
for a while we fill them.

In drawers full of linen and love,
in a stove which says no
and warms its own standpoint only,
in a telephone our ears have stayed behind
and listen, already conciliant,
to the new tone for busy.

Those days we slept in a trumpet.
Backward and forward we dreamed,
avenues, symmetrically planted.
On a tranquil unending back
we lay against that arch,
and never dreamed it would sound.

TR. CHRISTOPHER MIDDLETON

≈ In the Egg

We live in the egg.
We have covered the inside wall
of the shell with dirty drawings
and the Christian names of our enemies.
We are being hatched.

Whoever is hatching us
is hatching our pencils as well.
Set free from the egg one day
at once we shall make an image
of whoever is hatching us.

We assume that we're being hatched.
We imagine some good-natured fowl
and write school essays
about the colour and breed
of the hen that is hatching us.

When shall we break the shell?
Our prophets inside the egg
for a middling salary argue
about the period of incubation.
They posit a day called X.

Out of boredom and genuine need
we have invented incubators.
We are much concerned about our offspring inside the egg.
We should be glad to recommend our patent
to her who looks after us.

But we have a roof over our heads.
Senile chicks,
polygot embryos
chatter all day
and even discuss their dreams.

And what if we're not being hatched?
If this shell will never break?
If our horizon is only that
of our scribbles, and always will be?
We hope that we're being hatched.

Even if we only talk of hatching
there remains the fear that someone
outside our shell will feel hungry
and crack us into the frying pan with a pinch of salt.
What shall we do then, my brethren inside the egg?

TR. MICHAEL HAMBURGER AND CHRISTOPHER MIDDLETON

≈ Saturn

In this big house—
from the rats
who know about the drains,
to the pigeons
who know nothing—
I live and suppose much.

Came home late,
opened the house
with my key
and noticed as I hunted for my key
that I needed a key
to enter my own home.

Was quite hungry,
ate a chicken
with my hands
and noticed as I ate the chicken

that I was eating a chicken
which was cold and dead.

Then stopped,
took off both shoes
and noticed as I took off my shoes
that we have to stoop
if we want to take
shoes off.

I lay horizontal,
smoked the cigarette,
and in the darkness was certain
that someone held out his open hand
when I knocked the ashes
from my cigarette.

At night Saturn comes
and holds out his hand.
With my ashes, he
cleans his teeth, Saturn.
We shall climb
into his jaws.

TR. MICHAEL HAMBURGER AND CHRISTOPHER MIDDLETON

CHARLES SIMIC (1938–   )

Simic was born in Belgrade, Yugoslavia, at the beginning of World War
II. He came with his family to the United States in 1949 and was
educated at the University of Chicago and New York University. He is
now a professor at the University of New Hampshire. Simic was
awarded a Pulitzer Prize for his poetry in 1991 and has become one of
the most important American poets of his generation. These poems
refer, literally and figuratively, to the poet's memories of the war.

≈ Butcher Shop

Sometimes walking late at night
I stop before a closed butcher shop.
There is a single light in the store
Like the light in which the convict digs his tunnel.

An apron hangs on the hook:
The blood on it smeared into a map
Of the great continents of blood,
The great rivers and oceans of blood.

There are knives that glitter like altars
In a dark church
Where they bring the cripple and the imbecile
To be healed.

There is a wooden block where bones are broken,
Scraped clean—a river dried to its bed
Where I am fed,
Where deep in the night I hear a voice.

≈ The Lesson

It occurs to me now
that all these years
I have been
the idiot pupil
of a practical joker.

Diligently
and with foolish reverence
I wrote down
what I took to be
his wise pronouncements
concerning
my life on earth.
Like a parrot

I rattled off the dates
of wars and revolutions.
I rejoiced
at the death of my tormentors
I even become convinced
that their number
was diminishing.

It seemed to me
that gradually
my teacher was revealing to me
a pattern,
that what I was being told
was an intricate plot
of a picaresque novel
in installments,
the last pages of which
would be given over
entirely
to lyrical evocations
of nature.

Unfortunately,
with time,
I began to detect in myself
an inability
to forget even
the most trivial detail.
I lingered more and more
over the beginnings:
The haircut of a soldier
who was urinating
against our fence;
shadows of trees on the ceiling,
the day
my mother and I
had nothing to eat . . .
Somehow,
I couldn't get past
that prison train

that kept waking me up
every night.
I couldn't get that whistle
that rumble
out of my head . . .

In this classroom
austerely furnished
by my insomnia,
at the desk consisting
of my two knees,
for the first time
in this long and terrifying
apprenticeship,
I burst out laughing.
Forgive me, all of you!
At the memory of my uncle
charging a barricade
with a homemade bomb,
I burst out laughing.

≈ Begotten of the Spleen

The Virgin Mother walked barefoot
among the land mines.
She carried an old man in her arms.
The dove on her shoulder

barked at the moon.
The earth was an old people's home.
Judas was the night nurse.
He kept emptying bedpans into river Jordan.

The old man had two stumps for legs.
He was on a dog-chain. St. Peter pushed a cart
loaded with flying carpets.
They weren't flying carpets.

They were bloody diapers.
It was a cock-fighting neighborhood.
The Magi stood on street corners
cleaning their nails with German bayonets.

The old man gave Mary Magdalena
a mirror. She lit a candle,
and hid in the outhouse. When she got thirsty,
she licked the mist off the glass.

That leaves Joseph. Poor Joseph.
He only had a cockroach
to load his bundles on.
Even when the lights came on she wouldn't run
into her hole.

And the lights came on:
The floodlights
in the guard towers.

≈ **Prodigy**

I grew up bent over
a chessboard.

I loved the word *endgame*.

All my cousins looked worried.

It was a small house
near a Roman graveyard.
Planes and tanks
shook its windowpanes.

A retired professor of astronomy
taught me how to play.

That must have been in 1944.

In the set we were using,
the paint had almost chipped off
the black pieces.

The white King was missing
and had to be substituted for.

I'm told but do not believe
that that summer I witnessed
men hung from telephone poles.

I remember my mother
blindfolding me a lot.

She had a way of tucking my head
suddenly under her overcoat.

In chess, too, the professor told me,
the masters play blindfolded,
the great ones on several boards
at the same time.

≈ Toy Factory

My mother is here,
And so is my father.

They work the night shift.
At the end of the assembly line,
They wind toys
To inspect their springs.

Here's a mechanical
Firing squad.
They point their rifles.
They lower them.

The condemned man
Falls and gets up,

Falls and gets up.
He wears a plastic blindfold.

The china doll gravediggers
Don't work so well.
The spades are too heavy.
The spades are much too heavy.

Perhaps, that's how
It's supposed to be.

The Holocaust, The Shoah

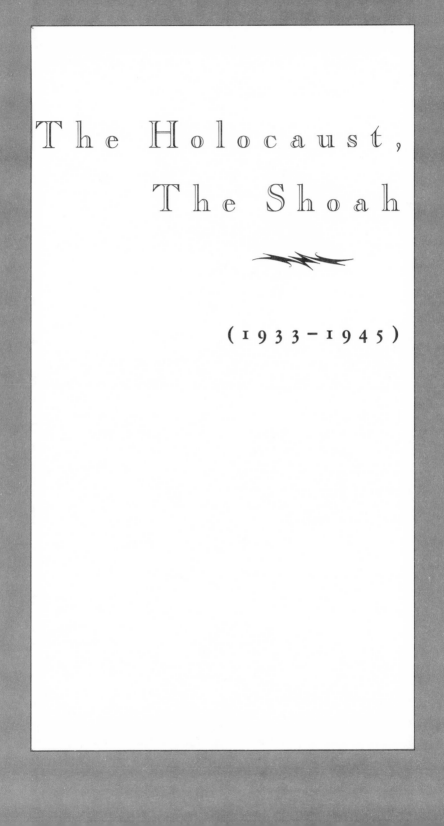

(1 9 3 3 – 1 9 4 5)

Anti-Semitism was officially sanctioned in Germany as early as 1920, as a plank in the first National Socialist Party platform. During the years of the Third Reich, the Nazis coupled racial hatred with new technologies of death and efficient means of bureaucratic organization in an unprecedented way. Close to twelve million people were killed in concentration, labor, and death camps and by special commando units that were formed to kill Jews (as well as Gypsies, Communists, the handicapped, homosexuals, Jehovah's Witnesses, and Mormons.) Of the dead, six million were Jews; by the end of World War II, the Nazis had exterminated three-quarters of the Jewish population of Europe.

The Nazis reserved their first concentration camp (Dachau) for political enemies of the Third Reich. During the first two years of Nazi rule, the Jews of Germany thought they might be able to live under the new government. Although they were persecuted, their sufferings (banishment, lynching, robbery, torture) were largely extrajudicial and extralegal. It was not until September 1935, with the passage of the infamous Nuremberg Laws, that Jews were deprived of their citizenship and therefore the protection of the state. In the years that followed, the expropriation of Jewish property proceeded, and restrictions on the Jews became harsher. Many tried to flee Germany (and Austria, after the Anschluss), but it was difficult to gain refuge: Palestinian Arabs, inflamed by German propaganda, resented the arrival of large groups of Jews; Britain and France wanted to appear neutral; and the United States had conflicting aims and policies that resulted in a grossly inadequate response to German and Austrian Jewish refugees. Although there was reliable information about the Nazi extermination program, German euphemisms and diplomatic pressure, in combination with general anti-Semitism, made it possible for foreign nations to ignore the plight of the Jews.

The worst misery began with the invasion of Poland in 1939. The Germans had various plans for resettlement and extermination, in both cases involving massive relocations of the Jewish population. In 1939, Jews were forced to wear the yellow Star of David: it was to serve as a badge of indignity, rendering Jews easily identifiable by local citizens and the Schutzstaffel (SS). A division of labor developed after the Polish campaign: the German army resisted executing civilians, and it was considered beneath the dignity of the civilian police, so the SS was given jurisdiction over such operations. Three thousand men were recruited for these Einsatzgruppen just before the invasion of Russia in the summer of 1941. When the attack came, these commando units were joined by Fascist and nationalist groups in Eastern Europe, including the Hungarian Arrow Cross party and the Romanian Black Shirts. As the German army advanced through Eastern Europe, the commandos slaughtered numerous Jews in spontaneous massacres. In September 1941, some thirty-four thousand Jews from Kiev were rounded up, marched to a ravine in nearby Babi Yar, stripped, and shot one by one in the neck. Their bodies were then cast into the chasm below. Similar massacres took place in cities such as Odessa and Rostov, as the Nazis moved toward total war against the Soviets and the Jews.

It was not until the Wannsee Conference in January 1942, however, that the mass extermination of the Jews—the "Final Solution"—became the declared policy of the Third Reich. The Germans had constructed an elaborate network of camps in Europe—some of the most notorious were Auschwitz-Birkenau, Treblinka, Chelmno, and Sobibor in Poland, and Dachau (in Germany)—which were operated in the manner of self-sufficient cities, but with varying functions (labor, transit, and extermination). Inmates were often worked to death, or starved. Executions were usually carried out by the use of Zyklon-B, a poison gas.

Gas chambers, crematoria, mass graves—all the apparatus of extermination—required massive organization and coordination. Moreover, the SS could do its work only if it received support and cooperation from local populations. The Germans were quick to exploit centuries of racial hatred among the Hungarians, Poles, and Romanians, as well as the Baltic peoples and Ukrainians. In fact, the SS sometimes had to "save" the Jews from the disorganized hatred of their neighbors, in order to send them to their deaths in a more orderly fashion. To a certain extent, the SS came to rely upon the complicity of the leaders of the Jewish community, who, in the hope of saving their ghettoes from complete destruction, delivered many of their fellow Jews for deportation.

In the midst of suffering, there were occasions of heroism and resistance. The Danes refused to give up their Jews to the Nazis: rather, they helped them escape to neutral Sweden in fishing boats. The Jews of the Warsaw Ghetto held a bloody uprising that they knew was hopeless. Within the camps themselves, there were acts of resistance under conditions that rendered such acts unlikely and in any event fruitless. In October 1943, more than one thousand women marked for death rose against their SS guards in the gas chambers and attacked three men. All the women were subsequently shot to death.

In the final days of the war in 1945, the extermination program was accelerated. At war's end, the camps were liberated, but many prisoners were too sick and weak to survive. In the end, the policy of "euthanasia," which began with the handicapped, elderly, and infirm, rendered mass murder by the state "acceptable," and allowed for the implementation of systematic genocide. This horror has been said to have "ruptured" history, and those who live in its aftermath cannot escape the knowledge that such atrocity is possible.

NELLY SACHS (1891–1970)

Sachs, born in Germany, had already published one book of poetry when the Nazis came to power. She continued to publish in Jewish periodicals, but persecution of the German Jewry was a constant threat. The man she loved was arrested and later died in a concentration camp, and Sachs herself narrowly escaped arrest. Able to emigrate to Sweden through the intercession of a noted Swedish writer, Sachs made a precarious living as a translator while writing poems about the Holocaust. Her work received recognition in the late 1950s, and she was awarded the Nobel Prize for Literature in 1966.

≈ O the Chimneys

And though after my skin worms destroy this body, yet in my flesh shall I see God.
  —Job 19:26

O the chimneys
On the ingeniously devised habitations of death
When Israel's body drifted as smoke
Through the air—
Was welcomed by a star, a chimney sweep,
A star that turned black
Or was it a ray of sun?

O the chimneys!
Freedomway for Jeremiah and Job's dust—
Who devised you and laid stone upon stone
The road for refugees of smoke?

O the habitations of death,
Invitingly appointed

For the host who used to be a guest—
O you fingers
Laying the threshold
Like a knife between life and death—

O you chimneys,
O you fingers
And Israel's body as smoke through the air!

TR. MICHAEL ROLOFF

≈ O Sister

O sister,
where do you pitch your tent?

In the black chicken-run
you call the brood of your madness
and rear them.

The cock's trumpet
crows wounds into the air—

You have fallen from the nest
like a naked bird
passers-by eye
the brazenness.

True to your native land
you sweep the roaring meteors
back and forth with a nightmare broom
before the flaming gates of paradise . . .

Dynamite of impatience
pushes you out to dance
on the tilted flashes of inspiration.

Your body gapes points of view
you recover the lost
dimensions of the pyramids

Birds
sitting in the branches of your eye
twitter to you the blossoming geometry
of a map of stars.

Night unfolds
a chrysalis of enigmatic moss
in your hand

until you hold the wing-breathing butterfly of morning
quivering—
quivering—
with a cry
you drink its blood.

TR. MATTHEW MEAD AND RUTH MEAD

≈ But Look

But look
but look
man breaks out
in the middle of the marketplace
can you hear his pulses beating
and the great city
on rubber tires
girded about his body—
for fate
has muffled
the wheel of time—
lifts itself
on the rhythm of his breathing.

Glassy displays
broken raven-eyes
sparkle
the chimneys fly black flags
at the grave of air.

But man
has said *Ah*
and climbs
a straight candle
into the night.

TR. MATTHEW MEAD AND RUTH MEAD

≈ You

You
in the night
busy unlearning the world
from far far away
your finger painted the ice grotto
with the singing map of a hidden sea
which assembled its notes in the shell of your ear
bridge-building stones
from Here to There
this precise task
whose completion
is left to the dying.

TR. MATTHEW MEAD AND RUTH MEAD

GERTRUD KOLMAR (1894–1943)

Born in Berlin, Kolmar was fluent in French, English, and Russian as well as her native German. She worked as a postal censor during World War I and published her first book in 1917. Her second did not appear until 1930, the year of her mother's death. Committed to caring for her elderly father, Kolmar chose not to emigrate with her sister after the Nazis came to power, and did forced labor in Berlin from 1941 to 1943. Her father was sent to Terezin camp in Czechoslovakia; she was deported in February 1943 and is presumed to have died at Auschwitz. Her highly allusive meditations on the Shoah (Holocaust) interrogate history through the figures of the Old Testament.

≈ **Judith**

Where is dew? Where is sand? Where the moon? Where a star?
Where are my servants, my former companions?
I cast screams at them, which echo insanely and vanish;
They all have sought other comrades and masters.

My feet grope along on scorpion-infested byways;
Darkness seeps from my toes.
They used to resemble little white lambs,
And now they are the feet of a murderess.

Where did I once look at the sunset of my people?
It gleamed bloodily, but I have lost it;
A head with temples and ears remains, in a sack.
The head is dead.

It speaks: its tongue speaks.
Words ascend amidst greyish vapours,
Writhe about like a woman with birth-pains,
Linger, and will not fade.

And the threat hangs over me.
The threat shall set in over Israel,
Like the wings of a raven, cawing, scrawny,
Shall stand before it as heavily as a horned steer.

The head shall be there again and again.
With senile curses, in reddish years,
With blonde strands or with shining black hairs,
It shall spit hate and destruction down on my cities.

Battered by courage, buried in dirt,
It shall rise up again and again.
I shake out the bag; here is no life,
My horror has called it awake.

The night is a long worm.
And the morning becomes iron, in order to slice it.
I, who dress myself in shame and my crime,
Step under the blade as soon as I remember.

My darkness hardly knew it any more;
But the daylight will tell it:
The beard and the forehead and the eyes lay
Asleep in you, there between breast and breast.

Why did you knock the forehead to the ground,
And shatter these eyes?
Your pride was the judge—and was not corrupt,
And did not cut short your heart?

Look back! Does your land kneel at your bed
With the weeping pleas of mothers and old people,
With the unjustly frightened gazes of orphans,
And pour thanks out of tattered garments?

It followed you childishly in quiet trust.
It wrapped itself up and has left you,
In order not to look at your lascivious smile,
Not to see your glistening loins' slander.

And although you were planted with the sword,
Your roots have already been ripped from the earth:
Now you must wander and no longer know
Where your homeland is.

TR. DAVID KIPP

≈ The Sacrifice

Her purple shoes know the way, and the metal band on her ankle
    knows it.
So she wanders without a will, captive, in dream.
So her coal-like, dimming eyes wander through rows of stony, winged
    cats and thick, painted columns to the temple forecourt,
Where a naked old man in a filthy loincloth hammers away on his tiny
    drum and chants without pause in a nasally pleading, sing-song
    voice.
A leprous woman, entangled in wildly hanging strands of hair,
    stretches out her arm with a moan.
Barren wives groan and pray.

A young man stands, tall and stiff, motionless, with a broad bronze
    sword,
And a lunatic squirms across the rose-granite threshold with a soft,
    ecstatic giggle.
As she presses by, sick, hooded figures snatch at her gown, at her
    amaranth-coloured hem;
But she drifts on, a cloud, toward unattainable evening skies.

Three times her questioning hand knocks on the copper door, and
    three times it receives a reply.
A priest opens it.
His beard flows, a blue stream, over the linen whiteness of his
    undergarment, over the saffron-yellow of his coat.
On his tall, black headdress a silver bird poses haughtily.
He pours milk into the red clay vessels, milk of the wax-white cows
    with gilded horns,
The drink of the sacred snakes
Which coil and writhe their sleek, ink-patterned bodies on the floor of
    the shadowy room.
And the largest, chysolite-eyed one raises itself, listens, and slowly
    sways to an inaudible sorrow.
The woman bends down to it, covers its eyes with her finger, and
    kisses it on the forehead.
She says nothing,
And walks out into the empty inner courtyard;
Only the mother-of-pearl pigeons peck grains of wheat from the
    leek-green nephrite.
They do not become frightened.
Between colourfully decorated walls a narrow, austere, ebony-wood
    door stands,
And three times the woman raps on its bolt with her ivory staff, but
    receives no answer.
She stays and waits.

She will go inside.
Beneath the image of the idol with the golden toad-legs,
In the smoke of smouldering sandalwood,
By the flickering light of the fire,
The stranger will approach her,
Will step slowly, and lay his right hand on her waist as a sign.
He will lead her into the burning circle,

And will look at her breasts,
And, with a wordless violence, smelt his pleasure from glowing
    embraces.
They kill . . .
That is her fate and she knows it.

She does not hesitate. Her arms and legs do not tremble; she does not
    look back,
Feels neither fortune nor misfortune.
She has filled herself completely with a burning darkness, with a
    numb, radiant humility, which wants only to serve the
    monster-god's wish, to die for the golden idol.

And yet God is in her heart.
On her grave and beautiful face his seal is stamped.
But she does not know it.

TR. DAVID KIPP

MIKLÓS RADNÓTI (1909–1944)

Radnóti, orphaned by age eleven, enrolled at the University of Szeged
in 1930, the year his first book of poetry appeared. For his second
book, Radnóti was tried for "effrontery to public modesty and incite-
ment to rebellion," and found guilty, whereupon his books were con-
fiscated. He was called to forced military labor intermittently from 1940
until his death. In 1944 he was sent to Yugoslavia to construct a railway,
but was force-marched with three thousand other men back to Hun-
gary because of the advancing Red Army. In early November 1944,
Radnóti and twenty other survivors of this march were put in the hands
of Hungarian noncommissioned officers, who, unable to place their
charges at a local hospital, shot them. Radnóti's body was exhumed
from a mass grave in 1946. His widow, going through his pockets,
discovered a notebook full of poems, which included "Forced March,"
"Letter to My Wife," "Picture Postcards," and "Seventh Eclogue."

≈ Forced March

The man who, having collapsed,   rises, takes steps, is insane;
he'll move an ankle, a knee,   an arrant mass of pain,
and take to the road again   as if wings were to lift him high;
in vain the ditch will call him: he simply dare not stay;
and should you ask, why not?   perhaps he'll turn and answer:
his wife is waiting back home,   and a death, one beautiful, wiser.
But see, the wretch is a fool,   for over the homes, that world,
long since nothing but singed   winds have been known to whirl;
his housewall lies supine;   your plum tree, broken clear,
and all the nights back home   horripilate with fear.
Oh, if I could believe   that I haven't merely borne
what is worthwhile, in my heart;   that there *is*, to return, a home;
tell me it's all still there: the cool verandah, bees
of peaceful silence buzzing,   while the plum jam cooled;
where over sleepy gardens   summer-end peace sunbathed,
and among bow and foliage   fruits were swaying naked;
and, blonde, my Fanni waited   before the redwood fence,
with morning slowly tracing   its shadowed reticence. . . .
But all that *could* still be—   tonight the moon is so round!
Don't go past me, my friend—   shout! and I'll come around!

Bor, 15 September 1944

TR. EMERY GEORGE

≈ Letter to My Wife

Down in the deep, dumb worlds are waiting, silent;
I shout; the silence in my ears is strident,
but no one can reply to it from far
Serbia, fallen into a swoon of war,
and you are far. My dream, your voice, entwine,
by day I find it in my heart again;
knowing this I keep still while, standing proudly,
rustling, cool to the touch, many great ferns surround me.

When may I see you? I hardly know any longer,
you, who were solid, were weighty as the psalter,
beautiful as a shadow and beautiful as light,

to whom I would find my way, whether deafmute or blind;
now hiding in the landscape, from within,
on my eyes, you flash—the mind projects its film.
You were reality, returned to dream
and, fallen back into the well of my teen years,

jealously question you: whether you love me,
whether, on my youth's summit, you will yet be
my wife—I am now hoping once again,
and, back on life's alert road, where I have fallen,
I know you are all this. My wife, my friend and peer—
only, far! Beyond three wild frontiers.
It is turning fall. Will fall forget me here?
The memory of our kisses is all the clearer;

I believed in miracles, forgot their days;
above me I see a bomber squadron cruise.
I was just admiring, up there, your eyes' blue sheen,
when it clouded over, and up in that machine
the bombs were aching to dive. Despite them, I am alive,
a prisoner; and all that I had hoped for, I have
sized up, in breadth. I will find my way to you;
for you I have walked the spirit's full length as it grew,

and highways of the land. If need be, I will render
myself, a conjurer, past cardinal embers,
amid nose-diving flames, but I will come back,
if I must be, I shall be resilient as the bark
on trees. I am soothed by the peace of savage men
in constant danger: worth the whole wild regimen ˘
of arms and power; and, as from a cooling wave of the sea,
sobriety's 2x2 comes raining down on me.

Lager Heidenau, above Zagubica in the mountains,
August–September 1944

TR. EMERY GEORGE

≈ Peace, Horror

As I stepped out the doorway it was ten o'clock,
a baker on a shiny wheel swept by, he sang,
above, a plane was droning, sun shone, ten o'clock,
my aunt who died came back to mind and all the souls
I'd loved, who lived no more, were flying overhead,
darkly a host of the silent dead flew by above,
and suddenly a shadow fell along the wall.
In silence morning halted, it was ten o'clock,
peace hung along the street, a touch of horror too.

1938

TR. EMERY GEORGE

≈ Picture Postcards

I

From Bulgaria thick, wild cannon pounding rolls.
It strikes the mountain ridge, then hesitates and falls.
A piled-up blockage of thoughts, animals, carts, and men;
whinnying, the road rears up; the sky runs with its mane.
In this chaos of movement you're in me, permanent,
deep in my conscious you shine, motion forever spent
and mute, like an angel awed by death's great carnival,
or an insect in rotted tree pith, staging its funeral.

30 August 1944. In the mountains.

II

Nine kilometers from here the haystacks and
houses are burning;
sitting on the field's edges, some scared and speechless
poor folk are smoking.
Here a little shepherdess, stepping onto the lake still
ruffles the water;
the ruffled sheep flock at the water drinks from
clouds, bending over.

Cservenka, 6 October 1944

III

Bloody saliva hangs on the mouths of the oxen.
Blood shows in every man's urine.
The company stands in wild knots, stinking.
Death blows overhead, revolting.

Mohacs, 24 October 1944

IV

I fell beside him; his body turned over,
already taut as a string about to snap.
Shot in the back of the neck. That's how you too will end,
I whispered to myself; just lie quietly.
Patience now flowers into death.
Der springt noch auf, a voice said above me.
On my ear, blood dried, mixed with filth.

Szentkirályszabadja, 31 October 1944

TR. EMERY GEORGE

≈ Seventh Eclogue

Look how evening descends and around us the barbed-wire-hemmed,
    wild
oaken fence and the barracks are weightless, as evening absorbs them.
Slowly the glance loses hold on the frame of our captive condition,
only the mind, it alone is alive to the tautness of wire.
See, Love: phantasy here, it too can attain to its freedom
only through dream, that comely redeemer who frees our broken
bodies—it's time, and the men in the prison camp leave for their
    homes now.

Ragged, with shaven heads, these prisoners, snoring aloud, fly,
leaving Serbia's blind peak, back to their fugitive homesteads.
Fugitive homesteads—right. . . . Oh, does that home still exist, now?
Still untouched by bombs? as it stood, back when we reported?
And will the men who now groan on my right, lie left, make it home
    yet?
Is there a home, where people can savor haxameter language?

No diacritics. Just one line under another line: groping,
barely, as I am alive, I write my poem in half-dark,
blindly, in earthworm-rhythm, I'm inching along on the paper.
Flashlights, books: the guards of the *Lager* took everything from us,
nor does the mail ever come. Only fog settles over the barracks.

Here among rumors and worms all live, be they Frenchmen or Polish,
loud-voiced Italian, partisan Serb, sad Jew, in the mountains,
bodies hacked and in fever; yet *one* life that all live in common:
waiting for good news, a womanly word, for a fate free and human,
waiting the end plumbing viscous dusk, or miracles—maybe.

Worm-ridden, captive beast: that is just how I lie on the bunk board.
Fleas will renew their siege; the battalion of flies is asleep now.
Evening is here; once again our serfdom has grown a day shorter,
so have our lives. The camp is asleep. On mountain and valley
bright moon shines; in its light once more all the wires pull tighter,
and through the window you see how the shadows of camp's armed,
        pacing
sentries are thrown on the wall in the midst of the night's lone voices.

Camp is asleep, dear one: can you see us? the dreams come rustling;
starting, one will snort on his narrow bunk, turn over;
sleeping again, his face shines. Lonely the vigil I'm keeping;
in my mouth I taste that half-smoked cigarette, not your
kisses, and dreams won't come, no sleep will come to relieve me,
since I can face neither death nor a life any longer without you.

Lager Heidenau, above Zagubica in the mountains,
July 1944

TR. EMERY GEORGE

PRIMO LEVI (1919–1987)

Born in Turin, Levi, a Jew, was trained as a chemist. Because of the
persecution of Italian Jews, he joined the partisans, with whom he
fought until his capture in 1944. He was sent to the Buna-Monowitz

concentration camp, where his background in chemistry helped him survive until his camp was liberated by the Russians in January 1945. Levi's first collection of poems was published privately. He made his living as the manager of a chemical factory until 1977. After that he devoted himself entirely to literature; he was most famous for his accounts of the death camps. Primo Levi committed suicide in his native Turin in April 1987.

≈ Buna

Torn feet and cursed earth,
The long line in the gray morning.
The Buna smokes from a thousand chimneys,
A day like every other day awaits us.
The whistles terrible at dawn:
'You multitudes with dead faces,
On the monotonous horror of the mud
Another day of suffering is born.'
Tired companion, I see you in my heart.
I read your eyes, sad friend.
In your breast you carry cold, hunger, nothing.
You have broken what's left of the courage within you.
Colorless one, you were a strong man,
A woman walked at your side.
Empty companion who no longer has a name,
Forsaken man who can no longer weep,
So poor you no longer grieve,
So tired you no longer fear.
Spent once-strong man.
If we were to meet again
Up there in the world, sweet beneath the sun,
With what kind of face would we confront each other?

28 December 1945

TR. RUTH FELDMAN AND BRIAN SWANN

≈ Shemà

You who live secure
In your warm houses,
Who return at evening to find
Hot food and friendly faces:

> Consider whether this is a man,
> Who labors in the mud
> Who knows no peace
> Who fights for a crust of bread
> Who dies at a yes or a no.
> Consider whether this is a woman,
> Without hair or name
> With no more strength to remember
> Eyes empty and womb cold
> As a frog in winter.

Consider that this has been:
I commend these words to you.
Engrave them on your hearts
When you are in your house, when you walk on your way,
When you go to bed, when you rise.
Repeat them to your children.
Or may your house crumble,
Disease render you powerless,
Your offspring avert their faces from you.

10 January 1946

TR. RUTH FELDMAN AND BRIAN SWANN

≈ For Adolf Eichmann

The wind runs free across our plains,
The live sea beats for ever at our beaches.
Man makes earth fertile, earth gives him flowers and fruits.
He lives in toil and joy; he hopes, fears, begets sweet offspring.

. . . And you have come, our precious enemy,
Forsaken creature, man ringed by death.

What can you say now, before our assembly?
Will you swear by a god? What god?
Will you leap happily into the grave?
Or will you at the end, like the industrious man
Whose life was too brief for his long art,
Lament your sorry work unfinished,
The thirteen million still alive?

Oh son of death, we do not wish you death.
May you live longer than anyone ever lived.
May you live sleepless five million nights,
And may you be visited each night by the suffering of everyone who
    saw,
Shutting behind him, the door that blocked the way back,
Saw it grow dark around him, the air fill with death.

20 July 1960

TR. RUTH FELDMAN AND BRIAN SWANN

≈ **Annunciation**

Don't be dismayed, woman, by my fierce form.
I come from far away, in headlong flight;
Whirlwinds may have ruffled my feathers.
I am an angel, yes, and not a bird of prey;
An angel, but not the one in your paintings
That descended in another age to promise another Lord.
I come to bring you news, but wait until my heaving chest,
The loathing of the void and dark, subside.
Sleeping in you is one who will destroy much sleep.
He's still unformed but soon you'll caress his limbs.
He will have the gift of words, the fascinator's eyes,
Will preach abomination and be believed by all.
Jubilant and wild, singing and bleeding,
They'll follow him in bands, kissing his footprints.
He will carry the lie to the farthest borders.
Evangelize with blasphemy and the gallows.
He'll rule in terror, suspect poisons
In spring-water, in the air of high plateaus.
He'll see deceit in the clear eyes of the newborn,

And die unsated by slaughter, leaving behind sown hate.
This is your growing seed. Woman, rejoice.

22 June 1979

TR. RUTH FELDMAN

≈ Voices

Voices mute for ever, or since yesterday, or just stilled;
If you listen hard you can still catch the echo.
Hoarse voices of those who can no longer speak,
Voices that speak and can no longer say anything,
Voices that think they're saying something,
Voices that speak and can't be understood:
Choruses and cymbals for smuggling sense
Into a senseless message.
Pure hubbub to pretend
That silence is not silence.
A vous parle, compaignes de galle:
I speak to you, companions of revelry,
Drunk like me on words,
Sword-words, poison-words,
Key-words, lockpicker-words,
Salt-words, mask and nepenthe.
The place we're going to is silent
Or deaf. It's the limbo of the lonely and the deaf.
You'll have to run the last lap deaf,
You'll have to run the last lap by yourself.

10 February 1981

TR. RUTH FELDMAN

JIŘÍ ORTEN (1919–1941)

Orten, born to a Czech Jewish family in a town near Prague, moved to
the capital as an adolescent and remained there after the German inva-
sion and the Munich Accords, which ceded Bohemia to the Nazis. As a

Jew, he was forced to publish his poetry under a pseudonym, and only four books appeared in his lifetime. After being struck by a German car in Prague, he was refused admission to a hospital because he was Jewish, and died in another hospital several days later. His reputation has suffered the vicissitudes of political history: he was widely read between 1945 and the rise of the Communists in 1948, was retrieved in the Prague Spring of 1968, fell into disfavor after the Soviet occupation, and is only now being discovered again.

≈ Whispered

Blood only blood is able to beat to strike the right note
And hands are useless you can tell at a glance
Here's the cloakroom Please leave your coat
Enter softly As though you were two-legged moss
And look about you the way a shadow looks about
glancing sideways here and there as if by chance
Become the soul of lamps whose light is almost out
And stop on every grave you come across

Music reaches up here through a crack of light
it's as if we were waiting for a concert to start
And the dead are astonished by the sight
of the green miracle of grass growing on them not to mention
all the grave-bugs making fast
work of everything—the dead whisper to us as if half in
jest—sparkling words are scattered on the vast
silence of the graves' comprehension

And oh you that are dead I am also there I too
touch only the blank internal side of things from where
I lie I too give up when confronted with singular despair
Perhaps only the wind that blows on me is new
it alone marks me as different as one of those
That the well of my life is full is true
here's my cover which You've almost managed to close
only it stays slightly askew

TR. LYN COFFIN

≈ The Last Poem

Darkness stares from everywhere and no one's here.
Now all is as it was—Suddenly
when I look crookedly around again, it's clear
my burning heart has turned to freezing me.

I hold my head in my hand. I keep weeping. Just
the same, no screams escape my throat but, at most, a kind
of shade—the shadow of a past voice like a meadow with a crust
of frost, the shade I was made to unwind.

—Over the hill, the river, the acrid heather, day after day
at first he persevered. Now he's untricked, forced to understand
in what kind of catacombs his future's been bricked away.
He longs for a peach like a child with a peach in his hand,

God, do you know how longing is? how the soul can long
for endless tenderness which all of a sudden burns low
and he is guilty!
        —I am guilty for the nice aroma, the wrong
fragrance, for the vain longing for my father, I know,
for verses, yes, for love that's lost to me,
for shame, for silence and a land full of those who yearn
to be without pain, for heaven, for God who shortened my days
and gave me a dead paradise in return—

and still! Do you believe me? In places I won't try to mention,
deep in my wounds, I keep finding a country, a small nation
of little songs to which only winter pays attention,
I ask and ask these songs for information!

TR. LYN COFFIN

PAUL CELAN (1920–1970)

Born Paul Antschel in a German-speaking part of Romania, Celan
studied medicine in France but returned to his native city in 1939 to
take up Romance languages and literature. The region was invaded by

the Russians in 1940 and then occupied by Romanian Fascists and the Nazis. A ghetto was established, and in 1942 Celan's parents were sent to a concentration camp, where his father died of typhus and his mother was shot. Celan himself, conscripted to forced labor, was freed in 1944, and settled in Paris in 1948. Although he became a French citizen, he continued to write poetry in German, in a fractured, painful play of syntax and neologism that made him the most important and influential poet in that language since the war. He drowned himself in the Seine in 1970.

≈ Night Ray

Most brightly of all burned the hair of my evening loved one:
to her I send the coffin of lightest wood.
Waves billow round it as round the bed of our dream in Rome;
it wears a white wig as I do and speaks hoarsely:
it talks as I do when I grant admittance to hearts.
It knows a French song about love, I sang it in autumn
when I stopped as a tourist in Lateland and wrote my letters to
     morning.

A fine boat is that coffin carved in the coppice of feelings.
I too drift in it downbloodstream, younger still than your eye.
Now you are young as a bird dropped dead in March snow,
now it comes to you, sings you its love song from France.
You are light: you will sleep through my spring till it's over.
I am lighter:
in front of strangers I sing.

       TR. MICHAEL HAMBURGER

≈ Death Fugue

Black milk of daybreak we drink it at evening
we drink it at midday and morning we drink it at night
we drink and we drink
we shovel a grave in the air there you won't lie too cramped
A man lives in the house he plays with his vipers he writes
he writes when it grows dark to Deutschland your golden hair
     Marguerite

he writes it and steps out of doors and the stars are all sparkling
      he whistles his hounds to come close
he whistles his Jews into rows has them shovel a grave in the ground
he orders us strike up and play for the dance

Black milk of daybreak we drink you at night
we drink you at morning and midday we drink you at evening
we drink and we drink
A man lives in the house he plays with his vipers he writes
he writes when it grows dark to Deutschland your golden hair
      Marguerite
your ashen hair Shulamith we shovel a grave in the air
                          there you won't lie too cramped
He shouts jab this earth deeper you lot there you others sing up and
      play
he grabs for the rod in his belt he swings it his eyes are blue
jab your spades deeper you lot there you others play on for the
      dancing

Black milk of daybreak we drink you at night
we drink you at midday and morning we drink you at evening
we drink and we drink
a man lives in the house your goldenes Haar Marguerite
your aschenes Haar Shulamith he plays with his vipers
He shouts play death more sweetly Death is a master from
      Deutschland
he shouts scrape your strings darker you'll rise then in smoke to the
      sky
you'll have a grave then in the clouds there you won't lie too cramped

Black milk of daybreak we drink you at night
we drink you at midday Death is a master aus Deutschland
we drink you at evening and morning we drink and we drink
this Death is ein Meister aus Deutschland his eye it is blue
he shoots you with shot made of lead shoots you level and true
a man lives in the house your goldenes Haar Margarete
he looses his hounds on us grants us a grave in the air
he plays with his vipers and daydreams
                  der Tod ist ein Meister aus Deutschland

dein goldenes Haar Margarete
dein aschenes Haar Shulamith

TR. JOHN FELSTINER

≈ THERE WAS EARTH INSIDE THEM, and they dug.

They dug and they dug, so their day
went by for them, their night. And they did not praise God,
who, so they heard, wanted all this,
who, so they heard, knew all this.

They dug and heard nothing more;
they did not grow wise, invented no song,
thought up for themselves no language.
They dug.

There came a stillness, and there came a storm,
and all the oceans came.
I dig, you dig, and the worm digs too,
and that singing out there says: They dig.

O one, o none, o no one, o you:
Where did the way lead when it led nowhere?
O you dig and I dig, and I dig towards you,
and on our finger the ring awakes.

TR. MICHAEL HAMBURGER

≈ I HEAR THAT THE AXE HAS FLOWERED, I hear that the place can't be named,

I hear that the bread which looks at him
heals the hanged man,
the bread baked for him by his wife,

I hear that they call life
our only refuge.

TR. MICHAEL HAMBURGER

≈ **A LEAF**, treeless
for Bertolt Brecht:

What times are these
when a conversation
is almost a crime
because it includes
so much made explicit?

TR. MICHAEL HAMBURGER

TADEUSZ BOROWSKI (1922–1951)

Born in Zytomierz, Poland, Borowski lived in the Ukraine during his childhood and studied literature at Warsaw University. His first volume of poems was published in 1942. The following year he was arrested, then sent to Auschwitz and Dachau, where he remained until the liberation. His second book of poetry appeared in 1945, and in 1946, the first of three volumes of concentration camp stories was published in Munich. The other two were published in Poland in 1948. He contributed actively to Polish literary magazines. In July 1951, he committed suicide by gassing himself, choosing as his death the fate he had miraculously escaped during his internment.

≈ **The Sun of Auschwitz**

You remember the sun of Auschwitz
and the green of the distant meadows, lightly
lifted to the clouds by birds,
no longer green in the clouds,
but seagreen white. Together
we stood looking into the distance and felt
the far away green of the meadows and the clouds'
seagreen white within us,
as if the color of the distant meadows
were our blood or the pulse
beating within us, as if the world
existed only through us and nothing changed

as long as we were there. I remember
your smile as elusive
as a shade of the color of the wind,
a leaf trembling on the edge
of sun and shadow, fleeting
yet always there. So you are
for me today, in the seagreen
sky, the greenery and
the leaf-rustling wind. I feel
you in every shadow, every movement,
and you put the world around me
like your arms. I feel the world
as your body, you look into my eyes
and call me with the whole world.

TR. LARRY RAFFERTY, MERYL NATCHEZ, AND
TADEUSZ PIORO

≈ Two Countries

That's your freedom—bootleg whiskey
and some slut in tricot lingerie.
My freedom—the vast, clear sky.
That's why we have different homelands.

Your country—a stock market transaction
and hoarded sacks of grain.
My country—the gas chamber
and the Auschwitz flame.

Your country—the Triumphal Arch
and parade music—banal, victorious.
My country—a rotting grave
in the Smolensk forest!

Your country—a quiet niche,
a neck that bows obediently,
and my country—a burned out house
and a file with the KGB.

TR. LARRY RAFFERTY, MERYL NATCHEZ, AND
TADEUSZ PIORO

≈ Project: Flag

(they're already threatening to lock up Communists)

We're fed up with national colors!
The pigment of life is what we want,
not what's on show for holidays.
Let's give every flag new colors—
The Polish flag will be striped!
The stripes, of course, are prison bars . . .

TR. LARRY RAFFERTY, MERYL NATCHEZ, AND
TADEUSZ PIORO

DAN PAGIS (1930–1986)

Pagis was born in Bukovina, first part of Austria, then of Romania, and now within the boundaries of the former Soviet Union. Sent to a concentration camp in the Ukraine, Pagis escaped after three years of incarceration in 1944. He emigrated to Israel in 1946 and taught on a kibbutz, then moved in 1956 to Jerusalem, where he earned a doctorate and was for many years a professor of Hebrew literature at the Hebrew University. Pagis also taught at Harvard University, the University of California at Berkeley, and the Jewish Theological Seminary. He died in July 1986. These poems bear witness to his camp experience.

≈ Autobiography

I died with the first blow and was buried
among the rocks of the field.
The raven taught my parents
what to do with me.

If my family is famous,
not a little of the credit goes to me.
My brother invented murder,
my parents invented grief,
I invented silence.

Afterward the well-known events took place.
Our inventions were perfected. One thing led to another,
orders were given. There were those who murdered in their own way,
grieved in their own way.

I won't mention names
out of consideration for the reader,
since at first the details horrify
though finally they're a bore:

you can die once, twice, even seven times,
but you can't die a thousand times.
I can.
My underground cells reach everywhere.

When Cain began to multiply on the face of the earth,
I began to multiply in the belly of the earth,
and my strength has long been greater than his.
His legions desert him and go over to me,
and even this is only half a revenge.

TR. STEPHEN MITCHELL

≈ A Lesson in Observation

Pay close attention: the world that appears now
at zero-point-zero-one degrees
was, as far as is known,
the only one
that burst out of the silence.

It hovered within a blue bubble, fairly large;
and sometimes there were clouds, sea breezes,
sometimes a house, perhaps a kite, children,
and here and there an angel,
or a garden, or a town.
Beneath these were the dead, beneath them
rock, beneath this the fiery prison.

Is that clear? I will repeat: outside there were
clouds, screams, air-to-air missiles,

fire in the fields, memory.
Far beneath these, there were houses, children. What else?

The little dot on the side? It seems to be
the only moon of that world.
It blew itself out even before this.

TR. STEPHEN MITCHELL

≈ Written in Pencil in the Sealed Railway Car

here in this carload
i am eve
with abel my son
if you see my other son
cain son of man
tell him that i

TR. STEPHEN MITCHELL

≈ Draft of a Reparations Agreement

All right, gentlemen who cry blue murder as always,
nagging miracle-makers,
quiet!
Everything will be returned to its place,
paragraph after paragraph.
The scream back into the throat.
The gold teeth back to the gums.
The terror.
The smoke back to the tin chimney and further on and inside
back to the hollow of the bones,   .
and already you will be covered with skin and sinews and you will live,
look, you will have your lives back,
sit in the living room, read the evening paper.
Here you are. Nothing is too late.
As to the yellow star:
it will be torn from your chest

immediately
and will emigrate
to the sky.

TR. STEPHEN MITCHELL

EDITH BRÜCK (1932–)

Born to a poor Jewish family on the border between Hungary and the Ukraine, Brück spent part of her childhood in a concentration camp, an experience addressed in these poems. After the liberation, she lived in Israel before settling in Italy in 1954. A filmmaker and playwright as well as a poet, she lives in Rome.

≈ Childhood

Your milk was already poisoned
by dark foreboding
your tired arms
offered me no protection
your eyes were consumed by tears
your heart pounded with fear
your mouth opened only to pray
or to curse me the last born seeking refuge
from human shapes that attacked in the dark
from dogs egged on by silent slow-witted masters
from the spittle of children fed on ignorance
from idiots let loose by families
who kept them in shame and chains
so they could take it out on the Jews
at the synagogue exit.

TR. RUTH FELDMAN

≈ Pretty Soon

Pretty soon
when people hear a quiz show expert
talk about Auschwitz
they'll ask themselves if they would have guessed
that name
they'll comment on the current champion
who never gets dates wrong
and always guesses the number of dead.
Yawning sleepily
they'll say maybe they would have preferred
Greco-Roman history
to these Jews
who have always gotten themselves talked about:
they really attract persecution.

TR. RUTH FELDMAN

≈ Equality, Father

Equality, father! Your dream has come true.
I glimpse you dimly, still see you walking
next to Roth the man of property who refused us
a little cottage cheese for the holidays,
Klein the shoemaker who wouldn't resole your only shoes
on credit, Goldberg the butcher
with his trimmed goatee who dragged you
into court for selling meat without a license,
Stein the teacher who gave us Hebrew lessons
in expectation of a heavenly reward and directed us
like a demoniac conductor
breaking dozens of pointers over the heads
of your children, illiterate in Hebrew, destined to hell.
And you, the poorest, most recognizable
by those skinny buttocks! The most agile,
most exploitable in forced labor.
Forward, father! You've been tried by every eventuality,
armed with experience

you know the front lines, rifles, trenches,
the daily struggle even in good times.
You know prison, the hard plank in the dark cell
where you picked off lice, licked your wounds,
unrolled cigarette butts.
You know the taste of blood in your mouth
from a rotten tooth
from a Fascist's fist
from a bullet you caught defending the homeland
you stubbornly believed was yours.

You know death lurking in ambush
the meanness of men
the power game
the bosses' exploitation.
You know the whole gamut of humiliation
the dark street with menacing shadows
ravenous wolves and skittish horses
on sleepless nights during your solitary trips
in the illusion of business deals
doomed to fail
the promises not kept
except for Jehovah's wrath!

Forward, father! You know the marches,
the cold, hunger! Hold your head high!
you no longer have to hide from your creditors:
they're all there, naked!

Ah, you turn toward me? Don't you know me?
I've grown up, my breasts are firm,
the down on my skin is pure and soft
like mama's when they brought her to you
as a bride. Take me, father!
I'll give you pleasure, not children,
love, not obligations,
love, not reproaches,
love undreamed of by you,
imagined by me. Run:

It is the time of the Apocalypse!
Let us commit a mortal sin
worthy of death.

TR. RUTH FELDMAN

IRENA KLEPFISZ (1941–   )

Born of Jewish parents in Warsaw, Klepfisz was an infant during the
Warsaw Uprising. After her father was killed in an air attack, mother
and child escaped the ghetto and were hidden by peasants. After the
war, they emigrated to Sweden, then entered the United States, where
Klepfisz was educated in New York public schools and Workmen's
Circle Yiddish schools. Her undergraduate work was at City College of
New York, and she earned her doctorate from the University of Chi-
cago. Klepfisz founded *Conditions,* a feminist-lesbian magazine. Her
previous books are *A Few Words in the Mother Tongue: Poems Selected and
New* (1971–1990) and *Dreams of an Insomniac: Jewish Feminist Essays,
Speeches, and Diatribes.* "Bashert," titled with the Yiddish word for
"inevitable" or "predestined," is the story of her survival during and after
the Holocaust.

≈ Bashert

These words are dedicated to those who died

These words are dedicated to those who died
because they had no love and felt alone in the world
because they were afraid to be alone and tried to stick it out
because they could not ask
because they were shunned
because they were sick and their bodies could not resist the
disease
because they played it safe
because they had no connections
because they had no faith
because they felt they did not belong and wanted to die

These words are dedicated to those who died
because they were loners and liked it

because they acquired friends and drew others to them
because they took risks
because they were stubborn and refused to give up
because they asked for too much

These words are dedicated to those who died
because a card was lost and a number was skipped
because a bed was denied
because a place was filled and no other place was left

These words are dedicated to those who died
because someone did not follow through
because someone was overworked and forgot
because someone left everything to God

because someone was late
because someone did not arrive at all
because someone told them to wait and they just couldn't
any longer

These words are dedicated to those who died
because death is a punishment
because death is a reward
because death is the final rest
because death is eternal rage

These words are dedicated to those who died

Bashert

These words are dedicated to those who survived

These words are dedicated to those who survived
because their second grade teacher gave them books
because they did not draw attention to themselves and got lost
in the shuffle
because they knew someone who knew someone else who could
help them and bumped them into a corner on a Thursday
afternoon
because they played it safe
because they were lucky

These words are dedicated to those who survived
because they knew how to cut corners
because they drew attention to themselves and always got
picked
because they took risks
because they had no principles and were hard

These words are dedicated to those who survived
because they refused to give up and defied statistics
because they had faith and trusted in God
because they expected the worst and were always prepared
because they were angry
because they could ask
because they mooched off others and saved their strength
because they endured humiliation
because they turned the other cheek
because they looked the other way

These words are dedicated to those who survived
because life is a wilderness and they were savage
because life is an awakening and they were alert
because life is a flowering and they blossomed
because life is a struggle and they struggled
because life is a gift and they were free to accept it

These words are dedicated to those who survived

Bashert

1. Poland, 1944: My mother is walking down a road.

My mother is walking down a road. Somewhere in Poland. Walking towards an unnamed town for some kind of permit. She is carrying her Aryan identity papers. She has left me with an old peasant who is willing to say she is my grandmother.

She is walking down a road. Her terror in leaving me behind, in risking the separation is swallowed now, like all other feelings. But as she walks, she pictures me waving from the dusty yard, imagines herself suddenly picked up, the identity papers challenged. And even if she were to survive that, would she ever find me later? She tastes the terror in her mouth again. She swallows.

I am over three years old, corn silk blond and blue eyed like any Polish child. There is terrible suffering among the peasants. Starvation. And like so many others, I am ill. Perhaps dying. I have bad lungs. Fever. An ugly ear infection that oozes pus. None of these symptoms is disappearing.

The night before, my mother feeds me watery soup and then sits and listens while I say my prayers to the Holy Mother, Mother of God. I ask her, just as the nuns taught me, to help us all: me, my mother, the old woman. And then catching myself, learning to use memory, I ask the Mother of God to help my father. The Polish words slip easily from my lips. My mother is satisfied. The peasant has perhaps heard and is reassured. My mother has found her to be kind, but knows that she is suspicious of strangers.

My mother is sick. Goiter. Malnutrition. Vitamin deficiencies. She has skin sores which she cannot cure. For months now she has been living in complete isolation, with no point of reference outside of herself. She has been her own sole advisor, companion, comforter. Almost everyone of her world is dead: three sisters, nephews, and nieces, her mother, her husband, her in-laws. All gone. Even the remnants of the resistance, those few left after the uprising, have dispersed into the Polish countryside. She is more alone than she could have ever imagined. Only she knows her real name and she is perhaps dying. She is thirty years old.

I am over three years old. I have no consciousness of our danger, our separateness from the others. I have no awareness that we are playing a part. I only know that I have a special name, that I have been named for the Goddess of Peace. And each night, I sleep secure in that knowledge. And when I wet my bed, my mother places me on her belly and lies on the stain. She fears the old woman and hopes her body's warmth will dry the sheet before dawn.

My mother is walking down a road. Another woman joins her. My mother sees through the deception, but she has promised herself that never, under any circumstances, will she take that risk. So she swallows her hunger for contact and trust and instead talks about the sick child left behind and lies about the husband in the labor camp.

Someone is walking towards them. A large, strange woman with wild red hair. They try not to look at her too closely, to seem overly curious. But as they pass her, my mother feels something move inside her. The movement grows and grows till it is an explosion of yearning that she cannot contain. She stops, orders her companion to continue without her. And then she turns.

The woman with the red hair has also stopped and turned. She is grotesque, bloated with hunger, almost savage in her rags. She and my mother move towards each other. Cautiously, deliberately, they probe past the hunger, the swollen flesh, the infected skin, the rags. Slowly, they begin to pierce five years of encrusted history. And slowly, there is perception and recognition.

In this wilderness of occupied Poland, in this vast emptiness where no one can be trusted, my mother has suddenly, bizarrely, met one of my father's teachers. A family friend. Another Jew.

They do not cry, but weep as they chronicle the dead and count the living. Then they rush to me. To the woman I am a familiar sight. She calculates that I will not live out the week, but comments only on my striking resemblance to my father. She says she has contacts. She leaves. One night a package of food is delivered anonymously. We eat. We begin to bridge the gap towards life. We survive.

2. Chicago, 1964: I am walking home alone at midnight.

I am walking home alone at midnight. I am a student of literature, and each night I stay in the library until it closes. Yet each night, as I return I still feel unprepared for the next day. The nature of literary movements eludes me. I only understand individual writers. I have trouble remembering genre definitions, historical dates and names, cannot grasp their meaning, significance. A whole world of abstractions and theories remains beyond my reach, on the other side of a wall I cannot climb over.

So each night, I walk home clutching my books as if I were a small school child. The city is alien. Since coming to America, this is my first time away from a Jewish neighborhood, Jewish friends, and I feel isolated, baffled at how to make a place for myself in this larger, gentile world which I have entered.

I am walking home alone at midnight. The university seems an island ungrounded. Most of its surrounding streets have been emptied. On some, all evidence of previous life removed except for occasional fringes of rubble that reveal vague outlines that hint at things that were. On others, old buildings still stand, though these are hollow like caves, once of use and then abandoned. Everything is poised. Everything is waiting for the emptiness to close in on itself, for the emptiness to be filled up, for the emptiness to be swallowed and forgotten.

Walking home, I am only dimly aware of the meaning of this strange void through which I pass. I am even less aware of the dangers for someone like me, a woman walking home alone at midnight. I am totally preoccupied with another time, another place. Night after night, protected by the darkness, I think only of Elza who is dead. I am trying to place a fact about her, a fact which stubbornly resists classification: nothing that happened to her afterwards mattered. All the agonized effort. All that caring. *None of that mattered!*

At the end of the war, friends come to claim her. With the cold, calculated cunning of an adult, the eight year old vehemently denies who she is. No she is not who they think. Not a Jew. They have made a mistake. Mixed her up with another Elza. This one belongs here, with her mother.

She is simply being scrupulous in following her parents' instructions. "Do not ever admit to anyone who you are. It is our secret. Eventually we will come for you. Remember! *Never admit who you are!* Promise!"

Four years later, the war is over. Her parents are dead. She is still bound by her promise. This woman is her mother. Her parents' friends know better. The woman has been kind, has saved her. But she is a Pole and Elza is a Jew. Finally, the bribe is big enough and the child released. Elza becomes an orphan.

And afterwards? She is adopted and finally seems to have everything. Two parents. Two handsome brothers. A house. Her own room. She studies Latin and does translations. Is valedictorian of her class. Goes away to college. Has boyfriends, affairs. Comes to New York. Works. Begins graduate school. Explicates Dylan Thomas, T.S. Eliot. Marries.

But none of it matters. She cannot keep up. The signs are clear. She is a poor housekeeper. Insists they eat off paper plates. She buys enough clothes to fill all her closets. But nothing soothes her. Finally she signs her own papers. Is released within a few months. I finish college and leave for Europe. Three weeks later, she checks into a hotel and takes an overdose. She is twenty-five years old.

Fearing I too might be in danger, my mother instructs Polish Jews resettled in Paris and Tel Aviv: "Don't tell her!" And to me she writes: "Elza is in the hospital again. There is no hope." I am suspicious, refer to her whenever I can. I am alert. Sense a discomfort, an edge I cannot define. I think I know, but I never dare ask. I come home. Seven months after her death, I finally know.

A story she once told me remains alive. During the war, the Polish woman sends her to buy a notebook for school. She is given the wrong change and points it out. The shopkeeper eyes her sharply: "Very accurate. Just like a Jew. Perhaps you are a little Jewess?" And Elza feels afraid and wonders if this woman sees the truth in her blue eyes.

Another memory. Elza is reading accounts of the war. She cannot help herself she tells me. An anecdote explains something to her. A woman in a camp requests a bandage for a wound. And the guard, so startled by her simplicity and directness, makes sure she gets one. That woman, Elza tells me, refused to stop acting like a human being. Jews, she concludes, made a terrible mistake.

I am walking home alone at midnight. I am raw with the pain of her death. I wonder. Is it inevitable? Everything that happened to us afterwards, to all of us, does none of it matter? Does it not matter what we do and where we live? Are there moments in history which cannot be escaped or transcended, but which act like time warps permanently trapping all those who are touched by them? And that which should have happened in 1944 in Poland and didn't, must it happen now? In 1964? In Chicago? Or can history be tricked and cheated?

These questions haunt me. Yet I persist with a will I myself do not understand. I continue reading, studying, making friends. And as the rawness of Elza's death eases and becomes familiar, as time becomes distance, I find myself more and more grounded in my present life, in my passion for words and literature. I begin to perceive the world around me. I develop perspective.

I see the rubble of this unbombed landscape, see that the city, like the rest of this alien country, is not simply a geographic place, but a time zone, an era in which I, by my very presence in it, am rooted. No one simply passes through. History keeps unfolding and demanding a response. A life obliterated around me of those I barely noticed. A life unmarked, unrecorded. A silent mass migration. Relocation. Common rubble in the streets.

I see now the present dangers, the dangers of the void, of the American hollowness in which I walk calmly day and night as I continue my life. I begin to see the incessant grinding down of lines for stamps, for jobs, for a bed to sleep in, of a death stretched imperceptibly over a lifetime. I begin to understand the ingenuity of it. The invisibility. The Holocaust without smoke.

Everything is poised. Everything is waiting for the emptiness to be filled up, for the filling-up that can never replace, that can only take over. Like time itself. Or history.

3. Brooklyn, 1971: I am almost equidistant from two continents.

I am almost equidistant from two continents. I look back towards one, then forward towards the other. The moment is approaching when I will be equidistant from both and will have to choose. Maintaining equidistance is not a choice.

By one of those minor and peculiar coincidences that permanently shape and give texture to our lives, I am born on my father's twenty-eighth birthday. Two years later, exactly three days after his thirtieth and my second birthday, he is dead in the brush factory district of the Warsaw Ghetto. His corpse is buried in a courtyard and eventually the spot blends with the rest of the rubble. The Uprising, my birth, his death—all merge and become interchangeable. That is the heritage of one continent.

In one of the classes that I teach, all the students are Black and Puerto Rican. I am the only white. Initially, the students are nervous, wondering if I will be a hard taskmaster. I am nervous too, though I do not yet have a name for it. After a few months together, we grow accustomed to each other. I am trying to understand my role here. That is the heritage of the other continent.

And now, approaching my own thirtieth birthday, approaching the moment when I will be equidistant from the two land masses, I feel some kind of cellular breakdown in my body, a sudden surging inside me, as if flesh and muscle and bone were losing definition. Everything in me yearns to become transparent, to be everywhere, to become like the water between two vast land masses that will never touch. I desire to become salt water, to establish the connection.

I am almost equidistant from two continents.

April 17, 1955. I have been asked to light one of the six candles. I stand on the stage in the large, darkened auditorium, wait to be called, wait to accept the flame, to pass it on like a memory. I am numb with terror at the spectacle around me. I fear these people with blue numbers on their arms, people who are disfigured and scarred, who have missing limbs and uneasy walks, people whose histories repel me. Here in this auditorium, they abandon all inhibitions, they transform themselves into pure sound, the sound of irretrievable loss, of wild pain and sorrow. Then they become all flesh, wringing their hands and covering their swollen eyes and flushed faces. They call out to me and I feel myself dissolving.

When it is time for me to come forward, to light the candle for those children who were burned, who were shot, who were stomped to death, I move without feeling. And as I near the candelabra, I hear them call out the common Yiddish names: *Surele. Moyshele. Channele. Rivkele. Yankele. Shayndele. Rayzl. Benyomin. Chavele. Miriam. Chaim.* The names brush against my face, invade my ears, my mouth. I breathe them into my lungs, into my bones. And as the list continues, guided by their sounds, I cross the stage and light the sixth and final candle. It is my fourteenth birthday.

I am almost equidistant from two continents.

March, 1971. There are twenty-eight people in the class. Eighteen women, ten men. Some married. Some single. Alone. With children. With parents and grandparents. Nieces. Nephews. They are here because they have not met the minimum standards of this college. This class is their special chance to catch up. Subject and verb agreement. Sentence fragments. Pronoun reference. Vocabulary building. Paragraph organization. Topic sentence. Reading comprehension. Study skills. Discipline. All this to catch up, or as one student said to me, his eyes earnest: "I want to write so that when I go for a job they won't think I'm lazy."

I am required to take attendance. I check through the names, call them out each morning: *James. Reggie. Marie. Simone. Joy. Christine. Alvarez. Ashcroft. Basile. Colon. Corbett. White. Raphael. Dennis. Juan. Carissa. Lamont. Andrea.* Fragments of their lives fall before me. The chaos and disorganization. A mother needing help in filling out forms in English. A sick child. Hospital regulations. A brother looking for a job. Another brother in trouble. Welfare red tape. Unemployment payment restrictions. Waiting lists. Eviction. SRO. The daily grind interrupting their catching-up, and the increasing sense that with each day missed, they fall further behind.

I am almost equidistant from two continents. I look back towards one, then forward towards the other. There is a need in me to become transparent like water, to become the salt water which is their only connection.

March, 1971. Marie wants to study medicine. She concedes it's a long haul, but, as she says, "It's only time. What difference does it make?" Slightly older than the others, she lives alone with her daughter. To some of the women's horror, she refuses to have a telephone, does not like to be intruded upon. When necessary, she can always be reached through a neighbor. She rarely misses class, on a few occasions brings her daughter with her who sits serenly drawing pictures. Facing Marie, I sometimes do not know who I am and wonder how she perceives me. She seems oblivious to my discomfort. She is only focused on the class, always reworking her assignments, reading everything twice, asking endless questions to make sure she really understands. One day, at the end of the hour, when we are alone, she asks: "What are you?" I am caught off guard, know the meaning of the question, but feel the resistance in me. I break it down and answer quietly: "A Jew." She nods and in that moment two vast land masses touch.

Each continent has its legacy. The day I reach my thirtieth birthday, the age of my father's death, I am equidistant from both. And as the moment passes, everything in me becomes defined again. I am once again muscle, flesh, bone. America is not my chosen home, not even the place of my birth. Just a spot where it seemed safe to go to escape certain dangers. But safety, I discover, is only temporary. No place guarantees it to anyone forever. I have stayed because there is no other place to go. In my muscles, my flesh, my bone, I balance the heritages, the histories of two continents.

4. Cherry Plain, 1981: I have become a keeper of accounts.

There are moments when I suddenly become breathless, as if I had just tricked someone, but was afraid the ruse would be exposed and I'd be hunted again. At those moments, the myths that propel our history, that turn fiction into fact, emerge in full force in me, as I stare into the eyes of strangers or someone suddenly grown alien. And when I see their eyes become pinpoints of judgments, become cold and indifferent, or simply distanced with curiosity, at those moments I hear again the words of the Polish woman:

Very accurate. Just like a Jew. You are perhaps a little Jewess?

At moments such as these I teeter, shed the present, and like rage, like pride, like acceptance, like the refusal to deny, I call upon the ancient myths again and say:

Yes. It's true. All true. I am scrupulously accurate. I keep track of all distinctions. Between past and present. Pain and pleasure. Living and surviving. Resistance and capitulation. Will and circumstances. Between life and death. Yes. I am scrupulously accurate. I have become a keeper of accounts.

Like the patriarchs, the shabby scholars who only lived for what was written and studied it all their lives

Like the inhuman usurers and dusty pawnbrokers who were quaran-
tined within precisely prescribed limits of every European town and
who were accurate as the magistrates that drew the boundaries of their
lives and declared them diseased

Like those men of stone who insisted that the *goyim* fulfill the contracts
they had signed and who responded to the tearful pleas of illness,
weakness, sudden calamity and poverty, with the words: "What are
these to me? You have made me a keeper of accounts. Give me my
pound of flesh. It says on this piece of paper, you owe me a pound of
flesh!"

Like those old, heartless, dried up merchants whose entire lives were
spent in the grubby *shtetl* streets that are now but memory, whose only
body softness was in their fingertips worn smooth by silver coins,
whose vision that all that mattered was on pieces of paper was proven
absolutely accurate, when their zloty, francs, and marks could not buy
off the written words *Żyd, Juif, Jude*

Like these, my despised ancestors
I have become a keeper of accounts

And like all the matriarchs, the wives and daughters, the sisters and
aunts, the nieces, the keepers of button shops, milliners, seamstresses,
peddlers of foul fish, of matches, of rotten apples, laundresses, mid-
wives, floor washers and street cleaners, who rushed exhausted all week
so that *shabes* could be observed with fresh *khalah* on the table, who
argued in the common tongue

and begged for the daughter run off to the revolution
and the daughter run off with a *sheygets*
who refused to sit *shiva* and say *kadish* for a living child
who always begged for life
who understood the accounts but saw them differently
who knew the power of human laws, knew they always counted
no matter what the revolution or the party or the state
who knew the power of the words *Żyd, Juif, Jude*

who cried whole lifetimes for their runaway children
for the husbands immobilized by the written word
for the brother grown callous from usury

for the uncle grown indifferent from crime, from bargaining,
from chiseling, from jewing them down

Like these, my despised ancestors
I have become a keeper of accounts

I do not shun this legacy. I claim it as mine   whenever I see the
photographs of nameless people. Standing staring off the edge of the
picture. People dressed in coats lined with fur. Or ragged at elbows and
collar. Hats cocked on one side glancing anxiously toward the lens. A
peasant cap centered and ordinary. Hair styled in the latest fashion. Or
standing ashamed a coarse wig awkwardly fitted. The shabby clothes.
Buttons missing. The elegant stance. Diamond rings. Gold teeth. The
hair being shaved. The face of humiliation. The hand holding the
child's hand. A tree. A track. A vague building in a photograph. A
facility. And then the fields of hair   the endless fields of hair   the
earth growing fertile with their bodies with   their souls

Old   rarely seen types.   Gone   they say   forever.   And yet I know
they can be revived again   that I can trigger them again.   That they
awaken in me   for I have felt it happen in the sight of strangers   or
someone suddenly grown alien.   Whenever I have seen the judgment
the coldness   and indifference   the distanced curiosity.   At those
moments I teeter   shed my present self   and all time merges   and
like rage   like pride   like acceptance   like the refusal to deny   I an-
swer

Yes. It is true. I am a keeper of accounts.

Bashert

Repression in Eastern and Central Europe

(1945 - 1991)

After World War II, a series of pacts divided the European continent into conflicting zones. The Russians had little difficulty installing client governments in Romania, Hungary, Bulgaria, Poland, and the Russian-occupied zone in eastern Germany. Yugoslavia had been liberated by Communist partisans (who were able to achieve a certain autonomy from Moscow), and Czechoslovakia came under Communist control after the coup d'état in 1948.

The installation of Stalinist regimes in what came to be known as the Eastern Bloc established a certain kind of state apparatus in Eastern Europe by 1949. A strong Party, rigid censorship, and a powerful secret police ensured that populations were kept under control. Strict limitations on travel made emigration virtually impossible.

With the ascendance of Nikita Khrushchev in the Soviet Union in 1956, there seemed to be an opportunity for reformists, but in Hungary (as in East Berlin three years earlier) the Soviets demonstrated no tolerance of external opposition. Soviet response was similar in 1968, when troops from other Warsaw Pact countries invaded Czechoslovakia to crush the liberal reforms of Alexander Dubcek during the "Prague Spring."

In the face of pervasive Party control of art, writers had limited options if they wanted to publish in their own countries. They could conform to the tenets of "socialist realism" and write works accessible to "the workers" (who were used as an excuse for such censorship); they could incur the wrath of the state by publishing their works abroad; or they could publish in *samizdat,* that is, in underground form. Manuscripts were often memorized, hand-typed, and secretly circulated. Works circulated in *samizdat* were presented abroad, infuriating the authorities and subjecting the authors to retaliation.

The first signs of weakness in the Eastern Bloc came with the rise of the independent Polish labor union Solidarity in 1980 and 1981. Although Poland subsequently came under martial law and the union was suppressed, the Poles had shown that change was possible. This became even more clear when Mikhail Gorbachev came to power in the Soviet Union in 1985: his attempt to save the Soviet economy through openness (*glasnost*) and reconstruction (*perestroika*), together with his recognition of the need for massive political reform, created opportunities for the revolutions in Eastern Europe that began in 1989; within two years, the countries of the Warsaw Pact achieved independence. It is not without significance that Vaclav Havel, the first president of the new government in Czechoslovakia, is a writer who was once imprisoned for dissent.

TUDOR ARGHEZI (1880–1967)

Arghezi, born to a peasant family in Bucharest, ran away from home as a teenager, held a number of jobs, put himself through school, and published his first book of poetry by the time he was sixteen. He spent four years as a monk, then left the monastery and worked as an editor and later became an itinerant laborer in Europe. A pacifist when World War I began, Arghezi argued against Romania's alliance with Britain and France and was jailed for treason after the Armistice. He was a committed anti-Fascist during the 1930s and was imprisoned in the concentration camp at Tirgu-Jiu in 1943. A prolific writer, he was Romania's most famous poet at the time of his death.

≈ Testament

I'll bequeath no goods to you when I am dead.
Only a name upon a book instead.
In the rebel evening which comes through
From my forefathers to you,
Past precipices and deep ravines,
Up which my folk have clambered on hands and knees,
And which await your climbing while you're young,
This book of mine, my son, will be a rung.

Enshrine it at the head of your bed,
It spells out the oldest charter have had,
From serfs in sheepskin coats burned only
By bones which flowed down years and into me.

So that for the first time we might exchange
The hoe for pen, the furrow for inkstand,
Our old folk laboring among the oxen
Stored much sweat over countless eons.
Out of their tongue with which they called their herds

I've woven into verse my fitting words,
And cradles for the masters yet to be.
I kneaded them for a thousand weeks,
I turned them into dreams and icons.
From tatters I've made buds and shining crowns.
Distilling honey from pent-up poison,
I stroke to keep in full its potency.
I've taken insult and spun it fine, with care
Sometimes to charm, sometimes to curse or swear.
From the hearth, ash of people dead and gone
I have shaped into a God of stone,
A lofty bourn with two worlds at its rim,
Keeping high watch on your duty to him.

All our bitter grief and mute pain
I heaped upon one single violin,
Which the master heard, and to every note
He thrashed and kicked like a new-stuck goat.
Out of slime, festering pustules, and mildew
I have brought forth beauties, values that are new.
The whip, so long endured, returns as words,
And slowly punishing, it thus redeems
The living spawn of everyone's misdeeds.
It sets the hidden forest bough aright
As it reaches out into the light,
Bearing on its end, like a clump of warts,
The fruits of grief from past eternities.

Recycling idly in her cozy nook,
The princess suffers in my book.
Words of fire and words forged by the mind
Are married in my book, and intertwined,
Like red-hot iron embraced by tongs.
What the serf has written, the master ponders,
Though unaware that buried deep within
Simmers the stored-up wrath of my ancient kin.

TR. ANDREI BANTAS AND THOMAS AMHERST PERRY

≈ **Psalm**

I ponder you in clamor and in silence
Tracking you through the course of time, like game,
To see: are you my much sought-after falcon?
Should I kill you? Or kneel down and pray.

For faith's sake or the sake of denial,
Stubborn I search for you, and uselessly.
Of all my dreams you are the loveliest
And I daren't shake the sky to let you fall.

As if reflected in the flow of water
Sometimes you seem to be and sometimes not;
I've glimpsed you in the stars, among the fish
Like the wild bull when he is taking water.

And now, us two alone, in your great story
I stay to match myself again with you,
Without my wanting to emerge the victor.
I want to touch you and to shout: 'He is!'

TR. ANDREI BANTAS AND THOMAS AMHERST PERRY

ALEKSANDER WAT (1900–1967)

Born Aleksander Chwat to a family of Polish Jews, Wat studied philosophy at the University of Warsaw and published his first book of poems in 1919. An enthusiast of the Russian revolution and a committed leftist, Wat was arrested and jailed by the Polish government for editing a Communist magazine. In 1939, he fled Warsaw into the Soviet Zone. He was arrested by the Russians the following year and sent to a number of prisons in Poland and the Soviet Union, including the dreaded Lubyanka in Moscow. After his release in 1941, he was reunited with his family, only to be arrested again for refusing to give up his Polish citizenship. He returned to Poland in 1946 but was silenced by the Communist government in 1949 until the post-Stalinist thaw allowed him to publish a book of poems in 1957. He lived in France, Italy, and the United States until his suicide in 1967.

≈ Before Breughel the Elder

Work is a blessing,
I tell you that, I—professional sluggard!
Who slobbered in so many prisons! Fourteen!
And in so many hospitals! Ten! And innumerable inns!
Work is a blessing.
How else could we deal with the lava of fratricidal love towards fellow
    men?
With those storms of extermination of all by all?
With brutality, bottomless and measureless?
With the black and white era which does not want to end
endlessly repeating itself *da capo* like a record
forgotten on a turntable
spinning by itself?
Or perhaps someone invisible watches over the phonograph? Horror!
How, if not for work, could we live in the paradise of social hygienists
who never soak their hands in blood without aseptic gloves?
Horror!
How else could we cope with death?
That Siamese sister of life
who grows together with it—in us, and is extinguished with it
and surely for that reason is ineffective.
And so we have to live without end,
without end. Horror!
How, if not for work, could we cope with ineffective death
(Do not scoff!)
which is like a sea,
where everyone is an Icarus, one of nearly three billion,
and, besides, so much happens all around us
and everything is equally unimportant, precisely, unimportant
although so difficult, so inhumanly difficult, so painful!
How then could we cope with all that?
Work is our rescue.
I tell you that—I, Breughel, the Elder (and I, for one,
your modest servant, Wat, Aleksander)—work is our rescue.

Saint-Mandé, July 1956

TR. CZESLAW MILOSZ AND LEONARD NATHAN

≈ To Be a Mouse

To be a mouse. Preferably a field mouse. Or a garden mouse—
but not the kind that live in houses.
Man exhales an abominable smell!
We all know it—birds, crabs, rats.
He provokes disgust and fear.
    Trembling.

To feed on wisteria flowers, on the bark of palm trees,
to dig up roots in cold, humid soil
and to dance after a fresh night. To look at the full moon,
to reflect in one's eyes the sleek light of lunar
    Agony.

To burrow in a mouse hole for the time when wicked Boreas
will search for me with his cold, bony fingers
in order to squeeze my little heart under the
               blade of his claw,
a cowardly mouse heart—
    A palpitating crystal.

Menton–Garavan, April 1956

TR. CZESLAW MILOSZ AND LEONARD NATHAN

≈ From Persian Parables

By a great, swift water
on a stony bank
a human skull was lying
and shouting: Allah la ilah.

And in that cry such horror
and such supplication
so great was its despair
that I asked the helmsman:

For what can it still cry out? Of what is it still afraid?
What divine judgment could strike it yet again?

Suddenly there came a wave
took hold of the skull
and tossing it about
smashed it against the bank.

Nothing is ultimate
—the helmsman's voice was hollow—
and there is no bottom to evil.

TR. CZESLAW MILOSZ AND LEONARD NATHAN

≈ Imagerie d'Epinal

On the death of Reik, Slansky and thousands of others.

The executioner yawned. From his axe the blood was still dripping.
"Don't cry, here's a lollipop, don't, my child."

He took her in his arms. Caressed her. And she looked at the head.
At the sightless eyes. At the dumb lips.

It was the head of her father. Later on, embalmed,
washed, it was put on a pole and nicely painted.

With that pole she marched in a parade on a sunny, populous road,
under her school placard:
                    "Happiness to all—death to enemies . . ."

1949

TR. CZESLAW MILOSZ AND LEONARD NATHAN

VÍTĚZSLAV NEZVAL (1900–1958)

Nezval began writing poetry in 1916 and moved from Moravia to
Prague four years later. A passionate polemicist for the Czech avant-
garde, Nezval called for a radical social transformation through aes-
thetic revolution. He joined the Communist Party in 1924 and founded

the Czech branch of the surrealist movement in the early 1930s. While
he defended surrealism at the International Writers' Congress in Mos-
cow in 1934, he disbanded the Czech surrealists in 1938 after the Nazi
invasion, in solidarity with his fellow Communists. His poetry was
banned by the Germans during the war. He remained a leading Czech
poet until his death.

≈ Walker in Prague

To climb and descend steps
Which lead nowhere
How often this nameless vertigo is conjured up

One day in April 1920 I arrived in Prague for the first time
At the station as sad as ashes huddled a dejected crowd
They were emigrants
And there I first saw the world I shall never understand
Midday was noisy but this was twilight and the station stretched far
    into the suburbs

You don't understand why they've shut you up in the morgue
Where you can smell boiled cabbage and the stench of the railway
The smell of my suitcase is making me cry
I shake like a pianola at the high notes
The yard hangs like an evil cloud outside the window from which I
    never lean
And everywhere I feel a stranger

Like a practical joke the Castle suddenly stands before me
I shut my eyes it was a mirage
A fragment of memory the tears are welling we are in Prague
I try in vain to sleep in the room where a man once shot himself

Thus I walked for days and nights on end
Unspeakably dejected
Everything was strange I did not dare to remember
Until one day
I met a memory
It was a friend
He took me along under his umbrella

We sat in a room the piano was playing at last I shall be able to love
    you Prague

Sitting on the embankment
It's past midnight we've come from a terrible cell
It was beautiful with a naked woman on a leather sofa
Under the water are strung garlands of lights
As if someone had folded an umbrella
Leaning over the Bridge of the Legions I shall watch this fiesta of
    parasols every day

It was difficult like the love a woman from whom you are fleeing
The countless lodgings you changed in the course of your flight
Before you allowed green eyes to trap you
Now in her footsteps the embankment changes into a terrace with
    Chinese lanterns
With the May-flies dying in the café windows
How often did you change your lodgings
Before you were bewitched by the ice-cream vendor in St Salvator
    Street

Thus I learned to love Prague
Thus I first heard the bird singing under an art-nouveau cornice of a
    shabby square
Thus the pain of your inconsolable sadness faded away
Thus in the sickly suburbs I found my Cinderella
Thus I became a walker in Prague
Thus I learned to have dates in your streets with adventure and love
Prague of my dreams

It is evening work has stopped the city is dancing
For your delight a thousand fans have opened
Your black coach is driving out from white houses
You'll be spinning round like a brilliant roundabout
The magnolia blossoms are bursting now they are dresses
They are dresses they are bonnets
They are your eyes they are your lips

Even on a rainy day she is radiant
She drops her roses I pick them up

She drops her roses everywhere even among the hideous laundry
    basements
My longing leads me about the city which seems to me as miraculous
    as a fountain playing over a cemetery
As a dragonfly over a sleeping woman as eyes in a lake
As a fire in a goldsmith's shop as a peacock on a belvedere
As a rainbow over a window where someone is playing the piano
As a comb from which sparks crackle on a bunch of carnations
As an umbrella with a hole burnt through by a meteor
As the fountain jet which you wave at me whenever I am sad
As Captain Corcoran's ship which has struck the Magnetic Mountain

TR. EWALD OSERS

≈ The Lilac by the Museum on St. Wenceslas Square

I don't love flowers
I love women
Yet I slept beneath the lilac
From afar came the breath of a cellar
Stuffy as main street apartments in the artificial night
Of your artificial eyes
Of your artificial lips
Of your artificial breasts and hair styles
I love you bunch of lilac
On the promenade where the gardens step out in the evening
With roses untold
Her breasts covered in rose petals
Prague breathes through open windows
Cool twilight
And while I was asleep
The lilac burst into flower on St. Wenceslas Square

TR. EWALD OSERS

≈ Prague in the Midday Sun

I have not woken from a dream nor arrived by express train
I am spared the bother of seeing the sights like a tourist
For years I have not opened a book of fairy-tales

I don't expect love to reveal the universe or even this world
I don't want to sing with the birds nor rave about undersea landscapes
I've no illusions about nations which rule the world or about foreign
  settlements
I don't regard the people whose language I speak as either better or
  worse than those of other countries
I'm linked with the fate of the world's disasters and only have a little
  freedom to live or die

It is late in the morning
I am sitting under a coloured parasol—Prague lies down there
After long rains an amethyst vapour is rising
I see her through the filigree of trees as a maniac sees his phantasm
I see her as a great ship whose mast is the Castle
Like the enchanted cities of my visions
Like the great ship of the Golden Corsair
Like the dream of delirious architects
Like the throned residence of Magic
Like Saturn's palace with its gates flung open to the sun
Like a volcano fortress hewn by a raving madman
Like a guide to solitary inspiration
Like an awakened volcano
Like a bracelet dangling before mirrors

It is noon
Prague is sleeping and yet awake like a fantastic dragon
A sacred rhinoceros whose cage is the sky
A stalacrite organ playing softly
A symbol of resurrection and of treasures of dried-up lakes
An army in panoply saluting the emperor
An army in panoply saluting the sun
An army in panoply turned into jasper

Magic city I have been gazing too long at you with blind eyes
Looking for you in the distance oh today I know it
You are obscure as the fires deep in the rocks as my fantasy
Your beauty has sprung from caverns and subterranean agates
You are old as the prairies over which song spreads its wings
When your tower clocks strike you are opaque as an island night
Exalted as the tombs as the crowns of Ethiopian kings
As if from a different world a mirror of my imagery

Beautiful as the mystery of love and improbable clouds
Beautiful as the mystery of speech and primordial memory
Beautiful as an erratic block marked by the rains
Beautiful as the mystery of sleep of stars and of phosphorescence
Beautiful as the mystery of thunder of the magic lamp and of poetry

TR. EWALD OSERS

≈ Moon over Prague

The decorator is mixing his plaster
He's lit an oil lamp on top of the stepladder
It is the moon
It moves like an acrobat
Wherever it appears it causes panic
It turns black coffee into white
It offers paste jewelry to women's eyes
It changes bedrooms into death chambers
It settles on the piano
It floodlights the Castle theatrically
Today Prague remembers its history
It's the river féte look at that bobbing Chinese lantern
The bells are as brittle as plates
There'll be a grand tourney
White carpets are laid throughout the city
Buildings have their roles in the great tragedy and all belongs to the
     underworld
The moon enters the tiny garrets
It gleams on the table it is an inkwell
A thousand letters will be written with its ink
And a single poem

TR. EWALD OSERS

JAROSLAV SEIFERT (1901–1986)

Born in a suburb of Prague, Seifert achieved fame with his first book, published when he was barely twenty. A political progressive, he found his allegiance to the Communist Party strained after 1925, and he was expelled from the Party in 1929. In the next decade he produced four books of poetry, then his work was banned by the Nazis. After the war, he worked as editor of a trade union journal, but was attacked for his "subjectivism" and his work was banned until 1954. After criticizing Party dogmatism during a Writers' Union Congress in 1956, he was once again forced to give up publishing poetry until the 1960s. During the Prague Spring of 1968, Seifert was president of the Union when it was disbanded under Soviet pressure, and in the years after the Soviet invasion his work was available only in underground editions. A signatory of Charter 77, which protested human rights abuses, Seifert was awarded the Nobel Prize for Literature in 1984.

≈ The Candlestick

God knows what happened to the candlestick
my mother brought with her from Kralupy.
It was made from an artillery shell-case
of the First World War
and for many years it stood on top of our cupboard.

Whenever we ran out of paraffin at home
we put a candle in the candlestick:
it burnt with a sooty flame.

By its poor light
I wrote my first verses.
And when my folk went to bed
I read, while it was burning,
novels about love.

Its trembling flame
became my inescapable will-o'-the-wisp

which lured me from my lessons,
at least in my dreams,
into Prague's mildewy little streets,
where love was quick and short.

But I was afraid.
        They were more mysterious
than the treacherous swamps of the Jizera
near its headwaters,
where even a bold horseman drowned
with his horse.

Whenever my mother buffed up the candlestick
with a velvet pad
she seemed to me to draw a deep sigh.
I did not ask her why.
Later I guessed the reason.
Let there be no more war.

But it came!

TR. EWALD OSERS

≈ Never Again

A hundred houses were in ruins,
nearly a thousand had been damaged
by aerial bombs.
No, I didn't count them myself.
I worked my way through the rubble
and circumnavigated the craters.
They were frightening
like gaping gates to fiery hell.

Speedily they cleared away the debris
but it was three days before
they broke into the little house
in Sverma Street,
the house of Mr Hrncír.
The whole family was dead.

Only the rooster, that fighting cock
whom the Apostle Peter did not
greatly love,
alone had saved himself.
Over the bodies of the dead he'd climbed
onto a pile of rubble.

He looked about the scene of the disaster
and spread his wings
to shake the heavy dust
from his golden feathers.

And I repeated softly to myself
what I had found written
in letters of grief and in letters of pain
upon the faces of the Kralupy people.

And into that silence of death
I screamed in a loud voice,
so loud the war should hear it:
Never again, war!

The rooster looked at me
with its black beady eye
and burst into horrible laughter.
He laughed at me
and at my pointless screaming.
Besides, he was a bird
and sided with the planes.
The bastard!

TR. EWALD OSERS

VLADIMIR HOLAN (1905–1980)

A native of Prague, Holan published his first book of poetry when he
was twenty-one. He worked in the government pension office from
1927 to 1933, then became editor of two arts journals. Surviving the

war on a small pension, he saluted the liberation with works in honor of the USSR. Nevertheless, he was attacked for "decadent formalism" by Communist Party dogmatists after 1948, and his work went unpublished for another fifteen years. He was rehabilitated in 1963 and honored by the state in 1964 and 1968. He had published ten volumes of poetry at the time of his death.

≈ In the Yard of the Policlinic

This morning I heard persistent and angry blows on a carpet
beaten in the yard of the policlinic—
and I had to think of all the hearts
persistently and angrily beating
shabby curtains of hope, hope for a kinder future
that wouldn't lie even if it were true.
And I had to think of all those people, people lost and begging,
and of those who can't beg, tired as a hand after the war,
I had to think of creatures stuck in the doors of those
who talk while eating and to whom they offered statuettes of
        gargoyles,
threads from virgins' blouses, or ice cream made of April snow,
I had to think of those who commune with the fickle grave only in the
        language of whores,
I had to think of all those constantly longing and constantly
        disappointed,
so they know only the anger of desire
and slippery mushrooms instead of May butter,
I had to think of all those *eternally* cheated, so they become spiritual,
so spiritual that they are in every body in coughing basement
        apartments
and in every body that hasn't eaten for a long time
and warms its raw hands
at the kitchen fire of imagination with its dipping flames,
I had to think of those desperate men who stumble
in the borrowed shoes of alcohol,
of all those who are so commonplace that they're invisible
in their humiliation, drowned by the goldsmith's selfish anvil,
I had to think of all those God could hear about

if children sent him a telegram, if children got hold of a radio,
if children weren't as merciless as adults—
I had to think of all those said to be riddles,
who are simply souls nobody feels any mercy for,
I had to think of pale girls in shops in empty passageways,
with lamps lit all day and no customers,
girls who are startled when someone enters to buy a roll,
I had to think of girls who try to hide their pregnancy
and yet produce illegitimate children out of nothingness,
the nothingness of nettles and graveyard plums,
while fate feels like wine
going up into your nose when you laugh,
I had to think of newsboys running beside streetcars
with the wretched servility of tubercular patients and with earwigs of
          cries,
of female singers who lost their voices
and lower their necklines to louden their breasts,
of women servants who, when tidying up the houses of the rich,
are only allowed to walk barefoot, on rags thrown on the floor,
so they won't dirty the parquet,
I had to think of all those with rings in their noses,
of all those dragged to places where they're needed like salt:
to salt mines, sewers, the sweatshops of Petrak Square,
yes, I had to think of all those, inside whom I am and always will be,
as long as there are old forgotten women who must beg pitifully
leaning against the railway station wall,
oh yes, there, where people are in such a hurry—
and as long as there are old men, who, though they're just the skin
          and bones of a tombstone epitaph,
have to live and are quickly shut up by dead men's mouths,
oh yes, there, where lazy pedestrians forgot to bring their
          compassion—
and as long as there is poverty and misery,
both apparently disappointed because they're misunderstood,
and misunderstood because they're unliberated—
and as long as there are poor people who out of pride save up
for a coffin and funeral music—
and as long as there are the wretched ones who are down and out,
whose fate boozed up the cashbox at St. Elegy's Church,
and who don't know when they were born or why they were named,

and who as adults in "times of peace" are buried in sugar crates,
and as children are buried in soapboxes.

TR. C.G. HANZLICEK AND DANA HABOVA

≈ Children at Christmas in 1945

I saw children at Christmas in 1945.
They stood in front of the only stall in Charles Square
and they stood in line. They were pale,
they borrowed shoes from each other and breathed
on the tips of fingers without nails,
but they stood there patiently, humbly, grateful in advance,
awaiting their turn to buy
cotton candy, that sweet air,
because there was nothing else for sale . . .
And I saw a hungry boy running with a briefcase
to get communion wafers at the baker's, looking forward
to eating all the broken pieces at the vicarage.
And I saw a mother who in the morning stuck
tenpenny nails into a sour crab apple
and in the evening gave the apple to her kids,
convinced they would at least get a little iron in their blood . . .

World, world, you bastard, what should I do with you?
What should I do with you, if I hear your blackmailing talk about
how to safeguard peace so military intervention won't become necessary!

TR. C.G. HANZLICEK AND DANA HABOVA

≈ To the Enemies

I've had enough of your baseness, and I haven't killed myself
only because I didn't give myself life
and I still love somebody because I love myself.
You may laugh, but only an eagle can attack an eagle
and only Achilles can pity the wounded Hector.
To be is not easy . . . To be a poet and a man
means to be a forest without trees
and to see . . . A scientist observes.

Science can only forage for truth:
forage yes, take wing no! Why?
It's so simple, and I've said it before:
Science is in probability, poetry in parables,
the large cerebral hemisphere
refuses the most exquisite poem by clamoring for sugar . . .
A rooster finds rain repulsive, but that's another story,
it is night, you might say: sexually mature,
and the young lady's breasts are so firm
you could easily break
two glasses of schnapps on them, but that's another story.
And imagine a ship's beacon,
a sailing beacon: but that's an entirely different story.
And your whole development from the stele for man
to the stele of a lichen: but that's an entirely different story!
A cloud is going to vomit, but there's not even a gas leak at your
    place,
you cannot be, you can't even be
strangled by snake scales,
what God conceived, he wants to be felt,
children and drunkards know this,
but they aren't brazen enough to ask
why a mirror fogs when a menstruating woman looks into it,
and poets, from love of life, do not ask
why wine moves in the barrels
when she passes by . . .

And I've had enough of your impudence
that permeates everything it wanted to contain
but couldn't embrace.
But a holocaust will come
that you couldn't have dreamed of
having no dreams,
what God conceived, he wants to be felt,
a holocaust will come, children and drunkards know it,
joy could come about only through love,
if love were not passion,
happiness could come about only through love,
if happiness were not passion,
children and drunkards know it . . .
In order to be, you would have to live,

but you won't because you don't live,
and you don't live because you don't love,
because you don't even love yourself, let alone your neighbor.
And I've had enough of your vulgarity,
and I haven't killed myself only because
I didn't give myself life
and I still love somebody because I love myself . . .
You may laugh, but only the female eagle can attack the male eagle
and only Briseis the wounded Achilles.
To be is not easy . . . Only shitting is easy . . .

TR. C.G. HANZLICEK AND DANA HABOVA

≈ Resurrection

After this life here, we're to be awakened one day
by the terrible screams of trumpets and bugles?
Forgive me, Lord, but I trust
that the beginning and the resurrection of us, the dead,
will be announced by the crowing of a rooster . . .

We'll lie on for a little longer . . .
The first one to rise
will be mother . . . We'll hear her
quietly making the fire,
quietly putting the kettle on,
and cozily taking the coffee grinder out of the cupboard.
We'll be at home again.

TR. C.G. HANZLICEK AND DANA HABOVA

PETER HUCHEL (1903–1981)

Huchel, a native of Brandenburg, withdrew his first book of poetry
from publication as a protest against the Nazi rise to power in 1933. He
was later conscripted into the German army in World War II and was a
prisoner of war in the Soviet Union. He edited East Germany's fore-

most literary magazine *Sinn und Form* from 1948 until he was dismissed in 1962 for refusing to adhere to the Party line. Driven into internal exile, he was permitted to emigrate to West Germany in 1971. He died in the West in 1981.

≈ Landscape Beyond Warsaw

March strikes the ice of the sky
With its sharp pick.
Light bursts through the cracks,
Surges low
Over the telegraph wires and empty roads.
White at noon, it nestles in the reeds,
A huge bird,
When it spreads its claws,
The webs shine in the thin mist.

Darkness comes fast.
Then the sky arches
Flatter than the roof of a dog's mouth.
A hill smokes
As though hunters
Were still sitting there by their damp fire.
Where have they gone?
The hare's tracks in the snow
Once told us where.

TR. DANIEL SIMKO

≈ Roads

Choked sunset
Of crashing time.
Roads. Roads.
Intersections of flight.
Cart-tracks across the fields
That saw the burned sky
Through the eyes
Of dead horses.

Nights with lungs full of smoke,
With the heavy breath of those fleeing,
When shots
Struck the twilight.
Out of a broken gate
Ash and wind came soundlessly,
A fire
Morosely chewed the darkness.

The dead
Thrown over the railroad tracks,
Their suffocated screams
Like a stone in the mouth.
A black
Humming cloth of flies
Closed their wounds.

TR. DANIEL SIMKO

≈ The Garden of Theophrastus

To my son

When the white flame of verses
Dances above the urns at noon,
Remember, my son. Remember those
Who once planted their conversations like trees.
The garden is dead, my breath is heavy,
Preserve the hours, here Theophrastus walked
Fertilizing the soil with oak-bark,
Binding the wounded bark to tree-trunks.
An olive tree splits the brittle ruins
Remaining a voice in the dusty heat.
Their orders were to cut it down and root it out.
Your light is fading, defenseless leaves.

TR. DANIEL SIMKO

≈ Psalm

That from the seed of men
No man,
And from the seed of the olive tree
No olive tree
Shall grow,
This must be measured
With the yardstick of death.

Those who live
Beneath the earth
In cement spheres,
Their strength like
A blade of grass
Lashed by snow.

The desert is history.
Termites write it
Into sand
With their pincers.

And no one will inquire
About a species
Eager
For self-destruction.

TR. DANIEL SIMKO

ATTILA JÓZSEF (1905–1937)

One of the greatest Hungarian poets, József was the son of a soap maker who abandoned his family when the boy was only three. József tried to commit suicide when he was nine years old. He lived in poverty with his mother until her death in 1919. When his first poems were published in 1922, he was tried for blasphemy. He became a member of the outlawed Hungarian Communist Party in 1930 but was forced out of the Party by Stalinists in 1931. He made a meager living as a writer

for years, and threw himself under a train in 1937. The poems here were
written toward the end of József's life.

≈ Attila József

I really love you,
believe me. It is something I inherited
from my mother.
She was a good woman. After all,
she was the one who brought me
into this world.

We may compare life
to a shoe, or a laundromat,
or whatever.
Nonetheless, we love it
for reasons of our own.

Saviours, there are
enough of them to save the world
three times a day and still nobody knows
how to light a match. I'll have to give up
on them.

It would be nice
to buy tickets for a trip to the
self. It must be somewhere inside us.

Every morning I wash
my thoughts
in cold water.
That way they come out fresh as a daisy.

Diamonds can sprout
good warm songs,
if you plant them under your heart.

Some people will stay
pedestrians no matter what they ride,
horse, car, or airplane.

Me, I just lie around
in the morning song of larks
and still make it over the abyss.

Let us carefully save our
true souls
like our best suit of clothes
to keep them spotless for the days of
celebration.

TR. JOHN BATKI

≈ To Sit, to Stand, to Kill, to Die

To shove this chair away from here,
to sit down in front of a train,
to climb a mountain with great care,
to shake my bag into the valley,
to feed a bee to my old spider,
to caress an old, old woman,
to sip a delicious bean soup,
to walk on tiptoes in the mud,
to place my hat on railroad tracks,
to stroll around the banks of a lake,
to sit all dressed up on the bottom,
to get a suntan while the waves ring,
to flower with the sunflowers,
or just to give off a deep sigh,
to scare away a single fly,
to wipe the dust from my old book,
to spit a gob into my mirror,
to make peace with my enemies,
to kill them all with a long knife,
to examine their blood gushing,
to watch a young girl as she walks,
to sit idle without stirring,
to set fire to Budapest,
to wait for birds to take my crumbs,
to hurl my stale bread to the ground,
to make my faithful woman cry,

to lift her little sister up high,
if the world wants explanations,
to run away and never be seen—
O you bind me and you free me,
you who write this poem in me,
you bring laughter, you bring weeping,
O my life, you make me choose.

TR. JOHN BATKI

≈ The Seventh

If you set out in this world,
better be born seven times.
Once, in a house on fire,
once, in a freezing flood,
once, in a wild madhouse,
once, in a field of ripe wheat,
once, in an empty cloister,
and once among pigs in a sty.
Six babes crying, not enough:
you yourself must be the seventh.

When you must fight to survive,
let your enemy see seven.
One, away from work on Sunday,
one, starting his work on Monday,
one, who teaches without payment,
one, who learned to swim by drowning,
one, who is the seed of a forest,
and one, whom wild forefathers protect,
but all their tricks are not enough:
you yourself must be the seventh.

If you want to find a woman,
let seven men go for her.
One, who gives his heart for words,
one, who takes care of himself,
one, who claims to be a dreamer,
one, who through her skirt can feel her,

one, who knows the hooks and snaps,
one, who steps upon her scarf:
let them buzz like flies around her.
You yourself must be the seventh.

If you write and can afford it,
let seven men write your poem.
One, who builds a marble village,
one, who was born in his sleep,
one, who charts the sky and knows it,
one, whom words call by his name,
one, who perfected his soul,
one, who dissects living rats.
Two are brave and four are wise;
you yourself must be the seventh.

And if all went as was written,
you will die for seven men.
One, who is rocked and suckled,
one, who grabs a hard young breast,
one, who throws down empty dishes,
one, who helps the poor to win,
one, who works till he goes to pieces,
one, who just stares at the moon.
The world will be your tombstone:
you yourself must be the seventh.

TR. JOHN BATKI

≈ Freight Trains

Freight trains are pulling in.
A slow clanking
lightly handcuffs
the silent landscape.

Like an escaped prisoner
the moon flies free.

Broken stones rest
on their shadows,

sparkling
for themselves.
They are in place
as never before.

From what huge darkness
was this heavy
night chipped?
It falls on us
as a piece of iron falls
on a speck of dust.

Desire,
born of the sun,
when the bed is embraced
by shadow,
could you keep watch
through that whole night as well?

TR. JOHN BATKI

ONDRA LYSOHORSKY (1905–1989)

Lysohorsky studied at the German University in Prague and cus-
tomarily wrote in German, but difficulties arose when he decided to
write in his native Lachian, an idiom closer to Polish than to Czech. His
first book was a success in 1934. In 1938, he refused to cooperate with
the pro-German authorities and was fired from his position as a
teacher. In 1939, Lysohorsky emigrated to Poland, and at the outbreak
of World War II, he joined a Czechoslovak military unit which was
interned by the Soviet army advancing in to Poland. After nine months,
he was released and given a teaching post in Moscow and although his
poetry was popular in Russian translation, the poet offended Czech
Communists by writing in Lachian. After the war, he was unable to
publish in Czechoslovakia and was harassed in his jobs. "22.6.1941" is
titled for the date of the German invasion of the USSR. "Ballad of Jan
Palach, Student and Heretic" eulogizes a young Czech student who
immolated himself in protest over the Soviet invasion of Czechoslova-
kia in 1968.

≈ 22.6.1941

That day I lost everything
because I lost you.
Like an orphaned child
with a dry crust
I stare into the mists.
And I see you,
staring into the mists,
an orphaned child
with a dry crust.
That day you lost everything
because you lost me.

But soon our eyes will see the sky again,
deep blue at noon or studded with silent stars,
that sky alone will always be above us,
above the sorrow of all our wanderings,
as we find our way to one another:
perhaps living to living,
perhaps living to dead,
perhaps two graves under a vaulted sky,
deep blue at noon or studded with silent stars.

TR. EWALD OSERS

≈ At a Sunlit Window

You say: I am sitting in a room,
with a handful of books,
a modest bed,
an empty table,
a window looking out on
a landscape of vine-clad hills,
and at their feet
some factory chimney's belching smoke
into a vast plain.

But I say to you: I am sitting in a prison.
My window is barred.

And if you follow the river
a little distance to the west
you will see the barbed wire
in double lines
and between them the earth ploughed and raked
and beyond them the minefields.
And if a man has tackled all these
and reached the river
in order to
swim to the far bank
the dogs will follow him
and tear him apart
on one of the many small islands
which already belong to our neighbour.

TR. EWALD OSERS

≈ Ballad of Jan Palach, Student and Heretic

A human torch
races through Prague.

Today's heretics are spared
the long journey to Constance.

Prague, city of the schism,
has become the city of the Council of Conscience.

The dead philosophy student
testifies louder

than debates in the Party Secretariat or in Parliament
where words are swept on the rubbish heap of history

and burnt in the vortex of the human pillar of fire
which will sweep through Prague

till the end of the history of this city steeped in fire and blood
where John Huss has preached in vain

for over five centuries:
'He that will not serve truth, conscience and humanity

shall lose his power.'
One man alone understood the eternal heretic:

the student whom yesterday no one knew
and whom the whole world knows today.

And he acted at once. And for ever.
Seeking the truth. A heretic. A hero.

    TR. EWALD OSERS

CZESLAW MILOSZ (1911–   )

Born into a Lithuanian family of Polish descent, Milosz began writing
and publishing as an undergraduate, earned a law degree, and became a
rather unorthodox Marxist in the 1930s. He lived in Warsaw during the
German occupation and served as a diplomat for the Communists after
the war. Defecting in 1951, he lived in Paris until 1960, then came to the
United States, where he teaches at the University of California at Berke-
ley. The author of novels, poetry, criticism, and a study of politics,
Milosz was awarded the Nobel Prize for Literature in 1980. In his book
The Witness of Poetry, Milosz wrote, "The poetic act changes with the
amount of background reality embraced by the poet's consciousness.
In our century that background is . . . related to the fragility of those
things we call civilization or culture. . . . . It could just as well not
exist—and so man constructs poetry out of the remnants found in
ruins."

≈ Dedication

You whom I could not save
Listen to me.
Try to understand this simple speech as I would be ashamed of
    another.

I swear, there is in me no wizardry of words.
I speak to you with silence like a cloud or a tree.

What strengthened me, for you was lethal.
You mixed up farewell to an epoch with the beginning of a new one,
Inspiration of hatred with lyrical beauty,
Blind force with accomplished shape.

Here is the valley of shallow Polish rivers. And an immense bridge
Going into white fog. Here is a broken city,
And the wind throws screams of gulls on your grave
When I am talking with you.

What is poetry which does not save
Nations or people?
A connivance with official lies,
A song of drunkards whose throats will be cut in a moment,
Readings for sophomore girls.
That I wanted good poetry without knowing it,
That I discovered, late, its salutary aim,
In this and only this I find salvation.

They used to pour on graves millet or poppy seeds
To feed the dead who would come disguised as birds.
I put this book here for you, who once lived
So that you should visit us no more.

Warsaw, 1945

TR. CZESLAW MILOSZ

≈ A Task

In fear and trembling, I think I would fulfill my life
Only if I brought myself to make a public confession
Revealing a sham, my own and of my epoch:
We were permitted to shriek in the tongue of dwarfs and demons
But pure and generous words were forbidden
Under so stiff a penalty that whoever dared to pronounce one
Considered himself as a lost man.

TR. CZESLAW MILOSZ

≈ Child of Europe

I

We, whose lungs fill with the sweetness of day,
Who in May admire trees flowering,
Are better than those who perished.

We, who taste of exotic dishes,
And enjoy fully the delights of love,
Are better than those who were buried.

We, from the fiery furnaces, from behind barbed wires
Upon which whined the winds of endless Autumns.
We, from battles when the wounded air roared in paroxysms of pain,
We, saved by our own cunning and knowledge.

By sending others to the more exposed positions,
Urging them loudly to fight on,
Ourselves withdrawing in certainty of the cause lost.

Having the choice of our own death and that of a friend,
We chose his, coldly thinking: let it be done quickly.

We sealed gas chamber doors, stole bread,
Knowing the next day would be harder to bear than the day before.

As befits human beings, we explored good and evil.
Our malignant wisdom has no like on this planet.

Accept it as proven that we are better than they,
The gullible, hot-blooded weaklings, careless with their lives.

II

Treasure your legacy of skills, child of Europe,
Inheritor of gothic cathedrals, of baroque churches,
Of synagogues filled with the wailing of a wronged people.
Successor of Descartes, Spinoza, inheritor of the word "honor,"
Posthumous child of Leonidas,
Treasure the skills acquired in the hour of terror.

You have a clever mind which sees instantly
The good and bad of any situation.
You have an elegant, skeptical mind which enjoys pleasures
Quite unknown to primitive races.

Guided by this mind you cannot fail to see
The soundness of the advice we give you:
Let the sweetness of day fill your lungs.
For this we have strict but wise rules.

III

There can be no question of force triumphant.
We live in the age of victorious justice.

Do not mention force, or you will be accused
Of upholding fallen doctrines in secret.

He who has power, has it by historical logic.
Respectfully bow to that logic.

Let your lips, proposing a hypothesis,
Not know about the hand faking the experiment.

Let your hand, faking the experiment,
Not know about the lips proposing a hypothesis.

Learn to predict a fire with unerring precision.
Then burn the house down to fulfill the prediction.

IV

Grow your tree of falsehood from a small grain of truth.
Do not follow those who lie in contempt of reality.

Let your lie be even more logical than the truth itself,
So the weary travelers may find repose in the lie.

After the Day of the Lie gather in select circles,
Shaking with laughter when our real deeds are mentioned.

Dispensing flattery called: perspicacious thinking.
Dispensing flattery called: a great talent.

We, the last who can still draw joy from cynicism.
We, whose cunning is not unlike despair.

A new, humorless generation is now arising,
It takes in deadly earnest all we received with laughter.

V

Let your words speak not through their meanings,
But through them against whom they are used.

Fashion your weapon from ambiguous words.
Consign clear words to lexical limbo.

Judge no words before the clerks have checked
In their card index by whom they were spoken.

The voice of passion is better than the voice of reason.
The passionless cannot change history.

VI

Love no country: countries soon disappear.
Love no city: cities are soon rubble.

Throw away keepsakes, or from your desk
A choking, poisonous fume will exude.

Do not love people: people soon perish.
Or they are wronged and call for your help.

Do not gaze into the pools of the past.
Their corroded surface will mirror
A face different from the one you expected.

VII

He who invokes history is always secure.
The dead will not rise to witness against him.

You can accuse them of any deeds you like.
Their reply will always be silence.

Their empty faces swim out of the deep dark.
You can fill them with any features desired.

Proud of dominion over people long vanished,
Change the past into your own, better likeness.

VIII

The laughter born of the love of truth
Is now the laughter of the enemies of the people.

Gone is the age of satire. We no longer need mock
The senile tyrant with false courtly phrases.

Stern as befits the servants of a cause,
We will permit ourselves only sycophantic humor.

Tight-lipped, guided by reasons only,
Cautiously let us step into the era of the unchained fire.

TR. JAN DAROWSKI

≈ On Angels

All was taken away from you: white dresses,
wings, even existence.
Yet I believe you,
messengers.

There, where the world is turned inside out,
a heavy fabric embroidered with stars and beasts,
you stroll, inspecting the trustworthy seams.

Short is your stay here:
now and then at a matinal hour, if the sky is clear,
in a melody repeated by a bird,
or in the smell of apples at close of day
when the light makes the orchards magic.

They say somebody has invented you
but to me this does not sound convincing
for the humans invented themselves as well.

The voice—no doubt it is a valid proof,
as it can belong only to radiant creatures,
weightless and winged (after all, why not?),
girdled with the lightning.

I have heard that voice many a time when asleep
and, what is strange, I understood more or less
an order or an appeal in an unearthly tongue:

day draws near
another one
do what you can.

TR. CZESLAW MILOSZ

JOHANNES BOBROWSKI (1917–1965)

Bobrowski, born in Tilsit (now on the border of Germany and Lith-
uania), was inducted into the Wehrmacht and served on the eastern
front in World War II. Captured by the Soviets, he spent four years as a
prisoner of war, then returned to East Berlin in 1949. His first collec-
tion of poems was not published until 1961, and his work did not
receive recognition until shortly before his death. "Kaunas 1941" in-
vokes the memory of the Pruzzians who were exterminated by the
Teutonic Knights. Bobrowski's terse, often elliptical poems chronicle
the violent history of Central Europe.

≈ Kaunas 1941

Town,
branches over the river,
copper-coloured, like branching candles.
The banks call from the deep.
Then the lame girl

walked before dusk,
her skirt of darkest red.

And I know the steps,
the slope, this house. There is no
fire. Under this roof
lives the Jewess, lives whispering
in the Jews' silence
—the faces of the daughters
a white water. Noisily
the murderers pass the gate. We walk
softly, in musty air, in the track of wolves.

At evening we looked out
over a stony valley. The hawk
swept round the broad dome.
We saw the old town, house after house
running down to the river.

Will you walk over
the hill? The grey processions
—old men and sometimes boys—
die there. They walk
up the slope ahead of the slavering wolves.

Did my eyes avoid yours
brother? Sleep struck us
at the bloody wall. So we went on
blind to everything. We looked
like gipsies at the villages
in the oakwood, the summer
snow on the roofs.

I shall walk on the stone banks
under the rainy bushes,
listen in the haze of the plains.
There were swallows upstream
and the woodpigeon called
in the green night:
My dark is already come.

TR. MATTHEW MEAD

≈ Pruzzian Elegy

To sing you
one song,
bright with angry love—
but dark, bitter with
grieving, like wet meadow—
herbs, like the bare pines
on the cliff, groaning
beneath the pale dawn-wind,
burning before evening—

your never sung
fall, which struck us once
in the blood as our days
of child's-play hung
dream-wide—

then in the forests of the homeland,
above the green sea's
foaming impact, we shuddered
where groves had smoked
with sacrifice, before stones,
by long sunken-in gravemounds,
grass-grown ramparts, under the linden
lightly bent with age—

how rumour hung in its branches!
So in the old women's songs
sounds yet
the scarcely to be fathomed
call of the Foretime—
how we heard then
the echo rotting, the cloudy
discoloured sediment!
So when the deep bells
break, a cracked
tinkle remains.

People of the black woods,
of heavy thrusting rivers,

of empty Haffs, of the sea!
People
of the night-hunt,
of the herds and summer fields!
People
of Perkun and Pikoll,
of the corn-crowned Patrimpe!
People, like no other, of joy!
People,
like no other, no other, of death!—

People
of smouldering groves,
of burning huts, greencorn
trampled, blood-stained rivers—
People, sacrificed to the singeing
lightning-stroke; your cries veiled
by clouds of flame—
People,
leaping before the strange
god's mother in the throat—

TR. MATTHEW MEAD

≈ Latvian Songs

My father the hawk.
Grandfather the wolf.
And my forefather the rapacious fish in the sea.

I, unbearded, a fool,
lurching against the fences,
my black hands strangling a lamb
in the early light, I,

who beat the animals
instead of the white
master, I follow the rattling caravans
on washed-out roads,

I pass through the glances
of the gipsy-women. Then
on the Baltic shore I meet Uexküll, the master.
He walks beneath the moon.

Behind him, the darkness speaks.

TR. MATTHEW MEAD

≋ Elderblossom

Here comes
Babel, Isaak.
He says: In the pogrom
when I was a child
they tore the head
off my pigeon.

Houses in a wooden street,
at the fences, elder.
Down the small steps
the white-scrubbed threshold—
then, you remember,
the flecks of blood.

People, you say: Forget it—
there are young people coming,
their laughter like elder-bushes.
People, the elder
might die
of your forgetfulness.

TR. MATTHEW MEAD

TADEUSZ RÓZEWICZ (1921–)

The son of a minor Polish official, Rózewicz held a number of menial jobs after the German invasion of 1939. He underwent clandestine military training and published poems in an underground press. As a partisan, he fought the Nazis throughout the war. This experience proved to be the formative impulse of Rózewicz's poetry.

≈ Massacre of the Boys

The children cried "Mummy!
But I have been good!
It's dark in here! Dark!"

See them They are going to the bottom
See the small feet
they went to the bottom Do you see
that print
of a small foot here and there

pockets bulging
with string and stones
and little horses made of wire

A great plain closed
like a figure of geometry
and a tree of black smoke
a vertical
dead tree
with no star in its crown.

The Museum, Auschwitz, 1948

TR. ROBERT A. MAGUIRE AND MAGNUS JAN KRYNSKI

≈ Pigtail

When all the women in the transport
had their heads shaved
four workmen with brooms made of birch twigs
swept up
and gathered up the hair

Behind clean glass
the stiff hair lies
of those suffocated in gas chambers
there are pins and side combs
in this hair

The hair is not shot through with light
is not parted by the breeze
is not touched by any hand
or rain or lips

In huge chests
clouds of dry hair
of those suffocated
and a faded plait
a pigtail with a ribbon
pulled at school
by naughty boys

The Museum, Auschwitz, 1948

TR. ROBERT A. MAGUIRE AND MAGNUS JAN KRYNSKI

≈ What Happens

It has happened
and it goes on happening
and will happen again
if nothing happens to stop it

The innocent know nothing
because they are too innocent

and the guilty know nothing
because they are too guilty

The poor do not notice
because they are too poor
and the rich do not notice
because they are too rich

The stupid shrug their shoulders
because they are too stupid
and the clever shrug their shoulders
because they are too clever

The young do not care
because they are too young
and the old do not care
because they are too old

That is why nothing happens
to stop it
and that is why it has happened
and goes on happening and will happen again

TR. ROBERT A. MAGUIRE AND MAGNUS JAN KRYNSKI

≈ Questions about Poetry since Auschwitz

Whether it rose up as a small brown bird
out of the smoke of cremation ovens
and then rested in one of the birches
of Birkenau

whether it flew closer
drawn by the screams of the girls
and saw them raped
and then sang

to the dust of the ruined cities
its song of quiet love
and to the starving
the lay of the ripening corn

whether it grew up in the shadow of money
and lent it its voice
for money had grown too big
to be able to jingle

whether it flew through the world
and learned its sense of beauty
from the vivid colours
of bodies torn to pieces

from the bright flames of village huts
or from the glint
of the changing daylight
in glazed eyes

whether at last in a tree
stripped by defoliants
it built its nest of hair
of paper shreds of rags and bloody feathers

and now waits for mating
for the time to sit on its eggs
and for the hatching of
its eternally innocent young

that only lyric poets know
who steadfastly call
for wild bird protection
in a world soon to be whole again

TR. ROBERT A. MAGUIRE AND MAGNUS JAN KRYNSKI

ION CARAION (1923–1986)

The Romanian poet Ion Caraion was an active journalist and defender of democratic causes during World War II. His bleak and outspoken poetry brought him into conflict with the Communist authorities, and he was imprisoned from 1949 until 1963. Although the tone of his poetry did not become less pessimistic over the years, he was rehabilitated by the Party and worked as an editor until his death.

≈ Song from the Occupation Time

What I would not give for this century, were it only to change!
How deep would my heart plow its field with life!
Had you ever felt the pains of an army in retreat,
you would not have imprisoned joy in any city.

Careful now: this is a thing and this is a passing.
The bow on the wall contains a musical forest, forgotten.
The poet went hunting with the lost
dogs—like railroad tracks.

What a fine thing to be aware!
In the Commons, they discussed De Gaulle,
tomorrow the banned newspapers shall come from Switzerland.
We'll read them during the bombing, in the cellar.

I hear there's hunger in France, I hear
that Pierre Drieu La Rochelle returned to Paris.
What has this to do with France?

On the borders of the Loire, much farther away—a presentiment
of skies that shall never again flap at the closed window.

The skies will laugh no longer . . . From now on
magnanimous, deep, the heart of France
shall travel under cover across the border
under the silence killed by the moon.

An exodus is expected from the North
alien people coming through the woods.
Paul Eluard has stopped his writing,
two thousand emigrants have crossed the Ocean,
from the Pyrenees one hears gunfire, and learns of executions.

I ask you: where is freedom for which the cities have burned
and where are the joys for which
our children, charred, have multiplied the carcasses of war?

Nowhere has silence hurt so darkly
nowhere was loneliness greater than here.
The eyes frowning speak of peace
as if speaking of the heroes in Sienkiewicz's books.

I ask you: where is the freedom for which the cities burned?

Unknown messengers brought news from Tunis:
hunger reigns in France; the newspapers declare:
"Three German Officers Shot In Paris."

What a fine thing: to be aware!

Great rains shall come to flood the cities,
the yellow drought shall come to dry the gardens,
the houses shall burn to the ground, the trees
through which the alien armies have invaded.
Only the menacing heart of France,
only, magnanimous and deep, the heart of France,
like the moon-white nights under the sun-white silence
shall travel across the borders under cover.

TR. MARGUERITE DORIAN AND ELLIOTT B. URDANG

≈ Remember

Delirious the drought raved birds stretched on the fence
the country rambled railway stations swathed in ghosts
bony animals like grandparents' fingers
led anti-history by the hand—

the earth had eaten its own wells.

TR. MARGUERITE DORIAN AND ELLIOTT B. URDANG

≈ The Enveloping Echo

A woman crossed the park and laughed.
With hoop, with kite, with sling,

the children ran about the sky.
A woman crossed the park and sang.

That fall was like a bunch of grapes.

TR. MARGUERITE DORIAN AND ELLIOTT B. URDANG

≈ Tomorrow the Past Comes

No longer for me is there anything late. All is late.
The blood runs like a subway through capitals.
And the past   is   everywhere   like the blood.
                 In the sunrise of the rivers red
with lightning   and croups   of centaurs
there was a kind of light—I don't know what kind of light that was.

In the fog much becomes clear.

TR. MARGUERITE DORIAN AND ELLIOTT R. URDANG

≈ Ultimate Argument

The years pass like donkeys.
the children have grown up—
here a homunculus, there a mongrel,
the years pass like pigs—

I am sleeping in a prophet from Egypt . . .

maybe the things I have not known
are just as dirty.

TR. MARGUERITE DORIAN AND ELLIOTT R. URDANG

WISLAWA SZYMBORSKA (1923–)

Szymborska's first book, ready for publication in 1948, was deemed incomprehensible and overly morbid by the Communist government. When a vicious campaign was launched against her, she withdrew the book. Subsequent work fared better, and Szymborska has been awarded a number of prizes. A native of Cracow, she has always lived in Poland.

≈ The Terrorist, He Watches

The bomb will go off in the bar at one twenty p.m.
Now it's only one sixteen p.m.
Some will still have time to get in,
some to get out.

The terrorist has already crossed to the other side of the street.
The distance protects him from any danger,
and what a sight for sore eyes:

A woman in a yellow jacket, she goes in.
A man in dark glasses, he comes out.
Guys in jeans, they are talking.
One seventeen and four seconds.
That shorter guy's really got it made, and gets on a scooter,
and that taller one, he goes in.

One seventeen and forty seconds.
That girl there, she's got a green ribbon in her hair.
Too bad that bus just cut her off.
One eighteen p.m.
The girl's not there any more.
Was she dumb enough to go in, or wasn't she?
That we'll see when they carry them out.

One nineteen p.m.
No one seems to be going in.
Instead a fat baldy's coming out.
Like he's looking for something in his pockets and
at one nineteen and fifty seconds
he goes back for those lousy gloves of his.

It's one twenty p.m.
The time, how it drags.
Should be any moment now.
Not yet.
Yes, this is it.
The bomb, it goes off.

TR. ROBERT A. MAGUIRE AND MAGNUS JAN KRYNSKI

≈ Still

In sealed box cars travel
names across the land,
and how far they will travel so,
and will they ever get out,
don't ask, I won't say, I don't know.

The name Nathan strikes fist against wall,
the name Isaac, demented, sings,
the name Sarah calls out for water for
the name Aaron that's dying of thirst.

Don't jump while it's moving, name David.
You're a name that dooms to defeat,
given to no one, and homeless,
too heavy to bear in this land.

Let your son have a Slavic name,
for here they count hairs on the head,
for here they tell good from evil
by names and by eyelids' shape.

Don't jump while it's moving. Your son will be Lech.
Don't jump while it's moving. Not time yet.
Don't jump. The night echoes like laughter
mocking clatter of wheels upon tracks.

A cloud made of people moved over the land,
a big cloud gives a small rain, one tear,
a small rain—one tear, a dry season.
Tracks lead off into black forest.

Cor-rect, cor-rect clicks the wheel. Gladeless forest.
Cor-rect, cor-rect. Through the forest a convoy of clamors.
Cor-rect, cor-rect. Awakened in the night I hear
cor-rect, cor-rect, crash of silence on silence.

TR. ROBERT A. MAGUIRE AND MAGNUS JAN KRYNSKI

≈ Children of the Epoch

We are children of the epoch.
The epoch is political.

All my daily and nightly affairs,
all your daily and nightly affairs,
are political affairs.

Whether you want it or not,
your genes have a political past,
your skin a political tone,
your eyes a political color,
What you say resounds,
what you don't say is also
politically significant.

Even coming through the rye,
you walk with political steps
on political ground.

Apolitical poems are also political,
and in the sky there's a moon

that's no longer moonlike.
To be or not to be, that is a question.
Oh darling, what a question, give a suggestion.
A political question.

You don't have to be human
to acquire a political meaning.
It's enough to be petroleum,
cattle fodder, raw material.
Or just a conference table whose shape
was disputed for months.

In the meantime, people were killed.
Animals died,
houses burned,
fields grew wild,
as in distant
and less political epochs.

TR. GRAZYNA DRABIK AND AUSTIN FLINT

≈ Any Case

It could have happened.
It had to happen.
It happened earlier. Later.
Closer. Farther away.
It happened, but not to you.

You survived because you were the first.
You survived because you were the last.
Because alone. Because the others.
Because on the left. Because on the right.
Because it was raining. Because it was sunny.
Because a shadow fell.

Luckily there was a forest.
Luckily there were no trees.
Luckily a rail, a hook, a beam, a brake,

a frame, a turn, an inch, a second.
Luckily a straw was floating on the water.

Thanks to, thus, in spite of, and yet.
What would have happened if a hand, a leg,
one step, a hair away—

So you are here? Straight from that moment still suspended?
The net's mesh was tight, but you—through the mesh?
I can't stop wondering at it, can't be silent enough.
Listen,
how quickly your heart is beating in me.

TR. GRAZYNA DRABIK AND SHARON OLDS

≈ Hunger Camp at Jasło

Write it. Write. In ordinary ink
on ordinary paper: they were given no food,
they all died of hunger. "All. How many?
It's a big meadow. How much grass
for each one?" Write: I don't know.
History counts its skeletons in round numbers.
A thousand and one remains a thousand,
as though the one had never existed:
an imaginary embryo, an empty cradle,
an ABC never read,
air that laughs, cries, grows,
emptiness running down steps toward the garden,
nobody's place in the line.

We stand in the meadow where it became flesh,
and the meadow is silent as a false witness.
Sunny. Green. Nearby, a forest
with wood for chewing and water under the bark—
every day a full ration of the view
until you go blind. Overhead, a bird—
the shadow of its life-giving wings
brushed their lips. Their jaws opened.

Teeth clacked against teeth.
At night, the sickle moon shone in the sky
and reaped wheat for their bread.
Hands came floating from blackened icons,
empty cups in their fingers.
On a spit of barbed wire,
a man was turning.
They sang with their mouths full of earth.
"A lovely song of how war strikes straight
at the heart." Write: how silent.
"Yes."

TR. GRAZYNA DRABIK AND AUSTIN FLINT

≈ Once we knew the world well

Once we knew the world well.
It was so small it could fit in a handshake,
so easy you could describe it with a smile,
it was ordinary as old truths in a prayer.

History did not welcome us with fanfares.
It threw filthy dust into our eyes.
Before us only dead-end roads,
poisoned wells, bitter bread.

Our war's booty is knowledge of the world.
It is so large it can fit in a handshake.
so difficult you can describe it with a smile,
it is extraordinary as old truths in a prayer.

TR. GRAZYNA DRABIK AND SHARON OLDS

ZBIGNIEW HERBERT (1924–)

Born in a Polish-speaking city that became part of the former Soviet
Union, Herbert fought the Nazis as a teenager with the partisans, an
experience that provided the themes of his work: "what a man is in the

face of death, how he behaves in the presence of a totalitarian threat, what moral values can and should be saved." After the war, he studied law, economics, and philosophy. During the Stalinist years, he earned a living as a journalist and a manual laborer. He did not publish his first book of poetry until 1956, although he had been writing for over a decade. Herbert is now recognized as one of Poland's leading poets.

≈ What I Saw

To the memory of Kazimierz Moczarski

I saw prophets tearing at their pasted-on beards
I saw impostors joining sects of flagellants
butchers disguised in sheepskin
who fled the anger of the people
playing on a block-flute

I saw I saw

    I saw a man who had been tortured
    he now sat safely in the family circle
    cracked jokes ate soup
    I looked at the opened mouth
    his gums—two bramble twigs stripped of bark
    I saw his whole nakedness
    the whole humiliation

    later
    a solemn meeting
    many people flowers
    stifling
    someone spoke incessantly about deviations
    I thought of his deviated mouth

is this the last act
of the play by Anonymous
flat as a shroud
full of suppressed sobbing

and the snickering of those
who heave a sigh of relief

that again it has worked out
and after clearing away the dead props
slowly
raise

the blood-drenched curtain

1956

TR. JOHN CARPENTER AND BOGDANA CARPENTER

≈ Report from the Besieged City

Too old to carry arms and fight like the others—

they graciously gave me the inferior role of chronicler
I record—I don't know for whom—the history of the siege

I am supposed to be exact but I don't know when the invasion began
two hundred years ago in December in September perhaps yesterday
    at dawn
everyone here suffers from a loss of the sense of time

all we have left is the place the attachment to the place
we still rule over the ruins of temples specters of gardens and houses
if we lose the ruins nothing will be left

I write as I can in the rhythm of interminable weeks
monday: empty storehouses a rat became the unit of currency
tuesday: the mayor murdered by unknown assailants
wednesday: negotiations for a cease-fire the enemy has imprisoned
    our messengers
we don't know where they are held that is the place of torture
thursday: after a stormy meeting a majority of voices rejected
the motion of the spice merchants for unconditional surrender
friday: the beginning of the plague saturday: our invincible defender
N.N. committed suicide sunday: no more water we drove back
an attack at the eastern gate called the Gate of the Alliance

all of this is monotonous I know it can't move anyone

I avoid any commentary I keep a tight hold on my emotions I write
    about the facts
only they it seems are appreciated in foreign markets
yet with a certain pride I would like to inform the world
that thanks to the war we have raised a new species of children
our children don't like fairy tales they play at killing
awake and asleep they dream of soup of bread and bones
just like dogs and cats

in the evening I like to wander near the outposts of the City
along the frontier of our uncertain freedom
I look at the swarms of soldiers below their lights
I listen to the noise of drums barbarian shrieks
truly it is inconceivable the City is still defending itself
the siege has lasted a long time the enemies must take turns
nothing unites them except the desire for our extermination
Goths the Tartars Swedes troops of the Emperor regiments of the
    Transfiguration
who can count them
the colors of their banners change like the forest on the horizon
from delicate bird's yellow in spring through green through red to
    winter's black

and so in the evening released from facts I can think
about distant ancient matters for example our
friends beyond the sea I know they sincerely sympathize
they send us flour lard sacks of comfort and good advice
they don't even know their fathers betrayed us
our former allies at the time of the second Apocalypse
their sons are blameless they deserve our gratitude therefore we are
    grateful
they have not experienced a siege as long as eternity
those struck by misfortune are always alone
the defenders of the Dalai Lama the Kurds the Afghan mountaineers

now as I write these words the advocates of conciliation
have won the upper hand over the party of inflexibles
a normal hesitation of moods fate still hangs in the balance

cemeteries grow larger the number of defenders is smaller
yet the defense continues it will continue to the end

and if the City falls but a single man escapes
he will carry the City within himself on the roads of exile
he will be the City
we look in the face of hunger the face of fire face of death
worst of all—the face of betrayal

and only our dreams have not been humiliated

1982

TR. JOHN CARPENTER AND BOGDANA CARPENTER

≈ Painter

Under walls white as a birch forest the ferns of paintings grow. In an odour of turpentine and oils Miron recreates the drama of a lemon condemned to coexistence with a green drapery. There is also a female nude.

—My fiancée, says Miron. She posed for me during the occupation. It was winter, without bread and coal. The blood gathered into small blue blots under her white skin. It was then that I painted the warm pink background.

TR. JOHN CARPENTER AND BOGDANA CARPENTER

≈ The Wall

We are standing under the wall. Our youth has been taken off like a shirt from the condemned men. We wait. Before the fat bullet will sit down on the nape of the neck, ten, twenty years pass. The wall is high and strong. Behind the wall is a tree and a star. The tree pries at the wall with its roots. The star nibbles the stone like a mouse. In a hundred, two hundred years there will already be a small window.

TR. JOHN CARPENTER AND BOGDANA CARPENTER

≈ The Trial

During his great speech the prosecutor
kept piercing me with his yellow index finger

I'm afraid I didn't appear self-assured
unintentionally I assumed a mask of fear and depravity
like a rat caught in a trap an informer a fratricide
the reporters were dancing a war dance
I slowly burned at a stake of magnesia
all of this took place in a small stifling room
the floor the benches creaked plaster fell from the ceiling
I counted knots in the boards holes in the wall faces
the faces were alike almost identical
assessors judges witnesses for the defence and the prosecution
and also the audience—they belonged to the same organization
I vainly hoped the defender was a man from town
but he too was a member of the union of magicians

in the first row sat an old fat woman
dressed up as my mother with a theatrical gesture
she kept raising a handkerchief to her dirty eyes
but she didn't cry
it must have lasted very long I don't know how long
the old blood of the West was rising in the gowns of the judges

the real trial went on in my cells
they certainly knew the verdict earlier
after a short rebellion they capitulated and slowly started to die
one after the other I looked in amazement
at my wax hands

I didn't speak the last word and yet
for so many months years I was composing the final speech
to God to the court of the world to the conscience
to the dead rather than the living
roused to my feet by the guards
I managed only to twist my head and then
the room burst out in healthy laughter
my adoptive mother laughed also
the gavel banged and this was really the end

I don't know if I was hung or if the punishment
was changed to a life sentence I'm afraid however
neither the one nor the other happened
therefore when I wake I don't open my eyes

I don't move my head my hands tightly against the body
I breathe lightly because truly I don't know
how many seconds of air I still have left

TR. JOHN CARPENTER AND BOGDANA CARPENTER

NINA CASSIAN (1924–)

Cassian was brought up in the multiethnic Romanian city of Brasov and then in Bucharest. Forced to leave her school because she was Jewish, she became an ardent Communist. When she published her first book of poetry, both she and her work were attacked as "enemies of the people." After a brief period of liberalization, Cassian wrote poetry, film criticism, and children's books. She came to the United States in 1985 for a short visit, and learned that a friend of many years had been arrested, tortured, and killed in Romania. Cassian's satirical verses aimed at the Romanian government had been among her friend's papers. She asked for and was awarded political asylum in the United States.

≈ Temptation

Call yourself alive? Look, I promise you
that for the first time you'll feel your pores opening
like fish mouths, and you'll actually be able to hear
your blood surging through all those lanes,
and you'll feel light gliding across the cornea
like the train of a dress. For the first time
you'll be aware of gravity
like a thorn in your heel,
and your shoulder blades will ache for want of wings.
Call yourself alive? I promise you
you'll be deafened by dust falling on the furniture,
you'll feel your eyebrows turning to two gashes,
and every memory you have—will begin
at Genesis.

TR. BRENDA WALKER AND ANDREA DELETANT

≈ Vowel

A clean vowel
is my morning,
Latin pronunciation
in the murmur of confused time.
With rational syllables
I'm trying to clear the occult mind
and promiscuous violence.
My linguistic protest
has no power.
The enemy is illiterate.

TR. BRENDA WALKER AND ANDREA DELETANT

HORST BIENEK (1930–   )

Born in what is now Poland, Bienek was a student at the Berliner
Ensemble, Bertolt Brecht's theater. In 1951, he was arrested and sen-
tenced to twenty-five years in a labor camp at Vorkuta. Released in
1955 in an amnesty following Stalin's death, he subsequently emigrated
to the Federal Republic of Germany. He has written novels and essays
as well as poetry.

≈ Vorkuta

In Vorkuta no disciple of the Lord
walks the green-foaming tundra.
Here there is no feeding of the five thousand.
Here a dream dies every day
in the still uncertain dawn.

In Vorkuta, no machine-guns rust.
Whoever tires listens to the cantata
of the snowstorm in the barbed wire
and embroiders with his own blood
an endless pattern in his black katorga-shirt.

Nor in Vorkuta
is the prayer of the dead a prayer
and the lips of the living
are rusting lips, iron bars,
behind which the tongue festers and rots.

In Vorkuta no widow
covers her hair with a veil.
Her breasts still tremble
when she thinks of the loneliness
beneath the arching body of a man.

In Vorkuta no one digs a grave
for crumbling hopes
And there is no one to weep
when the abandoned corpses
drift to the rivers with the melting snow.

Vorkuta, 1953

TR. MATTHEW MEAD

≈ Exodus

They drove us out
on nights when moons died.
Patiently we bore the cross
they had made for us
out of lies, violence and torture,
and beneath the blows of their rifle-butts
we broke down more than thrice—
On the endless road of graves
we met no Simon of Cyrene.

Who among you, the living, can say
that he saw us?
Who among you, the dead, can say
he recognized his brother?
Only our mothers
behind sorrow-curtained windows
sensed our departure

and startled prayers fled from their lips
into the darkness.

Encompassed by night we departed from all the cities
and memory went with us.
We were thirsty,
memory has quenched our thirst,
we were hungry
and memory fed us the meat of Job,
and when we were weary
memory spread for us
a bed of thistles.

We were blind,
memory created illusion,
we were deaf,
memory was the music of the Cherubim,
we were naked,
memory lent us the divided cloak of comfort,
we were innocent
and memory never let us be guilty
in the eyes of God.

They drove us out
on nights when moons died,
and around us sprouted
a forest of hostile bayonets.

Vorkuta, 1954

TR. MATTHEW MEAD

≈ Resistance

I

We have disconcerted
The revolutions with our prayers.

You escaped
Or betrayed your brothers

Or deserted the burning slopes,
Or crouched closer to your test-tubes,
Or you wept.

But we slept fearlessly in the fires
Wedded to the burning flames
And the white heat of secret avowals
Dwelt in our eyes alone.

When we awoke
We mingled with you,
We spoke loudly but no one understood us:

It was that language which turns the steely noon
Into evening pierced with triumph,
Which makes the snow and the forgotten burden
Of the flags fall black from the roofs,
Which brings leprous doubt to the traitor
And surprises the meek and the indulgent
As they sell their virtue.
The words were no more: poems.

They were: the birth of all things.
They became fish and mandragora
When we said *fish* and *mandragora,*
They became rocks and lightning, deer and drums
When we said *rocks* and *lightning, deer* and *drums,*
They became ashes and homeland, sorrow and trust
When we said *ashes* and *homeland, sorrow* and *trust.*

No one can say he did not see us:
Barbed wire was our crown.
Bayonets inscribed the formulae of death
Upon our foreheads,
And the impatient enemy bullets
Blossomed strangely in our bodies.

But we have set dreams in order
With our prayers.

II

We speak loudly but no one understands us.
But we are not surprised
For we are speaking the language
That will be spoken tomorrow.

III

But I ask you: what did you do?

You painted remote moonscapes
And wept.
You danced in bars, in cellars of lust,
And hummed with nuptial lips:
The song of the sweetest dream.
You read the murder-columns in the newspapers
And wept.
You talked in the tube
(Between Babel and Vineta)
Of being and not-being,
And wept.

You made football-pools a science
And science a football-pool
And wept.
You supplied clever diagnoses
But prescribed no remedies,
In your books are great words
About fear and death.

But you are unworthy of death
When so many die with dignity.

IV

None of us weeps.
None of us weeps.
None of us weeps!

V

We have conquered the revolutions
With our prayers.

1955

tr. Matthew Mead

≈ Our Ashes

Barbed-wire
      is the cloak of saints
whoever is covered by down
or darkness
      is living in sin
Only when the lamp blinds your eyes
can you deny your guilt
only when you are interrogated
      remain silent

No one speaks of the
forty days on bread and water
      (who painted the Tintorettos
      on the wall of your cell?)
No one speaks of the path
to the latrine-pits
      no one helps you carry
      the latrine-buckets
and carrying them
      you broke down
            more than thrice

No one came
      but a bird of black smoke
and later the murderers
      appeared punctually
they bore the sun
wounded/pierced/bleeding
      on their bayonets
      to the black wall

Walk
said a voice
five paces to the wall
and do not turn round
when you hear the shots
What will happen
when the cry crucifies the sky
what will happen
when the wind destroys the memory
what will happen
when the sun-fish leaps in the veins
and quick-lime deletes our faces?

The answer has
been given
but which of us
which of us has heard it?
Who among us, the living,
can say
he has heard it
who has seen it—
which of us?

We have chlorine in the eyes
and sand in the ears
and eternity
grows silently in our bodies

When will our ashes speak?

TR. MATTHEW MEAD

SARAH KIRSCH (1935–   )

After studying literature and biology at the universities of Halle and
Leipzig in what was then East Germany, German poet Sarah Kirsch
worked in a sugar factory. Her poetry was assailed for its commitment
to nature, which seemed to signal an apolitical passivity and resignation.

In 1977, however, Kirsch offended the state by supporting the dissident poet Wolf Biermann and was forced to emigrate to the Federal Republic of Germany. The poems here recall World War II and postwar life in Germany.

≈ Legend of Lilja

I

if she was beautiful is uncertain the more
so since the testimonies of surviving camp inmates
are contradictory even the color of her hair
is variously described in the card-file there
was no picture she supposedly
had been sent from Poland

II

in summer Lilja went barefoot as in winter and wrote
seven letters

III

six small wire-thin rolls wander
through prison uniforms across the parade ground stick
to tired skin disturb sleep reach
the one they don't know (he cannot
be a witness at the trial)

IV

the seventh someone traded for bread

V

Lilja in the writing-room Lilja walking Lilja in the bunker
lash with the whip the name why doesn't she say anything
    who knows
why is she silent in August when the birds
sing in the smoke

VI

one in uniform death's-head on the collar lover
of old plays (his dog with classical name) determined
they should let her eyes speak

VII

through the imprisoned men a road was made
a strange avenue of plundered trees opened up
here she was to walk and betray one

VIII

now use your eyes Lilja command
the muscles the blood indifference here you have often walked
know every stone every
stone

IX

her face passed by
the survivors said they
would have trembled Lilja as if dead walked walked
until the man whose dog was named Hamlet
howled commanded enough

X

after this she was seen no more

XI

other witnesses said on her way she had
smiled at everyone combed her hair with her fingers
was immediately gassed—that was
over twenty years ago—

XII

all spoke a long time about Lilja

XIII

in the year '65 the judges from Frankfurt stated on record
obviously

legends were told this point
was to be struck from the indictment

XIV

in the letter was said to be written we
will not get out of here we have
seen too much

TR. WAYNE KVAM

≈ Pictures

My mother drives the goat
never has she owned her
over the green leaf-tops
my father's clocks strike
one after another in the night
my brother died very young
his flowers grow wild
since he no longer counts
My city went up in flames
people ran into the churches
and burned up with the pictures
unafraid I saw them lying
I was small and mornings gleaned
ears of grain from the fields
when the midday hot was over
I practiced on the bike
or sat in our garden
wound jasmine to circular wreaths
laid them on the pretty
raised mounds of drowned birds
clatters the garden door now barks
this wandering dog
ah the father of my mother
drives me out of the full trees
and I stand before the rows
where the cold asters glisten

trample their late heads
under my postwar shoes

TR. WAYNE KVAM

≈ Mail

Somewhere in the world my tree stands, for I know that every person
has the right to a tree. Likewise a type of grass and a certain bird. Thus
my bird can already eat seeds, light on a tree, recognize an event. The
event of my bird in this damp cold February should be a pleasing one,
not a huge rain, rather the arrival of a mail truck with letters from Stan
and Ollie, descriptions of life in the country, the border officials paste a
decal of a protected bird- or person-type on the truck and signal "Red
Front," the outstretched thumbs indicate the way of the world.

TR. WAYNE KVAM

GOJKO DJOGO (1940–   )

Born in Vlahovići, Yugoslavia, Djogo studied literature at the Univer-
sity of Belgrade. He was the first writer in his country to be imprisoned
because of his poetry, for a book called *Woolly Times.* Although he was
released before his two-year sentence ended, his book remains banned.

≈ The National Hero

They cut off his left arm
and his right arm,
one, then the other leg,
finally his head
and they planted his neck in the soil
—to grow.

Children and scapegoats
hang on his stumps.

TR. MICHAEL MARCH AND DUŠAN PUVAČIĆ

≈ The Wooden Handle

Here,
Take it home and give it to your wife
So she may bear you sons
Without hiding the best man behind the door.

Tie it between your legs
So that your pants won't be empty
That you have something to lean on
When you stumble
Or stick it up on the ridge of the roof
To protect you from lightning.

You will have a poker for the yule log
And a pipe in your mouth.
You'll never find a better candlestick.
If its flame does not lick you
You'll take your Communion in the dark
And break your fast.

Take it, take it, you'll need it.
Whoever possesses the golden faucet
Will be the emperor's wine taster,
Whoever walks with a linden stick
Won't go to Constantinople on all fours.

If you fall to your knees, mount!
Bare-headed, in a bad mood
He boils stones
And saves the eggs for you.

He looks like you, too.
Could be your twin brother
A substitute in bed, at the church fair.
Just lend him your cap
And kiss his star-studded brow.

Here, take it,
Gouge out your eyes with it
And they will lead you home blind.

TR. MICHAEL MARCH AND DUŠAN PUVAČIĆ

≈ The Black Sheep

Here is the black sheep, master
Black are both her father and mother
Beneath her a black lamb
Sucking black milk.

And her blood is full of smoke
And her teeth are eye-teeth
And her eyes are cross-eyed
And she has horns
But no star on her forehead.

Whoever she kisses
Will catch the pox
In front of whosoever's house she dwells at dawn
His noon will grow dark.

Whether you lure her or not
She will not lick the salt from your palm
Nor manure your barren fields.

She prefers the wolf to the shepherd
She prefers the slaughterhouse to the sheepfold
And the blind leader
To the clairvoyant bell-wether.

—Hold out your hand to her,
You will have black on white.

TR. MICHAEL MARCH AND DUŠAN PUVAČIĆ

STANISLAW BARANCZAK (1946–   )

As a professor at Adam Mickiewicz University in Poznan, Baranczak had published several books by 1975, but he was blacklisted because of his activity in the Polish human rights movement: he was cofounder of KOR (Committee for the Defense of Workers' Rights) and the editor of underground journals. Fired from his teaching job in 1977, he was harassed and forbidden to publish. The Poles refused Baranczak an exit visa eight times, and he was not able to leave the country until 1981. His passport was revoked in 1984, and he has lived in the United States since then.

≈ If China

If china, then only the kind
you wouldn't miss under the movers' shoes or the treads of a tank;
if a chair, then one that's not too comfortable, or
you'll regret getting up and leaving;
if clothes, then only what will fit in one suitcase;
if books, then those you know by heart;
if plans, then the ones you can give up
when it comes time for the next move,
to another street, another continent or epoch
or world:

who told you you could settle in?
who told you this or that would last forever?
didn't anyone tell you you'll never
in the world
feel at home here?

TR. MAGNUS J. KRYNSKI

≈ December 14, 1979: A Poetry Reading

For the poet Leszek

They came, since there are certain matters, and you gentlemen have
   only yourselves to blame.
They entered, since there are certain laws and surely you don't want us
   to force the door.
They stopped the reading, since there are certain words and we're
   giving you some friendly advice.
They took away the poems, since there are certain limits and we might
   as well agree.

They took down everyone's name, since there are certain regulations
    and please sir don't try our patience.
They searched the apartment, since there are certain rules and ma'am
    kindly keep that child quiet.
They took a few people away, since there are certain special reasons
    and don't you worry, your husband will be back day after
    tomorrow.
They didn't strike anyone, since there are certain forms and of course
    you gentlemen would like nothing better.
They didn't work long, since there is a certain film on TV and a man
    is only human.

TR. MAGNUS J. KRYNSKI

≈ February 8, 1980: And No One Has Warned Me

And no one has warned me that freedom
may also consist of the fact that
I sit in a police station with a notebook of my own poems
hidden (what foresight) in the leg of my winter underwear,
while five civilians with a higher education
and even higher pay waste time
analyzing the junk removed from my pocket:
streetcar tickets, a laundry receipt, a dirty
handkerchief and a mysterious (I'll die laughing) scrap of paper:

> "greens
> can of peas
> tomato paste
> potatoes";

and no one has warned me that slavery
may also consist of the fact that
I sit in a police station with a notebook of my own poems
hidden (how grotesque) in the leg of my winter underwear,
while five civilians with a higher education
and even lower foreheads have the right
to paw the innards wrenched out of my life:
streetcar tickets, a laundry receipt, a dirty handkerchief,
and above all (no, this is more than I can take) that scrap of paper:

> "greens
> can of peas

                                                tomato paste
                                                potatoes";
and no one has warned me that my entire globe
is the space separating the opposing poles
between which there really is no space

TR. MAGNUS J. KRYNSKI

TOMASZ JASTRUN (1950–   )

Jastrun, a Pole, was already a published poet when he joined the striking workers at the Gdansk shipyards in 1980; he worked for Solidarity until martial law was declared a year later. He went into hiding, but was arrested and detained in 1982. Two later books of poetry were underground publications. He now lives and works as an editor in Warsaw.

≈ The Seed

Birds
Fly into the depths of our existence
Frightened
They fold and unfold
Their wings

Birds
Fly through the fading corridor

Dead tired
They rest on our shoulders
They are hungry

Our hands are already empty
The seed
Within our eyes and lips

TR. MICHAEL MARCH AND JAROSLAW ANDERS

≈ The Polish Knot

There was no good solution
Therefore it shrank and darkened
There was no good solution
Therefore uprisings broke out like sobs

There is no good solution
Therefore everyone wears
The Gordian Knot
On his neck

When you cut it
You cut the throat

TR. MICHAEL MARCH AND JAROSLAW ANDERS

≈ Scrap

After us there will be
Neither scrap metal
Nor laughter
From start to finish
We held no illusions
All our uprisings
Lie packed in the hall
With a toothbrush
and a towel

When someone knocks on the door
The echo pounds
Through the solitary years
But there is no call to action
No convoy to Siberia
Only the upstairs neighbour whose sink
Once again has overflowed
Comes wringing his hands to warn us

TR. DANIEL BOURNE

≈ Hat

This elderly gentleman
also takes walks in the Yard
But his hat clashes
with the barbed wire
and the bars muzzling the windows
as though they were afraid we might bite through
This man with a hat
is here because he sought
to overthrow the government by force
and violate our treaties.

Sixty years old
his hands furrowed like the earth
of pre-war Europe
and a very dangerous hat
on his head

TR. DANIEL BOURNE

JAN POLKOWSKI (1953–   )

Born in Krakow, Poland, Polkowski studied Polish literature and was
active in the Student Solidarity Committee at the Jagiellonian Univer-
sity. He was arrested in 1981; three volumes of his work were subse-
quently published by underground presses. He now lives in Krakow.

≈ The world is only air

The world is only air
shining, granular, transparent things,
fleeting breath, through which I see
time.

Thought is more material
(footprints in the snow, the smell

of crushed grass, a leaf caged
in the fist of the wind).

The silent word is more
palpable
than wood, wall, flesh—invisible
proof of Eden.

TR. MICHAEL MARCH AND JAROSLAW ANDERS

≈ I Don't Know That Man

I clearly hear the crowing of a rooster,
I have not misheard,
crowing in the middle of a concrete garden,
though invisible to sight.
I write it down, I freeze, I listen,
but someone writes with my hand:
'Haven't you renounced me, Galilean?'
(Are you afraid?)

TR. MICHAEL MARCH AND JAROSLAW ANDERS

≈ Noli Me Tangere

Gesture of an Ionic column returning your face
gesture of slender fire returning you, page by page,
the book of generations,
oval of a marble breast, the oval of a pregnant womb
    of an imprisoned woman
bestowing upon you the stony alphabet of humanity
the untouchable whiteness of a hostage's shirt (Goya, *The
Third of May 1808*) dressing the world in fountains of colour,
dark chant of a psalmist,
damp taste of a couplet—indestructible blade which cuts you
into good and evil.

TR. MICHAEL MARCH AND JAROSLAW ANDERS

War and Dictatorship in the Mediterranean

(1 9 0 0 – 1 9 9 1)

The apparently self-evident prime tenet of nationalism that members of one linguistic and regional group should have their own nation becomes confusing in the Mediterranean, because the boundaries between languages and ethnic loyalties are pronounced but difficult to establish. So it was that C. P. Cavafy was a Greek brought up in Egypt, Nazim Hikmet was a Turk born in Greece, and George Seferis was a Greek born in what is now Turkey.

In the 1920s, Greece was a constitutional monarchy. Turkey, under the strong rule of Kemal Atatürk, was about to begin a long period of enforced Europeanization, which entailed an often violent secularization and an industrial revolution overseen by the state. The Turkish method of modernization demanded strong state control. Political dissent was treated severely and opposition parties were not legalized until 1950. By 1960, political restrictions were again enforced and the military has been intermittently in power for the last three decades, though the recent return to civilian rule seems secure.

In 1924, Greece was proclaimed a republic with George II as nominal monarch, but by the end of the 1930s the country had reverted to military dictatorship under General Ioannis Metaxas. He was successful in defeating the Italians when they tried to invade at the start of World War II, but the Germans were able to overrun the country in 1941. The Nazis were not forced to leave until 1944, and as the best-organized resistance to the occupation was led by the Communists, there was a bloody civil war between the Communists and the Royalists after World War II. The Communists were defeated in 1949, and Greece was a parliamentary democracy until a military coup d'état in 1967. The army did not relinquish power until 1974.

The island of Cyprus, whose population was Greek and Turkish, was officially established as an independent republic in 1960, to avoid annexation by Greece or Turkey. Although the Greek president of Cyprus, Archbishop Makarios III, refused union with Greece, the Turkish Cypriots felt oppressed. In 1964, the Turkish air force attacked Greek Cypriots, but the United Nations was able to avert war until 1974, when tensions between Greek and Turkish Cypriots led to an invasion of Cyprus by Turkey, which claimed 40 percent of the island's territory. The United Nations established a buffer zone between the two populations, which govern themselves autonomously, while the island remains partitioned.

CONSTANTINE P. CAVAFY (1863–1933)

The greatest of modern Greek poets, Cavafy was born in Alexandria. His father, an exporter, benefited strongly from the monopolies given to Greeks in what is now Egypt. His success did not, however, cushion the family when he died in 1870. They moved to England, then returned to Alexandria impoverished in 1879, but were forced to flee again in 1882 when military harassment of foreigners drove the English to bombard the city. The Cavafy family lived in Istanbul for three years, after which time Cavafy returned to Alexandria, never to leave again. An odd, reclusive man, Cavafy worked in the Department of Irrigation. He published only limited editions of his work during his lifetime, while carefully cultivating his reputation; he was revered by Auden, Seferis, and Ritsos. He died of cancer on his seventieth birthday.

≈ Waiting for the Barbarians

What are we waiting for, assembled in the forum?

> The barbarians are due here today.

Why isn't anything going on in the senate?
Why are the senators sitting there without legislating?

> Because the barbarians are coming today.
> What's the point of senators making laws now?
> Once the barbarians are here, they'll do the legislating.

Why did our emperor get up so early,
and why is he sitting enthroned at the city's main gate,
in state, wearing the crown?

> Because the barbarians are coming today
> and the emperor's waiting to receive their leader.

He's even got a scroll to give him,
loaded with titles, with imposing names.

Why have our two consuls and praetors come out today
wearing their embroidered, their scarlet togas?
Why have they put on bracelets with so many amethysts,
rings sparkling with magnificent emeralds?
Why are they carrying elegant canes
beautifully worked in silver and gold?

      Because the barbarians are coming today
      and things like that dazzle the barbarians.

Why don't our distinguished orators turn up as usual
to make their speeches, say what they have to say?

      Because the barbarians are coming today
      and they're bored by rhetoric and public speaking.

Why this sudden bewilderment, this confusion?
(How serious people's faces have become.)
Why are the streets and squares emptying so rapidly,
everyone going home lost in thought?

      Because night has fallen and the barbarians haven't come.
      And some of our men just in from the border say
      there are no barbarians any longer.

Now what's going to happen to us without barbarians?
Those people were a kind of solution.

    TR. EDMUND KEELEY AND PHILIP SHERRARD

≈ The City

You said: "I'll go to another country, go to another shore,
find another city better than this one.
Whatever I try to do is fated to turn out wrong
and my heart lies buried like something dead.
How long can I let my mind moulder in this place?

Wherever I turn, wherever I look.
I see the black ruins of my life, here,
where I've spent so many years, wasted them, destroyed them totally."
You won't find a new country, won't find another shore.
This city will always pursue you.
You'll walk the same streets, grow old
in the same neighborhoods, turn gray in these same houses.
You'll always end up in this city. Don't hope for things elsewhere:
there's no ship for you, there's no road.
Now that you've wasted your life here, in this small corner,
you've destroyed it everywhere in the world.

TR. EDMUND KEELEY

GEORGE SEFERIS (1900–1971)

Born in Smyrna (now Izmir in Turkey), Seferis studied law at the Sorbonne in Paris. In 1922, the Greek population of his native city was displaced when the Turks recaptured it; he was to live in exile for the rest of his life. He entered the Greek foreign service and after the German invasion of Greece served the government-in-exile in Egypt, South Africa, and Italy. After the war, Seferis held a number of diplomatic posts, including the ambassadorship to Great Britain. His poetry, Greek in theme but influenced by all the currents of European modernism, has been recognized internationally. He was awarded the Nobel Prize for Literature in 1963.

≈ A Word for Summer

We've returned to autumn again; summer,
like an exercise book we're tired of writing in, remains
full of deletions, abstract designs,
question marks in the margin; we've returned
to the season of eyes gazing
into the mirror under the electric light
closed lips and people strangers
in rooms in streets under the pepper-trees

while the headlights of cars massacre
thousands of pale masks.
We've returned; we always set out to return
to solitude, a fistful of earth, to the empty hands.

And yet I used to love Syngrou Avenue
the double rise and fall of the great road
bringing us out miraculously to the sea
the eternal sea, to cleanse us of our sins;
I used to love certain unknown people
met suddenly at the end of day
talking to themselves like captains of a sunken armada,
evidence that the world is large.
And yet I used to love these roads here, these columns,
even though I was born on the other shore, close
to reeds and rushes, islands
where water gushed from the sand to quench
the thirst of a rower, even though I was born
close to the sea that I unwind and wind on my fingers
when I'm tired—I no longer know where I was born.

There still remains the yellow essence, summer,
and your hands touching medusas on the water
your eyes suddenly open, the first
eyes of the world, and the sea caves:
feet naked on the red soil.
There still remains the blond marble youth, summer,
a little salt dried in the rock's hollow
a few pine needles after the rain
scattered and red like broken nets.

I don't understand these faces I don't understand them,
sometimes they imitate death and then again
they gleam with the low life of a glow-worm
with a limited effort, hopeless,
squeezed between two wrinkles,
between two stained café tables;
they kill one another, grow smaller,
stick like postage stamps to window panes—
the faces of the other tribe.

We walked together, shared bread and sleep
tasted the same bitterness of parting
built our houses with what stones we had
set out in ships, knew exile, returned
found our women waiting—
they scarcely knew us, no one knows us.
And the companions wore statues, wore the naked
empty chairs of autumn, and the companions
destroyed their own faces: I don't understand them.
There still remains the yellow desert, summer,
waves of sand receding to the final circle
a drum's beat, merciless, endless,
flaming eyes sinking into the sun
hands in the manner of birds cutting the sky
saluting ranks of the dead who stand at attention
hands lost at a point beyond my control and mastering me:
your hands touching the free wave.

Autumn 1936

TR. EDMUND KEELEY AND PHILIP SHERRARD

≈ **The Last Day**

The day was cloudy. No one could come to a decision;
a light wind was blowing. "Not a north-easter, the sirocco," someone
    said.
A few slender cypresses nailed to the slope and the sea,
gray with shining pools, beyond.
The soldiers presented arms as it began to drizzle.
"Not a north-easter, the sirocco," was the only decision heard.
And yet we knew that by the following dawn
nothing would be left to us, neither the woman drinking sleep at our
    side
nor the memory that we were once men,
nothing at all by the following dawn.

"This wind reminds me of spring," said my friend
as she walked beside me gazing into the distance, "the spring

that came suddenly in winter by the closed-in sea.
So unexpected. So many years have gone. How are we going to die?"

A funeral march meandered through the thin rain.

TR. EDMUND KEELEY AND PHILIP SHERRARD

≈ Our Sun

This sun was mine and yours; we shared it.
Who's suffering behind the golden silk, who's dying?
A woman beating her dry breasts cried out: "Cowards,
they've taken my children and torn them to shreds, you've killed them
gazing at the fire-flies at dusk with a strange look,
lost in blind thought."
The blood was drying on a hand that a tree made green,
a warrior was asleep clutching the lance that flared against his side.

It was ours, this sun, we saw nothing behind the gold embroidery
then the messengers came, dirty and breathless,
stuttering unintelligible words

twenty days and nights on the barren earth with thorns only
twenty days and nights feeling the bellies of the horses bleeding

TR. EDMUND KEELEY AND PHILIP SHERRARD

≈ Last Stop

Few are the moonlit nights that I've cared for:
the alphabet of the stars—which you spell out
as much as your fatigue at the day's end allows
and from which you gather new meaning and hope—
you can then read more clearly.
Now that I sit here, idle, and think about it,
few are the moons that remain in my memory:
islands, color of a grieving Virgin, late in the waning
or moonlight in northern cities sometimes casting
over turbulent streets, rivers, and limbs of men

a heavy torpor.
Yet here last evening, in this our final port
where we wait for the hour of our return home to dawn
like an old debt, like money lying for years
in a miser's safe, and at last
the time for payment comes
and you hear the coins falling onto the table;
in this Etruscan village, behind the sea of Salerno
behind the harbors of our return, on the edge
of an autumn squall, the moon
outstripped the clouds, and houses
on the slope opposite became enamel:
Amica silentia lunae.

This is a train of thought, a way
to begin to speak of things you confess
uneasily, at times when you can't hold back, to a friend
who escaped secretly and who brings
word from home and from the companions,
and you hurry to open your heart
before exile forestalls you and alters him.
We come from Arabia, Egypt, Palestine, Syria;
the little state
of Kommagene, which flickered out like a small lamp,
often comes to mind,
and great cities that lived for thousands of years

and then became pasture land for cattle,
fields for sugar-cane and corn.
We come from the sand of the desert, from the seas of Proteus,
souls shriveled by public sins,
each holding office like a bird in its cage.
The rainy autumn in this gorge
festers the wound of each of us
or what you might term differently: nemesis, fate,
or simply bad habits, fraud and deceit,
or even the selfish urge to reap reward from the blood of others.
Man frays easily in wars;
man is soft, a sheaf of grass,
lips and fingers that hunger for a white breast
eyes that half-close in the radiance of day

and feet that would run, no matter how tired,
at the slightest call of profit.
Man is soft and thirsty like grass,
insatiable like grass, his nerves roots that spread;
when the harvest comes
he would rather have the scythes whistle in some other field;
when the harvest comes
some call out to exorcise the demon
some become entangled in their riches, other deliver speeches.
But what good are exorcisms, riches, speeches
when the living are far away?
Is man ever anything else?
Isn't it this that confers life?
A time for planting, a time for harvesting.

"The same thing over and over again," you'll tell me, friend.
But the thinking of a refugee, the thinking of a prisoner, the thinking
of a person when he too has become a commodity—
try to change it; you can't.
Maybe he would have liked to stay king of the cannibals
wasting strength that nobody buys,
to promenage in fields of agapanthi
to hear the drums with bamboo overhead,
as courtiers dance with prodigious masks.
But the country they're chopping up and burning like a
      pine-tree—you see it
either in the dark train, without water, the windows broken, night
      after night
or in the burning ship that according to the statistics is bound to
      sink—

this is riveted in the mind and doesn't change
this has planted images like those trees
that cast their branches in virgin forests
so that they take root in the earth and sprout again;
they cast their branches that sprout again, striding mile after mile;
our mind's a virgin forest of murdered friends.
And if I talk to you in fables and parables
it's because it's more gentle for you that way, and horror
really can't be talked about because it's alive,
because it's mute and goes on growing:

memory-wounding pain
drips by day drips in sleep.

To speak of heroes to speak of heroes: Michael
who left the hospital with his wounds still open,
perhaps he was speaking of heroes—the night
he dragged his foot through the darkened city—
when he howled, groping over our pain: "We advance in the dark,
we move forward in the dark . . ."
Heroes move forward in the dark.

Few are the moonlit nights that I care for.

Cava dei Tirreni, 5 October 1944

TR. EDMUND KEELEY AND PHILIP SHERRARD

NAZIM HIKMET (1902–1963)

Born in Salonika (now in Greece), the Turkish poet Hikmet began
writing poems while at a naval academy, from which he was expelled
for taking part in a strike. He taught in Anatolia (Turkey), became a
socialist, and published his first book of poetry in 1922. He enrolled at
the University of the Workers of the East in Moscow and returned to
Turkey in 1924. The years 1925 and 1933 were marked by exile (in the
USSR) and imprisonment (in Turkey). Finally he was arrested in 1938
for allegedly fomenting revolt among naval cadets; his trial, a legal
scandal, resulted in a thirty-five-year sentence. He wrote a great deal in
prison and was released in 1951, thanks in part to the efforts of Jean-
Paul Sartre, Pablo Neruda, and Pablo Picasso. For the remainder of his
life he lived in Eastern Europe. After his death, his poetry was pub-
lished in Turkey, where it had not been available since 1937.

≈ Letters from a Man in Solitary

I

I carved your name on my watchband
with my fingernail.

Where I am, you know,
I don't have a pearl-handled jacknife
(they won't give me anything sharp)
               or a plane tree with its head in the clouds.
Trees may grow in the yard,
but I'm not allowed
                    to see the sky overhead . . .
How many others are in this place?
I don't know.
I'm alone far from them,
they're all together far from me.
To talk to anyone besides myself
                    is forbidden.
So I talk to myself.
But I find my conversation so boring,
               my dear wife, that I sing songs.
And what do you know,
that awful, always off-key voice of mine
               touches me so
                         that my heart breaks.
And just like the barefoot orphan
          lost in the snow
in those old sad stories, my heart
—with moist blue eyes
and a little red runny nose—
               wants to snuggle up in your arms.
It doesn't make me blush
          that right now
                    I'm this weak,
                         this selfish,
                              this *human* simply.

No doubt my state can be explained
physiologically, psychologically, etc.
Or maybe it's
          this barred window,
               this earthen jug,
                    these four walls,
               which for months have kept me from hearing
               another human voice.

It's five o'clock, my dear.
Outside,
      with its dryness,
            eerie whispers,
                    mud roof,
and lame, skinny horse
      standing motionless in infinity
—I mean, it's enough to drive the man inside crazy with grief—
outside, with all its machinery and all its art,
a plains night comes down red on treeless space.

Again today, night will fall in no time.
A light will circle the lame, skinny horse,
And the treeless space, in this hopeless landscape
stretched out before me like the body of a hard man,
will suddenly be filled with stars.
We'll reach the inevitable end once more,
which is to say the stage is set
again today for an elaborate nostalgia.
Me,
the man inside.
once more I'll exhibit my customary talent,
and singing an old-fashioned lament
in the reedy voice of my childhood,
once more, by God, it will crush my unhappy heart
to hear you inside my head,
so far
away, as if I were watching you
                    in a smoky, broken mirror . . .

II

It's spring outside, my dear wife, spring.
Outside on the plain, suddenly the smell
of fresh earth, birds singing, etc.
It's spring, my dear wife,
the plain outside sparkles . . .
And inside the bed comes alive with bugs,
               the water jug no longer freezes.
and in the morning sun floods the concrete . . .
The sun—

every day till noon now
it comes and goes
from me, flashing off
         and on . . .
And as the day turns to afternoon, shadows climb the walls,
the glass of the barred window catches fire,
            and it's night outside,
         a cloudless spring night . . .
And inside this is spring's darkest hour.
In short, the demon called freedom,
with its glittering scales and fiery eyes,
possesses the man inside
         especially in spring . . .
I know this from experience, my dear wife,
         from experience . . .

III

Sunday today.
Today they took me out in the sun for the first time.
And I just stood there, struck for the first time in my life
         by how far away the sky is,
         how blue
         and how wide.
Then I respectfully sat down on the earth.
I leaned back against the wall.
For a moment no trap to fall into,
no struggle, no freedom, no wife.
Only earth, sun, and me . . .
I am happy.

1938

    TR. RANDY BLASING AND MUTLU KONUK

≈ Since I Was Thrown Inside

Since I was thrown inside
    the earth has gone around the sun ten times.
If you ask it:
        "Not worth mentioning—
          a microscopic span."

If you ask me:
        "Ten years of my life."
I had a pencil
        the year I was thrown inside.
I used it up after a week of writing.
If you ask it:
        "A whole lifetime."
If you ask me:
        "What's a week."

Since I've been inside
    Osman did his seven-and-a-half
        for manslaughter and left,
        knocked around on the outside for a while,
        then landed back inside for smuggling,
        served six months, and got out again;
        yesterday we had a letter—he's married,
        with a kid coming in the spring.

They're ten years old now
    the children who were born
        the year I was thrown inside.
And that year's foals, shaky on their spindly long legs,
    have been wide-rumped, contented mares for some time.
But the olive seedlings are still saplings,
                  still children.

New squares have opened in my far-off city
                since I was thrown inside.
And my family now lives
    in a house I haven't seen
        on a street I don't know.

Bread was like cotton, soft and white,
                the year I was thrown inside.
Then it was rationed,
and here inside men killed each other
           over black loaves the size of fists.
Now it's free again
but dark and tasteless.

The year I was thrown inside
   the SECOND hadn't started yet.

The ovens at Dachau hadn't been lit,
nor the atom bomb dropped on Hiroshima.

Time flowed like blood from a child's slit throat.
Then that chapter was officially closed.
Now the American dollar talks of a THIRD.

Still, the day has gotten lighter
           since I was thrown inside,
And "at the edge of darkness,
    pushing against the earth with their heavy hands,
           THEY've risen up" halfway.

Since I was thrown inside
   the earth has gone around the sun ten times.
And I repeat once more with the same passion
      what I wrote about THEM
         the year I was thrown inside:
"They who are numberless like ants in the earth,
         fish in the sea,
            birds in the air,
who are cowardly, brave,
     ignorant, wise,
         and childlike,
and who destroy
   and create,
my songs tell only of their adventures."
          And anything else,
            such as my ten years here,
            is just so much talk.

1947

TR. RANDY BLASING AND MUTLU KONUK

≈ **Things I Didn't Know I Loved**

it's 1962 March 28th
I'm sitting by the window on the Prague-Berlin train
night is falling
I never knew I liked
night descending like a tired bird on a smoky wet plain
I don't like
comparing nightfall to a tired bird

I didn't know I loved the earth
can someone who hasn't worked the earth love it
I've never worked the earth
it must be my only Platonic love

and here I've loved rivers all this time
whether motionless like this they curl skirting the hills
European hills crowned with chateaus
or whether stretched out flat as far as the eye can see
I know you can't wash in the same river even once
I know the river will bring new lights you'll never see
I know we live slightly longer than a horse but not nearly as long
    as a crow
I know this has troubled people before
                    and will trouble those after me
I know all this has been said a thousand times before
                    and will be said after me

I didn't know I loved the sky
cloudy or clear
the blue vault Andrei studied on his back at Borodino
in prison I translated both volumes of War and Peace into Turkish
I hear voices
not from the blue vault but from the yard
the guards are beating someone again

I didn't know I loved trees
bare beeches near Moscow in Peredelkino
they come upon me in winter noble and modest
beeches are Russian the way poplars are Turkish
"the poplars of Izmir

losing their leaves . . .
they call me The Knife..
                    lover like a young tree . . .
I blow stately mansions sky-high"
in the Ilgaz woods in 1920 I tied an embroidered linen handkerchief
                                to a pine bough for luck

I never knew I loved roads
even the asphalt kind
Vera's behind the wheel we're driving from Moscow to the Crimea
                                Koktebele
                    formerly "Goktepe ili" in Turkish
the two of us inside a closed box
the world flows past on both sides distant and mute
I was never so close to anyone in my life
bandits stopped me on the red road between Bolu and Geredé
                                when I was eighteen
apart from my life I didn't have anything in the wagon they could take
and at eighteen our lives are what we value least
I've written this somewhere before
wading through a dark muddy street I'm going to the shadow play
Ramazan night
a paper lantern leading the way
maybe nothing like this ever happened
maybe I read it somewhere an eight-year-old boy
                                going to the shadow play
Ramazan night in Istanbul holding his grandfather's hand
    his grandfather has on a fez and is wearing the fur coat
        with a sable collar over his robe
    and there's a lantern in the servant's hand
    and I can't contain myself for joy

flowers come to mind for some reason
poppies cactuses jonquils
in the jonquil garden in Kadikoy Istanbul I kissed Marika
fresh almonds on her breath
I was seventeen
my heart on a swing touched the sky
I didn't know I loved flowers
friends sent me three red carnations in prison

I just remembered the stars
I love them too
whether I'm floored watching them from below
or whether I'm flying at their side

I have some questions for the cosmonauts
were the stars much bigger
did they look like huge jewels on black velvet
                              or apricots on orange
did you feel proud to get closer to the stars
I saw color photos of the cosmos in *Ogonek* magazine now don't
     be upset comrades but nonfigurative shall we say or abstract
     well some of them looked just like such paintings which is to
     say they were terribly figurative and concrete
my heart was in my mouth looking at them
they are our endless desire to grasp things
seeing them I could even think of death and not feel at all sad
I never knew I loved the cosmos

snow flashes in front of my eyes
both heavy wet steady snow and the dry whirling kind
I didn't know I liked snow

I never knew I loved the sun
even when setting cherry-red as now
in Istanbul too it sometimes sets in postcard colors
but you aren't about to paint it that way

I didn't know I loved the sea
                              except the Sea of Azov
or how much

I didn't know I loved clouds
whether I'm under or up above them
whether they look like giants or shaggy white beasts

moonlight the falsest the most languid the most petit-bourgeois
strikes me
I like it

I didn't know I liked rain
whether it falls like a fine net or splatters against the glass my
    heart leaves me tangled up in a net or trapped inside a drop
    and takes off for uncharted countries I didn't know I loved
    rain but why did I suddenly discover all these passions sitting
    by the window on the Prague-Berlin train
is it because I lit my sixth cigarette
one alone could kill me
is it because I'm half dead from thinking about someone back in
    Moscow
her hair straw-blond eyelashes blue

the train plunges on through the pitch-black night
I never knew I liked the night pitch-black
sparks fly from the engine
I didn't know I loved sparks
I didn't know I loved so many things and I had to wait until sixty
    to find it out sitting by the window on the Prague-Berlin train
    watching the world disappear as if on a journey of no return

Moscow, 19 April 1962

TR. RANDY BLASING AND MUTLU KONUK

≈ The Evening Walk

You no sooner got out of prison
than you made your wife
        pregnant;
she's on your arm,
        and you're out for an evening walk around the
                neighborhood.
The lady's belly comes up to her nose.
She carries her sacred charge coyly.
You're respectful and proud.
The air is cool
—cool like baby hands.
You'd like to take it in your palms
        and warm it up.
The neighborhood cats are at the butcher's door,
and upstairs his curly wife

has settled her breasts on the window ledge
        and is watching the evening.
Half-light, spotless sky:
smack in the middle sits the evening star,
      sparkling like a glass of water.
Indian summer lasted long this year—
the mulberry trees are yellow,
        but the figs are still green.
Refik the typesetter and the milkman Yorgi's middle daughter
      have gone out for an evening stroll,
    their fingers locked.
The grocer Karabet's lights are on.
This Armenian citizen has not forgiven
      the slaughter of his father in the Kurdish mountains.
But he loves you,
because you also won't forgive
      those who blackened the name of the Turkish
             people.
The tuberculars of the neighborhood and the bedridden
      look out from behind the glass.
The washwoman Huriye's unemployed son,
       weighed down by his sadness
          goes off to the coffeehouse.
Rahmi Bey's radio is giving the news:
in a country in the Far East,
moon-faced yellow people
      are fighting a white dragon.
Of your people,
      four thousand five hundred Mehmets
        have been sent there to murder their brothers.
You blush
      with rage and shame
and not in general either—
   this impotent grief
   is all yours.
It's as if they'd knocked your wife down from behind
        and killed her child,
or as if you were back in jail
and they were making the peasant guards
            beat the peasants again.

All of a sudden it's night.
The evening walk is over.
A police jeep turned into your street,
your wife whispered:
                    "To our house?"

1950

            TR. RANDY BLASING AND MUTLU KONUK

YANNIS RITSOS (1909–1990)

Ritsos, a committed socialist, saw his books burned by the Fascist
government of Greece in 1936, and his work was banned until 1954.
During World War II, his health did not permit him to join the parti-
sans—he suffered from tuberculosis—but he was active politically.
During the civil war after World War II, he was forced to go into
hiding; he was captured in 1948 and spent four years in concentration
camps. Released in 1952, he began receiving official recognition and
prizes for his poetry. He was imprisoned again after the coup of 1967
and was released only because of ill health. The recipient of many
awards, Ritsos, along with Cavafy and Seferis, is considered among the
greatest modern Greek poets.

≈ Unanswered

Why are you taking me this way? Where does this road go? Tell me.
I can't see a thing. This isn't a road. Just stones.
Black beams. Lamp bracket. At least if I had
that cage—not this bird cage but that other one
with the heavy wire netting, with the naked statues. Back then
when they threw the dead bodies down from the roof terrace, I didn't
        say anything,
I gathered up those statues—felt sorry for them. Now I know:
the last thing that dies is the body. So speak to me.

Why are you taking me this way? I can't see a thing. It's great I can't
see.
The biggest obstacle against thinking to the end is glory.

TR. EDMUND KEELEY

≈ **Underneath Oblivion**

The only evidence remaining from his existence was his coat.
They hung it there in the large closet. It was forgotten,
shoved deeper by our own clothes, summer, winter,
new clothes each year for our fresh needs. Until,
one day, it caught our eye—perhaps because of its strange color,
perhaps because of its old-fashioned cut. On its buttons
there remained three circular, identical scenes:
the wall of the execution with four holes, and around it our memories.

TR. MINAS SAVAS

≈ **Audible and Inaudible**

A sudden, unexpected movement; his hand
clutched the wound to stop the bleeding,
though we had not heard the gunburst at all
or the whistling of a bullet. A short time later
he lowered his hand and smiled;
but again slowly he placed his palm
on that same spot, pulled out his wallet,
paid the waiter politely, and went out.
Just then the small coffee cup cracked by itself.
That at least we heard clearly.

TR. MINAS SAVAS

≈ **Afternoon**

The afternoon is all fallen plaster, black stones, dry thorns.
The afternoon has a difficult color made up of old footsteps halted in
mid-stride,
of old jars buried in the courtyard, covered by fatigue and straw.

Two killed, five killed, twelve—so very many.
Each hour has its killing. Behind the windows
stand those who are missing, and the jug full of water they didn't
    drink.

And that star that fell at the edge of evening
is like the severed ear that doesn't hear the crickets,
doesn't hear our excuses—doesn't condescend
to hear our songs—alone, alone,
alone, cut off totally, indifferent to condemnation or vindication.

    TR. EDMUND KEELEY

≈ The Missing

Others made the decisions, others spoke on their behalf. They,
as though missing, as though outside the law (truly, outside the law),
heard their names called out on the megaphones, heard the charges,
    their sentence,
saw notices piled up—how many long-winded threats and
    prohibitions—
metal notices, unreadable. Far, so far away, exiled,
foreigners in their own country, strangers to themselves,
    indifferent—they
who once believed in their responsibility, and generally, in the
    responsibility of citizens,
they with the broad knowledge (once learned by heart), the handsome
    ones, the naive ones. And now,
no temple dedicated to Amphiaraus; and on the small stony hill,
    asphodels everywhere,
no black ram for some sort of sacrifice, nor afterward lying down
inside the warm hide of the slaughtered animal, staying up all night
    waiting
to find a way out even through the gleam of some hallucination, to
    find an herb
to heal their country, and the whole world (as they said in those days),
and then finally to throw large gold coins in the fountain
to show their gratitude. Even though, all along, as far as we could
    remember
the sacristans found only copper pennies in the Amphiaraus fountain.

That was to be expected—people would forget, and gold was always
  needed.

March 19, 1968

TR. EDMUND KEELEY

≈ After the Defeat

After the heavy losses that the Athenians suffered at Aegospotami,
  and a little later,
after our final defeat, free talk is dead, so too is the Periclean glory,
the flowering of Art, the Gymnasia and the Symposia of our learned
  men. Now
deep silence and gloom in the Agora, and the Thirty Tyrants
  unaccountable.
Everything, even what is most ours, becomes ours by default, without
the possibility of any appeal, any defense or vindication,
any formal protest even. Our papers and books are burned,
our country's honor thrown out in the garbage. And if we might ever
  be allowed
to bring in an old friend as a witness, he would refuse to come
for fear of finding himself in our situation—and rightly so. That's why
it's really all right to be here: maybe we can establish a new
  relationship with nature,
gazing out, beyond the barbed wire, at a bit of sea, the stones, the
  grass,
or maybe a cloud at sunset, heavy, violet, touching. And maybe
someday we'll find a new Kimon, secretly guided
by the same eagle, to dig down and uncover the iron point of our
  spear,
rusted, that too eaten away, so that he can carry it officially through
  Athens
in a funeral procession or victory celebration, with music and wreaths.

March 21, 1968

TR. EDMUND KEELEY

≈ Not Even Mythology

The day ends that way, with brilliant colors, so lovely, without
anything at all happening for us. The guards forgotten in the
    guardhouses.
A boat floats in the shallows, the light golden and rose, foreign;
the nets in the slime gather black fish, fat and oily,
reflecting the glimmer of twilight. And later, when the lamps were lit,
we went inside and again returned to Mythology, searching
for some deeper correlation, some distant, general allegory
to soothe the narrowness of the personal void. We found nothing.
The pomegranate seeds and Persephone seemed cheap to us
in view of the night approaching heavily and the total absence.

Leros, March 31, 1968

TR. EDMUND KEELEY

ODYSSEAS ELYTIS (1911–1991)

Elytis was born on the island of Crete to a well-known industrial family.
Raised in Athens, he studied law and began publishing poetry in 1935.
In World War II he served as an officer during the so-called Albanian
Campaign, when the Greek army fought heroically to repel an Italian
invasion. After the war, he devoted himself almost exclusively to writing, as part of the generation that included Seferis. He was awarded the
Nobel Prize for Literature in 1979.

≈ Anniversary

I brought my life this far
To this spot which struggles
Forever near the sea
Youth upon the rocks, breast
To breast against the wind
Where is a man to go
Who is nothing other than a man
Reckoning with the coolness his green

Moments, with waters the visions
Of his hearing, with wings his remorse
O Life
Of a child who becomes a man
Forever near the sea when the sun
Teaches him to breathe there where the shadow
Of a seagull vanishes.

I brought my life this far
White addition, black total
A few trees and a few
Wet pebbles
Gentle fingers to caress a forehead
What forehead
Anticipation wept all night and is no more
Nor is anyone.
Would that a free footstep be heard
A rested voice rise
The poops ripple at the jetty, inscribing
A name in darker blue upon their horizon
A few years, a few waves
Sensitive rowing
In the bays surrounding love.

I brought my life this far
Bitter furrow in the sand that will vanish
—Whoever saw two eyes touch his silence
And mixed with their sunshine, closing a thousand worlds
Let him remind his blood in other suns
Nearer the light
There is a smile that pays for the flame—
But here in this ignorant landscape that loses itself
In an open and merciless sea
Success sheds
Whirling feathers
And moments that have become attached to the earth
Hard earth under the soles of impatient feet
Earth made for vertigo
A dead volcano.

I brought my life this far
A stone pledged to the liquid element
Beyond the islands
Lower than the waves
Next to the anchors
—When keels pass, splitting with passion
Some new obstacle, and triumph over it
And hope dawns with all its dolphins
The sun's gain in a human heart—
The nets of doubt draw in
A figure in salt
Carved with effort
Indifferent, white,
Which turns toward the sea the void of its eyes
Supporting infinity.

TR. EDMUND KEELEY AND PHILIP SHERRARD

≈ The March toward the Front

At daylight on St. John's, the day after Epiphany, we got our orders to move up to the front again, out there where you don't find weekdays or holidays. We were to take over the line the Artans had been holding till then, from Khimara to Tepeleni. The reason being they'd been fighting since the first day, without a break, and only about half of them were left and they couldn't take it any longer.

Twelve whole days we'd been back there, in the villages. And just as our ears were again getting used to the sweet creaking of the earth and just as we'd begun gingerly to make sense out of a dog's barking or the clang of a distant church bell, they tell us we have to go back to the only sound we really knew: the slow and heavy cannon, the dry and quick machineguns.

Night after night we trudged ahead without stopping, one behind the other, like the blind—sweating to pull our feet out of the mud, sometimes in it up to our knees. Because it was usually drizzling out there on the road, just as it was inside us. And the few times we'd pull up for a rest, not a word, everyone serious and silent, we'd share our raisins one by one under the light from a bit of pine kindling. Or sometimes, when we got the chance, we'd rip off our gear and scratch ourselves wildly until we drew blood. Because the lice were up to our ears, and that was even harder to take than being tired. Finally, through the darkness you'd hear a whistle signalling us to move out, and we'd push off again like pack animals to gain ground before daylight, when we'd make an open target for the planes. Because God didn't know about targets and things, so he'd stick to his habit of making the light come up at the same time every day.

Then, hidden in the ravines, we'd lay our heads down on the heavy side, the one that doesn't give out dreams. And the birds would get mad at us, thinking we weren't taking their talk seriously—and maybe also because we were disfiguring nature for no reason. We were farmers of a different kind, carrying picks and tools of a different kind, damn them.

Twelve whole days back there in the villages we'd gazed for hours on end at the shape of our faces in the mirror. And just as our eyes were getting used again to the old familiar features, and just as we'd begun gingerly to make sense of the bare upper lip or the sleep-filled cheek, they tell us we have to move, so that by the second night we began to feel we were changing again, more so by the third, until on the last, the fourth, it was clear we were no longer the same. Except it seemed we were marching along like a gang made up of all generations and ages, some from now and some from ancient times, turned white by too much beard. Scowling mountain chieftains with their headbands, tough priests, sergeants from the wars of '97 and '12, grim pioneers swinging their axes, Byzantine border guards with their maces and shields still covered with the blood of Turks and Bulgars. Together, no one speaking, groaning on side by side numberless years, crossing mountain ridges and the gorges between, no thought about anything else. Because just as people who get the bad breaks again and again become used to Evil and end up changing its name to Destiny or Fate, so we kept heading straight ahead for what we called the Plague, as we might have said the Fog or the Cloud—sweating to pull our feet out of the mud, sometimes in it up to our knees. Because it was usually drizzling out there on the road, just as it was inside us.

That we were very near the place where you don't find weekdays or holidays, sick people or healthy people, poor or rich, we now knew. Because the roar ahead, like a storm beyond the mountains, kept growing, so that in the end we could clearly read the slow and heavy cannon, the dry and quick machineguns. Also because more and more we started coming across the slow procession of the wounded, heading out the other way. And the medics, with the red cross on their arm bands, would set their stretchers down and spit on their hands, eyes wild for a cigarette. And when they'd hear where we were going, they'd shake their heads and start their tales of blood and terror. But we, the only thing we listened to were those other voices rising in the darkness, still scalding from the fire and brimstone of the depths. "Oi, oi, mana mou," "Oi, oi, mana mou." And sometimes, less often, the sound of stifled breathing, like a snore, and those who knew said that was the rattle of death.

Sometimes they dragged along with them prisoners captured a few hours before in surprise raids by our patrols. Their breath stank of wine and their pockets were full of canned goods or chocolates. But we had nothing, the bridges cut off behind us and our few mules helpless in the snow and the slippery muck.

Finally the moment came when we saw smoke rising here and there in the distance, and along the horizon the first bright red flares.

TR. EDMUND KEELEY AND GEORGE SAVIDIS

≈ The Autopsy

And so they found that the gold of the olive root had dripped in the recesses of his heart.

And from the many times that he had lain awake by candlelight waiting for the dawn, a strange heat had seized his entrails.

A little below the skin, the blue line of the horizon sharply painted. And ample traces of blue throughout his blood.

The cries of birds which he had come to memorize in hours of great loneliness apparently spilled out all at once, so that it was impossible for the knife to enter deeply.

Probably the intention sufficed for the evil.

Which he met—it is obvious—in the terrifying posture of the innocent. His eyes open, proud, the whole forest moving still on the unblemished retina

Nothing in the brain but a dead echo of the sky.

Only in the hollow of his left ear some light fine sand, as though in a shell. Which means that often he had walked by the sea alone with the pain of love and the roar of the wind.

As for those particles of fire on his groin, they show that he moved time hours ahead whenever he embraced a woman.

We shall have early fruit this year.

TR. EDMUND KEELEY AND PHILIP SHERRARD

≈ The Sleep of the Brave

They still smell of incense, and their faces are burnt by their crossing through the Great Dark Places.

There where they were suddenly flung by the Immovable

Face-down, on ground whose smallest anemone would suffice to turn the air of Hades bitter

(One arm outstretched, as though straining to be grasped by the future, the other arm under the desolate head, turned on its side,

As though to see for the last time, in the eyes of a disemboweled horse, the heap of smoking ruins)—

There time released them. One wing, the redder of the two, covered the world, while the other, delicate, already moved through space,

No wrinkle or pang of conscience, but at a great depth

The old immemorial blood that began painfully to etch, in the sky's blackness,

A new sun, not yet ripe,

That couldn't manage to dislodge the hoarfrost of lambs from live clover, but, before even casting a ray, could divine the oracles of Erebus . . .

And from the beginning, Valleys, Mountains, Trees, Rivers,

A creation made of vindicated feelings now shone, identical and re-
versed, there for them to cross now, with the Executioner inside
them put to death,

Villagers of the limitless blue:

Neither twelve o-clock striking in the depths nor the voice of the pole
falling from the heights retracted their footsteps.

They read the world greedily with eyes now open forever, there where
they were suddenly flung by the Immovable,

Face-down, and where the vultures fell upon them violently to enjoy
the clay of their guts and their blood.

TR. EDMUND KEELEY AND PHILIP SHERRARD

The Indo-Pakistani Wars

(1947–1972)

In 1947, India was proclaimed independent, and partitioned into India, East Pakistan, and West Pakistan, in an attempt to satisfy self-rule demands of Hindus and Moslems. Kashmir, an independent kingdom of Moslems ruled by a Hindu, was claimed by both India and West Pakistan (which bordered Kashmir). In October 1947, fighting began when Kashmiri Moslems revolted against Hindu landlords, drawing Pakistan and India into the battle. India's Hindu leader Mahatma Gandhi, who advocated peace between Hindus and Moslems, was assassinated by a Hindu factionalist in 1948. His death, mourned by both Hindus and Moslems, united the factions long enough for United Nations intervention to effect a cease-fire.

In 1965, General Muhammad Ayub Khan took power in Pakistan and aligned his nation with China, which led to war between India and Pakistan. The United States, the Soviet Union, and Great Britain mediated a settlement at Tashkent in 1966, but in 1971, a civil war erupted in Pakistan, which resulted in the establishment of East Pakistan as the new nation of Bangladesh. The United States supported Pakistan and, accusing India of attempting to destabilize that country, cut off India's American credit. Pakistani war planes then attacked Indian bases in Kashmir, which led to a twelve-day war between India and both Bangladesh and West Pakistan, until India was able to impose a cease-fire.

FAIZ AHMAD FAIZ (1911–1984)

Born in Punjab, Faiz served in the Indian army during World War II. After the partition of India and Pakistan, Faiz chose to live in Pakistan. He worked as a newspaper editor until 1951, when he was arrested for suspected involvement in the Rawalpindi conspiracy, in which a number of army officers and others allegedly planned an antigovernment coup d'état. Sentenced to death, he spent four years in prison, much of the time in solitary confinement. Committed to the ideals of social revolution, he was jailed again by a new military government in 1958. After the fall of President Zulfikar Ali Bhutto, Faiz lived in Beirut until the Israeli invasion and then in Lahore, where he died. Noted for skill with traditional Arabic and Persian forms, Faiz also worked in support of the recognition of regional languages such as Punjabi, Sindhi, Balochi, and Pashto.

≈ Once Again the Mind

Today, as usual, the mind goes hunting for a word,
one filled with venom, a word
sultry with honey, heavy with love,
    smashing with fury.
The word of love must be brilliant as a glance
which greets the eye like a kiss on the lips,
bright as a summer river, its surface streaming gold,
joyous as the moment when the beloved enters
    for the appointed meeting.

The word of rage must be a ferocious blade
that brings down for all time the oppressor's citadel.
This word must be dark as the night of a crematorium;
if I bring it to my lips
    it will blacken them forever.

Today every instrument is forsaken by its melody,
and the singer's voice goes searching for its singer.
Today the chords of every harp are shredded
like a madman's shirt. Today
the people beg each gust of wind
to bring any sound at all, even a lamentation,
even a scream of anguish,
or the last trump crying the hour of doom.

   TR. NAOMI LAZARD

≈ No Sign of Blood

Nowhere, nowhere is there any trace of blood.
Neither on the hands of the assassin,
    nor under his fingernails,
not a spot on his sleeve, no stain on the walls.
No red on the tip of his dagger,

no dye on the point of his bayonet.
There is no sign of blood anywhere.
This invisible blood was not given in the service of kings
for a reward of bounty, nor as a religious sacrifice
        to obtain absolution.
It was not spilled on any battlefield for the sake of honor,
celebrated later in script on some banner.
The orphaned blood of murdered parents screamed out
        for justice;
no one had time or patience to listen to its cries.
There was no plaintiff, no witness;
        therefore no indictment.
It was the blood of those whose homes are made of dust,
blood that in the end became the nourishment for dust.

    TR. NAOMI LAZARD

≈ The Tyrant

This is the festival; we will inter hope
with appropriate mourning. Come, my people.
We will celebrate the massacre of the multitudes.
Come, my people.
I have caused the ghost city known as Limbo
to be inhabited. I have liberated you
from night and from day.

You desire something from dawn's first brushstrokes?
You make a wish on your bed of dreams?
I have decreed death to vision;
all eyes have been excised.
I have sent all dreams to the gibbet.

No bough will display its wealth of blossoms.
The spring that is near will not bring
the embers of Nimrod's fire.
This season's beads of rain will not shimmer
like pearl drops; its clouds
will cover you with dust and ashes.

Mine is the new religion, the new morality.
Mine are the new laws, and a new dogma.
From now on the priests in God's temple
will touch their lips to the hands of idols.
Proud men, tall as Cypress trees, will bend
to lick the dwarves' feet, and taste the clay.

On this day all over earth the door
                    of beneficent deeds is bolted.
Every gate of prayer throughout heaven
                    is slammed shut today.

TR. NAOMI LAZARD

≈ A Prison Daybreak

Night wasn't over
when the moon stood beside my bed
and said, "You've drunk your sleep to the dregs,
your share of that wine is finished for this night."

My eyes tore themselves from a dream of passion—
they said farewell to my lover's image, still
lingering in the night's stagnant waters
that were spread, like a sheet, over the earth.
Silver whirlpools began their dervish dance
as lotuses of stars fell from the moon's hands.
Some sank. Some rose to the surface,
floated, and opened their petals.
Night and daybreak had fallen desperately
into each other's arms.

In the courtyard,
the prisoners emerged slowly
from a backdrop of gloom. They were shining,
for the dew of sleep had washed, for that moment,
all grief for their country from their eyes,
all agony of separation from their lovers.

But there's a drum, far off. A siren wails.
The famished guards, their faces pale,

begin their reluctant rounds, in step
with stifled screams from torture rooms.
The cries of those who'll be broken on the rack awake,
just as light breezes intoxicated with sleep awake.
Poison awakes. Nothing in the world is asleep.
A door opens in the distance, another is shut.
A chain rasps, then shrieks.
A knife opens a lock's heart, far off,
and a window begins to break its head,
like a madman, against the wind.

So it is the enemies of life awake
and crush the delicate spirit
that keeps me company in my barren despair
while the prisoners and I wait, all day and night,
for a rebel prince of legends to come
with burning arrows, ready to pierce
these tyrant hearts of stone and steel.

TR. AGHA SHAHID ALI

War in the

Middle East

(1948–1991)

As a consequence of World War I and the defeat of the Ottoman Empire, the British and French gained a political foothold in the Middle East. This colonial period (which did not last long past World War II) had a long-term effect on the region, as France and Britain established the boundaries of future countries according to their own needs for influence and oil. The British, then in control of Palestine, promised a portion to the Jews, who had begun to settle in Palestine during the 1890s. The French created the state of Lebanon by effecting a compromise between Christians and Arabs, who were traditionally suspicious of each other. Similarly, Syria was formed from a loose coalition of disputing factions, tribes, and groups.

The constitutive rift came in 1948 with the foundation of the state of Israel by the United Nations. The original agreement called for separate Palestinian and Jewish states. With the declaration of Jewish independence, however, the neighboring Arab countries attacked Israel. They were defeated, and Israel, the victor, was able to occupy and claim the land intended for the Palestinian state. Dispossessed and disenfranchised, many Palestinians fled, and the refugees, now stateless and homeless, were forced to settle in Arab countries—the majority on the bank of the Jordan River, others in Egypt and in the Gaza Strip. As a result of another victory, in the Six-Day War of 1967, Israel began occupation of the West Bank and the Gaza Strip (as well as the relatively unpopulated Golan Heights) and found itself with an even larger Palestinian population.

After a relatively brief but difficult war in 1973, the region settled into a fitful peace: the Palestinian Liberation Organization launched attacks on Israel and fought against its hosts and supporters; the Arab states were permanently at war with Israel; and the Jewish state had to come to terms with its increasing Palestinian population. There was a diplomatic break in 1978, when Anwar Sadat of Egypt came to Jerusalem; a peace treaty was signed between Egypt and Israel in 1979. Sadat was later assassinated.

Because most of the world had mistakenly seen the Arabs as a united bloc after 1948, deep tensions between Arabs were often ignored. They became clearer after the Six-Day War; when the Jordanians expelled the Palestinian Liberation Organization in 1970, the Lebanese Moslems accepted them into their country. The Moslem faction saw them as an instrument against Israel and, more important, against the Lebanese Christians. The fragile constitution of Lebanon, which had granted hegemony to the Christians, had become outdated. There were more Arabs than Christians in the country, and even then, the Moslems belonged to different (and frequently warring) sects: the Sunni Moslems and the Shiites were positioned against one another (a tension that became clearer during the Iranian revolution in 1979), and both were at direct odds with the Maronite Christians.

The inevitable civil war began in 1975. In 1982, Israel invaded Lebanon with the objective of destroying the Palestinian Liberation Organization and ensuring the supremacy of Israel's allies, the Maronites. The Israelis occupied the southern part of the country and the Syrians the northern half. The country began to fall apart, in spite of American hopes of halting the disintegration—hopes that faded when the U.S. Marine barracks were attacked by suicide bombers in Beirut in 1983, killing over two hundred American soldiers. Lebanon would continue to decline until the late 1980s. The Israelis withdrew into southern Lebanon in 1985.

The neutralization of the Palestinian Liberation Organization in 1982 seemed, for a time, to limit any Palestinian threat to Israel. In the 1980s, however, frustrated Palestinians, reduced to second-class citizenship, harassed by the Israeli authorities, and limited in their economic prospects, began to take their future into their own hands. Rather than rely on their compatriots in other countries, they began in 1987 to rebel against the occupation of the West Bank and the Gaza which had endured for two decades. Their new resistance, the Intifada, has been met by harsh Israeli retaliation: the massacre of Palestinians on the Temple Mount in 1990 was the result of an accident, but the use of live ammunition against unarmed crowds was judged excessive by an Israeli court.

Military occupation has taken its toll on both the Palestinians and the Israelis, just as constant war has been difficult for the Jewish state. The complicated loyalties that the situation requires have exacted an extraordinary human price.

EDMOND JABÈS (1912–1991)

Born into a French-speaking community of Jews in Egypt, Jabès studied in Paris in the early 1930s and became a friend of the surrealists, especially of Max Jacob. He served as an officer in the British army in Palestine during World War II. In 1956, as a result of the Suez Crisis, he was forced to leave Egypt and emigrate to France with his family.

Gradually, he broke away from the traditional formal strictures of poetry and started to write in a format that included aphorisms, dialogues, and narratives, all reminiscent of the Jewish tradition of Biblical and legal commentary.

≈ The Beginning of the Book

"The book does not begin," he replied.
"All beginnings are already in the book."

A priori doubtful, interpretation of the book, because, at every turn, it is challenged by the opaque light of some word that might well be the key.
The text is rich where it shares this darkness.

"To know that we can only penetrate the book after it has been taken from us.
"That we inhabit only our losses," he said.

Light needs much dark in order to dazzle.

We shall have written on the wavy surface of a breath!

TR. ROSEMARIE WALDROP

≈ The Book

Someone said, "Our right hand is in the book. But the left has the privilege of opening and closing.
"Thus both hands preside over the morrow of the book."
Another replied: "If I figure in the book, my name must be quoted somewhere.
"But nowhere do I find a trace of this word."

Dialogue recovered its place, which had long stood empty. It resurfaced suddenly, on its own.

It was again the first day of the word.

... dialogue constantly thwarted like the cork
left to the whim of the wave.
      Perpetual. Perpetuated.

"The sea is my memory, my awesome memory," thought the swimmer heading out from the shore.

We shall never master the horizons.

    TR. ROSEMARIE WALDROP

≈ The Desert

Hidden language, not that of hands or eyes, a language beyond gesture, beyond looks, smiles or tears that we had to learn! Ah, what desert will revive it now?

We thought we were done with crossing the desolate stretch of land where the word had dragged us, making us and our wanderings bear amazed witness to its perennial nature.

And here silence leads us into its glass kingdom, vaster yet at first sight, breaking all trace of our passage.

... primal silence which we cannot escape.

Do not confuse *hothouse* and *desert, plant* and *speech*. Silence shelters, sand shifts.

Princely, the plant; the word, a particle of dust.

Image stripped of its verbal eloquence—don't we speak of a telling likeness?—representing nothing. Yellowed. Does forgetting have a color? Ah, this yellow, color of awakened sand.

There lies the better part of my past. What persists, writing recovers in fragments.

Write, write, write in order to remember.

You only understand what you destroy.

    TR. ROSEMARIE WALDROP

≈ Notebook, II

To talk alone, at the threshold, with already-gone, has-been, to-be-announced. To be your own legend.

Close in on the real: vocation of vocables.

"We share the same language. You only use it to state who you are, I, to find out who I am. We are both wrong. Perhaps this is why we are drawn to each other," he wrote.

"My mother tongue is foreign. Hence I am on easy terms with my strangeness," he said.

And added: "I have patiently forged my language out of words that were foreigners, making them into brothers."

And had he not written earlier: "I did not take your soul: I gave it to you?"

What is a foreigner?—One who makes you think you are at home.

(Creation is play of light and dark, of war zone and zone of peace. But who will define them?

Cries and laughter—ah, all my books blur into the word "write."

To take the contradictions into our keeping.

At the edge of Emptiness.)

TR. ROSEMARIE WALDROP

≈ The Desert, II

You might imagine the desert as a rectangle without angles, as a circle without circumference, but you could never imagine it as a square or a triangle. Because thinking of it as a square would immediately wall it in your memory, and approaching it as a triangle would assign this formless memory a base and a peak.

Death is a whirlwind with life for its air mass or water ration.

Passive, our life in its most split duration; dynamic in its fury to live, our death.

The desert gives us an image of flat, immovable eternity.

Was there an end to my road?
"Sandstorms blind us," said a sage, "to teach us to walk with lowered head, in the footsteps of the man before us. For the goal comes only after the goal."

Despair hatches hope, as, in a mountain cave, an eagle wounded by a hunter's bullet, her eggs red with blood.

"When, in the desert, you hear a grain of sand tell you the history of every grain of sand, you know that you have finally become infinite listening. Readiness regained!" he said.

Scooping up a handful of sand the nomad said: "This is my life," then, repeating the gesture with his other hand: "And this my death. All the rest is mirage."

What else to add for those who know all about me?
Ah, this else: the power of nothingness, the impotence of the word.

TR. ROSEMARIE WALDROP

FADWA TUQUAN (1917–)

The sister of Ibrahim Tuquan, a well-known Palestinian poet of the 1930s and 1940s, Fadwa Tuquan spent her childhood in Nablus on the West Bank, in what was then Jordan. After the Six-Day War in 1967, when Israel began to occupy the West Bank and Gaza, Fadwa Tuquan felt the pressure of her prominence within the Palestinian community. She is considered a major voice for the Palestinians, one of the finest writers in the Arab world.

≈ Face Lost in the Wilderness

Do not fill postcards with memories.
Between my heart and the luxury of passion
stretches a desert where ropes of fire
blaze and smoulder, where snakes
coil and recoil, swallowing blossoms
with poison and flame.

No! Don't ask me to remember. Love's memory
is dark, the dream clouded;
love is a lost phantom
in a wilderness night.
Friend, the night has slain the moon.
In the mirror of my heart you can find no shelter,
only my country's disfigured face
her face, lovely and mutilated,
her precious face . . .

How did the world revolve in this way?
Our love was young. Did it grow in this horror?
In the night of defeat, black waters
covered my land, blood on the walls
was the only bouquet.
I hallucinated: 'Open your breast,
open your mother's breast for an embrace
priceless are the offerings!'
The jungle beast was toasting in the
tavern of crime; winds of misfortune
howled in the four corners.
He was with me that day.

I didn't realise morning
would remove him.
Our smiles cheated sorrow
as I raved: 'Beloved stranger!
Why did my country become a gateway
to hell? Since when are apples bitter?
When did moonlight stop bathing orchards?
My people used to plant fields and love life
Joyfully they dipped their bread in oil

Fruits and flowers tinted the land
with magnificent hues—
will the seasons ever again
give their gifts to my people?

Sorrow—Jerusalem's night is silence and smoke.
They imposed a curfew; now nothing beats in the
heart of the City but their bloodied heels
under which Jerusalem trembles
like a raped girl.

Two shadows from a balcony
stared down at the City's night.
In the corner a suitcase of clothes,
souvenirs from the Holy Land—
his blue eyes stretched like sad lakes.
He loved Jerusalem. She was his mystical lover.
On and on I ranted. 'Ah, love! Why did God abandon
my country? Imprisoning light, leaving us
in seas of darkness?'
The world was a mythical dragon standing
at her gate. 'Who will ever solve this mystery,
beloved, the secret of these words?'

Now twenty moons have passed,
twenty moons, and my life continues.
Your absence too continues. Only one memory remaining:
The face of my stricken country filling my heart.

And my life continues—
the wind merges me with my people
on the terrible road of rocks and thorns.
But behind the river, dark forests of spears
sway and swell; the roaring storm
unravels mystery, giving to dragon-silence
the power of words.

A rush and din, flame and sparks
lighting the road—
one group after another
falls embracing, in one lofty death.

The night, no matter how long, will continue
to give birth to star after star
and my life continues,
my life continues.

TR. NAOMI SHIHAB NYE

≈ After Twenty Years

Here the foot prints stop;
Here the moon
Lies with the wolves, the dogs, and the stones,
Behind the rocks and the tents, behind the trees.
Here the moon
Sells its face every night,
For a dagger, a candle, a braid of rain.
Don't throw a stone in their fire;
Don't steal the glass rings
From the gypsies' fingers.
They slept, and so did the fish and the stones and the trees.

Here the foot prints stop;
Here the moon was in labour.
Gypsies!
Give her then the glass rings
And the blue bracelets.

TR. UNKNOWN

≈ I Won't Sell His Love

What chance
Sweet dreamlike chance
Joined us here in this distant land
Here two strange souls we
Were united by the Muse
Who carried us away
Our souls becoming a song
Floating on a Mozart air
In its precious world

You said: How deep your eyes
How sweet you are
You said it with hushed, echoing desire
For we were not alone
And in your eyes an invitation
And in my depths intoxication
What intoxication
I am a woman so forgive my heart its vanity
When your murmur caresses it: How deep your eyes
How sweet you are

O Poet, in my country
My beloved country
I have a sweetheart waiting
He is my countryman I won't squander
His heart
He is my countryman I won't sell
His love
For the world's treasures
For the shining stars
For the Moon
Yet intoxication grips my heart
As in your eyes drift love's shadows
Or invitation glimmers

I am a woman so forgive my heart its vanity
When your murmur caresses it: How deep your eyes
How sweet you are

TR. MOUNAH AIKHOURI AND HAMID ALGAR

≈ Behind Bars, Sel.

I

My mother's phantom hovers here
her forehead shines before my eyes
like the light of stars
She might be thinking of me now,
dreaming

(Before my arrest
I drew letters in a book
new and old
I painted roses
grown with blood
and my mother was near me
blessing my painting)
I see here
on her face silence and loneliness now
and in the house
silence and loneliness
My satchel there on the bookshelf
and my school uniform
on the hanger
I see her hand reaching out
brushing the dust from it
I follow my mother's steps
and listen to her thoughts
yearn to her arms and the face of day

TR. HATEM HUSSAINI

≈ Song of Becoming

They're only boys
who used to frolic and play
releasing in the western wind
their blue red green kites
the colour of the rainbow
jumping, whistling, exchanging spontaneous jokes
and laughter
fencing with branches, assuming the roles
of great heroes in history.

They've grown suddenly now
grown more than the years of a lifetime
grown, merged with a secret word of love
carried its letters like a Bible, or a Quran
read in whispers

They've grown more than the years of a lifetime
become the trees plunging deep into the earth
and soaring high towards the sun
They're now the voice that rejects
they're the dialectics of destruction and building anew
the anger burning on the fringes of a blocked horizon
invading classroom, streets, city quarters
centering on the squares
and facing sullen tanks with a stream of stones.

With plain rejection they now shake the gallows of the dawn
assailing the night and its deluge
They've grown, grown more than the years of a lifetime
become the worshipped and the worshipper
When their torn limbs merged with the stuff of our earth,
they became a legend
They grew, and became the bridge
they grew, grew and became
larger than all poetry.

TR. NAOMI SHIHAB NYE

ABBA KOVNER (1918–1987)

Kovner's family, attempting to flee from the Crimea to Palestine, were caught in Sebastopol at the outbreak of World War I. After the war, they returned to what was then Vilnius, where Kovner grew up and joined the Zionist Socialist youth movement. In 1943, during the German occupation, he became the leader of the armed resistance movement in Vilnius, the United Partisan Organization. In 1947, he tried to enter Palestine secretly, but was arrested while still aboard ship and imprisoned by the British, first in Cairo, then in Jerusalem. He was freed by the Jewish underground and went to live on a kibbutz.

≈ What's Not in the Heart

I

I do not hold a mirage in my hand—
my shirt's in my hand. The plain filled
with my wheat. All of it. Soaked by dew
flat at my feet. Its beauty
turns each image pale. The returning heron
and the apple garden. Sun
plucks at my shoulders like my daughter's fingers.
And this day
recalling soon
the smell of the harvest:
this morning (I say to myself)
even in the burned forest the bird
has come back to sing.

II

Useless. I try now to understand that what happened
happened. We declared two minutes of silence
so silence would not grow in the windows
of our homes. And no way out, my brother.
The world does not stand on a cry

at night. On a man
with something in his heart, because
what's in the heart is nothing. Because
the living live by the will of those who go
where they were not willing to go.

Useless: I try now to define who you were—
word-shadows! Only your returning shadow
exists. My hands will never
touch you. Your coffin
never leaves my shoulders.

        TR. SHIRLEY KAUFMAN

≈ **It's Late**

Naked soil is the way to my beloved.
I come to her like someone coming to a tryst.
I quietly try to rebuild
a city, transparent. To sail confused houses
in two-way streets. To give them back
their faces, to arrange
rotating crops, to let the sea
break through into the small square
rooms and wash the frost flowers
and sand stripes alternately from the windows
like an old-fashioned devoted servant. Already

there is a road.
A road sign.
It's really possible to go. I will only hang
my hat to sway
on the acacia branch. I will mount
the new streetlights in my eyes so they won't close
in difficult moments. On the neck of the weather vane
I have already fastened my tie
with the pure gold pin
I inherited from my father. I will spread

my shirt before the first policeman's
dog who comes on time
running in front of his master. And my shoes
I will leave my shoes—
for the cat
until a better story is found
for the city children
and you
only you, my little sister, will I take with me
on my back. To carry you beyond
my naked plot of soil.

TR. SHIRLEY KAUFMAN

≈ Potato Pie

I

The father wore an overcoat with a narrow velvet collar.

II

Once in a while there was a striped suit underneath and a shirt,
always neatly pressed.

III

Sorrow already on his clothes
like an eternal crease.

IV

There was no radio at home. And no end to his curiosity,
his thoughts awake at night walking
everywhere.

V

In his time he figured out correctly
the results of the Russo-Japanese War, a bit late.

VI

He liked potato pie with salt herring.

VII

When he couldn't have herring he made do
with the brine.

VIII

Suddenly the first World War
was over. A year later
Poland's liberation began. In 1919
he inherited a stone building

IX

in the capital. On the bank of the river, with 22
condemned apartments. When he was already
a landlord, with tenants

X

and creditors

XI

he still loved the potato pie his wife
made in all seasons.

XII

They loved the sea
because another country came close
reflected in its waters.

XIII

He dreamed he'd go back

XIV

. . . .

XV

So he went back. The day he imagined
his father returned
he lost his voice. And more.

XVI

He stood on the threshold.

XVII

There was no witness to see
the father
still standing on the threshold

XVIII

not remembering the time. How long
his mouth was wide open

XIX

and silent.
Until he moved his lips. Until his tongue
began to work, until his voice was back
and the echo
the father

XX

behind the muslin curtain and the boy,
a buzzing in his head.

XXI

From that time on he feels a buzzing
in his head. Like pieces of a heart scraping his temples
and not only when

XXII

there's an uninvited guest,
present without having come. Or
when he plays with his grandson: all the colors of the rainbow
in a soap bubble ready to burst
on the window screen.
Then
it's there—this buzzing in his head!

XXIII

The pain passes as it comes.
Often
there's nothing in its place.

TR. SHIRLEY KAUFMAN

≈ To Myself

Mathematicians take a huge area like a whole world
and divide it into smaller areas, identical,
smaller than the eye can see.
Parts so exact don't need
an empty space between them.
Mathematicians
do it with only three forms:
isosceles triangle, square,
and hexagon, reliable instruments,
of course. My fear taught me
to try something else: when I could no longer bear
the space surrounding me, I wanted to manage
something smaller
like a cell, dividing itself
without fission. Not looking for answers
to every question. Only to discover what is
nagging me. Still trying: forty years
and more. Why did I want to get rid
of that hidden fear?
After all, if I fall dead in the empty space
it's not the mathematicians who'll be surprised.

TR. SHIRLEY KAUFMAN

YEHUDA AMICHAI (1924–)

Israel's foremost living poet was born in Germany in 1924. His family fled the Nazis and emigrated to what was then Palestine in 1936. Educated in Jerusalem, Amichai served with the Jewish Brigade during World War II and fought during the Israeli War of Independence in 1956 as well as in the Six-Day War in 1967. The author of several novels and plays, he lives in Jerusalem and has frequently taught in the United States. His poetry is deeply spiritual, and often engages in conversations, sometimes comedic, with the Supreme Being.

≈ Ibn Gabirol

Sometimes pus
Sometimes a poem.

Something always bursts out.
And always pain.

My father was a tree in a forest of fathers
Covered in green cotton wool.

Oh, widows of the flesh, orphans of the blood,
I must escape.

Eyes sharp as tin openers
Opened heavy secrets.

But through the wound on my chest
God peers into the world.

I am the door
to his apartment.

TR. ASSIA GUTMANN

≈ Like Our Bodies' Imprint

Like our bodies' imprint,
Not a sign will remain that we were in this place.
The world closes behind us,
The sand straightens itself.

Dates are already in view
In which you no longer exist,
Already a wind blows clouds
Which will not rain on us both.

And your name is already on the passenger lists of ships
And in the registers of hotels
Whose names alone
Deaden the heart.

The three languages I know,
All the colors in which I see and dream:

None will help me.

TR. ASSIA GUTMANN

≈ God Has Pity on Kindergarten Children

God has pity on children in kindergartens,
He pities school children—less.
But adults he pities not at all.

He abandons them,
Sometimes they have to crawl on all fours
In the roasting sand
To reach the dressing station,
And they are streaming with blood.

But perhaps
He will have pity on those who love truly
And take care of them
And shade them,
Like a tree over the sleeper on the public bench.

Perhaps even we will spend on them
Our last pennies of kindness
Inherited from mother,

So that their own happiness will protect us
Now and on other days.

TR. ASSIA GUTMANN

≈ Two Songs of Peace

I

My son smells of peace when I lean over him.
It isn't just the soap.

Everybody was once the child with the smell of peace.
(And in the whole country there isn't a single windmill which turns.)

O torn country, like torn clothes
Which can't be mended,
And hard, lonely forefathers in Hebron's grave
In childless silence.

My son smells of peace.
His mother's womb
Promised him that
Which God can't promise us.

II

My love was not in the war.
She learns love and history
Off my body, which was in two, or three.
And at night.
When my body makes battles into peace
She is bewildered.
Her perplexity is her love. And her learning.
Her wars and her peace, her dream.

And I am now in the middle of my life.
The time when one begins to collect
Facts, and many details,
And exact maps
Of a country we shall never occupy
And of an enemy and lover
Whose borders we shall never cross.

TR. ASSIA GUTMANN

≈ If I Forget Thee, Jerusalem

If I forget thee, Jerusalem,
Then let my right be forgotten.
Let my right be forgotten, and my left remember.
Let my left remember, and your right close
And your mouth open near the gate.

I shall remember Jerusalem
And forget the forest—my love will remember,
Will open her hair, will close my window,
Will forget my right,
Will forget my left.

If the west wind does not come
I'll never forgive the walls,
Or the sea, or myself.
Should my right forget,
My left shall forgive,
I shall forget all water,
I shall forget my mother.

If I forget thee, Jerusalem,
Let my blood be forgotten.
I shall touch your forehead,
Forget my own,
My voice change
For the second and last time
To the most terrible of voices—
Or silence.

TR. ASSIA GUTMANN

ADONIS (ALI AHMAD SA'ID) (1930–   )

Adonis, the pseudonym of Ali Ahmad Sa'id, was born in a village in Syria. He attended the lycée in Tartus, studied law and philosophy at the University of Damascus, and began writing poetry early. After emigrating to Lebanon in 1956, he founded the journal *Shi'ir,* which was pivotal in establishing modern Arabic poetry. He was an influential member of the first generation of Arabs to break with the traditional Arabic forms and write free verse. His work is also marked by a strongly nontraditional sense of social commitment.

≈ The New Noah

I

We sailed in the Ark
Our oars were God's promises.
Under the rain and dirt
We survived, but not mankind.
We went along with the waves
And the sky was like a rope of dead people
On which we tied our lives.
Through a window of prayers we reached the sky.

'Lord, why did you save us above all other
People and creatures?
Where will you throw us, to your other land,
To our original home,
To the leaves of death, to the wind of life?
Lord, our fear of the sun
Runs in our blood. We have lost faith in light,
We have lost faith in tomorrow
Where we used to begin a new life.
Oh, if only we had not been a seed
Of creation, of the earth,
If only we had remained soil or live coals,
If only we had stayed half-way
So as not to see the world,
So as not see its hell and its God twice.'

II

If time was to start all over again
And life's face was covered with water
And the earth trembled and God was mad
And Noah asked me: 'Save the living'
I would not listen to God,
I would go about on my Ark
Clearing the pebbles and dirt
From the sockets of the dead,
Opening their souls to the flood,
Whispering in their veins:
We have returned from our wanderings,

We have come out of the cave
And changed the sky of years,
We are sailing and fear cannot bend us,
And we do not listen to God's word.

We have an appointment with death,
We have become familiar with our shores of despair,
We have grown to accept its frozen sea with iron water
And we sail through it to its end.
We carry on moving and never listen to that God,
We long for a new god.

TR. ABDULLAH AL-UDHARI

≈ Elegy for the Time at Hand

I

Chanting of banishment,
exhaling flame,
the carriages of exile
breach the walls.

Or are these carriages
the battering sighs of my verses?

Cyclones have crushed us.
Sprawled in the ashes of our days,
we glimpse our souls
passing
on the sword's glint
or at the peaks of helmets.
An autumn of salt spray
settles on our wounds.
No tree can bud.
No spring . . .

Now in the final act,
disaster tows our history
toward us on its face.
What is our past

but memories pierced like deserts
prickled with cactus?
What streams can wash it?
It reeks with the musk
of spinsters and widows
back from pilgrimage.
The sweat of dervishes
begrimes it as they twirl
their blurring trousers into miracles.

Now blooms the spring of the locust.
Over the dead nightingales
the night itself weighs and weighs.
The day inches to birth
while the shut and bolted door
of the sea
rejects us.

We scream.
We dream of weeping,
but tears refuse our eyes.
We twist our necks
in zero hurricanes.

O my land,
I see you as a woman in heat,
a bridge of lust.

The pharaohs take you when they choose,
and the very sand applauds them.
Through the clay of my eyeshells,
I see what any man can see:
libations at the graves of children,
incense for holy men,
tombstones of black marble,
fields scattered with skeletons,
vultures,
mush corpses with the names of heroes.

Thus we advance,
chests to the sea,

grieving for yesterday.
Our words inherit nothing,
beget nothing.
We are islands.

From the abyss we smell ravens.
Our ships send out their pleas
to nothing but the moon's crescent
of despair that broods
a devil's spawn.
At riverfall, at the dead sea,
midnight dreams its festivals,
but sand and foam and locusts
are the only brides.

Thus we advance,
harvesting our caravans
in filth and tears,
bleeding the earth
with our own blood
until the green dam of the sea
alone
stops us.

II

What god shall resurrect us
in his flesh?
After all, the iron cage is shrinking.
The hangman will not wait
though we wail from birth
in the name of these happy ruins.

What narrow yesterdays,
what stale and shriveled years . . .
Even storms come begging
when the sky matches the gray
of the sand,
leaving us stalled between seasons,
barricaded by what we see,
marching under clouds that move

like mules and cannon.
The dust of graveyards blinds us
until our eyes rhyme
with ash.
No lashes fringe the sun.
No brows can shade the day,
and life comes moment by moment
as it comes to the poor only.
Shadowed by ice and sand,
we live.

And so live all men.

All men . . . mere scraps from everywhere,
fresh baits of arsenic.
Under their sky what green can sprout?

All men . . . choked by ashes,
crushed by the rocks of silence,
mounted by empire builders,
paraded in arenas for their sport,
so many footstools,
so many banners . . .
No one whispers in Barada or the Euphrates.
Nothing breeds or stirs.
O my dry and silent land,
who left you like a fossil?
On the map you're virile,
rich with wheat, oil, ports,
countercolored by migrations.
Shall a new race grow in the poppy fields?
Shall fresh winds rearrange the sand?

Let the rain come.
Let rain wash us in our ruins,
wash the corpses, wash our history.
Let the poems strangled on our lips
be swept away like rocks in the street.
Let us attend to cows, doves, flowers, gods.
Let sounds return
to this land of starving frogs.

Let bread be brought by locusts
and the banished ants . . .

My words become a spear in flight.
Unopposable as truth,
my spear returns to strike me
dead.

III

Braid your hair, my boys, with greener leaves.
We still have verse among us.
We have the sea.
We have our dreams.
"To the steppes of China
we bequeath our neighing horses,
and to Georgia, our spears.
We'll build a house of gold
from here to the Himalayas.
We'll sail our flags in Samarkand.
We'll tread the treasured mosses
of the earth.
We'll bless our blood with roses.
We'll wash the day of stains
and walk on stones as we would walk on silk.

"This is the only way.
For this we'll lie with lightning
and anoint the mildewed earth
until the cries of birth
resound, resound, resound.

"Nothing can stop us.
Remember,
we are greener than the sea,
younger than time.
The sun and the day are dice
between our fingers."

Under the exile's moon
tremble the first wings.

Boats begin to drift
on a dead sea, and siroccos
rustle the gates of the city.
Tomorrow the gates shall open.
We'll burn the locusts in the desert,
span the abyss
and stand on the porch
of a world to be.

"Darkness,
darkness of the sea,
be filled with the leopard's joy.
Help us to sacrifice,
name us anew.
The eagle of the future waits,
and there are answers in its eyes.

"Darkness,
darkness of the sea,
ignore this feast of corpses.
Bring the earth to blossom
with your winds.
Banish plague and teach the very rocks
to dance and love."

The goddess of the sand prostrates herself.
Under brichthorn
the spring rises like clocynth from the lips
or life from the sea.
We leave the captive city
where every lantern is a church
and every bee more sacred than a nun.

IV

"Where is your home?
Which country?
Which camp without a name?"

"My country is abandoned.
My soul has left me.
I have no home."

When pharoahs ruled and men were cannibals,
the words of poets died.
While pharoahs rule,
I take my books and go,
living in the shade of my heart,
weaving from my verse's silk
a new heaven.

The sea cleanses our wounds
and makes of wounds the salt's kin. . . .
The white sea,
the daily Euphrates,
the Orontes in its cradle,
the Barada—
I have tasted them all,
and none could slake me.
Yet I learned their love,
and my despair deserved such waters.

Though desperate, I still hate death.
Though lost, I seek my way
through all the lies and doubts
that are the crust and quicksand
of the earth.

Give me the exile's sail,
the pilgrim's face.
I turn my back on jails and holocausts.
I leave the dead to death.

And I go,
keeping my endless sorrows,
my distance from the stars,
my pilgrimage,
my girl
and my verses.
I go with the sweat
of exile on my forehead
and with a lost poem
sleeping in my eyes.
I go,

dreaming of those buried
in orchards and vineyards,
and I remember those I love,
those few.
When the sea rages my blood
and the wind kisses my love's hair,
I remember my mother,
and I weave in memory for her
a mat of straw
where she can sit and weep.

Amen to the age of flies.

Because the earth survives beneath my feet,
the pale god of my despair rejoices.
A new voice speaks my words.
My poems bloom naked as roses.

Find me some paper,
some ink.
Despair is still my star,
and evil is always being born.
Silence rises on the sand.
There are hearts to touch.
Some ink. . . .
Some paper. . . .

"Where is your home?
What camp without a name?"

"My country is abandoned.
My soul has left me.
I have no home."

TR. SAMUEL HAZO

≈ A Mirror for the Twentieth Century

A coffin bearing the face of a boy
A book

Written on the belly of a crow
A wild beast hidden in a flower

A rock
Breathing with the lungs of a lunatic:

> This is it
> This is the Twentieth Century

TR. ABDULLAH AL-UDHARI

MAHMOUD DARWISH (1941–   )

Darwish, born in Palestine in a village razed by the Israelis in 1948, fled with his family to Lebanon and subsequently returned to Galilee. His first book of poetry was published when he was nineteen. A noted voice of Palestinian resistance and a committed Marxist (he joined the Communist Party in 1961), Darwish went into exile, and served as director of the Research Center of the Palestine Liberation Organization.

≈ Earth Poem

A dull evening in a run-down village
Eyes half asleep
I recall thirty years
And five wars
I swear the future keeps
My ear of corn
And the singer croons
About a fire and some strangers
And the evening is just another evening
And the singer croons

And they asked him:
Why do you sing?

And he answered:
I sing because I sing

. . . .

And they searched his chest
But could only find his heart
And they searched his heart
But could only find his people
And they searched his voice
But could only find his grief
And they searched his grief
But could only find his prison
And they searched his prison
But could only see themselves in chains

TR. ABDULLAH AL-UDHARI

≈ We Travel Like Other People

We travel like other people, but we return to nowhere. As if travelling
Is the way of the clouds. We have buried our loved ones in the
    darkness of the clouds, between the roots of the trees.
And we said to our wives: go on giving birth to people like us for
    hundreds of years so we can complete this journey
To the hour of a country, to a metre of the impossible.
We travel in the carriages of the psalms, sleep in the tent of the
    prophets and come out of the speech of the gypsies.

We measure space with a hoopoe's beak or sing to while away the
    distance and cleanse the light of the moon.
Your path is long so dream of seven women to bear this long path
On your shoulders. Shake for them palm trees so as to know their
    names and who'll be the mother of the boy of Galilee.
We have a country of words. Speak speak so I can put my road on the
    stone of a stone.
We have a country of words. Speak Speak so we may know the end of
    this travel.

TR. ABDULLAH AL-UDHARI

≈ Prison

The address of my house has changed,
And the time when I eat,
Changed too the amount of my tobacco,
The colour of my clothes, my face, the look of me.
Even the moon,
So dear to me here,
Has become larger, more beautiful,
And the smell of the earth: Perfume,
And the taste of nature: Sugar.
It is as though I am on the roof of my old house
And a new star
Has riveted itself upon my eye.

TR. DENYS JOHNSON-DAVIES

≈ Psalm 2

Now I find myself dried
Like trees growing out of books.
The wind is just a passing thing.
Shall I fight or shall I not fight?
That is not the question.
The important thing is to have a strong throat.
Shall I work or shall I not work?
That is not the question.
The important thing is to rest eight days a week
Palestine time.
Country, turning up in songs and massacres,
Show me the source of death;
Is it the dagger or the lie?

Country, turning up in songs and massacres,
Why do I smuggle you from airport to airport
Like opium,
Invisible ink,
A radio transmitter?

I want to draw your shape,
You, scattered in files and surprises.

I want to draw your shape,
You, flying on shrapnel and birds' wings.
I want to draw your shape
But heaven snatches my hand.
I want to draw your shape
You, trapped between the dagger and the wind.
I want to draw your shape
To find my shape in yours
And get blamed for being abstract,
For forging documents and photos,
You, trapped between the dagger and the wind.

Country, turning up in songs and massacres,
How could you be a dream, rob me of the thrill
And leave me like a stone?
Perhaps you are more sweet than a dream,
Perhaps you're sweeter!

There isn't a name in Arab history
I haven't borrowed
To help me slip through your secret windows.
All the code-names are kept
In air-conditioned recruiting offices.
Will you accept my name—
My only code-name—
Mahmoud Darwish?
The police and Carmel's pines
Have whipped my real name
Off my skin.

Country, turning up in songs and massacres,
Show me the source of death;
Is it the dagger
Or the lie?

    TR. DENYS JOHNSON-DAVIES

Repression and Revolution in Latin America

(1 9 0 0 - 1 9 9 1)

On his deathbed, Simón Bolívar, who had led much of the South American continent to freedom, complained that he had done nothing more than plow the sea, for the old social structures of colonialism had remained intact. Bolívar's distress was perhaps overstated, but the deep societal divisions between landowning oligarchies and landless peasants, liberal city dwellers and conservative farmers, the very rich and the very poor, were solidly in place at the time of the nineteenth-century revolutions.

During the first two decades of the twentieth century, the United States intervened militarily in the affairs of Latin nations more than twenty times. After World War I, however, American interest became more recognizably economic: the United States was the largest investor in Central and South America when the Great Depression of the 1930s led many governments to default on their loans. The fall in commodity prices for Latin American cash crops and the subsequent social unrest led to apparently conflicting movements: nationalist fervor, a desire for revolutionary reform, and a call for order. Almost every country in the region suffered a military coup in the decade following 1930.

The renewal of world markets during World War II brought new wealth, as well as new pressures. In Argentina, Venezuela, and Colombia, the military formed alliances with the labor force under such strong leaders as Argentina's President Juan Perón. In less industrialized nations, the military and the landed elites maintained their power, wary of each other and fearful of possible disruption by the impoverished multitudes. The Cold War between the United States and the Soviet Union also revitalized North American interest in the affairs of its southern neighbors. While ostensibly supportive of reformist movements, the United States provided material aid (directly, as in the Dominican Republic in 1965, or covertly, as in Guatemala in 1954) to the military governments viewed as most capable of protecting American economic and political interests.

With the success of the Cuban revolution in 1959 and Fidel Castro's subsequent alliance with the Soviet Union, right-wing fears of insurgency and leftist dreams of reform intensified. In some countries, the latter took the form of parliamentary mandates for change (as in Chile); in others, they appeared as armed insurgencies (as in Nicaragua and El Salvador). Reaction was commensurate: Salvador Allende's government in Chile was overthrown by a U.S.-supported military coup d'état in 1973, and the army took control of Argentina in 1976. The military governments and the elites they supported have waged wars of terrorism against suspected subversives. In Argentina alone, more than five thousand people were "disappeared" (murdered, with no recovery of the remains) between 1976 and 1981. In El Salvador, ex officio "death squads" have become notorious for their mutilations, murders, and sexual abuse of nuns, priests, peasants, industrial workers, and human rights activists. According to Amnesty International, during the early years of the 1980s, torture was common in Argentina, Chile, El Salvador, Guatemala, and Colombia. Cuba also demonstrated a disregard for human rights, although there does not seem to have been the same incidence of torture and extrajudicial murder there as in El Salvador and Argentina.

The victory of the Sandinistas in Nicaragua turned North American attention to Central America, where the United States supported counterrevolutionary forces in Nicaragua and right-wing forces in El Salvador. During the 1980s, military and right-wing forces took the lives of eighty thousand people in El Salvador and over one hundred thousand in Guatemala. While countries such as Brazil, Argentina, and Chile have become more liberal, others, such as Colombia, Peru, El Salvador, Guatemala, and Nicaragua, have suffered two decades of "low-intensity conflict," that is, a state of civil war and harassment marked by terror and the abuse of human rights.

A historic peace agreement was signed in Mexico City on January 15, 1992, bringing to an end twelve years of war in El Salvador.

CESAR VALLEJO (1892–1937)

Born to a rural Peruvian family, Vallejo studied medicine, but finally earned a degree in literature. He was arrested in 1920, falsely accused of complicity in a riot and jailed for four months. The charges against him were never proved. He left Peru for France in 1923, became a Marxist at the end of the decade, and was expelled from France with his French wife because of their political activities. They were allowed to return after two years of exile in 1932. The Spanish Civil War rekindled Vallejo's ardor for poetry, and he worked assiduously for the Republican cause. He died of a mysterious intestinal ailment in Paris in 1937.

≈ The Black Riders

There are blows in life so violent—I can't answer!
Blows as if from the hatred of God; as if before them,
the deep waters of everything lived through
were backed up in the soul . . . I can't answer!

Not many; but they exist . . . They open dark ravines
in the most ferocious face and in the most bull-like back.
Perhaps they are the horses of that heathen Attila,
or the black riders sent to us by Death.

They are the slips backward made by the Christs of the soul,
away from some holy faith that is sneered at by Events.
These blows that are bloody are the crackling sounds
from some bread that burns at the oven door.

And man . . . poor man! . . . poor man! He swings his eyes, as
when a man behind us calls us by clapping his hands;
swings his crazy eyes, and everything alive
is backed up, like a pool of guilt, in that glance.

There are blows in life so violent . . . I can't answer!

TR. ROBERT BLY

≈ The Rollcall of Bones

They demanded in loud voices:
"We want him to show both hands at the same time."
And that simply couldn't be done.
"We want them to check the length of his steps while he cries."
And that simply couldn't be done.
"We want him to think one identical thought during the time a zero
    goes on being useless."
And that simply couldn't be done.
"We want him to do something crazy."
And that simply couldn't be done.
"We want a mass of men like him to stand in between him and
    another man just like him."

And that simply couldn't be done.
"We want them to compare him with himself."
And that simply couldn't be done.
"We want them to call him finally by his own name."
And that simply couldn't be done.

TR. ROBERT BLY

≈ Have You Anything to Say in Your Defense?

Well, on the day I was born,
God was sick.

They all know that I'm alive,
that I'm vicious; and they don't know
the December that follows from that January.
Well, on the day I was born,
God was sick.

There is an empty place
in my metaphysical shape
that no one can reach:
a cloister of silence
that spoke with the fire of its voice muffled.

On the day I was born,
God was sick.

Brother, listen to me, Listen . . .
oh, all right. Don't worry, I won't leave
without taking my Decembers along,
without leaving my Januaries behind.
Well, on the day I was born,
God was sick.

They all know that I'm alive,
that I chew my food . . . and they don't know
why harsh winds whistle in my poems,
the narrow uneasiness of a coffin,

winds untangled from the Sphinx
who holds the desert for routine questioning.

Yes, they all know . . . Well, they don't know
that the light gets skinny
and the darkness gets bloated . . .
And they don't know that the Mystery joins things together . . .
that he is the hunchback
musical and sad who stands a little way off and foretells
the dazzling progression from the limits to the Limits.

On the day I was born,
God was sick,
gravely.

TR. JAMES WRIGHT

PABLO NERUDA (1904–1973)

Neruda, brought up in the frontier city of Tamuco, Chile, published his
first book of poetry when he was twenty. After consular appointments
to Burma, Ceylon, and Spain, his chief, realizing that the poet did not
have a facility for numbers, sent him to Madrid, where, he said, "the
poetry was." There Neruda continued his friendship with García Lorca
and met Rafael Alberti and Miguel Hernandez. They won him over to
leftist politics and a commitment to the Republican cause during the
Spanish Civil War. He lost his consular post because of his partisan
stand, and worked for the Loyalists in Chile in 1937. After diplomatic
service in Paris and Mexico, Neruda returned to Chile, where he was
elected a senator and became a member of the Communist Party. He
was charged with treason by the president of Chile in 1947 and was
forced to go into hiding; he did not return to his homeland until 1950.
He was named ambassador to France by Salvador Allende in 1971, the
year he won the Nobel Prize for Literature. In ill health, Neruda re-
turned to Chile in 1972. He died two weeks after the military coup
against Allende.

≈ The Dictators

An odor has remained among the sugarcane:
a mixture of blood and body, a penetrating
petal that brings nausea.
Between the coconut palms the graves are full
of ruined bones, of speechless death-rattles.
The delicate dictator is talking
with top hats, gold braid, and collars.
The tiny palace gleams like a watch
and the rapid laughs with gloves on
cross the corridors at times
and join the dead voices
and the blue mouths freshly buried.
The weeping cannot be seen, like a plant
whose seeds fall endlessly on the earth,
whose large blind leaves grow even without light.
Hatred has grown scale on scale,
blow on blow, in the ghastly water of the swamp,
with a snout full of ooze and silence

TR. ROBERT BLY

≈ America, I Do Not Call Your Name Without Hope

America, I do not call your name without hope.
When I hold the sword against the heart,
when I live with the faulty roof in the soul,
when one of your new days
pierces me coming through the windows,
I am and I stand in the light that produces me,
I live in the darkness which makes me what I am,
I sleep and awake in your fundamental sunrise:
as mild as the grapes, and as terrible,
carrier of sugar and the whip,
soaked in the sperm of your species,
nursed on the blood of your inheritance.

TR. ROBERT BLY

≈ Letter to Miguel Otero Silva, in Caracas

(1948)

Nicolas Guillen brought me your letter, written
invisibly, on his clothes, in his eyes.
How happy you are, Miguel, both of us are!
In a world that festering plaster almost covers
there is no one left aimlessly happy but us.
I see the crow go by; there's nothing he can do to harm me.
You watch the scorpion, and polish your guitar.
Writing poetry, we live among the wild beasts, and when we touch
a man, the stuff of someone in whom we believed,
and he goes to pieces like a rotten pie,
you in the Venezuela you inherited gather together
whatever can be salvaged, while I cup my hands
around the live coal of life.
                                    What happiness, Miguel!
Are you going to ask where I am? I'll tell you—
giving only details useful to the State—
that on this coast scattered with wild rocks
the sea and the fields come together, the waves and the pines,
petrels and eagles, meadows and foam.
Have you ever spent a whole day close to sea birds,
watching how they fly? They seem
to be carrying the letters of the world to their destinations.
The pelicans go by like ships of the wind,
other birds go by like arrows, carrying
messages from dead kings, viceroys,
buried with strands of turquoise on the Andean coasts,
and seagulls, so magnificently white,
they are constantly forgetting what their messages are.
Life is like the sky, Miguel, when we put
loving and fighting in it, words that are bread and wine,
words they have not been able to degrade even now,
because we walk out in the street with poems and guns.
They don't know what to do with us, Miguel.
What can they do but kill us; and even that
wouldn't be a good bargain—nothing they can do
but rent a room across the street, and tail us
so they can learn to laugh and cry like us.

When I was writing my love poems, which sprouted out from me
on all sides, and I was dying of depression,
nomadic, abandoned, gnawing on the alphabet,
they said to me: "What a great man you are, Theocritus!"
I am not Theocritus: I took life,
and I faced her and kissed her,
and then went through the tunnels of the mines
to see how other men live.
And when I came out, my hands stained with garbage and sadness,
I held my hands up and showed them to the generals,
and said: "I am not a part of this crime."
They started to cough, showed disgust, left off saying hello,
gave up calling me Theocritus, and ended by insulting me
and assigning the entire police force to arrest me
because I didn't continue to be occupied exclusively with metaphysical
    subjects.
But I had brought joy over to my side.
From then on I started getting up to read the letters
the sea birds bring from so far away,
letters that arrive moist, messages I translate
phrase by phrase, slowly and confidently: I am punctilious
as an engineer in this strange duty.
All at once I go to the window. It is a square
of pure light, there is a clear horizon
of grasses and crags, and I go on working here
among the things I love: waves, rocks, wasps,
with an oceanic and drunken happiness.
But no one likes our being happy, and they cast you
in a genial role: "Now don't exaggerate, don't worry,"
and they wanted to lock me in a cricket cage, where there would be
    tears,
and I would drown, and they could deliver elegies over my grave.

I remember one day in the sandy acres
of the nitrate flats; there were five hundred men
on strike. It was a scorching afternoon
in Tarapaca. And after the faces had absorbed
all the sand and the bloodless dry sun of the desert,
I saw coming into me, like a cup that I hate,
my old depression. At this time of crisis,

in the desolation of the salt flats, in that weak moment
of the fight, when we could have been beaten,
a little pale girl who had come from the mines
spoke a poem of yours in a brave voice that had glass in it and steel,
an old poem of yours that wanders among the wrinkled eyes
of all the workers of my country, of America.
And that small piece of your poetry blazed suddenly
like a purple blossom in my mouth,
and went down to my blood, filling it once more
with a luxuriant joy born from your poem.
I thought of you, but also of your bitter Venezuela.
Years ago I saw a student who had marks on his ankles
from chains ordered on him by a general,
and he told me of the chain gangs that work on the roads
and the jails where people disappeared forever. Because that is what
    our America has been:
long stretches with destructive rivers and constellations
of butterflies (in some places the emeralds are heavy as apples).
But along the whole length of the night and the rivers
there are always bleeding ankles, at one time near the oil wells,
now near the nitrate, in Pisagua, where a rotten leader
has put the best men of my country under the earth to die, so he can
    sell their bones.
That is why you write your songs, so that someday the disgraced and
    wounded America
can let its butterflies tremble and collect its emeralds
without the terrifying blood of beatings, coagulated
on the hands of the executioners and the businessmen.
I guessed how full of joy you would be, by the Orinoco, singing
probably, or perhaps buying wine for your house,
taking your part in the fight and the exaltation,
with broad shoulders, like the poets of our age—
with light clothes and walking shoes.
Ever since that time, I have been thinking of writing to you,
and when Guillen arrived, running over with stories of you,
which were coming loose everywhere out of his clothes
—they poured out under the chestnuts of my house—
I said to myself: "Now!" and even then I didn't start a letter to you.
But today has been too much for me: not only one sea bird,
but thousands have gone past my window,

and I have picked up the letters no one reads, letters they take along
to all the shores of the world until they lose them.
Then in each of those letters I read words of yours,
and they resembled the words I write, and dream of, and put in
     poems,
and so I decided to send this letter to you, which I end here,
so I can watch through the window the world that is ours.

    TR. ROBERT BLY

≈ They Receive Instructions Against Chile

But we have to see behind all them, there is something
behind the traitors and the gnawing rats,
an empire which sets the table,
and serves up the nourishment and the bullets.
They want to repeat in you their great success in Greece.
Greek playboys at the banquet, and bullets
for the people in the mountains: we'll have to destroy the flight
of the new Victory of Samothrace, we'll have to hang,
kill, lose men, sink the murderous knife
held to us from New York, we'll have to use fire
to break the spirit of the man who was emerging
in all countries as if born
from the earth that had been splashed with blood.
We have to arm Chiang and the vicious Videla,
give them money for prisons, wings
so they can bomb their own populations, give them
a handout, a few dollars, and they do the rest,
they lie, bribe, dance on the dead bodies
and their first ladies wear the most expensive minks.
The suffering of the people does not matter: copper
executives need this sacrifice: facts are facts:
the generals retire from the army and serve
as vice-presidents of the Chuquicamata Copper Firm,
and in the nitrate works the "Chilean" general
decides with his trailing sword how much the natives
may mention when they ask for a raise in wages.
In this way they decide from above, from the roll of dollars,

in this way the dwarf traitor receives his instructions,
and the generals act as the police force,
and the trunk of the tree of the country rots.

TR. ROBERT BLY AND JAMES WRIGHT

NICANOR PARRA (1914–)

Parra was educated in Chile, England, and the United States, imparting
to his poetry a quality of multiple estrangement: he is cosmopolitan,
and deeply committed to what he calls "antipoetry," a rejection of
poetic language and conventions. Trained as a physicist, with strong
leftist leanings (though his faith in individualism has alienated his Marx-
ist supporters), Parra refused to leave Chile after the coup that brought
Pinochet to power. Instead he established himself as a voice of dissent
within the university and within Chile itself.

≈ Warnings

No praying allowed, no sneezing.
No spitting, eulogizing, kneeling
Worshipping, howling, expectorating.

No sleeping permitted in this precinct
No inoculating, talking, excommunicating
Harmonizing, escaping, catching.

Running is absolutely forbidden.

No smoking. No fucking.

TR. MILLER WILLIAMS

≈ Inflation

Bread goes up so bread goes up again
Rents go up
This brings an instant doubling of all rents

The cost of clothes goes up
So the cost of clothes goes up again.
Inexorably
We're caught in a vicious circle.
In the cage there is food.
Not much, but there is food.
Outside are only great stretches of freedom.

TR. MILLER WILLIAMS

≈ Letters from the Poet Who Sleeps in a Chair

I

I tell it the way it is
Either we know everything beforehand
Or we never know anything.

The only thing they let us do
Is learn to speak correctly.

II

I dream of women all night
Some laugh in my face
Others give me rabbit punches
They won't leave me alone.
They're making war on me all the time.

I get up with a face like a thundercloud.

Which makes people think I'm crazy
Or anyway scared to death.

III

It's pretty hard work to believe
In a god that leaves his creatures
To their own devices
At the mercy of waves of age
And all the infirmities
Not to mention death.

IV

I am one of those who greet the hearse.

V

Young poets
Write any way you want to
In whatever style you please
Too much blood has gone under the bridge
To go on believing—I believe—
That only one road is right:
In poetry everything is permitted.

VI

Infirmity
        Decrepitude
                and Death
Dance like innocent maidens
Around Swan Lake
Half-naked
         drunk
With their coral lascivious lips.

VII

It's clear enough
That there are no people on the moon

That chairs are tables
That butterflies are flowers in perpetual motion
That truth is a collective error

That the spirit dies with the body

It's clear enough
That wrinkles are not scars.

VIII

Whenever for whatever reason
I've had to climb down

From my little wooden tower
I've drawn back shivering from the cold
From loneliness
           from fear
                from pain.

IX

The trolley tracks have all disappeared
They've cut down the trees
The horizon is filled with crosses.

Marx has been denied seven times
And we keep on keeping on.

X

Raise bees on bile
Inoculate semen into the mouth
Kneel in a puddle of blood
Sneeze in a funeral parlor.
Milk a cow
And throw the milk in its face

XI

From the thunderheads of breakfast
On to the thunder of noon
On to the lightning of supper.

XII

I don't get sad very easily
To tell you the truth
Even skulls make me laugh.
The poet asleep on the cross
Greets you with tears which are blood.

XIII

The poet's duty is this
To improve on the blank page
I doubt if it's possible.

XIV

I go along only with beauty
Ugliness hurts me.

XV

I say it for the last time
Maggots are gods
Butterflies are flowers in perpetual motion
Decayed teeth
easily broken
I belong to the days of the silent movie.

Fucking is a literary act.

XVI

Chilean aphorisms:
All redheads have freckles
The telephone knows what it says
The turtle never lost more time
Than when it stopped to learn speed from the eagle.

The automobile is a wheelchair.

And the traveler who looks back
Runs the grave risk
That his shadow will not follow him.

XVII

To analyze is to renounce yourself
One can reason only in a circle
One sees only what one wants to see
Birth solves nothing
I admit I'm crying.

Birth solves nothing.
Only death tells the truth
Even poetry is not convincing

We are taught that space does not exist
We are taught that time does not exist
But just the same
Old age is a *fait accompli.*

Let science say what it will

It makes me sleepy to read my poems
Even though they were written in blood.

TR. MILLER WILLIAMS

≈ Sentences

Let's not fool ourselves
The automobile is a wheelchair
A lion is made of lambs
Poets have no biographies
Death is a collective habit
Children are born to be happy
Reality has a tendency to fade away
Fucking is a diabolical act
God is a good friend of the poor

TR. MILLER WILLIAMS

≈ Modern Times

These are calamitous times we're living through
you can't speak without committing a contradiction
or keep quiet without complicity with the Pentagon.
Everyone knows there's no alternative possible
all roads lead to Cuba
but the air is dirty
breathing is a futile act.
The enemy says
the country is to blame
as if countries were men.
Accursed clouds circle accursed volcanoes
accursed embarkations launch accursed expeditions

accursed trees crumble on accursed birds:
it was all polluted to begin with.

TR. MILLER WILLIAMS

≈ Manifesto

Ladies and gentlemen
This is our final word
—Our first and final word—
The poets have come down from Olympus.

For the old folks
Poetry was a luxury item
But for us
It's an absolute necessity
We couldn't live without poetry.

Unlike our elders
—And I say it with all respect—
We maintain this
A poet is no alchemist
A poet is a man like all men
A bricklayer building his wall:
A maker of windows and doors.

We talk
With everyday words
We don't believe in cabalistic signs.

And one thing more:
The poet is there
To see to it the tree does not grow crooked.

This is our message.

We denounce the godlike poet
The Cockroach poet
The bookworm poet.

All of these gentlemen
—And I say it with great respect—
Must be arraigned and tried
For building castles in the air
For wasting time and space
By composing sonnets to the moon
For putting words together by chance
Following the latest Paris fashion.
That's not for us!
A thought is not born in the mouth
It is born in the heart.

We repudiate
The poetry of dark glasses
The poetry of the cape and sword
The poetry of the plumed hate
We propose instead
The poetry of the naked eye
The poetry of the hairy chest
The poetry of the bare head.

We don't believe in nymphs or tritons.
Poetry has to be this:
A girl in a wheatfield—
Or it's absolutely nothing.

Well now, on the political level
They, our immediate forebears,
Our good immediate ancestors,
Refracted themselves, dispersed themselves
Passing through crystal prisms.
A few came out communists.
I don't know if they actually were.
Let's assume they were communists.
All I know is this:
They were not poets of the people
They were nothing but touted bourgeois poets

Let's face it:
Only one or two
Ever found a place

In the hearts of the people.
Whenever they could
They declared themselves by word and by deed
Against the poetry of purpose
Against the poetry of the present
Against the poetry of the proletariat.

Let's say they were communists
But the poetry was a disaster
Second-hand surrealism
Third-hand decadence
Old planks washed up by the sea.
Adjective poetry
Nasal and guttural poetry
Arbitrary poetry
Poetry copies from books
Poetry based on the revolution of words
—But in fact
Poetry must spring from the revolution of ideas—
Poetry of the endless circle
For half a dozen chosen people:
"Absolute freedom of expression."

Today we scratch our heads and wonder
Why would they write such stuff
To frighten the petit bourgeois?
What a waste of time!
The petit bourgeois won't react
unless his stomach is at stake.

After all who's afraid of poetry!

TR. MILLER WILLIAMS

CLARIBEL ALEGRÍA (1924–   )

Daughter of a Nicaraguan political refugee, Alegría moved to El Salvador as an infant, and exile has been the hallmark of her life. At nineteen, Alegría attended George Washington University, and she has lived in

Mexico, Uruguay, Argentina, France, Spain, and Nicaragua. She remained in Managua during the Contra war against the Sandinista government. A novelist as well as a poet, she won the Casa de las Americas poetry award in 1978. "We Were Three" is a poem of mourning and exile, written in Deya, Mallorca. In "From the Bridge," the poet warns and admonishes her younger self.

≈ We Were Three

To Paco and Rodolfo

It was winter,
there was snow,
it was night,
this is a green day
of doves and sun
of ashes and cries.
The wind pushes me
across the bridge
over the cracked earth
through a dry streambed
strewn with cans.

Death comes to life
here in Deya.
the *torrente*
the stone bridge.
My dead wait
at every corner,
the innocent grillwork of balconies
the filmed mirror of my dead.
They smile from the distance
and wave to me,
they leave the cemetery,
a wall of the dead.
My flesh emits light
and they come to my door
waving their arms.

The bridge was stone,
it was night,

our arms circled each other,
we swayed to our songs,
our breath rose from our mouths
in small, crystalline clouds,
it was winter,
there was snow,
we were three.
Today the earth is dry
and resounds like a drum,
my arms fall to my sides,
I am alone.
My dead stand watch
and send signals to me,
they assail me
in the radio and paper.
The wall of my dead
rises and reaches from Aconcagua to Izalco.
The bridge was stone,
it was night,
no one can say
how they died.
Their persecuted voices are one voice
dying by torture in prison.
My dead arise, they rage.
The streets are empty
but my dead wink at me.
I am a cemetery,
I have no country
and they are too many to bury.

    TR. CAROLYN FORCHÉ

≈ From the Bridge

I have freed myself at last
it has been hard to break free:
near the end of the bridge
I pause
the water flows below
a turbulent water

sweeping fragments with it:
the voice of Carmen Lira
faces I loved
that disappeared.
From here
from the bridge
the perspective changes
I look backward
toward the beginning:
the hesitant silhouette
of a little girl
a doll
dangling from her hand
she lets it drop
and walks toward me
now she's an adolescent
gathers up her hair
and I recognize this gesture
stop girl
stop right there
if you come any closer
it will be difficult to talk
Don Chico died
after seven operations
they let him die
in a charity hospital
they closed Ricardo's school
and he died
during the earthquake
his heart failed.
Do you remember the massacre
that left Izalco without men?
You were seven.
How can I explain to you
nothing has changed
they keep on killing people daily?
It's better if you stop there
I remember you well at that age
you wrote honeyed poems
were horrified by violence

taught the neighborhood children
to read.
What would you say
if I told you that Pedro
your best student
rotted in jail
and that Sarita
the little blue-eyed girl
who made up stories
let herself be seduced
by the eldest son
of her employers
and afterwards sold herself
for twenty-five cents?
You've taken another step
you wear your hair short
have textbooks under your arm
poor deluded thing
you learned the consolations
of philosophy
before understanding
why you had to be consoled
your books spoke to you
of justice
and carefully omitted
the filth
that has always surrounded us
you went on with your verses
searched for order in chaos
and that was your goal
or perhaps your sentence.
You are coming closer now
your arms filled with children
it is easy to distract yourself
playing mother
and shrink the world
to a household.
Stop there
don't come any closer
you still won't recognize me

you still have to undergo
the death of Roque
of Rodolfo
all those innumerable deaths
that assail you
pursue you
define you
in order to dress in this plumage
(my plumage of mourning)
to peer out
through these pitiless
scrutinizing eyes
to have my claws
and this sharp beak.
I never found the order
I searched for
but always a sinister
and well-planned disorder
a prescribed disorder
that increases in the hands
of those who hold power
while the others
who clamor for
a more kindly world
a world with less hunger
and more hope
die tortured
in the prisons.
Don't come any closer
there's a stench of carrion
surrounding me.

TR. DARWIN FLAKOLL

ANGEL CUADRA (1931–)

Trained as a lawyer, Cuadra was an early supporter of the Cuban revolution, but was arrested in 1967 and sentenced to death for conspiracy against the government. His sentence was commuted to hard labor and he was released in 1976, but forbidden to write poetry. Nevertheless, he smuggled a book of poetry out of the country and was arrested again in 1977. He was allowed to go into exile in the early 1980s and now lives in Miami, Florida.

≈ In Brief

The common man I might have been
reproaches me now,
blaming me for his ostracism
his solitary shadow,
his silent exile.

I put my common man and the other man together.
I took the latter's hand and moved away,
as if to honor my brilliant friend,
my wished-for double,
my important, chosen self.
And the common man I told
to shut the door behind him,
to be quiet behind the panes,
or rather, to give up his place in the window
and, if possible, to wipe away his image with a cloth.

Time passed in its hurried way,
planetary time that is,
or simply,
the time spent on the road.

I have retraced my footsteps now—
with my other, my own self—
not sure if I am proud or sad.
It has rained on my face,
many nights have fallen.
Above the dust only one cold star
that seems like dust itself, like the mute dust
I brought back with me.
And I find my common man still there, where I left him,
the one I denied, the unimportant man I might have been;
and in his eyes of exile I can see

a stupor of sand and time and emptiness.
I look then at the other, the important man,
the one I chose to be.
I put my common man and the other man together . . .
and find they are one and the same.

17 March 1978

TR. KATHERINE RODRIGUEZ NIETO

≈ Brief Letter to Donald Walsh (in memoriam)

(Translator of my poems)

My friend:
In what language shall we begin our conversation?
How can I begin to celebrate
the support your voice gives me
in sending out my songs, drenched in your accents,
to live in this world?
And not know what the warmth of your hand is like in friendship;
only this music shining from the soul,
stretching like a bridge between us:
you in your country open to the stars,
I behind bars of rancor,
dying since the dawn.
Yet even so we meet.
The hands of friends
brought your name to me with the morning dew.
And you are here, and I am talking to you.

Because I've learned that not everything is hatred.
I want to declare another word,
sow it as it were in furrows
of goodness and of hope.

There are some men who crush my words,
tear me to pieces for producing beauty,
bring my poem to trial
and sentence it to run the gauntlet:
the drops of blood my poem sheds
form a constellation among the stars.

But there are other men who rescue me
and save my poem like unransomed light,
who gather up its pieces of suffering clay
and, like Prometheus, lend me fire for it.
The fire of love, I proclaim it now,
that is the word I will defend
in martyrdom, among the thorns.
My poem, the grape of pain
for which I bleed and grow.

And you exist, Donald Walsh.
I knew nothing of your musical being,
of that gemstone clear and high, transparent.
Don't leave now
that I have found days dawning in my heart
that were sent me by your hand
Don't leave now
that we begin to speak in a language
that unites the souls of Whitman and Marti.
And on the streets of all the world
—without bars, without bitterness or fear
—you and I will walk together, speaking
the word of Love that has existed since before the age of man.

22 March 1980, Boniato Prison

TR. KATHERINE RODRIGUEZ NIETO

HEBERTO PADILLA (1932–   )

Born in 1932, Padilla first moved to the United States in 1949, but
returned to his native Cuba after the revolution. From 1959 to 1961, he
was an editor of a literary magazine, which was suppressed. Padilla was
then sent abroad to Prague and Moscow as a correspondent. In 1967,
he criticized a novel that had strong government support, and when his
second book was published the following year, it included an introduc-
tion proclaiming it counterrevolutionary. He was arrested in 1971 and
sent into internal exile until 1980, when he was allowed to go to the

United States. His poems address the sweep of twentieth-century history.

≈ In Trying Times

They asked that man for his time
so that he could link it to History.
They asked him for his hands,
because for trying times
nothing is better than a good pair of hands.
They asked him for his eyes
that once had tears
so that he should see the bright side
(the bright side of life, especially)
because to see horror one startled eye is enough.
They asked him for his lips,
parched and split, to affirm,
to belch up, with each affirmation, a dream
(the great dream);
they asked him for his legs
hard and knotted
(his wandering legs),
because in trying times
is there anything better than a pair of legs
for building or digging ditches?
They asked him for the grove that fed him as a child,
with its obedient tree.
They asked him for his breast, heart, his shoulders.
They told him
that that was absolutely necessary.
They explained to him later
that all this gift would be useless
unless he turned his tongue over to them,
because in trying times
nothing is so useful in checking hatred or lies.
And finally they begged him,
please, to go take a walk.
Because in trying times
that is, without a doubt, the decisive test.

TR. ALASTAIR REID

≈ Nuclear Umbrella

Travelers perhaps,
but I am not sure of finding
                    a shelter zone.
The world no longer has any shelter zones.
When I go up the stairs in any building
                        in any city
in Europe,
        I gratefully read "Shelter Zone" (in another language)
and breathe easy;
but when I come to the last step
I turn to the sign,
which survives like a relic.
The shelter signs
are artifacts which decorate our screwed-up ethics.
There are not any modern cities.
The streets are all laid in antiquity,
but we live now in the yet-to-come.
More than once I realize
that I am opening doors and windows
in a ruined house.
The awnings of sidewalk cafés have begun to whirl,
merchants fly over the streets,
they cut through the traffic as though it were a flower.
But I am not a prophet or magician
to unknot contemporary enigmas,
or explain somehow this explosion.
I am not more than a traveler for Foreign Trade,
a political agent with a diplomatic passport,
a terrorist with a bookish look,
a Cuban (let's make no bones about it),
the guy the customs always watch.
They spend three hours
                    taking apart my bags.

II

You, sir,
        Undersecretary of Commerce,

young, slightly jaundiced, respected,

> with past experience,

could not have suspected this scene.
You, sir, discussed the plan, fixed the trip
> for the 20th of January
> but you did not know
that all the projects would be ruined today.
> My only error
consisted in not advising you, sir, that on the 20th of January
> I was born.

III

By fortunetelling,
by the little cheat of immortality,
old people lived;
and we are their future and continue
living by the superstition of the old.
We are
Marx's dream, the stench of the great corpses
that rotted
> on the banks of the Neva
so that a high official could be right or wrong,
or so that I could embark and challenge posterity,
> which studies me
through the eyes of an Agent
> that at this very moment
has read my name and rank on a visiting card.

IV

Hours go by so rapidly that I'm behind in my life.
I still feel something like horror
and even remorse for the day after tomorrow.
I surprise myself, suddenly, analyzing the mechanism of my
> serenity
traveling
between East and West,
at such and such an altitude
watched by the smiling stewardess who doesn't know
that I come from a continent of struggles and blood.
Could it be that the flower in my lapel betrays me?

And who the devil put this flower in my lapel
like a wheel tacked onto my bed?

V

That man who couples desperately in motels,
that confused man who wrings his hands,
the sarcastic and often gloomy charlatan,
alone like a prophet,
is, of course, me.
I am dressing in a hotel in Budapest, deformed
by another moon, a different mirror,
ugly; but the Danube is lovely and runs under the bridges.
Old man in a cassock, Berkeley, you were right: those waters
do not exist, I re-create them, just as I re-create this city.
        On one side Buda
        on the other side Pest, a little farther on is Obuda—
        here there was a counterrevolution in 1956;
        but only old men remember it.
Try, sir, to tell it to these adolescents who devour
                  themselves
in open-air cafés in high summer.
A Jewish girl tells me that she has a visa to go to Vienna
        (and fifty dollars).
A poet tells me that throughout the country
books from foreign publishers circulate now
        ("and many exiles have returned")
He drinks; he comes alive and recites to me the Ode to Bartok,
                by Gyula Illyés.
Another man tells me that it is almost forbidden to talk
            about guerrillas,
that he has written a poem
requesting notice in the press
        for the dead of Vietnam.
Later we go to a restaurant; we drink wine
            with apples;
we have lamb
        with plum brandy.
"But this peace"—shouts Judith, like one escaping
             from Lake Balaton—
     "is a piece of shit!"

VI

I have seen ballet dancers, in Paris,

                                buying

nylon windbreakers.
They would sell them later for a hundred rubles in Moscow.
In a huge square
they wanted to buy my little nylon windbreaker.
He was a teenager. He spoke to me in English.
I told him I was Cuban
and he stared at me a second.
Suddenly he took off.

In the middle of the cold, of the really beautiful, cold
Moscow spring,
I have seen those jackets
blue,
yellow,
brown.
I was there, watching them
till summer ended. They floated
over the passers-by,
Western, warm
(they looked like a fringe),
cheap in Rome, cheap in London,
cheap in Madrid;
the chemical industry engaged
in the clever machinations of the market
so that a ballet dancer might hastily buy them,
as he left a rehearsal,
in the Paris department stores.
Thousands of dancers like agile demons
reselling, buying them, hiding them in their frumpy suitcases.

VII

Impossible, Carlos Drummond, to compose a poem
        at this late stage of civilization.
The last troubadour died in 1914.
Impossible to stop to find,
        I will not say the calm that one gets
from excessive scorn,

but rather a simple wood cabin,
a window with no radar,
a pine table with no maps, no calculations.
Which side will someday have my head?
How much will the CIA give for the head of a poet,
       dead or alive?
In what language will we hear one night, or afternoon,
      the alert
  in the harsh voice of the loudspeakers?
Because no one will come to calm the lovers or the desperate.
(Sauve qui peut, and screw the rest.)
Now it is not even a secret that the folklore groups
  were indoctrinated
  and any melody whatever may pave the way to disaster.
Where can you go, when you've crossed the street
and heard the latest news?
Certainly,
  you might hide in the drains,
  or in the sewers,
  or in the chimney stacks.
Armed men have been seen coming out of caves,
      pulling down
their grubby caps;
  they make rapid maps in the dust, they are experts
in the fierce alliance of a stick and a stone
  (in everything that ruins and lays waste).
We are the children of these cities
      wonderfully made
  for the bomb.
The best thing
  (and the only thing we can do for the moment)
  is to get out of our libraries
to shake out the bookworms that crawl through our pages;
  for already, forever,
we have missed the only train that could escape the explosion.

TR. ALASTAIR REID

≈ History

—Tomorrow
you will walk toward other evenings
and all your questions
will flow like the last river of the world.

—Tomorrow, yes tomorrow . . .

—And, before daybreak,
in front of the great ovens,
among the sweating men,
you will hear the song
that they knead bread by.
You will meet
the much-loved dead,
my son; History
which covers its follies
its errors with dust.

—Tomorrow, yes, tomorrow . . .

In the darkening
room, the gloom
descends on the boy
who sees arms, shields.
His grandfather
gestures and foretells
as in eternity.

TR. ALASTAIR REID

≈ Sometimes I plunge into the ocean . . .

Sometimes I plunge into the ocean, for a long time,
and emerge suddenly gasping, breathing,
and swim as far as I can from the coast
and see the distant blurred line of the shore
and the sun making the oily water boil.
The shoreline drowns in the vapor

and I close my eyes blinded by the light.
Then, a handsbreadth from those waves, the country appears
that for so long we thought
we were carrying on our shoulders: white, like a warship,
shining against the sun and against poets.

TR. ALASTAIR REID

≈ Song of the Juggler

General, dein Tank ist ein starker Wagon.
—Brecht

General, there's a battle
between your orders and my songs.
It goes on all the time:
night, day.
It knows neither tiredness nor sleep—
a battle that has gone on for many years,
so many that my eyes have never seen a sunrise
in which you, your orders, your arms, your trenches
did not figure.

A rich battle
in which, aesthetically speaking, my rags
and your uniform face off.
A theatrical battle—
it only lacks dazzling stage sets
where comedians might come on from anywhere
raising a rumpus as they do in carnivals,
each one showing off his loyalty and valor.

General, I can't destroy your fleets or your tanks
and I don't know how long this war will last
but every night one of your orders dies without
being followed,
and, undefeated, one of my songs survives.

TR. ALASTAIR REID

ROQUE DALTON (1935–1975)

For most of his adult life, Salvadoran poet Roque Dalton was in conflict with the military government, suffering imprisonment several times and narrowly escaping execution more than once. Between 1960 and 1973, he lived in exile. He returned to Salvador and joined a guerrilla group, and was assassinated by a faction of this same group in May 1975. A poet of those who suffer from political repression, he is considered a major voice in Salvadoran literary history.

≈ My Neighbor

He has a rather plain wife.

He has two boys who drive him out of his mind
who these days chase the cats all over the neighborhood.

He works, reads a lot, he sings in the mornings,
and he asks after the ladies;
he likes bread *and* the baker,
he usually drinks
beer at noon;
he knows his soccer, he loves the sea,
he'd like to have his own car,
he goes to concerts, he has a small dog,
he has lived in Paris, and he's written a book—I believe
it was poetry—
he relaxes by watching the birds,
he pays his bills at the end of the month,
he helped repair the belfry . . .

Now he's in prison:
he's also a communist, so they say . . .

TR. RICHARD SCHAAF

≈ Love Poem

Those who widened the Panama Canal
(and were on the 'silver roll' not the 'gold roll')
those who repaired the Pacific fleet
in California bases,
those who rotted in prisons in Guatemala,
Mexico, Honduras, Nicaragua
for stealing, smuggling, swindling,
for starving,
those always suspected of everything
("Allow me to place him in your custody
for suspicious loitering
aggravated by the fact of being Salvadoran")
those who pack the bars and whorehouses
in every port and capital
('The Blue Grotto,' 'The G-String,' 'Happyland')
the sowers of corn deep in foreign forests,
the crime barons of the scandal sheets,
those who nobody ever knows where they're from,
the best artisans in the world,
those who were riddled with bullets crossing the border,
those who died from malaria
or scorpion bites or swarming bees
in the hell of banana plantations,
those who got drunk and wept for the national anthem
under a Pacific cyclone or up north in the snow,
the spongers, beggars, pot-heads,
the stupid sons of whores,
those who were barely able to get back,
those who had a little more luck,
the forever undocumented,
those who do anything, sell anything, eat anything,
the first ones to pull a knife,
the wretched the most wretched of the earth,
my compatriots,
my brothers.

TR. RICHARD SCHAAF

OTTO RENE CASTILLO (1936–1967)

Castillo was exiled from Guatemala for political activities with a student association. He won the coveted Central American Poetry Prize in 1955 and the Autonomia Prize the following year. He returned to Guatemala in 1958 and entered law school, but was exiled again. After some years in Germany, he went back to Guatemala in 1964 and worked as a student organizer for a year, until the military dictatorship arrested, imprisoned, and expelled him. Castillo returned clandestinely to fight with an insurgent group but was captured, brutally tortured for an extended period, and then burned alive. His poem "Apolitical Intellectuals" is an indictment of those who would hold themselves above political struggle.

≈ Before the Scales, Tomorrow

When the enthusiasm
of our time
is recounted
for those
yet to be born,
but who announce themselves
with a kinder face,
we will come out winners,
we who have suffered most.

To be ahead
of one's time
is to suffer much.

But it is beautiful to love the world
with the eyes
of those
    still
to be born.

And splendid
to know oneself already victorious
when everything around
is still so cold, so dark.

TR. BARBARA PASCHKE AND DAVID VOLPENDESTA

≈ Apolitical Intellectuals

One day,
the apolitical
intellectuals
of my country
will be interrogated
by the humblest
of our people.

They will be asked
what they did
when their country was slowly
dying out,
like a sweet campfire,
small and abandoned.

No one will ask them
about their dress
or their long
siestas
after lunch,
or about their futile struggles
against "nothingness,"
or about their ontological
way
to make money.
No, they won't be questioned
on Greek mythology,
or about the self-disgust they felt
when someone deep inside them
was getting ready to die
the coward's death.

They will be asked nothing
about their absurd
justifications
nurtured in the shadow
of a huge lie.

On that day,
the humble people will come,
those who never had a place
in the books and poems
of the apolitical intellectuals

but who daily delivered
their bread and milk,
their eggs and tortillas;
those who mended their clothes,
those who drove their cars,
those who took care of their dogs and gardens,
and worked for them,
and they will ask:
"What did you do when the poor
suffered, when tenderness and life
were dangerously burning out in them?"

Apolitical intellectuals
of my sweet country,
you will have nothing to say.

A vulture of silence
will eat your guts.
Your own misery
will gnaw at your souls.
And you will be mute
in your shame.

TR. MARGARET RANDALL

≈ Distances

I

In 1935 Hitler said
"The Third Reich
will last a thousand years."

What did Hitler say
ten years later
under the ruins of Berlin?

A few years later
Mister Dulles, snoring
like a caterpillar
said "This decade will see the end
of the slavery of communism."

What did Yuri Gagarin
do a few years later,
sending his greetings to men
over the wide oceans
and vast territories of America?

Thomas Mann was right
when he said
"Anti-communism
is the most ridiculous mode
of the twentieth century."
Still
    the interests
    the profit
continue their fanfare

continue killing
           still.

II

Under the bitter December air
a friend says
"I'm disillusioned. Everything goes
so slowly. The dictatorship is strong.
I'm desperate and pained
by the calvary of my people."

And I, sensing his anguish, the gray
and noble sadness of my friend,
knowing his fight
                    to keep on fighting,
do not say: coward or go to the mountains
or lazy or pessimist,
rigid, poor devil.

I only put my arm around his shoulder,
so the tearing cruelty of his cold
be less.

III

A knock
           at the door.

Before me, two sore eyes.
And behind them, a child whose six years
barely support national misery,
the national infamy, the cowardly nation.
He extends his hand
and on the face of my country
the pieces of my heart
fall split by blows
protesting this man's death
already dead.

Still
       when I give him bread

his tender eyes speak to me
from the depths of his ignorance.

IV

Someone hums the National Anthem.
In the street. I get up
and look from the window
of the house where I live now.
He who sings is barefoot.
Surely also without breakfast.
He is a hawker of lies

                  morning
                  and afternoon.

Fifteen years at best.
Fifteen years of misery, I bet on that.
And from his hoarse throat,
like a Greek god well fed,
emerges the National Anthem of Guatemala.
If I hadn't seen it, surely
I'd have said: "A soldier singing."

V

Recently returned from Europe
one of my nephews asks me
if I know Madrid.

I say no, brusquely,
and continue talking about Paris.

But my story goes pale.
The blood, hitting hard
and sudden in my heart,
the horrible bleeding.

VI

In the days of Ubico the tyrant,
end of '42, as the story goes,
there was a mason in the parish
who dared paint "*Liverty,*

Doun with th blody jenral"
on the city walls.
The mason was caught,
questioned,
—why was he so crazy
as to hate the General
if the General had complete military support
and his power was invincible.

And the mason said: Ubico will fall.
And everyone laughed. This is a crazy man,
they said. The General will rule forever
in Guatemala. Until he dies. Like God,
he is all powerful.
No one will lift a finger against him.
His power is infinite
and the people are cowardly, resigned,
afraid of his granite strength.

But the stubborn mason said: Ubico will fall.
He will not rule forever in Guatemala.
The people will rise against him.

And they shot him, in the morning,
in the barracks,
more for disbeliever than subversive,
the mason of the parish who wrote:
"Liverty, Doun with th blody jenral"
on the walls of the city.

VII

In the street someone stops me
and cries against my chest.
Those who pass look and close a bit more
the obscure rose of their nonconformist blood.

"They've killed him, my son.
They've killed him, those gorillas!"
she tells me, letting the ashes
of her voice fall, blackened forever.

And I, who love life so,
who fight so that all will love it
and no one will have to complain of it,
feel the desire to kill
he who killed, blind, awkward,
                                    rude indian
desire to revenge the killed
                        by killing.

But I say and do nothing.

I stroke the white head
of the old woman crying on my chest,
and life is more painful than ever.
And still I know: there are many ways
to give life for life.
The important thing:
to give it as it must be given!

TR. MARGARET RANDALL

ARIEL DORFMAN (1942–   )

Although born in Argentina, Dorfman is a Chilean. The coup d'état of
1973 that brought General Augusto Pinochet to power forced Dorf-
man, a strong supporter of socialist president Salvador Allende, into
exile. He lived in the United States and Europe until 1983, when he
returned to Chile, but was arrested and deported in 1987. He has since
been allowed to return, and divides his time between teaching at Duke
University and visits to Chile. He considers himself a resident of the
United States, where he has become well known as a novelist as well as
a poet.

≈ **I Just Missed the Bus and I'll Be Late for Work**

I'd have to piss through my eyes to cry for you
salivate, sweat, sigh through my eyes,

I'd have to waterfall
I'd have to wine
I'd have to die like crushed grapes
through my eyes,
cough up vultures spit green silence
and shed a dried-up skin
no good to animals
no good for a trophy
I'd have to cry these wounds
this war
to mourn for us.

TR. ARIEL DORFMAN AND EDITH GROSSMAN

≈ Last Waltz in Santiago

All that you've danced they take from you
they just take it
just like that.

They kill the dancer in you
they crush her slowly,
they skeleton, smoke,
before she can
                    dance this dance
                        with you

They break your rhumba, tango
                            they break you,
they dissolve your carnival in urine,
they put needles through the skin of your record,
they use the trumpet like a knife
                            and they shatter your violin
just like that.

They lock you in walls
that have no number,
among mirrors and songs covered with ashes,
they lock your hands, your feet, your collarbone,
and they tell you now dance you cripple

dance now you motherfucker,
they sentence you to tomb, they scrape you with sand.

Let's dance, then,
my dear,
because they're taking away all that we've danced
—right now, listen to the footsteps coming closer
and someone is trying out shiny soldier's boots
right now—

      right now.

TR. ARIEL DORFMAN AND EDITH GROSSMAN

≈ Vocabulary

I

But how can I tell their story
           if I was not there?

When two of them met
        far away
on an unfamiliar street corner
they could not know if it was
        a first meeting
        or a farewell.
They could not know who was looking at them
        from the quadrangle
           of that window.
Reporting every movement
      every movement of their lips.

      I was looking at them from another country
      and I cannot tell their story.
      I was calling from another country
      and the phone was always busy.

II

Show me a word I can use.
Show me one verb.

An adjective as clear as a ray of light.
Listen carefully to the bottom of every sentence,
to the attic and the dust in the furniture
of every sentence,
                              perk up your ears,
listen and look under the bed
of every sentence
at the soldiers waiting their turn
at the foot
of the bride's bed.

                    To preserve just one word.
                    What is it to be?
                    Like a question on a quiz show.
                    If you could take one word with you
                    to the future,
                    what is it to be?
Find it.
Plunge into the garbage heap.
Stick your hands deep into the ooze.
Close your fist around the fragment of a mirror
fractured by feet that dance on what should have been
a wedding night.

                    Let me tell you something.
                    Even if I had been there
                    I could not have told their story.

III

                    I was calling from another country
                    and the phone was still busy.
                    I was trying to call home
                    and the machine had just swallowed
                                        my last dime.

IV

As for the story I cannot tell,
They accumulated tenderness
                    as others accumulate money.

Ask them.
Even if the phone is busy.
Even if the machine has just swallowed your last dime.

Even if the operator drowns out all the other voices.
Ask them for the verse our lovers will still need
if we are ever again to bathe
                    in the same river.

Let them speak for themselves.

TR. ARIEL DORFMAN AND EDITH GROSSMAN

TERESA DE JESÚS

Teresa de Jesus is the pseudonym of a Chilean poet about whom little is known. These poems were smuggled out of Chile after the coup of 1973. Her poetry confronts the silencing of political dissent. "Mummy" in the poem "Proverbs" refers to a rightist, and Tres Alamos is the name of a prison.

≈ Proverbs

Chile, 1973 on

1) It's altogether something else with shrapnel
2) In closed mouth no bullets enter
3) In the house of the worker: knife & bullet
4) See not, hear not, speak not
5) The mummy, though dressed as a worker, is a mummy still
6) When the mummy sounds off, the shit carries
7) One hand betrays the other & both betray the face
8) One alone shuts up well, but two shut up better
9) The undercover agent who falls asleep gets carried off to Tres
    Alamos
10) Better one airplane on the ground than a hundred flying

11) Breed soldiers & they'll kill your sons
12) When one cell is shut, two hundred open up
13) By your mouth you die
14) Don't look a gift Mercedes in the teeth

TR. MARIA PROSER, ARLENE SCULLY, AND JAMES SCULLY

≈ Curfew

It is the heart of the night
wounded by silence.
The trees were left alone
with the butterflies of night.
The moon, at times, peeps through
and weeps among the trees.
But the houses too
are blackened by silence.
The moon cries sometimes
by the darkened houses.
A car goes by
parting the silence,
it's the night patrol
starved for victims.
The sacrificial stone is laid out
quietly in the silent night.
The barbarian god wants
hearts
in the infinite night.
Police cars search out
people.
The noise stops,
they knock at the door.
A man in pajamas comes out,
yes, they saw him go away.
He was whole and sound
as when he was born.
His voice trembled a little.
The silence. The silence.
The silence covers everything.

The relatives make inquiries
quietly.
They have cried on the table
and they have not screamed.
The children at their games
don't mention it.
They've learnt the new game
which is to hush.
The neighbors don't mention it,
correctly.
Friends draw back
discreetly.
There is a new game, sirs:
to keep silence.
The new moon sobs
over them all.

TR. MARIA PROSER, ARLENE SCULLY, AND JAMES SCULLY

≈ The Flag of Chile

Chile's flag has three colors.
Everyone knows it
and so do I.
It has three colors and a star.
Everyone knows it
and so do I.

The white certainly expresses
hunger: with mask, and without,
hunger disguised
and in civvies.

Everyone knows it
and so do I.

The blue represents neurosis
assembled minute by minute
and at the end of each month, confirmed
by an assassin over the blue.

Everyone knows it
and so do I.

The red wears away in waves
of blood, of torture and pain,
the red flames in poppies
opened by gunshots,
the red rises from tombs.

Everyone knows it
and so do I.

TR. MARIA PROSER, ARLENE SCULLY, AND JAMES SCULLY

The Struggle for Civil Rights and Civil Liberties in the United States

(1900–1991)

Although dissent is constitutionally protected in the United States by the Bill of Rights, such protection has at times seemed more theoretical than actual. There was a concerted campaign against political radicals, for instance, after World War I. Seditious activities came under scrutiny again in 1938, when Congress set up the House Un-American Activities Committee (HUAC), which devoted most of its attention to the investigation of the political left. HUAC subpoenaed people from all walks of life and subjected them to well-publicized inquiries about their loyalty to the government of the United States. During its first fifteen years, HUAC, establishing guilt by association, presented a startling contravention of the Constitution.

When the Cold War increased anti-Communist tensions, HUAC gained unprecedented exposure. The search for subversives was given motive force by the United States Chamber of Commerce, which in 1946 began publishing reports on Communist influence in different areas of American life. In the following year, the notorious hearings on members of the film industry were held, and former Communists, alleged Communists, and "fellow travelers" were asked to recant and inform on friends, colleagues, and associates or face industry blacklisting. The federal government instituted loyalty oaths; the Taft-Hartley Act forbade union officials to have ties with the Communist Party.

The early 1950s also brought national prominence to Senator Joseph McCarthy and his virulent attacks on the government, intellectuals, and what he claimed was the "Eastern Establishment." By the time he was censured by the Senate in 1954, McCarthy had drastically altered the terms of political debate. According to the historian Godfrey Hodgson, McCarthyism's "principal effect was to transform what ought to have been an issue of foreign policy—namely, how to deal with Communist power abroad—into the most emotional and dangerous issue in American domestic politics."

Soon after Senator McCarthy was condemned by Senate resolution, the modern civil rights movement began. The United States had been, until very recently, a country whose laws sanctioned overt racism and discrimination on the basis of skin color. This was clearest in the South after Reconstruction: the urgent separation of the races by law was upheld in the famous Supreme Court case *Plessy* v. *Ferguson,* which permitted segregation with "separate but equal" facilities. Although permitted to vote by statute, African-Americans were in effect disenfranchised by the application of numerous tests of their qualifications.

Throughout this century, African-Americans have differed about the best means of overcoming the obstacles erected by a racist society: separatism, self-help, nonviolent confrontation, assimilation, and violent confrontation have all seemed viable options to a group that has endured lynchings, unfair trials, and economic neglect.

Following World War II, in which African-Americans had once again served their country (as they had since the Revolutionary War), soldiers returned with the expectations of the loyal and victorious. Many left the South for the promise of greater wealth and success in the industrial North. Most historians accept that the modern civil rights movement began in 1955 (one year after the Supreme Court overturned *Plessy* v. *Ferguson* in the groundbreaking *Brown* case), when a woman named Rosa Parks refused to comply with a city ordinance in Montgomery, Alabama, and took a seat in the "white section" of the bus. The African-American community, under the strong leadership of Martin Luther King, Jr., boycotted the bus lines. This first mass movement against segregation was answered by intense violence: bombs were set off in African-American churches and King's home was attacked by rifle fire. The boycott prevailed, however, and in 1956 the Supreme Court outlawed discrimination on local bus lines.

The second milestone for the civil rights movement came in 1960, when four teenagers staged a sit-in at a segregated lunch counter in Greensboro, North Carolina. By the end of the year, more than fifty thousand people had taken part in demonstrations, and more than three thousand had gone to jail. The mobilization of the nation's African-American population was spontaneous and led to a number of actions. In the spring and summer of 1961, CORE (the Congress of Racial Equality) and SNCC (the Student Nonviolent Coordinating Committee) organized "Freedom Rides"—mixed-race demonstrations to desegregate Southern buses. Organizations registered voters and organized boycotts. National attention became acute when in 1963 the commissioner of public safety of Birmingham, Alabama, set police dogs against children in a demonstration. After that, the federal government signaled its commitment to civil rights, underscored by two voting-rights acts in 1964 and 1965.

The legislation proved difficult to enforce: racists called the new laws a violation of "states' rights," and there were many violent attacks against civil rights workers, who were arrested, beaten, and sometimes killed.

Changes in voting laws do not necessarily cure economic hardship. The frustration of African-Americans surfaced during the 1960s, a period of uprisings in cities from Newark, New Jersey, to Oakland, California. The frustrations of militant African-Americans became apparent when in 1965 the SNCC gave up its commitment to nonviolence and the Black Panther Party was formed. By 1966, CORE, which had always been multiracial, became wary of white membership and proclaimed its endorsement of the "Black Power" movement.

Despite the efforts of civil rights activists, the work of societal transformation by necessity continues, bequeathing its force to women, Native Americans, Latin Americans, Asian-Americans, and others.

LANGSTON HUGHES (1902–1967)

The foremost African-American writer of his day, Hughes was openly sympathetic to radical causes in the 1930s, visiting the Soviet Union and serving as a journalist during the Spanish Civil War. He was frequently denounced by the House Un-American Activities Committee and was finally called before the committee in 1953. He survived his interrogation by Senator Joseph McCarthy, but at a price: although he did not openly criticize leftist political views, he did seem to recant them. Nevertheless, Hughes was and remained a staunch defender of civil rights in the United States and of human rights worldwide.

≈ Letter to the Academy

The gentlemen who have got to be classics and are now old
     with beards (or dead and in their graves) will kindly
     come forward and speak upon the subject

Of the Revolution. I mean the gentlemen who wrote lovely
     books about the defeat of the flesh and the triumph of
     the spirit that sold in the hundreds of thousands and
     are studied in the high schools and read by the best
     people will kindly come forward and

Speak about the Revolution—where the flesh triumphs (as
     well as the spirit) and the hungry belly eats, and there
     are no best people, and the poor are mighty and no
     longer poor, and the young by the hundreds of
     thousands are free from hunger to grow and study and

love and propagate, bodies and souls unchained
without My Lord saying a commoner shall never
marry my daughter or the Rabbi crying cursed be the
mating of Jews and Gentiles or Kipling writing never
the twain shall meet—

For the twain have met. But please—all you gentlemen with
beards who are so wise and old and who write better
than we do and whose souls have triumphed (in spite
of hungers and wars and the evils about you) and
whose books have soared in calmness and beauty aloof
from the struggle to the library shelves and the desks
of students and who are now classics—come forward
and speak upon

The subject of the Revolution.

We want to know what in the hell you'd say?

Moscow, 1933

≈ **Madrid—1937**

*Damaged by shells, many of the clocks on the public buildings in Madrid have
stopped. At night, the streets are pitch dark.*

—News Item

Put out the lights and stop the clocks.
Let time stand still,
Again man mocks himself
And all his human will to build and grow.
　　Madrid!
The fact and symbol of man's woe.
　　Madrid!
Time's end and throw-back,
Birth of darkness,
Years of light reduced:
The ever minus of the brute,
The nothingness of barren land
And stone and metal,
Emptiness of gold,

The dullness of a bill of sale:
BOUGHT AND PAID FOR! SOLD!
Stupidity of hours that do not move
Because all clocks are stopped.
Blackness of nights that do not see
Because all lights are out.
   Madrid!
Beneath the bullets!
   Madrid!
Beneath the bombing planes!
   Madrid!
In the fearful dark!

Oh, mind of man!
So long to make a light
Of fire,
    of oil,
       of gas,
And now electric rays.
So long to make a clock
Of sun-dial,
    sand-dial,
       figures,
And now two hands that mark the hours.
Oh, mind of man!
So long to struggle upward out of darkness
To a measurement of time—
And now:
These guns,
These brainless killers in the Guardarrama hills
Trained on Madrid
To stop the clocks in the towers
And shatter all their faces
Into a million bits of nothingness
In the city
That will not bow its head
To darkness and to greed again:
That dares to dream a cleaner dream!
Oh, mind of man
Moulded into a metal shell—
Left-overs of the past

That rain dull hell and misery
On the world again—
Have your way
And stop the clocks!
Bomb out the lights!
And mock yourself!
Mock all the rights of those
Who live like decent folk.
Let guns alone salute
The wisdom of our age
With dusty powder marks
On yet another page of history.
Let there be no sense of time,
Nor measurement of light and dark,
In fact, no light at all!
Let mankind fall
Into the deepest pit that ignorance can dig
For us all!
Descent is quick.
To rise again is slow.
In the darkness of her broken clocks
Madrid cries NO!
In the timeless midnight of the Fascist guns,
Madrid cries NO!
To all the killers of man's dreams,
Madrid cries NO!

> To break that NO apart
> Will be to break the human heart.

Madrid, September 24, 1937

≈ Let America Be America Again

Let America be America again.
Let it be the dream it used to be.
Let it be the pioneer on the plain
Seeking a home where he himself is free.

(America never was America to me.)

Let America be the dream the dreamers dreamed—
Let it be that great strong land of love
Where never kings connive or tyrants scheme
That any man be crushed by one above.

(It never was America to me.)

O, let my land be a land where Liberty
Is crowned with no false patriotic wreath,
But opportunity is real, and life is free,
Equality is in the air we breathe.

(There's never been equality for me,
Nor freedom in this "homeland of the free.")

Say who are you that mumbles in the dark?
And who are you that draws your veil across the stars?

I am the poor white, fooled and pushed apart,
I am the Negro bearing slavery's scars.
I am the red man driven from the land,
I am the immigrant clutching the hope I seek—
And finding only the same old stupid plan
Of dog eat dog, of mighty crush the weak.

I am the young man, full of strength and hope,
Tangled in that ancient endless chain
Of profit, power, gain, of grab the land!
Of grab the gold!
Of grab the ways of satisfying need!
Of work the men! Of take the pay!
Of owning everything for one's own greed!

I am the farmer, bondsman to the soil.
I am the worker sold to the machine.
I am the Negro, servant to you all.
I am the people, worried, hungry, mean—
Hungry yet today despite the dream.
Beaten yet today—O, Pioneers!
I am the man who never got ahead,
The poorest worker bartered through the years.

Yet I'm the one who dreamt our basic dream
In that Old World while still a serf of kings.
Who dreamt a dream so strong, so brave, so true,
That even yet its mighty daring sings
In every brick and stone, in every furrow turned
That's made America the land it has become.
O, I'm the man who sailed those early seas
In search of what I meant to be my home—
For I'm the one who left dark Ireland's shore,
And Poland's plain, and England's grassy lea,
And torn from Black Africa's strand I came
To build a "homeland of the free."

The free?

A dream—
Still beckoning to me!

O, let America be America again—
The land that never has been yet—
And yet must be—
The land where every man is free.
The land that's mine—
The poor man's, Indian's, Negro's ME—
Who made America,
Whose sweat and blood, whose faith and pain,
Whose hand at the foundry, whose plow in the rain,
Must bring back our mighty dream again.
Sure, call me any ugly name you choose—
The steel of freedom does not stain.
From those who live like leeches on the people's lives,
We must take back our land again,
America!

O, yes,
I say it plain,
America never was America to me,
And yet I swear this oath—
America will be!
An ever-living seed,

Its dream
Lies deep in the heart of me.

We, the people, must redeem
Our land, the mines, the plants, the rivers,
The mountains and the endless plain—
All, all the stretch of these great green states—
And make America again!

RICHARD WRIGHT (1908–1960)

Son of an illiterate Southern sharecropper, Wright left home during his teens and worked in Chicago at a number of jobs, including public relations man for the Federal Theater Project and writer for the Works Progress Administration (WPA). He joined the Communist Party in 1932; he later became disaffected, but remained adamantly leftist. His greatest achievement was the best-selling novel *Native Son.* The result-ing fame led to notoriety and harassment in the United States, and Wright (in his own words) "chose exile" in France from 1947 until his death. Although he was not as prolific as a poet, Wright's poetic work is widely anthologized.

≈ I Have Seen Black Hands

I am black and I have seen black hands, millions and millions of
    them—
Out of millions of bundles of wool and flannel tiny black fingers have
    reached restlessly and hungrily for life.
Reached out for the black nipples at the black breasts of black mothers,
And they've held red, green, blue, yellow, orange, white, and purple
    toys in the childish grips of possession,
And chocolate drops, peppermint sticks, lollypops, wineballs, ice cream
    cones, and sugared cookies in fingers sticky and gummy,
And they've held balls and bats and gloves and marbles and jack-knives
    and slingshots and spinning tops in the thrill of sport and play,

And pennies and nickels and dimes and quarters and sometimes on New Year's, Easter, Lincoln's Birthday, May Day, a brand new green dollar bill,

They've held pens and rulers and maps and tablets and books in palms spotted and smeared with ink,

And they've held dice and cards and half-pint flasks and cue sticks and cigars and cigarettes in the pride of new maturity . . .

II

I am black and I have seen black hands, millions and millions of them—

They were tired and awkward and calloused and grimy and covered with hangnails,

And they were caught in the fast-moving belts of machines and snagged and smashed and crushed,

And they jerked up and down at the throbbing machines massing taller and taller the heaps of gold in the banks of bosses,

And they piled higher and higher the steel, iron, the lumber, wheat, rye, the oats, corn, the cotton, the wool, the oil, the coat, the meat, the fruit, the glass, and the stone until there was too much to be used,

And they grabbed guns and slung them on their shoulders and marched and groped in trenches and fought and killed and conquered nations who were customers for the goods black hands made.

And again black hands stacked goods higher and higher until there was too much to be used,

And then the black hands held trembling at the factory gates the dreaded lay-off slip,

And the black hands hung idle and swung empty and grew soft and got weak and bony from unemployment and starvation,

And they grew nervous and sweaty, and opened and shut in anguish and doubt and hesitation and irresolution . . .

III

I am black and I have seen black hands, millions and millions of them—

Reaching hesitantly out of days of slow death for the goods they had made, but the bosses warned that the goods were private and did not belong to them,

And the black hands struck desperately out in defence of life and there

was blood, but the enraged bosses decreed that this too was
    wrong,
And the black hands felt the cold steel bars of the prison they had
    made, in despair tested their strength and found that they could
    neither bend nor break them,
And the black hands fought and scratched and held back but a thou-
    sand white hands took them and tied them,
And the black hands lifted palms in mute and futile supplication to the
    sodden faces of mobs wild in the revelries of sadism,
And the black hands strained and clawed and struggled in vain at the
    noose that tightened about the black throat,
And the black hands waved and beat fearfully at the tall flames that
    cooked and charred the black flesh . . .

IV

I am black and I have seen black hands
Raised in fists of revolt, side by side with the white fists of white
    workers,
And some day—and it is only this which sustains me—
Some day there shall be millions and millions of them,
On some red day in a burst of fists on a new horizon!

≈ Between the World and Me

And one morning while in the woods I stumbled suddenly upon the
    thing,
Stumbled upon it in a grassy clearing guarded by scaly oaks and elms.
And the sooty details of the scene rose, thrusting themselves between
    the world and me. . . .

There was a design of white bones slumbering forgottenly upon a
    cushion of ashes.
There was a charred stump of a sapling pointing a blunt finger accus-
    ingly at the sky.
There were torn tree limbs, tiny veins of burnt leaves, and a scorched
    coil of greasy hemp;
A vacant shoe, an empty tie, a ripped shirt, a lonely hat, and a pair of
    trousers stiff with black blood.

And upon the trampled grass were buttons, dead matches, butt-ends of
  cigars and cigarettes, peanut shells, a drained gin-flask, and a
  whore's lipstick;
Scattered traces of tar, restless arrays of feathers, and the lingering smell
  of gasoline.
And through the morning air the sun poured yellow surprise into the
  eye sockets of a stony skull. . . .
And while I stood my mind was frozen with a cold pity for the life that
  was gone.
The ground gripped my feet and my heart was circled by icy walls of
  fear—
The sun died in the sky; a night wind muttered in the grass and fumbled
  the leaves in the trees; the woods poured forth the hungry yelping
  of hounds; the darkness screamed with thirsty voices; and the
  witnesses rose and lived:
The dry bones stirred, rattled, lifted, melting themselves into my bones.
The grey ashes formed flesh firm and black, entering into my flesh.
The gin-flask passed from mouth to mouth; cigars and cigarettes
  glowed, the whore smeared the lipstick red upon her lips,
And a thousand faces swirled around me, clamoring that my life be
  burned. . . .

And then they had me, stripped me, battering my teeth into my throat
  till I swallowed my own blood.
My voice was drowned in the roar of their voices, and my black wet
  body slipped and rolled in their hands as they bound me to the
  sapling.
And my skin clung to the bubbling hot tar, falling from me in limp
  patches.
And the down and quills of the white feathers sank into my raw flesh,
  and I moaned in my agony.
Then my blood was cooled mercifully, cooled by a baptism of gasoline.
And in a blaze of red I leaped to the sky as pain rose like water, boiling
  my limbs.
Panting, begging I clutched childlike, clutched to the hot sides of death.
Now I am dry bones and my face a stony skull staring in yellow surprise
  at the sun. . . .

MURIEL RUKEYSER (1913–1980)

Poet, activist, biographer, playwright, Rukeyser was nineteen when she
contracted typhoid fever in an Alabama jail for protesting during the
second trial (1933) of the so-called Scottsboro boys, a celebrated case
involving nine African-American youths accused of raping two white
women. Rukeyser was jailed again, thirty years later, for a protest
against the Vietnam War. She became president of the P.E.N.-Ameri-
can Center, and in the 1970s traveled to South Korea on behalf of a
dissident poet Kim Chi-Ha, but was not permitted to see him. She
profoundly influenced a number of American women poets and is
esteemed as a model for poet-activists.

≈ Breaking Open

I come into the room   The room stands waiting
river   books   flowers   you are far away
black river   a language just forgotten
traveling blaze of light   dreams of endurance
racing into this moment ˙ outstretched faces
and you are far away
                        The stars cross over
fire-flood   extremes of singing
filth and corrupted promises   my river
A white triangle of need
                        my reflected face
laced with a black triangle   of need

Naked among the silent of my own time
and Zig Zag Zag that last letter
   of a secret or forgotten alphabet
   shaped like our own last letter but it means
Something in our experience you do not know
When will it open open opening
River-watching all night
                        will the river

swing open we are Asia and New York
Bombs, roaches, mutilation   River-watching

———

Looking out at the river
the city-flow seen as river
the flow seen as a flow of possibility
and I too to that sea.

———

Summer repetitive. The machine screaming
Beating outside, on the corrupted
Waterfront.
On my good days it appears digging
And building,
On others, its monstrous word
Says on one note Gone, killed, laid waste.

———

The whole thing—waterfront, war, city,
sons, daughters, me—
Must be re-imagined.
Sun on the orange-red roof.

———

Walking into the elevator at Westbeth
Yelling in the empty stainless-steel
Room like the room of this tormented year.
Like the year
The metal nor absorbs nor reflects
My yelling.
My pulled face loose at me
From the steel walls.

———

And then we go to Washington as if it were
Jerusalem;
and then we present our petition, clearly,
rightfully;
and then some of us walk away;
and then do others of us stay;

and some of us lie gravely down
on that cool mosaic floor,
the Senate.
Washington! Your bombs rain down!
I mourn, I lie down, I grieve.

————

Written on the plane:

The conviction that what is meant by the unconscious is the same
as what is meant by history. The collective unconscious is the
living history brought to the present in consciousness, waking or
sleeping. The personal "unconscious" is the personal history.
This is an identity.
We will now explore further ways of reaching our lives, the new
world. My own life, yours; this earth, this moon, this system,
the "space" we share, which is consciousness.

Turbulence of air now. A pause of nine minutes.

————

Written on the plane. After turbulence:

The movement of life: to live more fully in the present. This
movement includes the work of bringing this history to "light"
and understanding. The "unconscious" of the race, and its traces
in art and in social structure and "inventions"—these are our
inheritance. In facing history, we look at each other, and in facing
our entire personal life, we look at each other.

I want to break open. On the plane, a white cloud seen through
rainbow. The rainbow is, optically, on the glass of the window.

————

The jury said Guilty, Guilty, Guilty,
Guilty, Guilty.   Each closed face.
I see myself in the river-window. River
Slow going to its sea.
And old, crushed, perverse, waiting,
In loss, in dread, dead tree.

Columbus

Inner greet.   Greenberg said it,
Even the tallest man needs inner greet.
This is the great word
brought back, in swinging seas.   The new world.

End of summer.
Dark-red butterflies on the river
Dark-orange butterflies in the city.
The young men still going to war
Or away from war, to the prisons, to other countries.
To the high cold mountains, to the source of the river, I too go,
Deeper into this room.

A dream remembered only in other dreams.
The voice saying:
All you dreaded as a child
Came to pass in storms of light;
All you dreaded as a girl
Falls and falls in avalanche—
Dread and the dream of love will make
All that time and men may build,
All that women dance and make.
They become you.   Your own face
Dances through the night and day,
Leading your body into this
Body-led dance, its mysteries.
Answer me.   Dance my dance.

River-watching from the big Westbeth windows:
Powerful miles of Hudson, an east-blowing wind
All the way to Asia.
No.   Lost in our breath,
Sobbing, lost, alone.   The river darkens.
Black flow, bronze lights, white lights.
Something must answer that light, that dark.

Love,
The door opens, you walk in.

————————

The old man said, "The introversion of war
Is the main task of our time."
Now it makes its poem, when the sky stops killing.
I try to turn my acts inward and deeper.
Almost a poem.   If it splash outside,
All right.
My teacher says, "Go deeper."
The day when the salmon-colored flowers
Open.
I will essay.   Go deeper.
Make my poem.

————————

Going to prison. The clang of the steel door.
It is my choice. But the steel door does clang.
The introversion of this act
Past its seeming, past all thought of effect,
Until it is something like
Writing a poem in my silent room.

————————

In prison, the thick air,
still, loaded, heat on heat.
Around your throat
for the doors are locks,
the windows are locked doors,
the hot smell locked around us,
the machine shouting at us,
trying to sell us meat and carpets.
In prison, the prisoners,
all of us, all the objects,
chairs, cots, mops, tables.
Only the young cat.
He does not know he is locked in.

————————

In prison, the prisoners.
One black girl, 19 years.
She has killed her child
and she grieves, she grieves.
She crosses to my bed.
"What do *Free* mean?"
I look at her.
"You don't understand English."
"Yes, I understand English."
"What do *Free* mean?"

———

In prison a
brown paper bag
I put it beside my cot.
All my things.
Comb, notebook, underwear,
letterpaper, toothbrush, book.
I am rich—
they have given me another toothbrush.
The guard saying:
"You'll find people share here."

———

Photos, more precise than any face can be.
    The broken static moment, life never by
    any eye seen.

———

My contradictions set me tasks, errands.

This I know:
What I reap, that shall I sow.

———

How we live:
I look into my face in the square glass.
Under it, a bright flow of cold water.
At once, a strong arrangement of presences:
I am holding a small glass
under the little flow

at Fern Spring, among the western forest.
A cool flaw among the silence.
The taste of the waterfall.

————————

Some rare battered she-poet, old girl in the Village
racketing home past low buildings some freezing night,
come face to face with that broad roiling river.
Nothing buried in her but is lit and transformed.

Burning the Dreams

on a spring morning of young wood, green wood
it will not burn, but the dreams burn.
My hands have ashes on them.
They fear it
and so they destroy the nearest things.

Death and the Dancer

Running from death
throwing his teeth at the ghost
dipping into his belly, staving off death with a throw
tearing his brains out, throwing them at Death
death-baby is being born
scythe clock and banner come
trumpet of bone   and drum made of something—
the callous-handed goddess
her kiss is resurrection

Rational Man

The marker at Auschwitz
The scientists torturing male genitals
The learned scientists, they torture female genitals
The 3-year-old girl, what she did to her kitten
The collar made of leather for drowning a man in his chair
The scatter-bomb with the nails that drive into the brain
The thread through the young man's splendid penis
The babies in flames.   The thrust
Infected reptile dead in the live wombs of girls
We did not know we were insane.

We do not know we are insane.
We say to them: you are insane
Anything you can imagine
      on punishable drugs, or calm and young
      with a fever of 105, or on your knees,
      with the world of Hanoi bombed
      with the legless boy in Bach Mai
      with the sons of man torn by man
Rational man has done.

Mercy, Lord.   On every living life.

———

In tall whirlpools of mirrors
Unshapen body and face
middle of the depth
of a night that will not turn
the unshapen all night
trying for form

———

I do and I do.
Life and this under-war.
Deep under protest, make.
For we are makers more.

but touching teaching going
the young and the old
they reach they break they are moving
to make the world

———

something about desire
something about murder
something about my death
something about madness

something about light
something of breaking open

sing me to sleep and morning
my dreams are all a waking

———————

In the night
wandering room to room of this world
I move by touch
and then something says
let the city pour
the sleep of the beloved
Let the night pour down
all its meanings
Let the images pour
the light is dreaming

The Hostages

When I stand with these three
My new brothers my new sister
These who bind themselves offering
Hostages to go at a word, hostages
to go deeper here among our own cities
When I look into your faces
Karl, Martin, Andrea.

When I look into your faces
Offered men and women, I can speak,
And I speak openly on the church steps,
At the peace center saying: We affirm
Our closeness forever with the eyes in Asia,
Those who resist the forces we resist.
One more hostage comes forward, his eyes: Joe,
With Karl, Martin, Andrea, me.

And now alone in the river-watching room,   ·
Allen, your voice comes, the deep prophetic word.
And we are one more, Joe, Andrea, Karl, Martin,
Allen, me.   The hostages.   Reaching.   Beginning.

———————

That I looked at them with my living eyes.
That they looked at me with their living eyes.
That we embraced.
That we began to learn each other's language.

It is something like the breaking open of my youth
but unlike too, leading not only to consummation
of the bed and of the edge of the sea.
Although that, surely, also.

But this music is
itself
needing only other selving
It is defeated but a way is open:
transformation

———————

Then came I entire to this moment
process and light
    to discover the country our waking
breaking open

THOMAS MCGRATH (1916–1990)

McGrath's self-described "unaffiliated far left" politics were formed
during the 1930s, when he worked as a labor organizer on the docks of
Manhattan's West Side. He served in the Army Air Forces in World
War II, then spent two years in England as a Rhodes Scholar. He had
already published six books of poetry when he was fired from his
teaching job at Los Angeles State College because he had been black-
listed: in 1954, he had refused to provide information to the House
Committee on Un-American Activities, declaring that he would prefer
to ally himself with the great revolutionary poets of the past. He
resumed teaching six years later and lived in North Dakota and Min-
nesota until his death. His powerful narrative poems record a lifetime
of political engagement.

≈ Nocturne Militaire

Miami Beach: wartime

Imagine or remember how the road at last led us
Over bridges like prepositions, linking a drawl of islands.
The coast curved away like a question mark, listening slyly
And shyly whispered the insomniac Atlantic.
But we were uncertain of both question and answer,
Stiff and confused and bemused in expendable khaki,
Seeing with innocent eyes, the walls gleaming,
And the alabaster city of a rich man's dream.

Borne by the offshore wind, an exciting rumor,
The legend of tropic islands, caresses the coast like hysteria,
Bringing a sound like bells rung under sea;
And brings the infected banker and others whose tenure
Is equally uncertain, equally certain: the simple
And perfect faces of women—like the moon
Whose radiance is disturbing and quite as impersonal:
Not to be warmed by and never ample.

They linger while in the dazzling sepulchral city,
Delicately exploring their romantic diseases,
The gangster, the capitalist and their protégés
With all their doomed retainers:
       not worth your hate or pity
Now that they have to learn a new language—
And they despise the idiom like an upper class foreigner:
The verb *to die* baffles them. We cannot mourn,
But their doom gives stature at last, moon-dazzled,
       silhouette on the flaming Atlantic.

Something is dying. But in the fierce sunlight,
On the swanky golf-course drill-field, something is being born
Whose features are anonymous as a child's drawing
Of the lonely guard whose cry brings down the enormous night.
For the sentry moonlight is only moonlight, not
Easy to shoot by. But our devouring symbols
(Though we walk through *their* dying city
       and *their* moonlight lave us like lovers)

Are the loin-spring spotlight sun and the hangman sack-hooded
    blackout.

    * * *

Now in the east the dark, like many waters,
Moves, and uptown, in the high hotels, those few
Late guests move through their remembered places
But their steps are curiously uncertain, like a sick man's
    or a sleepwalker's.
Down the beach, in rooms designed for their masters,
The soldiers curse and sing in the early blackout.
Their voices nameless but full of fear or courage
Ring like calm bells through their terrible electric idyll.

They are the nameless poor who have been marching
Out of the dark, to that possible moment when history
Crosses the tracks of our time. They do not see it approaching,
But their faces are strange with a wild and unnoticed mystery.
And now at the Casino the dancing is nice and no one
Notices the hunchback weeping among the bankers,
Or sees, like the eye of an angel, offshore, the burning tanker,
As the night patrol of bombers climbs through the rain and is gone.

≈ Blues for Warren

Killed spring 1942, North Sea

I

The beasts in the schoolroom, whose transparent faces
Revealed the gesture in the hands of history,
Made love to us across calendars where lately
They'd planted minefields around our childhood mysteries.
We fell from innocence into the trap of the State,
From Blind Man's Bluff and legends, stepped into the war of the
    Thirties.
Moving among the murders to the sound of broken treaties—
Shame of our kid's inexperience was all we knew at the start.

Opening at opportunity's knock—
That was the banker for our mortgaged love
That was the priest of our money or our life:
All this to teach us that nervous knack
A bourgeois culture keeps in stock—
Honest living in a thieves' society.
But under the academic acanthus, among the books and dubiety,
We summoned the value of man, his loss and luck.
Now, after alarums and plots, the obscure future—
The time which is Now—places awards and banners,
Emblems across our past; the time-shortened figures
Are decorated with light which none can feel.
And now we must condemn all those whose handsome dishonest
      features
Flowered on the stalk of our youth; their rentier manners
Calling alike to ruin and forgiveness
Placing across our lives their iron seal.

II

Spotlight on midnight Europe: the furred boreal gleams
Of names on fallen monuments. A shaft of stallion's shriek
Nailed in the naked sheen of indifferent weather,
A weather of starvation. And among the ruins and the broken
      columns,
The betrayals, incrustations, the harps of the nineteenth century,
And among the treachery and hideous moneys of the world,
The Judas flags, the parliaments of beasts,
Devils with Oxford diplomas and diplomats' visas
He moved to the accompaniment of dispossessed angels:
The Angel of Love who issued no marriage licenses
The Angel of Reason with the brutal face of a child
The Angel of Hope who carried a gun in his fist
The Angel of the Fifth Season with his red flag
The Angel of Your Death who looks like your friend or your lover.
A kid knee-deep in the rotting dreams of dead statesmen,
In the First Imperialist War, thinking of home.

Home then after food queues and the cries of the starving
Lost like birds in the lord's infinite heaven

(Where no sparrow falls, etc.). But he wrote it down in his book,
Framed to remember: who were the false magicians;
What children had starved; what workers been murdered.
But what can a boy know in our time? The hawk wheels
An eye in the casual blue; the fox waits in the forest—
What can he know but the lost cries of the victims?

Down then to the matchless cold Atlantic,
Its oiled incredible reciprocating motion,
And the white ship, passage of hope, shape of return and departure
Gathered him into its hold like the seas's maw.
And the night came in like the seas's paw, gathering
The light away, and the ship, and the ocean's plunging mustangs.
By gullcry, by wavecry the littoral, the statues, the statements
The tide of the darkness gathers, are gathered into his heart.

To a barbaric rhythm of light the seafarer slowly
Tammuz . . . Adonis, going away in the dark
With a few ears of maize, a wreath of barley leaves,
A bouquet of terror from Europe's autumn garden.
Return in Spring, or on Spring-side of ocean, America,
With the ritual wheat, with a dictionary of hopes;
Tammuz . . . Adonis . . . Warren . . . comes up the lordly Hudson
Bringing the summer in to the music of dancing light.

But the summer was unemployed that year—
June and July; and a million happinesses of weather,
Inventing lovers, filling all straights and flushes,
Knocked at the hearts where no one was at home.
At noon the roads ran over the hills like rabbits;
At midnight the clock's tongue spat out the clanging hours:
They ran to the dark interior, the back bush-country;
They fell at the feet of statues like a flight of iron flowers.

Those summers he rode the freights between Boston and Frisco
With the cargoes of derelicts, garlands of misery,
The human surplus, the interest on dishonor,
And the raw recruits of a new century.
The Boss's machine gun split open the human midnight
And the darkness bled its bland alarms and hours

Calling always to resistance and decision
Falling across his brief unhoused years.

III

The bells of darkness gather their iron garlands
In the stone jungles of the blacked-out cities:
Now, after the lockout in Frisco, after the strike in New Orleans,
After the Wobblies, after the Communist Party,
After the Dorniers and Junkers, after the bomb with his number,
After the North Sea had him, after the ship went under.

The child's picture looks for itself in the old man's features,
Eye looks for sight; hand for its family fingers.
Our loves are memorialized in casual gestures
And the lost letter cries in the trunk at what it remembers.
Our loss weeps for itself, but it weeps without tongue or eyes
And the heart in its dark cave mourns. There is nothing to give it ease.

For the sea bird is not alone on the moonless waters,
Nor the fox alone in the high hills of the desert
Nor is even the soldier alone on his lone night watches
Holding with terrible integrity to his bland hazard.
The foxes have holes: the birds of the air their nests,
            and we will sometime go home.
But O in the timeless night, in the dark nothing, Warren, you are
    alone.

IV

These envy the wild birds; these, the shy life of the mole—
The blind night fugue of flight or the mothering cave in the hill.
These dream the fast fadeout, blessed by distance:
They see space as saviour, negation of form and identity,
            an underground existence.
For these ran away at childhood, seeking a stranger's country
But arrived as the masked Prince or the son of southern gentry.
These others whose progressive alienation,
            centripetal and strict,
Divorces the world instead of themselves,
            prefer the abstract

And feuding heresy. They turn from the world and find
Health in their high foreheads, or their indifference to hope,
      but their fond
Elaborate and humdrum disguises can never bandage their wounds.

These escape from themselves in the world; these others
      from the world in themselves,
But are haunted by a small disquieting awareness that nothing saves—
The explorer who escapes geography, the hophead
      who shoots up the town,
The sage on his pillar, the professor in his tower
      where his thoughts go round and round—
They are shadowed by a sinister familiar they remember but
      cannot place,
He appears in their nightmares; if they think of his name
      they are certain to fall from grace.
And between one pole and the other, as between desire and desire,
The Socially Necessary Man is hanging in chains of fire.
(His candle burns for the saviour whose birthday is drawing near.)

Oh, hell has many doorways, the key is under the mat,
And a light is burning darkly for the wandering boy tonight.
And you yearn like a tramp under the happy window
Wanting the warmth and the voices and shelter from the wild winter.
But the final achievement of each is his own damnation;
There is a family devil attendant on every private notion.
To the saint withdrawn in himself, the hero in his passage of exile,
Comes the questioner they fear to remember:
      and the terrible judgments fall.
For turning and turning in their monstrous hells of negation
They escape the glory and guilt of human action.
They haply escape salvation, escape the Fall.
But you, Warren, in the general affirmative hell
(Which includes all others) escaped these common infections
Avoiding Pride's Scylla, Fear's Charybdis, Hope's defection,
Though fiends with Kiwanis masks howled from the parlor lair,
Or tried to hold your hands across a war,
And the professors in their towers let down their long dark hair.

You moved in the light of your five angels as when the mythical great
Jesus, his common worker's clothes embroidered all over with hot

Big eyes of the poor and insulted moved on earth; or as later
Lenin arose again in the Finland Station
Thrones, Powers, Dominions, Soviets, Unions and Risings
Attended his coming and between two hells in fiery
Chains the Man of the Third Millennium stirred in his hell—

But the Fifth angle blows
And a star falls in the burning sea . . .

V

A star falls in the sea. Beyond the window
The clocks of a thousand cities record their minute advantages.
The dawn wind lifts and the lawns of the Fifth decade
Prepare for a congress of sunlight. The workers awake,
Groaning to a day of sweat and statistics.

The early flowers make a fool of our Progress. The clocks condemn it.
But the lockout imposed by Natural Grace admits no scabs,
No hiding place down here and no retreat
Beyond the fence of apes, to the animals' innocence.
And we have given hostages to the shadowing future
(You Warren, and my brother, and the comrades
        in a hundred countries—
In the casualty lists all names are manifestoes)
And burnt offerings to the shocking, sublime
Instinct of brotherhood, the human desire for perfection.

Accept then, brother, this heavy burden,
This crucifixion we put upon you: Man
Who was, in the university in the lost South,
And among the poor in the middle hell of Europe,
And among the strikers in the American Winter,
And among the fighters in this long war
Who was in our sin and death and at the hour of our birth
Was, is now and ever shall be
Scapegoat and Saviour.

Therefore I praise you as one of whom death was required,
Who descended into hell for our sakes; awakener
Of the hanging man, the Man of the Third Millennium.

Who chose the difficult damnation and lived on that narrow margin
While the cries went up from the poor and it snowed in the churches
And hysterical roses mourned from the bankers' lapels.

A star falls in the sea. The darkness takes it, takes you—
As the sea of the primitives gathered their flowers and Adonis,
Leaving the sea knell only, a submarine tolling of bells—
Takes you to transmutations in the wild interior uplands,
Down fathomless dreaming funnels of the tides,
To new planes of struggle, levels of organization,
And the nodal point of qualitative change:
Toward a richer fulfillment, to more definitive capes,
Clamoring loud where on tomorrow's littoral reaches
Are beached the spring-tide flowers of our hopes.

≈ Go Ask the Dead

I

The soldier, past full retreat, is marching out of the grave
As he lies under dying grass in the slow judgment of time
On which he has lost his grasp.
                              And lost his taste as well—
For, tell-tale as fast as it will, no tongue can put salt on his name.
The captain sun has done with this numberless underground.

II

He has seeded out of that flesh where the flashing lights first fade
In the furry sky of the head.
                              And the orient admiral brain
Has seen its images go like ensigns blown from a line—
Those raving signals.
                      All quality's bled from his light,
And number (he's all thumbs now) divides where infinities fail.

III

Grand winds of the sky might claim; or the blue hold
Of ocean accept;
                  or fire sublime—
                                      though it's earth

Now hinders and halters
                    him.
                              But those underground birds, his bones,
(Homeless all havens save here) fly out of their low-hilled heavens
And shine up into the light to blaze in his land's long lie.

IV

And long they lie there but not for love in the windy contentions
Of sun and rain, shining. This endless invasion of death
Darkens our world. There is no argument that will move them.
"You are eating our light!" they cry. "Where have you taken the sun?
You have climbed to the moon on a ladder of dead men's bones!"

≈ Fresco: Departure for an Imperialist War

They stand there weeping in the stained daylight.
Nothing can stop them now from reaching the end of their youth.

Somewhere the Mayor salutes a winning team.
Somewhere the diplomats kiss in the long corridors of history.

Somewhere a politician is grafting a speech
On the green tree of American money.

Somewhere prayer; somewhere orders and papers.
Somewhere the poor are gathering illegal arms.

Meanwhile they are there on that very platform.
The train sails silently toward them out of American sleep,

And at last the two are arrived at the very point of departure.
He goes toward death and she toward loneliness.

Weeping, their arms embrace the only country they love.

≈ The End of the World

The end of the world: it was given to me to see it.
Came in the black dark, a bulge in the starless sky,
A trembling at the heart of the night, a twitching of the webby flesh
    of the earth.
And out of the bowels of the street one beastly, ungovernable cry.

Came and I recognized it: the end of the world.
And waited for the lightless plunge, the fury splitting the rock.
And waited: a kissing of leaves: a whisper of man-killing ancestral
    night—
Then: a tinkle of music, laughter from the next block.

Yet waited still: for the awful traditional fire,
Hearing mute thunder, the long collapse of sky.
It falls forever. But no one noticed. The end of the world provoked
Out of the dark a single and melancholy sigh

From my neighbor who sat on his porch drinking beer in the dark.
No: I was not God's prophet. Armageddon was never
And always: this night in a poor street where a careless irreverent
    laughter
Postpones the end of the world: in which we live forever.

DANIEL BERRIGAN (1921–)

Jesuit priest, peace activist, playwright, and poet, Daniel Berrigan was cofounder of the Catholic Peace Fellowship in 1964. He was first arrested at a Pentagon protest against the Vietnam War in 1967. A year later, he and eight others (including his brother, the priest Philip Berrigan) burned draft files at the Selective Service office in Catonsville, Maryland. Berrigan, arrested and sentenced, went underground and was finally sent to a federal prison in Connecticut, where he remained four years. During the 1970s' peace protests, he was arrested a number of times. His prison poems reflect his commitment to nonviolence and social justice.

≈ My Name

If I were Pablo Neruda
or William Blake
I could bear, and be eloquent

an American name in the world
where others perish
in our two murderous hands

Alas Berrigan
you must open those hands
and see, stigmatized in their palms
the broken faces
you yearn toward

you cannot offer
being powerless as a woman
under the rain of fire—
life, the cover of your body.

Only the innocent die.
Take up, take up
the bloody map of the century.
The long trek homeward begins
into the land of unknowing.

≈ Prayer

I left Cornell
with half a wit; six mismated socks
ski underwear, a toothbrush,
passport, one hundred good
green dollars, their faces
virtuous as ancestors,
the chamois sack
Karl Meyer gave me years ago, handmade
by dispossessed Georgia blacks.

Later, dismay; no Testament.
I must construct, out of oddments, abrasions,
vapor trails, dust, pedicabs
three crosshatch continents, Brooks Brothers embassies
their male models dressed to kill—

all He meant and means. I touch
shrapnel and flesh, and risk my reason
for the truth's sake, an ignorant hung head.

Man of one book, stand me in stead.

≈ Rehabilitative Report: We Can Still Laugh

In prison you put on your clothes
and take them off again.
You jam your food down
and shit it out again.
You round the compound right
to left and right again.
The year grows irretrievably old
so does your hair burn white.
The mood; one volt above
one volt below survival,
roughly per specimen, space
sufficient for decent burial.

GALWAY KINNELL (1927–   )

Kinnell, who served briefly in the U.S. Navy at the end of World War
II, was arrested in Louisiana in 1963 while working for the Congress of
Racial Equality. In the late 1960s, he actively protested the war in
Vietnam, a conflict which haunts his poem "Vapor Trail Reflected in
the Frog Pond." In recent years he received a Pulitzer Prize and a
National Book Award. Kinnell is a professor of English at New York
University.

≈ **Another Night in the Ruins**

I

In the evening
haze darkening on the hills,
purple
of the eternal, a last bird
crosses over, '*flop flop*',
adoring
only the instant.

II

Nine years ago,
in a plane that rumbled all night
above the Atlantic,
I could see, lit up
by lightning bolts jumping out of it,
a thunderhead formed like the face
of my brother, looking nostalgically down
on blue,
lightning-flashed moments of the Atlantic.

III

He used to tell me,
"What good is the day?
On some hill of despair
the bonfire
you kindle can light the great sky—
though it's true, of course, to make it burn
you have to throw yourself in . . ."

IV

Wind tears itself hollow
in the eaves of my ruins, ghost-flute
of snowdrifts
that build out there in the dark:
upside-down
ravines into which night sweeps
our torn wings, our ink-spattered feathers.

V

I listen.
I hear nothing. Only
the cow, the cow
of nothingness, mooing
down the bones.

VI

Is that a
rooster? He
thrashes in the snow
for a grain. Finds
it. Rips
it into
flames. Flaps. Crows.
Flames
bursting out of his brow.

VII

How many nights must it take
one such as me to learn
that we aren't, after all, made
from that bird which flies out of its ashes,
that for a man
as he goes up in flames, his one work
is
to open himself, to *be*
the flames?

≈ **Vapor Trail Reflected in the Frog Pond**

I

The old watch: their
thick eyes
puff and foreclose by the moon. The young, heads
trailed by the beginnings of necks,
shiver,
in the guarantee they shall be bodies.

In the frog pond
the vapor trail of a SAC bomber creeps,

I hear its drone, drifting, high up
in immaculate ozone.

II

And I hear,
coming over the hills, America singing,
the varied carols I hear:
crack of deputies' rifles practicing their aim on stray dogs at night,
sput of cattleprod,
TV groaning at the smells of the human body,
curses of the soldier as he poisons, burns, grinds, and stabs
the rice of the world,
with open mouth, crying strong, hysterical curses.

III

And by rice paddies in Asia
bones
wearing a few shadows
walk down a dirt road, smashed
bloodsuckers on their heel, knowing
the flesh a man throws down in the sunshine
dogs shall eat
and the flesh that is upthrown in the air
shall be seized by birds,
shoulder blades smooth, unmarked by old feather-holes,
hands rivered
by blue, erratic wanderings of the blood,
eyes crinkled up
as they gaze up at the drifting sun that gives us our lives,
seed dazzled over the footbattered blaze of the earth.

Imamu Amiri Baraka (Leroi Jones) (1934–   )

Born Leroi Jones in Newark, New Jersey, Baraka spent time at Rutgers and in the U.S. Air Force. Moving to New York, he soon became famous as a jazz reviewer, essayist, playwright, and poet. At first associated with the Beats, he became more overtly political in the early 1960s, and embraced black nationalism in 1965. He founded the Black Arts Repertory Theater, which was closed by the police in 1966, on the charge that arms had been hidden on the premises. He returned to Newark, where he formed a publishing house and a theater company and a local coalition of political groups. In 1967, he was arrested, beaten by police, and charged with unlawfully carrying firearms. His trial became a *cause célèbre*: he was found guilty, appealed, and was acquitted. He remains one of the most important African-American poets of his generation.

≈ Incident

He came back and shot. He shot him. When he came
back, he shot, and he fell, stumbling, past the
shadow wood, down, shot, dying, dead, to full halt.

At the bottom, bleeding, shot dead. He died then, there
after the fall, the speeding bullet, tore his face
and blood sprayed fine over the killer and the grey light.

Pictures of the dead man are everywhere. And his spirit
sucks up the light. But he died in darkness darker than
his soul and everything tumbled blindly with him dying

down the stairs.

We have no word

on the killer, except he came back, from somewhere
to do what he did. And shot only once into his victim's
stare, and left him quickly when the blood ran out. We know

the killer was skillful, quick, and silent, and that the victim
probably knew him. Other than that, aside from the caked sourness
of the dead man's expression, and the cool surprise in the fixture

of his hands and fingers, we know nothing.

≈ Balboa, the Entertainer

It cannot come
except you make it
from materials
it is not
caught from. (The philosophers
of need, of which
I am lately
one,
        will tell you. "The People,"
(and not think themselves
liable
to the same
trembling flesh). I say now, "The People,
as some lesson repeated, now,
the lights are off, to myself,
as a lover, or at the cold wind.

Let my poems be a graph
of me. (And they keep
to the line, where flesh
drops off. You will go
blank at the middle. A
dead man.

        But
die soon, Love. If
what you have for
yourself, does not
stretch to your body's
end.
        (Where, without
preface,

music trails, or your fingers
slip
from my arm

≈ Political Poem

(For Basil)

Luxury, then, is a way of
being ignorant, comfortably.
An approach to the open market
of least information. Where theories
can thrive, under heavy tarpaulins
without being cracked by ideas.

(I have not seen the earth for years
and think now possibly "dirt" is
negative, positive, but clearly
social. I cannot plant a seed, cannot
recognize the root with clearer dent
than indifference. Though I eat
and shit as a natural man. (Getting up
from the desk to secure a turkey sandwich
and answer the phone: the poem undone
undone by my station, by my station,
and the bad words of Newark.) Raised up
to the breech, we seek to fill for this
crumbling century. The darkness of love,
in whose sweating memory all error is forced.

Undone by the logic of any specific death. (Old gentlemen
who still follow fires, tho are quieter
and less punctual. It is a polite truth
we are left with. Who are you? What are you
saying? Something to be dealt with, as easily.
The noxious game of reason, saying, "No, No,
you cannot feel," like my dead lecturer
lamenting thru gipsies his fast suicide.

QUINCY TROUPE (1943–)

Born in New York City, Troupe was jailed and beaten for his activities during the civil rights movement. In 1964, *Paris Match* published his first poem, "What Is a Black Man?" Troupe taught writing in the Watts Writers' Movement in Los Angeles between 1966 and 1968. His own writing includes poems about the assassination of Martin Luther King, African-American identity, urban life, music, and drug addiction. His acclaimed biography of jazz musician Miles Davis was published in 1991.

≈ Poem for My Father

For Quincy T. Troupe, Sr.

father, it was honor to be there, in the dugout
with you, the glory of great black men swinging their lives
as bats, at tiny white balls
burning in at unbelievable speeds, riding up & in & out
a curve breaking down wicked, like a ball falling off a table
moving away, snaking down, screwing its stitched magic
into chitling circuit air, its comma seams spinning
toward breakdown, dipping, like a hipster
bebopping a knee-dip stride, in the charlie parker forties
wrist curling, like a swan's neck
behind a slick black back
cupping an invisible ball of dreams

& you there, father, regal, as an african, obeah man
sculpted out of wood, from a sacred tree, of no name, no place, origin
thick branches branching down, into cherokee & someplace else lost
way back in africa, the sap running dry
crossing from north carolina into georgia, inside grandmother mary's
womb, where your mother had you in the violence of that red soil
ink blotter news, gone now, into blood graves
of american blues, sponging rococo

truth long gone as dinosaurs
the agent-oranged landscape of former names
absent of african polysyllables, dry husk, consonants there
now, in their place, names, flat, as polluted rivers
& that guitar string smile always snaking across
some virulent, american, redneck's face
scorching, like atomic heat, mushrooming over nagasaki
& hiroshima, the fever blistered shadows of it all
inked, as etchings, into sizzled concrete

but you, there, father, through it all, a yardbird solo
riffing on bat & ball glory, breaking down the fabricated myths
of white major league legends, of who was better than who
beating them at their own crap
game, with killer bats, as bud powell swung his silence into beauty
of a josh gibson home run, skittering across piano keys of bleachers
shattering all manufactured legends up there in lights
struck out white knights, on the risky edge of amazement
awe, the miraculous truth sluicing through
steeped & disguised in the blues
confluencing, like the point at the cross
when a fastball hides itself up in a slider, curve
breaking down & away in a wicked, sly grin
curved & posed as an ass-scratching uncle tom, who
like old satchel paige delivering his famed hesitation pitch
before coming back with a hard, high, fast one, is slicker
sliding, & quicker than a professional hitman
the deadliness of it all, the sudden strike
like that of the "brown bomber's" crossing right
of sugar ray robinson's, lightning, cobra bite

& you, there, father, through it all, catching rhythms
of chono pozo balls, drumming, like conga beats into your catcher's
    mitt
hard & fast as cool papa bell jumping into bed
before the lights went out

of the old, negro baseball league, a promise, you were
father, a harbinger, of shock waves, soon come

≈ Boomerang: A Blatantly Political Poem

eye use to write poems about burning
down the motherfucking country for crazy
horse, geronimo & malcolm king
x, use to (w)rite about stabbing white folks
in their air-conditioned eyeballs with ice picks
cracking their sagging balls with sledgehammer blows
now, poems leap from the snake-tip of my tongue
bluesing a language twisted tighter than braided hope
hanging like a limp-noosed rope down the question mark
back of some coal miner's squaw, her razor slanted
killer shark eyes swollen shut with taboos
she thought she heard & knew
the sun in a voice looking like bessie smith's severed arm
on that mississippi back road, screaming, like a dead man's son
who had to watch his old man eat his own pleading heart
& sometimes eye wonder if it's worth the bother
of it all, these poems eye (w)rite holding
language percolating & shaped
into metaphoric rage
underneath, say
a gentle simile, like a warm
spring day, soft as balm or talcum
on the edge of a tornado that hits quicker
than the flick of a bat's wing nicking the eye

eye use to write poems about killing fools like ronald reagan
duffy duck grinning off 30 million sucked down
the whirlpooling black holes of cia space
director casey taking a lobotomy
hit, slash to protect
the gipper
dumb
motherfuckers
everywhere tying bombs
to their own tongues, lighting fuses
of staged events that lye of peace & saving
money in the s & l pirateering, like president gipper & scud butt bush
they are metaphors for all that's wrong in america right now, all this
cloning, brouhaha, paid mouthpieces on wall street & the gipper

giving frying skillet speeches, others that ray gun reagan
ray gunning america, now, cannibalizing air waves
with mouthpieces fronting slimy churches
building up humongous bank accounts
in the name of the holy bones
of jesus christ, long gone
& dead
& it is a metaphor
boomeranging jimmy
& tammy bakker, sleazy swaggert
vacuuming pocketbooks of the old & the dead
like medusa meese heads picked off and sluicing like bad faith
they dangle heads from "freedom fighter" mouths
tell the black bird press herded up on a wire
that it's okay, it's okay, it's okay
& them believing it

eye use to write poems about burning
down the motherfucking country for crazy
horse, geronimo & malcolm king
x marks the spot where "coons" signed away
their lives on dotted lines, black holes
sucking away their breath
for a sack of cotton
full of woe
eye
sit here
now, (w)riting
poems of the soft
calm beauty welling
in my son's innocent 4 year
old eyes, thinking, perhaps of the time
when this rage will strike him, driving him towards madness
knowing all the while it will come quick
sooner than expected
& nothing
absolutely nothing
will have been undone

RAY A. YOUNG BEAR (1950–   )

Ray Young Bear has lived much of his life in the Mesquakie Tribal Settlement (Red Earth), in Iowa. His poems appear frequently in literary magazines, and he has published two books of poetry, *Winter of the Salamander* and *The Invisible Museum,* as well as an autobiographical account, *Black Eagle Child: The Facepaint Narratives* (1992). Young Bear has taught at the Institute of American Indian Arts, Eastern Washington University, and the University of Iowa. He is also a singer and cofounder of the Woodland Song and Dance Troupe of Arts Midwest, which performs in nine states.

≈ The Song Taught to Joseph

I was born unto this snowy-red earth
with the aura and name of the Black Lynx.
When we simply think of each other,
night begins. My twin the Heron
is on a perpetual flight northward,
familiarizing himself with the landscape
of Afterlife, but he never gets there . . .
because the Missouri River descends
from the Northern Plains
into the Morning Star.

One certain thing though,
he sings the song of the fish
below him in the mirror
of Milky Way.

It goes:

In this confrontation,
the gills of the predator
overtake me in daylight near home;
in this confrontation,

he hinders my progress with a cloud of mud he stirs.
Crying, I ask that I not feel each painful part
he takes, at least not until I can grasp
in the darkness the entrance
of home.

≈ From the Spotted Night

In the blizzard
while chopping wood
the mystical whistler
beckons my attention.
Once there were longhouses
here. A village.
In the abrupt spring floods
swimmers retrieved our belief.
So their spirit remains.
From the spotted night
distant jets transform
into fireflies who float
towards me like incandescent
snowflakes.
The leather shirt
which is suspended
on a wire hanger
above the bed's headboard
is humanless; yet when one
stands outside the house,
the strenuous sounds
of dressers and boxes
being moved can be heard.
We believe someone wears
the shirt and rearranges
the heavy furniture
although nothing
is actually changed.
Unlike the Plains Indian shirts
which repelled lead bullets,
ricocheting from them

in fiery sparks,
this shirt is the means;
this shirt *is* the bullet.

≈ A Drive to Lone Ranger

Everyone knows the Indian's existence is bleak.
In fact, there are people who have taken it upon themselves to speak for us; to let the
universe know how we live, eat and think, but the Bumblebee—elder of the Black
Eagle Child Nation—thinks this sort of representation is repulsive. This past
winter, after our car conked out in 80 below zero winds, we decided to pay him our
yearly visit. Although part of it was done for amusement, we soon found out there
were serious things in life to consider. The poem which follows was written without
much revision. In fact, most of it was composed in his earth lodge. I can still
remember the warmth of his antique woodstove, as well as the silence after he shut off
his generator. He smiled at us as he accepted a carton of Marlboro cigarettes.

For listening and instructional purposes,
the Bumblebee confesses that he sleeps
with earphones attached to his apian body.
"As the crisp December wind makes the constellations
more visible, so too, are the senses. Our vision
and hearing benefits from this natural
purification. Hence, the earphones."
In a lethargic tone someone offers
the standard "so they say" answer.
But the old man is unaffected,
and he continues to animate
what is in his Winter Mind.
"Ever since the Stabs Back clan
made the decision to accept education
for the tribal reserve in the late 1800s
there has always been an economic
depression. And now, when the very land
we stand on could reverse this congenital
inequity, the force which placed us here
seeks to take back this land with force
disguised as sympathy."
From communal weatherization

to peyote songs, regional and world
affairs, his bilingual eloquence
made topical events old news.
Every other topic a prophecy come true.

After an incident in the Badlands
(on a roadside town noted for its
commercialized springwater) when
cinder rocks had been deliberately
placed in his food—some of which
he had already ingested—he no longer
believes *trapping* is limited to his kind.
"I distrust capsules to begin with, and now
I am wary of cooks who are able to look out
at customers from their greasy kitchens.
But aspirins are my salvation. Rural
physicians refuse to prescribe codeine
and Valium on the premise that *we* have no
reason to get headaches or depression."
We respond with an analogy:
if we were in Russia, the allotment
of vodka could not even begin to alleviate
our pain. Gravel is basically harmless,
but the message from the Badlands
restaurant is lucid.

Over pheasant omelettes and wine
he offers an explanation about his obsession
with technology.
"It may seem a contradiction,
but those cassette tapes on the wall
are the intellectual foundation
of my progeny."
Everyone laughs at the subliminal
connection to the earphones
and where they are placed,
breaking the tension.
We are accustomed
to his condescending attitude,
but underneath our Transformation Masks
we respect the old man, Bumblebee,

for he has retained the ability to understand
traditional precepts and myths. Moreover,
he understands the need to oppose
"outside" mining interests.

As he lights the candle on the mirrored
sconce, he translates our thoughts.
"Adjusting and manipulating
the strings and pulleys
of the exterior/interior masks
requires work at all levels.
The best test in the supernatural:
how to maintain calmness during its
manifestation; to witness and experience it
as it simply is, rather than camouflage it through
rational explanation."

In the gradual darkness our conversation
centers on Northern Lights:
celestial messengers in green atomic oxygen,
highlighted by red—the color of our impending
nuclear demise.
A hand-rolled cigarette begins
to glow from Bumblebee's lips.
Silhouetted against a white kitchen
cabinet, he rises from the sofa chair
and unfolds his transparent wings.
Just when we feel the motion of his wings
the candle goes out.

Before suggesting a drive in his pickup
to Lone Ranger to see the Helena Whiteskins
gamble in handgames with the Continental Dividers,
he reviews the strategy of the tripartite powers:
the Lynx claims Afganistan and Poland;
the Serpent feels threatened and cannot
choose sides. Having ravaged what he
can't ravage anymore, the Eagle
becomes vulnerable. Once the Three
(volcanic) Sisters in California,
Oregon and Washington decide

to speak, the Missouri River
will reroute itself.
Satellites are taking photographs
of our sacred minerals from space,
revealing what we can't see but know
is there.
"In time we'll become prosperous,
or else we'll become martyrs
protecting vast resources
of the Well-Off Man Mountains . . .
The force that placed us here
cannot be trusted."

JIMMY SANTIAGO BACA (1952–   )

Chicano and Native American, born in New Mexico, Baca ran away
from an orphanage when he was eleven. After living on the streets for
nine years, he was arrested for drug possession with intent to sell and
sent to Florence, a maximum-security prison in Arizona. While there,
he requested permission to take literacy classes and study for the Grad-
uate Equivalent degree. He was told that his request would be granted,
but his subsequent pleas were answered with an assignment to field
labor. When he refused, he was sent to the notorious "dungeon,"
where—in four years in solitary confinement—he taught himself to
read and write. Baca is the recipient of the 1989 International Hispanic
Heritage Award and a Wallace Stevens Yale Poetry Fellowship.

≈ Immigrants in Our Own Land

We are born with dreams in our hearts,
looking for better days ahead.
At the gates we are given new papers,
our old clothes are taken
and we are given overalls like mechanics wear.
We are given shots and doctors ask questions.
Then we gather in another room
where counselors orient us to the new land

we will now live in. We take tests.
Some of us were craftsmen in the old world,
good with our hands and proud of our work.
Others were good with their heads.
They used common sense like scholars
use glasses and books to reach the world.
But most of us didn't finish high school.

The old men who have lived here stare at us,
from deep disturbed eyes, sulking, retreated.
We pass them as they stand around idle,
leaning on shovels and rakes or against walls.
Our expectations are high: in the old world,
they talked about rehabilitation,
about being able to finish school,
and learning an extra good trade.
But right away we are sent to work as dishwashers,
to work in fields for three cents an hour.
The administration says this is temporary
So we go about our business, blacks with blacks,
poor whites with poor whites,
chicanos and indians by themselves.
The administration says this is right,
no mixing of cultures, let them stay apart,
like in the old neighborhoods we came from.

We came here to get away from false promises,
from dictators in our neighborhoods,
who wore blue suits and broke our doors down
when they wanted, arrested us when they felt like,
swinging clubs, and shooting guns as they pleased.
But it's no different here. It's all concentrated.
The doctors don't care, our bodies decay,
our minds deteriorate, we learn nothing of value.
Our lives don't get better, we go down quick.

My cell is crisscrossed with laundry lines,
my T-shirts, boxer shorts, socks and pants are drying.
Just like it used to be in my neighborhood:
from all the tenements laundry hung window to window.
Across the way Joey is sticking his hands

through the bars to hand Felipé a cigarette,
men are hollering back and forth cell to cell,
saying their sinks don't work,
or somebody downstairs hollers angrily,
about a toilet overflowing,
or that the heaters don't work.

I ask Coyote next door to shoot me over
a little more soap to finish my laundry.
I look down and see new immigrants coming in,
mattresses rolled up and on their shoulders,
new haircuts and brogan boots,
looking around, each with a dream in their heart,
thinking they'll get a chance to change their lives.

But in the end, some will just sit around
talking about how good the old world was.
Some of the younger ones will become gangsters.
Some will die and others will go on living
without a soul, a future, or a reason to live.
Some will make it out of here as human
as they came in, they leave wondering what good they are now
as they look at their hands so long away from their tools,
as they look at themselves, so long gone from their families,
so long gone from life itself, so many things have changed.

≈ **Like an Animal**

Behind the smooth texture
Of my eyes, way inside me,
A part of me has died:
I move my bloody fingernails
Across it, hard as a blackboard,
Run my fingers along it,
The chalk white scars
That say I AM SCARED,
Scared of what might become
Of me, the real me,
Behind these prison walls.

≈ How We Carry Ourselves

To Others in Prisons

> I am the broken reed in this deathly organ,
> I am those mad glazed eyes staring from bars,
> the silent stone look

that knows like other stones the smell of working feet,
knows how long and wide a human can spread
over centuries,

> each step, until we now step on dust
> and rock of prisons.

> I could not throw my feelings away,
> shoot them like wild horses,
> stone them like weeping dirty prophets,
> could not machete them pioneering a new path,
> I sought no mountain, no brave deed,

I sought to remain human, to look and feel wind bless me. . . .

> Chicanos, Blacks, Whites, Indians,
> we are all here, our blood all red,
> we are all filled with endurance
> and have tasted the blade,
> smelled the gun's oily smoke of death.

> We are steel hunks of gears and frayed ropes,
> our hands the toolsheds,
> our heads the incessant groan
> of never ending revolving wheels
> in an empty, gaunt warehouse,
> our blood dripping from steel joints
> like grease and oil onto granite floors.

I meant to say, you can turn away from this:

> if you can take the hammering, they will give,
> if you can hold on while they grip you
> and hurl you ragefully at the ground,
> if you can bite your teeth when they bend you,
> and still, you do not fit,
> you can be who you are.

You can see the morning and breathe in God's grace,
        you can laugh at sparrows, and find love
        in yourself for the sun, you can learn
        what is inside you, you can know silence,
        you can look at the dark gray machine around you,
        souls going up like billows of black smoke,
        and decide what you will do next,
        you who are the main switch, who turns
        everything off.
But you breathing, smiling, struggling,
turning yourself on. . . . . .

≈ Oppression

Is a question of strength,
of unshed tears,
of being trampled under,

and always, always,
remembering you are human.

Look deep to find the grains
of hope and strength,
and sing, my brothers and sisters,

and sing. The sun will share
your birthdays with you behind bars,
the new spring grass

like fiery spears will count your years,
as you start into the next year;
endure my brothers, endure my sisters.

War in Korea and Vietnam

(1945-1979)

Postwar American foreign policy was predicated on the assumption that Communist aggression must be contained at all costs short of all-out nuclear war. The wars in Korea and Vietnam, while historically specific and complex, both developed in divided countries engaged in civil wars that drew the superpowers into conflict by proxy. As was often the case in the postcolonial period after World War II, nationalist aspirations were wedded to radical politics and so were vulnerable to the larger power struggles between the Soviet Union, China, and the United States.

At the end of World War II, the Allies, in order to disarm Japanese occupation forces, temporarily divided Korea at the 38th parallel. Communist North Korea invaded democratic South Korea after attempts by the United Nations to unite them failed. Member nations sent troops to support South Korea, under the command of General Douglas MacArthur of the United States. The People's Republic of China came to the aid of the North, and a bitter war was fought, ending with an armistice in 1953 which left Korea divided.

American attention then turned to Vietnam, where the French colonial government, debilitated by World War II, was collapsing. The Chinese nationalists and the Communists occupied the northern half of the country. The dividing line between the sectors, established at the Potsdam Conference and intended as a jurisdictional boundary for the disarmament of Japanese troops, became a firmer border when the Communists used their positions to launch a war of liberation against the French. After the victory of the Chinese Communists in 1949, the North Vietnamese were provided bases from which to attack the South. Although the United States gave significant aid to the French, France withdrew from Vietnam after a disastrous defeat at Dien Bien Phu in 1954.

The United States saw Vietnam as a strategic interest, a bulwark against the spread of Communism in Asia. The Americans took over the training of the South Vietnamese army in 1955 and escalated their involvement during the next few years. Meanwhile, the autocratic government of South Vietnam lost the support of its people. There was a major coup attempt in 1961 and a successful coup in 1963. President John F. Kennedy had sworn to defend South Vietnam in 1961, and therefore increased American involvement, while trying to pressure for reforms. The situation did not change significantly after Kennedy's assassination. Not only did President Johnson promise to continue

American aid, he stepped up the American war effort—the Tonkin Gulf Resolution of 1964 gave him the authority to take whatever measures he deemed necessary in Southeast Asia.

The United States started bombing North Vietnam in 1965. By June of that year, American forces numbered 47,000 in the South, and they increased almost sixfold in the following twelve months. The United States was fighting on a number of fronts: it was striking against the regular North Vietnamese army, which was supported by Russian aid, and it was combating a flexible guerrilla army in the South, the Vietcong, which had been founded in 1960. At the height of the war, there were more than 500,000 American troops in Vietnam and American bombing raids were almost continuous. The troops in combat were increasingly drawn from the poorer sectors of American society, and as the war became less and less popular, the morale of the soldiers suffered. Frequently they seemed to be fighting an invisible enemy in support of a corrupt and unstable indigenous government. The American military command was not always candid: while it tried to maintain that the war was "winnable" and "being won," the experience of the soldiers on the ground was hardly triumphant.

The first antiwar demonstrations were held in 1965, and a poll that year revealed that 60 percent of adult Americans wanted the fate of Vietnam to be settled by the United Nations. Distaste for the war grew as television news coverage brought images of combat into American homes.

In spite of the antiwar movement, the government's inability to achieve credibility, and the enemy's durability in the face of the most technologically advanced weapons and defoliants (such as napalm and Agent Orange), the war continued after Richard Nixon was elected President in 1968. Even though Nixon decreased the number of American ground troops and claimed to be searching for "peace with honor," he increased the bombing of the North, took the war into neighboring Laos and Cambodia, and mined the harbors of North Vietnam. The American military role in Vietnam did not end until 1973. Saigon fell to the North Vietnamese in 1975, two weeks after the Communists were victorious in Cambodia.

For the Vietnamese, victory did not bring peace. In 1978 they went to war against Pol Pot, the brutal leader of Cambodia's Communist government. The Vietnamese and the Cambodians have been historical enemies, and the Vietnamese occupied their neighbor until they agreed to withdraw after 1988. In 1979, the Vietnamese fought a brief war against the Chinese. As they have been denied access to American markets and deprived of aid from the Chinese, the Vietnamese have been faced with rebuilding their country under grave economic hardships.

ETHERIDGE KNIGHT (1931–1991)

Born in Mississippi, Knight dropped out of school in the eighth grade, became addicted to drugs, and enlisted in the U.S. Army when he was seventeen. He received a shrapnel wound in the Korean War, fell back into addiction after his discharge, and was sent to prison in 1960 for robbery. While in prison, he discovered poetry; his first two books were framed by his time there and by the rise of the Black Power movement. His work, however, is scored by what he has called his "psyche wound," the damage resulting from the experience of war.

≈ The Idea of Ancestry

I

Taped to the wall of my cell are 47 pictures: 47 black
faces: my father, mother, grandmothers (1 dead), grand-
fathers (both dead), brothers, sisters, uncles, aunts,
cousins (1st & 2nd), nieces, and nephews. They stare
across the space at me sprawling on my bunk. I know
their dark eyes, they know mine. I know their style,
they know mine. I am all of them, they are all of me;
they are farmers, I am a thief, I am me, they are thee.

I have at one time or another been in love with my mother,
1 grandmother, 2 sisters, 2 aunts (1 went to the asylum),
and 5 cousins. I am now in love with a 7 yr old niece
(she sends me letters written in large block print, and
her picture is the only one that smiles at me).

I have the same name as 1 grandfather, 3 cousins, 3 nephews,
and 1 uncle. The uncle disappeared when he was 15, just took
off and caught a freight (they say). He's discussed each year
when the family has a reunion, he causes uneasiness in
the clan, he is an empty space. My father's mother, who is 93
and who keeps the Family Bible with everybody's birth dates

(and death dates) in it, always mentions him. There is no
place in her Bible for "whereabouts unknown."

II

Each fall the graves of my grandfathers call me, the brown
hills and red gullies of mississippi send out their electric
messages, galvanizing my genes. Last yr / like a salmon quitting
the cold ocean-leaping and bucking up his birthstream / I
hitchhiked my way from L.A. with 16 caps in my pocket and a
monkey on my back. And I almost kicked it with the kinfolks.
I walked barefooted in my grandmother's backyard / I smelled the old
land and the woods / I sipped cornwhiskey from fruit jars with the
        men/
I flirted with the women / I had a ball till the caps ran out
and my habit came down. That night I looked at my grandmother
and split / my guts were screaming for junk / but I was almost
contented / I had almost caught up with me.
(The next day in Memphis I cracked a croaker's crib for a fix).

This yr there is a gray stone wall damming my stream, and when
the falling leaves stir my genes, I pace my cell or flop on my bunk
and stare at 47 black faces across the space. I am all of them,
they are all of me, I am me, they are thee, and I have no children
to float in the space between.

≈ A Poem for Myself

(or Blues for a Mississippi Black Boy)

I was born in Mississippi;
I walked barefooted thru the mud.
Born black in Mississippi,
Walked barefooted thru the mud.
But, when I reached the age of twelve
I left that place for good.
Said my daddy chopped cotton
And he drank his liquor straight.
When I left that Sunday morning
He was leaning on the barnyard gate.

Left her standing in the yard
With the sun shining in her eyes.
And I headed North
As straight as the Wild Goose Flies,

I been to Detroit & Chicago
Been to New York city too.
I been to Detroit & Chicago
Been to New York city too.
Said I done strolled all those funky avenues
I'm still the same old black boy with the same old blues.
Going back to Mississippi
This time to stay for good
Going back to Mississippi
This time to stay for good—
Gonna be free in Mississippi
Or dead in the Mississippi mud.

≈ To Make a Poem in Prison

It is hard
To make a poem in prison.
The air lends itself not
to the singer.
The seasons creep by unseen
And spark no fresh fires.

Soft words are rare, and drunk drunk
Against the clang of keys;
Wide eyes stare fat zeroes
And plead only for pity.

But pity is not for the poet;
Yet poems must be primed.
Here is not even sadness for singing,
Not even a beautiful rage rage,
No birds are winging. The air
Is empty of laughter. And love?
Why, love has flown,
Love has gone to glitten.

≈ Hard Rock Returns to Prison from the Hospital for the Criminal Insane

Hard Rock / was / "known not to take no shit
From nobody," and he had the scars to prove it:
Split purple lips, lumbed ears, welts above
His yellow eyes, and one long scar that cut
Across his temple and plowed through a thick
Canopy of kinky hair.

The WORD / was / that Hard Rock wasn't a mean nigger
Anymore, that the doctors had bored a hole in his head,
Cut out part of his brain, and shot electricity
Through the rest. When they brought Hard Rock back,
Handcuffed and chained, he was turned loose,
Like a freshly gelded stallion, to try his new status.
And we all waited and watched, like a herd of sheep,
To see if the WORD was true.

As we waited we wrapped ourselves in the cloak
Of his exploits: "Man, the last time, it took eight
Screws to put him in the Hole." "Yeah, remember when he
Smacked the captain with his dinner tray?" "He set
The record for time in the Hole—67 straight days!"
"Ol Hard Rock! man, that's one crazy nigger."
And then the jewel of a myth that Hard Rock had once bit
A screw on the thumb and poisoned him with syphilitic spit.

The testing came, to see if Hard Rock was really tame.
A hillbilly called him a black son of a bitch
And didn't lose his teeth, a screw who knew hard Rock
From before shook him down and barked in his face.
And Hard Rock did *nothing*. Just grinned and looked silly,
His eyes empty like knot holes in a fence.

And even after we discovered that it took Hard Rock
Exactly 3 minutes to tell you his first name,
We told ourselves that he had just wised up,
Was being cool; but we could not fool ourselves for long,
And we turned away, our eyes on the ground. Crushed.
He had been our Destroyer, the doer of things

We dreamed of doing but could not bring ourselves to do,
The fears of years, like a biting whip,
Had cut deep bloody grooves
Across our backs.

WALTER McDONALD (1934–   )

McDonald was born in Lubbock, Texas. He became a pilot in the U.S. Air Force, earned his doctorate at the University of Iowa in 1966, then returned to the Air Force Academy to teach until 1969, when he left for Vietnam. Returning in 1970 after a tour of duty, he taught one more year at the Air Force Academy and then was granted a medical retirement. He has published seven volumes of poetry and teaches at Texas Tech University in Lubbock.

≈ The Children of Saigon

Always at night I found them
    climbing the piles of junk burning
        on the base. Around a flat track

I ran for miles, tight muscles
    jogging past bleachers
        where French soldiers

in parades for years
    passed out in the sun. Children
        climbed those bulldozed heaps

for food, for clothes, for trash
    piled up to blaze. I saw them
        crawling the last flare of the sun

spangled on garbage, the dump
    blazing in the sweat and blink
        of my eyes, children and old men

ragged and golden, clawing
   through flames long after sundown,
      no matter how many nights

I went without supper,
   how many leftovers I begged
      and carried in darkness

out past the tarmac and bleachers,
   passing it all to children
      who grabbed it and backed away.

≈ Christmas Bells, Saigon

Buses came late, each driver sullen,
head shaved above the ears. At the French
country club on base we nursed warm drinks
while French and their Viet Cong cousins
ignored us, strolling from room to room.

The maître d' said wait, he'd find a place
for us. For hours, we stumbled around outside
trying to get drunk. After weeks of rockets
we needed to celebrate. Someone joked
the clerk who took our reservation

died in last night's rockets. People I knew
kept disappearing. I asked what's going on.
Vietnamese friends all looked at me
and shrugged. Men who'd been in Vietnam
for years kept dancing off with girls.

I listened for gunfire above the band's
loud brassy mist of Beatles and Japanese.
I studied guards buried in cages
ten feet above us in trees. Five minutes apart
they rattled bells to signal—what?—

We are alive? How could anyone believe
in bells dangled on barbed wires?

Sappers smart enough to count
could slit the guards and keep it up,
ring-ring, till all guard stations fell.

Two sergeants and I sat on a verandah
and wondered where all the girls had gone,
when a bus to the barracks would come,
blamed bad French planters for the war.
Even with rockets, I wanted to lie down

and dream of peace, rumors of good will
toward men. We agreed on all things true
and noble, sober on gin and French vermouth,
listening to Japanese Beatles and the bells,
the bells all through the night.

≈ The Last Still Days in a Bunker

All morning we saw flames in the distance,
rockets or mortars, not bombs, which curl
and billow up like clouds. We left the door
wide open for a breath of air,
the heavy monsoon threatening Saigon

like a flood, the only breeze
the secret files we fanned our faces with,
and shredded. I shook my head at our schemes
and sweat flew. For weeks, rockets
had fallen on the base like Sodom.

Secretaries slept nude in this walk-in vault.
At dawn when we opened eight-bolt locks
we found them dressed, their torsos
outlined in sweat on the concrete.
Now, we were alone in khaki and black shoes

scuffed dull from days of shredding orders,
like trying to hide our tracks
in the jungle. We listened for news,

but all we heard piped in
were the same old country and western tunes

that kept us human. I flung cold sweat
and fed another sealed order
into the whirring shredder, wondering
how many tons of bombs we'd abandon,
how many battles we might stop.

JOHN BALABAN (1943–   )

John Balaban went to Vietnam in 1967 as a civilian conscientious objec-
tor with the International Voluntary Services and then with the Com-
mittee of Responsibility to Save War-Injured Children. He returned to
the United States in 1969, then went again to Vietnam from 1971 to
1972 on a National Endowment for the Humanities Fellowship to col-
lect Vietnamese oral poetry. This project resulted in the book *Ca Dao
Vietnam,* published by Unicorn Press in 1974.

≈ The Guard at the Binh Thuy Bridge

How still he stands as mists begin to move,
as morning, curling, billows creep across
his cooplike, concrete sentry perched mid-bridge
over mid-muddy river. Stares at bush green banks
which bristle rifles, mortars, men—perhaps.
No convoys shake the timbers. No sound
but water slapping boat sides, bank sides, pilings.
He's slung his carbine barrel down to keep
the boring dry, and two banana-clips instead of one
are taped to make, now, forty rounds instead
of twenty. Droplets bead from stock to sight;
they bulb, then strike his boot. He scrapes his heel,
and sees no box bombs floating towards his bridge.
Anchored in red morning mist a narrow junk
rocks its weight. A woman kneels on deck
staring at lapping water. Wets her face.

Idly the thick Rach Binh Thuy slides by.
He aims. At her. Then drops his aim. Idly.

≈ News Update

For Erbart, Gitelson, Flynn and Stone,
happily dead and gone.

Well, here I am in the *Centre Daily Times*
back to back with the page one refugees
fleeing the crossfire, pirates, starvation.
Familiar faces. We followed them
through defoliated forests, cratered fields
past the blasted water buffalo,
the shredded tree lines, the human head
dropped on the dusty road, eyes open,
the dusty road which called you all to death.

One skims the memory like a moviola
editing out the candid shots: Sean Flynn
dropping his camera and grabbing a gun
to muster the charge and retake the hill.
"That boy," the black corporal said,
"do in real life what his daddy do in movies."
Dana Stone, in an odd moment of mercy,
sneaking off from Green Beret assassins
to the boy they left for dead in the jungle.
Afraid of the pistol's report, Stone shut his eyes
and collapsed the kid's throat with a bayonet.
Or, Erhart, sitting on his motorcycle
smiling and stoned in the Free Strike Zone
as he filmed the ammo explosion at Lai Khe.
It wasn't just a macho game. Marie-Laure de Decker
photographed the man aflame on the public lawn.
She wept and shook and cranked her Pentax
until a cop smashed it to the street. Then
there was the girl returned from captivity
with a steel comb fashioned from a melted-down tank,
or some such cliché, and engraved: "To Sandra
From the People's Fifth Battalion, Best Wishes."

Christ, most of them are long dead. Tim Page
wobbles around with a steel plate in his head.
Gitelson roamed the Delta in cut-away blue jeans
like a hippy Johnny Appleseed with a burlap sack
full of seeds and mimeographed tips for farmers
until we pulled him from the canal. His brains
leaked on my hands and knee. Or me, yours truly,
agape in the Burn Ward in Danang, a quonset hut,
a half a garbage can that smelled like Burger King,
listening to whimpers and nitrate fizzing on flesh
in a silence that simmered like a fly in a wound.

And here I am, ten years later,
written up in the local small town press
for popping a loud-mouth punk in the choppers.
Oh, big sighs. Windy sighs. And ghostly laughter.

≈ For the Missing in Action

Hazed with harvest dust and heat
the air swam with flying husks
as men whacked rice sheaves into bins
and all across the sunstruck fields
red flags hung from bamboo poles.
Beyond the last treeline on the horizon
beyond the coconut palms and eucalyptus
out in the moon zone puckered by bombs
the dead earth where no one ventures,
the boys found it, foolish boys
riding buffaloes in craterlands
where at night bombs thump and ghosts howl.
A green patch on the raw earth.
And now they've led the farmers here,
the kerchiefed women in baggy pants,
the men with sickles and flails, children
herding ducks with switches—all
staring from a crater berm; silent:
In that dead place the weeds had formed a man
where someone died and fertilized the earth, with flesh
and blood, with tears, with longing for loved ones.

No scrap remained; not even a buckle
survived the monsoons, just a green creature,
a viny man, supine, with posies for eyes,
butterflies for buttons, a lily for a tongue.
Now when huddled asleep together
the farmers hear a rustly footfall
as the leaf-man rises and stumbles to them.

YUSEF KOMUNYAKAA (1947–   )

Born in Bogalusa, Louisiana, Komunyakaa served in the U.S. Army in
Vietnam in 1969 and 1970. He has published three books of poetry and
teaches at the University of Indiana at Bloomington.

≈ Starlight Scope Myopia

Gray-blue shadows lift
shadows onto an ox cart.

Making night work for us,
the starlight scope brings
men into killing range.

The river under Vi Bridge
takes the heart away

like the Water God
riding his dragon.
Smoke-colored

Viet Cong
move under our eyelids,

lords over loneliness
winding like coralvine through
sandalwood & lotus,

inside our skulls years
after this scene ends.

The brain closes down
to get the job done. What
looks like one step into the trees,

they're lifting crates of ammo
& sacks of rice, swaying

under their shared weight.
Caught in the infrared,
what are they saying?

Are they talking about women
or calling the Americans

beaucoup dien cai dau?
One of them is laughing.
You want to place a finger

to his lips & say "shhhh."
You try reading ghost-talk

on their lips. They say
"up-up we go," lifting as one.
This one, old, bowlegged,

you feel you could reach out
& take him into your arms. You

peer down the sights of your M-16,
seeing the full moon
loaded on an ox cart.

≈ **After the Fall of Saigon**

An afternoon storm has hit
the Pearl of the Orient
& stripped nearly everybody.

Bandoliers, miniskirts, tennis shoes,
fatigue jackets, combat boots—
the city's color bruised, polyester
suits limping down sidestreets.
Even the ragpicker is glad
to let his Australian bush hat
with the red feather float away.

Something deeper than sadness
litters the alleys.
The old mama-san who always
collected scraps of yellow paper,
cigarette butts & matchsticks
through field-stripped years
hides under her cardboard box.
Cowboys park new Harleys
along Lam Son Square
& do their disappearing act.

Dzung leaves the Continental Hotel
in a newspaper dress,
hoping for a hard rain.
Moving through broken colors
flung to the ground,
she sings, tries not to,
mixing up the words to Trinh's
"Mad Girl's Love Song"
& "Stars Fell on Alabama,"
trying to bite off her tongue.

≈ Boat People

After midnight they load up.
A hundred shadows move about blindly.
Something close to sleep
hides low voices drifting
toward a red horizon. Tonight's
a blue string, the moon's pull—
this boat's headed somewhere.

Lucky to have gotten past
searchlights low-crawling the sea,
like a woman shaking water
from her long dark hair.

Calm over everything, a change
of heart. Twelve times in three days
they've been lucky,
clinging to each other in gray mist.
Now Thai fishermen gaze out across
the sea as it changes color,
hands shading their eyes
like sailors do,
minds on robbery & rape.
Sunlight burns blood-orange
till nothing makes sense.
Storm warnings crackle from a radio.
Gold shines in their teeth.
The Thai fishermen turn away.
Not enough water for the trip.
The boat people cling to each other,
their faces like yellow sea grapes,
wounded by doubt & salt air.
Dusk hangs over the water.
Sea sick, they daydream Jade Mountain
a whole world away, half-drunk
on what they hunger to become.

GEORGE EVANS (1948–)

Evans is a veteran of the Vietnam War and the author of four poetry
collections, three published in England and one in the United States. In
1980, he received a Monbusho Research Fellowship for the study of
Japanese poetry from the Japanese Ministry of Education in Tokyo. He
lived in Japan for over two years, studying independently in Kyoto and
as a visiting scholar at Oita University (Kyushu). He now lives in San
Francisco.

≈ Revelation in the Mother Lode

I walk into the vineyard at night, into acres of cordoned vines
    against their stakes at pruning time, but see, stretching
    off through tule fog, only cross-marked graves.

How did it come to be that my generation would be stiff
    under hoarfrost, and that I should come across them
    twenty years after watching them die to remember and feel
    I've truly wasted my time, have left no mark upon the earth
    in their name, have left only the small craters of a boot
    sucking vineyard mud.

And is this guilt, or the product of being swept up
    in a time on human earth when few do more than raise
    the cause of their own names—and am I one, or is all this
    death just sloth which one pretends
    to work against the belly of
    but which in fact
    controls?

You who return to me as vines in the deep night under fog
    have come at a bad time, a time when the world is obsessed
    with rubbing you smooth, and its concentration
    on ceremony brings you to nothing.

Somewhere, mixed in with all the rest I'd meant to get to
    which is receding, is a day floating above jungle, flak
    exploding in small fists from the trees, rocking
    the chopper where I sit in shock and blood and urine
    staring into patchwork fields.

I stand behind bamboo shaking, thinking of Nguyet
    in a Saigon bar, worried how willingly we forget,
    bombs dropping like hair straight down   a shadow
    a black sheet   everything about us muscle   hot
    prick and resolve   and have no idea where I am
    but am everywhere   and she   wobbling on spiked heels
    around the bar stools and smoke has everything I cannot
    not the least of which is a reason
                        which makes her more beautiful

than possible, but also quite a bit like the ragged edge
of a ruined wall, and like the crisp brown bamboo leaves
dropping after terrible heat, dripping with an ache I love
which is more for youth than anything   certainly not war,
which also feels like dropping.

How tired I am of hearing about that war,
   which one should struggle
   to keep the nightmare of, suffer from rather than forget.
   I don't want to heal, and am sick of those who do.
   Such things end in license.

Back here it turns out newspapers
   and monuments are taxidermy;
   there is little retribution, little learning; what is lost
   is forgotten; sometimes it gets so bad I'm not sure
   I'm the one who lived . . . then come upon you in a field
   —a one-time soldier with a trick knee, flagging humor,
   monsoon debt—and find you enfolded by fog as if by spirits,
   and become the visage of all that's been
   thrown from the world.

≈ Eye Blade

*In the years after the war earth kept shaking. Landscapes shifted, windows shat-
tered. It was unpopular to be unpopular. Strong words disappeared like bees into
hives. Films were made, songs written, clubs formed, monuments erected. Objects
slipped in and out of the sacred, in and out of the picture. Everyone paid to wait to
get in then paid again and maybe got in. Cliffs dropped, mills shut, pots fell from
windows, cars from bridges, hearts fell like coins through grating—earth kept
shaking, wind rising. Weapons replaced gods, instruments people, TV replaced
distance and the mind. The missile lines grew long, long, long as a child's breath long.*

Air hazed by seed and bug, arms heavy
after work he sits, denting a can with his thumb
on the steps of the house which owns him
watching a figure inch uphill across the valley.
Skateboards scrape, spark, evening news begins
its tally, its explosions, the world exploding

block by block towards him, thing so large
the whole will not be seen.

Up blacktop as up a wall the figure climbs
cobblestone knuckled street, toting a sack.
San Francisco glitters in a circle below.
Hunchbacked splinter on a hill, inebriate
wandering, bottles clanking, moving but still:
dot, insect, man, instrument, subject.

A shadow. It peels and approaches
gathering shape: edges emerge,
throwing-star whizzing, it grows,
wheels away dragging its shadow—
a hawk, holding the world
in its eye: an island.

A blind man, stick tapping, stops, jerks
rapping, tap
              tap, fishing, reaching, scraping
ahead, edge against edge, feeling the world
through his stick, the whole black sphere
attached to its tip.

A child in the shape of a bowl.
A powdered form, body striped with ribs,
eating dust without protest
in forced geophagy, eyes shut,
no world beyond its plain
littered with blanket shacks.
Stone. Ripened fig. Speck in the cosmos.
Pair of eyes like planets.

A black mark bouncing through forest
leaps over root and vine, ferns snapping
between her toes she runs from a village,
whose life is food, who longs for the north
with its malls, who covets abstract visions
of Texas, hears gunfire and looks back thinking
of a water pot on her table flowering as it bursts,
and of TV, if its figures, like water, are stored within.

A farmer marching to a cadence beyond the trees,
chanting, fluting, shirt frayed, dissolving through hills
to revolt, to reach the capital grown in him like a fist,
ignorant of what he'll face: that everyone wants control,
and no one wants control—what everyone really wants is money.
His voice is smaller than a pin's tip, a bird's beak
drilling air, waving its words like a flag,
a target lighting its center.

The figure moves deeper away through the hills
wandering farther, mapless, sighting blue and gray
peaks to measure how far, or remember nothing
is far, everything far: arriving isn't the point,
the point's to move not away from or to, but constantly
in the place where the mind centers,
driving it through mountains.

The road becomes a dot. Red-winged blackbirds
stick to the wires then explode across the field.
He's walking in extreme states through the landscape.
The beauty is painful. He recognizes long-denied voids
spanned or camouflaged for love or attention. He's stuck,
confused between grief and self-pity, knowing patience
can turn to bitterness and vanity greed, but what
of aimlessness and sentimental truth which have
become his sack, and what of the journey
which has become his destination?

The poet Tu Fu, grain of dust to China,
watching chaos cross the horizon, pain
real and imagined, pities himself, hair
too thin to tie back, wanting his art
to bring fame, lost in the dead Li Po
drowned grabbing the moon where it blazed
like a white leaf past his boat, Li Po,
who drunk could make a ragpicker king.

Its nature is that it's outside, outside the outside.
Not a vehicle but a motion. No meaning, no correlative,
no use, no rejection, no acceptance, no form, no intention,
no morality, no religion, no school, no forebears, no

value, no price, no time, no bones. It is its own
future and purpose, own audience and shill.
It has no nature. It has the world.

  Crowds: unanchored islands.
    Trees: loci underpinning land.
   Stones: silence continues.
  Ground: departing map.
     Sky: motion's room.
 Animals: revolt subdued, and
   Wind: the mountain finally arrives.

Plowing uphill the runner blurs
the world, losing sense of the motionless, everything
moves: islands of flattened gum, discarded fruit,
exploding paper, statues jumping on lawns,
fences and clouds stream by. No distinguishing
what's forced to move from what itself is moving,
every speck of the world falling apart,
gathering, falling apart.

A mockingbird in its tree, long tail flicking:
guitars, cork pop, telephone, jackhammer, nail
squealed from wood, snoring. Creature of sound:
door squeak, hose spray, cop whistle, siren, jazz:
picks what has passed and sings back
over power line, building, car: voice
of the times on a twig, rocking,
returning what won't be had.

The Wall, the black wall rising. Dead list
in the capital, black list, stone mirror
faces float across searching its columns,
names to touch, lean upon and fall through
into space. Rolling stone which will not roll.
Wound which doesn't close except in sleep.
Numbers small for war, somehow unforgivable
for something perceived as error, though all
battle is all error. And when its shine dulls,
its sting fades, and those who weep go dry,
what good will be a wall?

An orchid in light
its veins are bones
the world is mad we
live on air unwinding
and resist the dark
but touch the dark
for death's the stem
and root, impatient
growling thing.

Bosatsu of a thousand whirling arms,
windmill on a hillside, each arm an event,
skill, perspective: world of a thousand
eyes viewing a thousand things at once
and each thing equal; world of a thousand
windows opened on as many things meaningless
one by one as there are self-obsessions;
the world which will not tolerate one view.

The obsessed turning in circles, gathering
chips as if this is Reno and somebody wins:
I'll take one of those, one of those, and
one of those. The rest of you take a hike,
get fucked, bug off, hit the road corpse—
this is my movie, this is me and me me me.
The Master said, getting up from where
he'd been kicked across the casino through
sawdust into a corner under a slot machine:
It's a bridge, all road and no sidewalk.
Don't fall asleep.

A flying ant crawls over an ash, stops,
washes its wings then goes on, lives to live
exceeding neither limits nor potential,
excoriating nothing in its pursuits.

A boy in a tree at night above Main Street,
Peru. Below, a woman with a sack of sugar
on her head waddles to a traffic light and waits.
He has entered the world of the dead, and hears

drums on the ground below, drums lined up in rows,
each with a drummer: enemies of the Inca,
gutted then stretched in a smokehouse
until their stomachs are taut, fit
to drum through the jungle.

Inches above the water the osprey hangs,
then dropping locks its talons in,
but the fish is strong, heavy,
and drags it into the liquid sky
through rings of impact down
to silence.

An old woman wobbles up, air bending
as she bends, wind pushing her down,
each moment stops, each step
an arrival she takes the hill
hobbling, teetering and suffers
the incurable: her skin.

A clump of weeds breaks the pavement
throwing lower worlds to light.
The rough the unwanted struggle most
but last by the effort, translating
land into landscape, revolting
underfoot. Things which are deep
and will not be cut.

Sparks fly from a guitar
player's fingers in a Chuck Berry duckwalk
across the skyline, wind shears
him, wind harp blown to life
on a high ridge culture dances,
twists, the passions course,
blood pounds and words drop
like hammer blows. Rock & Roll.

It's the specter of death. More than a cloud, a second
sky; Rangda, breasts like hanging knee-socks, shaking
her ass, whipping a trance on reason, stabbing the world

in full view of the world; Kali, popping her cheeks
like a drum, dangling life by its skin, flaying,
peeling the planet, palms out, hips in frenzy,
watching the world blow apart
as if on a screen.

In slo-mo the column rises into a ball, sweeping
cows from their fields, babies from cribs, hands
from their bodies, charring wallpaper, melting
the fence: no more flowers, trees or lawns, no more
houses, cars, or baseball. No more music, no more
sex, books, computers, airplanes, insects and birds
a vapor, elephants fried to a crisp, whales thrown
aloft: the reverse of the world.

A voice struggles to be heard,
but which mechanism detects it as a lie,
and how is it recognized? Patience
is the power of the eye, naiveté
skill when it comes to observing men
not given to truth, as silence is skill
in the wilderness, watching. A spot,
a mirror in light among mirrors, the eye.

Off your high horse, mister.
Yours is no profession or branch,
and you no bird to piss down
on fields and peasants, there are
peasants only to the stupid
who know prices, sizes, ways
to squeeze through, get in,
suck up, and nothing else.
Yours is not to perfect,
but to know you can't
and not why.

The evening shakes
and glows on the bay.
Buildings, colors, people
gild the moving sea

pours away then back
holding all in one shimmer, one
wave, as the world itself will not,
which slips away, then slips away.

BRUCE WEIGL (1949–   )

Weigl served in the First Air Cavalry during the years 1967 and 1968 of
the Vietnam War. The recipient of numerous awards and the author of
several books of poetry, including *Voices of Napalm,* he teaches English
at Pennsylvania State University. He has returned to Vietnam twice, in
1985 and 1990, on the second occasion with writers Tim O'Brien and
Larry Heineman.

≈ **Burning Shit at An Khe**

Into that pit
        I had to climb down
with a rake and matches; eventually,
        you had to do something
because it just kept piling up
        and it wasn't our country, it wasn't
our air thick with the sick smoke
        so another soldier and I
lifted the shelter off its blocks
        to expose the homemade toilets:
fifty-five-gallon drums cut in half
        with crude wood seats that splintered.
We soaked the piles in fuel oil
        and lit the stuff
and tried to keep the fire burning.
        To take my first turn
I paid some kid
        a CARE package of booze from home.
I'd walked past the burning once
        and gagged the whole heart of myself—

it smelled like the world
     was on fire,
but when my turn came again
     there was no one
so I stuffed cotton up my nose
     and marched up that hill. We poured
and poured until it burned and black
     smoke curdled
but the fire went out.
     Heavy artillery
hammered the evening away in the distance,
     Vietnamese laundry women watched
from a safe place, laughing.
     I'd grunted out eight months
of jungle and thought I had a grip on things
     but we flipped the coin and I lost
and climbed down into my fellow soldiers'
     shit and began to sink and didn't stop
until I was deep to my knees. Liftships
     cut the air above me, the hacking
blast of their blades
     ripped dust in swirls so every time
I tried to light a match
     it died
and it all came down on me, the stink
     and the heat and the worthlessness
until I slipped and climbed
     out of that hole and ran
past the olive-drab
     tents and trucks and clothes and everything
green as far from the shit
     as the fading light allowed.
Only now I can't fly.
     I lay down in it
and fingerpaint the words of who I am
     across my chest
until I'm covered and there's only one smell,
     one word.

≈ The Way of Tet

Year of the monkey, year of the human wave,
the people smuggled weapons in caskets through the city
in long processions undisturbed
and buried them in Saigon graveyards.
At the feet of their small Buddhas
weary bar girls burned incense
before the boy soldiers arrived
to buy them tea and touch them
where they pleased. Twenty years
and the feel of a girl's body
so young there's no hair
is like a dream, but living is a darker thing,
the iron burning bee who drains the honey,
and he remembers her
twisting in what evening
light broke into the small room in the shack
in the labyrinth of shacks
in the alley where the lost and corrupted kept house.
He undressed her for the last time,
each piece of clothing
a sacrifice she surrendered to the war
the way the world had become.
Tomorrow blood would run in every province.
Tomorrow people would rise from tunnels everywhere
and resurrect something ancient from inside them,
and the boy who came ten thousand miles to touch her
small self lies beside the girl whose words he can't understand,
their song a veil between them.

She is a white bird in the bamboo, fluttering.
She is so small he imagines
he could hold all of her
in his hands and lift her to the black
sky beyond the illumination round's white light
where she would fly from her life
and the wounds from the lovers would heal,
the broken skin grow back.
But he need only touch her, only
lift the blanket from her shoulders

and the automatic shape of love unfolds,
the flare's light burning down on them,
lost in a wave that arrives
after a thousand years of grief
at their hearts.

≈ The Last Lie

Some guy in the miserable convoy
raised up in the back of our open truck
and threw a can of C rations at a child
who called into the rumble for food.
He didn't toss the can, he wound up and hung it
on the child's forehead and she was stunned
backwards into the dust of our trucks.

Across the sudden angle of the road's curving
I could still see her when she rose,
waving one hand across her swollen, bleeding head,
wildly swinging her other hand
at the children who mobbed her,
who tried to take her food.

I grit my teeth to myself to remember that girl
smiling as she fought off her brothers and sisters.
She laughed
as if she thought it were a joke
and the guy with me laughed
and fingered the edge of another can
like it was the seam of a baseball
until his rage ripped
again into the faces of children
who called to us for food.

≈ Her Life Runs Like a Red Silk Flag

Because this evening Miss Hoang Yen
sat down with me in the small
tiled room of her family house

I am unable to sleep.
We shared a glass of cold and sweet water.
On a blue plate her mother brought us
cake and smiled her betel black teeth at me
but I did not feel strange in the house
my country had tried to bomb into dust.
In English thick and dazed as blood
she told me how she watched our planes
cross her childhood's sky,
all the children of Hanoi
carried in darkness to mountain hamlets, Nixon's
Christmas bombing. She let me hold her hand,
her shy unmoving fingers, and told me
how afraid she was those days and how this fear
had dug inside her like a worm and lives
inside her still, won't die or go away.
And because she's stronger, she comforted me,
said I'm not to blame,
the million sorrows alive in her gaze.
With the dead we share no common rooms.
With the frightened we can't think straight;
no words can bring the burning city back.
Outside on Hung Dao street
I tried to say goodbye and held her hand
too long so she looked back through traffic
towards her house and with eyes
she told me I should leave.
All night I ached for her and for myself
and nothing I could think or pray
would make it stop. Some birds sang morning
home across the lake. In small reed boats
the lotus gatherers sailed out
among their resuming white blossoms.

Hanoi, 1990

JAMES FENTON (1949–   )

James Fenton, the son of an Anglican priest, attended Oxford University, where he began writing poetry. With the prize money for his first book, he went to Southeast Asia in 1973. While there, he covered the American withdrawal from Saigon and the civil wars in Cambodia. He returned to England in 1976 and soon found a position covering German politics. He now lives in England, and in addition to poetry, has written a book of memoirs.

≈ Cambodia

One man shall smile one day and say goodbye.
Two shall be left, two shall be left to die.

One man shall give his best advice.
Three men shall pay the price.

One man shall live, live to regret.
Four men shall meet the debt.

One man shall wake from terror to his bed.
Five men shall be dead.

One man to five. A million men to one.
And still they die. And still the war goes on.

≈ Dead Soldiers

When His excellency Prince Norodom Chantaraingsey
Invited me to lunch on the battlefield
I was glad of my white suit for the first time that day.
They lived well, the mad Norodoms, they had style.
The brandy and the soda arrived in crates.

Bricks of ice, tied around with raffia,
Dripped from the orderlies' handlebars.

And I remember the dazzling tablecloth
As the APCs fanned out along the road,
The dishes piled high with frogs' legs,
Pregnant turtles, their eggs boiled in the carapace,
Marsh irises in fish sauce
And inflorescence of a banana salad.

On every bottle, Napoleon Bonaparte
Pleaded for the authenticity of the spirit.
They called the empties Dead Soldiers
And rejoiced to see them pile up at our feet.

Each diner was attended by one of the other ranks
Whirling a table-napkin to keep off the flies.
It was like eating between rows of morris dancers—
Only they didn't kick.

On my left sat the prince;
On my right, his drunken aide.
The frogs' thighs leapt into the sad purple face
Like fish to the sound of a Chinese flute.
I wanted to talk to the prince. I wish now
I had collared his aide, who was Saloth Sar's brother.
We treated him as the club bore. He was always
Boasting of his connections, boasting with a head-shake
Or by pronouncing of some doubtful phrase.
And well might he boast. Saloth Sar, for instance,
Was Pol Pot's real name. The APCs
Fired into the sugar palms but met no resistance.

In a diary, I refer to Pol Pot's brother as the Jockey Cap.
A few weeks later, I find him 'in good form
And very skeptical about Chantaraingsey.'
'But one eats well there,' I remark.
'So one should,' says the Jockey Cap:
'The tiger always eats well,
It eats the raw flesh of the deer,
And Chantaraingsey was born in the year of the tiger.

So, did they show you the things they do
With the young refugee girls?'

And he tells me how he will one day give me the gen.
He will tell me how the prince financed the casino
And how the casino brought Lon Nol to power.
He will tell me this.
He will tell me all these things.
All I must do is drink and listen.

In those days, I thought that when the game was up
The prince would be far, far away—
In a limestone faubourg, on the promenade at Nice,
Reduced in circumstances but well enough provided for.
In Paris, he would hardly require his private army.
The Jockey Cap might suffice for café warfare,
And matchboxes for APCs.

But we were always wrong in these predictions.
It was a family war. Whatever happened,
The principals were obliged to attend its issue.
A few were cajoled into leaving, a few were expelled,
And there were villains enough, but none of them
Slipped away with the swag.

For the prince was fighting Sihanouk, his nephew,
And the Jockey Cap was ranged against his brother
Of whom I remember nothing more
Than an obscure reputation for virtue.
I have been told that the prince is still fighting
Somewhere in the Cardamoms or the Elephant Mountains.
But I doubt that the Jockey Cap would have survived his good
   connections.
I think the lunches would have done for him—
Either the lunches or the dead soldiers.

≈ Lines for Translation into Any Language

   1. I saw that the shanty town had grown over the graves and that the
crowd lived among the memorials.

2. It was never very cold—a parachute slung between an angel and an urn afforded shelter for the newcomers.

3. Wooden beds were essential.

4. These people kept their supplies of gasoline in litre bottles, which their children sold at the cemetery gates.

5. That night the city was attacked with rockets.

6. The firebrigade bided its time.

7. The people dug for money beneath their beds, to pay the firemen.

8. The shanty town was destroyed, the cemetery restored.

9. Seeing a plane shot down, not far from the airport, many of the foreign community took fright.

10. The next day, they joined the queues at the gymnasium, asking to leave.

11. When the victorious army arrived, they were welcomed by the firebrigade.

12. This was the only spontaneous demonstration in their favour.

13. Other spontaneous demonstrations in their favour were organised by the victors.

Repression in
Africa and
the Struggle
against
Apartheid in
South Africa

(1900–1991)

The first colonists came to South Africa in the seventeenth century, but the potential for exploitation of the continent's resources was not apparent until the nation-states of the nineteenth century divided the region to establish their preemptive monopolies. Each colonial power sought a captive market for buying raw materials and selling manufactured wares.

The rhetoric of empire frequently mirrors the rhetoric of racism: the occupiers must convince themselves and others that their rule is legitimate (they are "natural" rulers) and beneficial (they will civilize the "backward" natives). South Africa was first settled by the Dutch, who sought in their religion the justification for their rule, and enslaved or dispossessed the Africans who had inhabited the land before them. (South African political mythology falsely claims that the land was uninhabited.) In the nineteenth century there were four states in what is now South Africa, and the British first gained control in 1806. Nevertheless, the Afrikaners (the descendants of the Dutch) remained the majority, fighting an unsuccessful civil war against the British between 1899 and 1902. The Union of South Africa was formed in 1910 and was relatively autonomous within the British Commonwealth of Nations. South African laws became increasingly restrictive after 1913, even though the indigenous Africans and the Indians (who had been brought from India to work as indentured servants on the plantations in the second half of the nineteenth century) had already been given few political rights under the Act of Union. The Africans were forced off their farms and onto "reserves" in 1913, and they were allowed to work only in certain professions. The legal pillars of apartheid (Afrikaans for "apartness"), however, were only constructed after 1948, with the electoral victory of the Afrikaners' Nationalist Party. After that time, all South Africans had to be classified by race (although this has sometimes proved difficult in a multiracial society), they were not allowed to marry outside their racial designations, and they could live (or own property) only in designated areas. This restriction on abode and movement was enforced through the "Pass Laws."

The indigenous people had long opposed their subjugation, and finally founded the African National Congress (ANC) in the aftermath of the Act of Union. But the apartheid system tolerated no opposition. The government granted itself a number of rights: it banned and deported activists and critics, banned political parties, detained "suspects" for unlimited amounts of time, and resorted to torture and murder of its opponents.

Recently, the white minority government reorganized itself. It has been forced to repeal the Pass Laws, the Group Areas Act, and the laws on race classification and mixed marriages. Furthermore, the ANC, which had been banned in 1960, has been allowed to function in the open again. It must be noted, however, that any number of restrictions, both legal and economic, still remain enforced, and the South African government has had a history of changing the names of its laws without changing their effects.

South Africa is probably the most extreme example of postcolonial racial repression left in Africa, but the disjunctions that resulted from the experience of colonialism have left their mark on other African states. The newly emergent countries had boundaries that reflected the limits of European rule, not indigenous alliances. The strains of ethnic and tribal conflict have been evident in Nigeria, which won independence in 1960, suffered under a military dictatorship between 1966 and 1979, fought a civil war between 1967 and 1970, and was ruled by military dictatorship after 1983. If Nigeria has swung between internal conflict and dictatorship, Malawi has been dominated by one man, Hastings Banda (born in 1906), for the past twenty-five years; he has maintained his power through censorship, detention, and terror.

Colonialism has bequeathed to Africa a legacy of border disputes and multicultural conflict. Uneven development has ensured socioeconomic inequity: the majority suffer extreme poverty, while a privileged minority benefit from modernization.

Es'kia Mphahlele (1919–   )

A novelist, short story writer, and dramatist as well as literary critic and poet, Mphahlele, born in Pretoria, South Africa, began writing works of protest against apartheid in the late 1940s and early 1950s. He applied for an "exit visa"—a permit to leave the country permanently—in the mid-1950s and went into exile in 1957. He lived in Nigeria, Kenya, Zambia, France, and the United States before deciding to return to South Africa in 1978.

≈ A Poem

For all the victims of racist tyranny in southern Africa

What is there that we can do or say
will sustain them
in those islands
where the sun was made for janitors?

What is there that we can say or do
will tear the years
from out the hands
of savages who man the island galleys,

will bring them home and dry and mend them
bring them back
to celebrate
with us the song and dance and toil of living?

What is it that we can do or say
will send the plague
among the bandits
that watch and wait to wreck the freedom train?

The hounds are breeding where our house is fallen
ourselves we roam
the wilderness
"Go tell them there across the seas go tell him

tell them that his mother's dead six years
hounds are watching
hounds are waiting—
she told him not write no more no more."

You who fell before the cannon or
the sabered tooth
or lie on hallowed
ground: O tell us what to say or do.

So many routes have led to exile since
your day, our Elders,

we've been here
and back in many cycles oh so many

Cheap and easy answers have been chewed up
ready to
pop like bubble gum
for exile is   a ghetto of the mind: *(*

new terrain different drummers borrowed
dreams, and there
behind us now
the hounds have diamond fangs and paws of steel.

Perhaps we still can sing *a better day's*
a-coming soon
so *we* don't break:
in our deflated days we want a center.

No time for dirge or burial without corpses:
teach us, Elders,
how to wait
and feel the center, tame the time like masters.

Suspended self like fireflies must come
to earthy center,
sing the blues
so pain will bleed and let the islands in.

≈ **Homeward Bound**

The mountains that I like
and do not fear
don't stoop over me
like giant apes marooned
on a patch of Time;

they are the forms beyond,
holding down
the edge of blue

and etching with a light
of ever-changing tints;

—they can look the way I want them.

I do not like the lights
that come at me
and stab and flail
and blind the eyes of night
that bounce and cling on tarmac;

those shimmering faraway bodies
softly throbbing
tell me and love
that coffee's on the boil,
she's listening for my footsteps;

—they can look the way I want them.

But you beside me here—
the contours of
your mountainscape
lead me to sniff at the corners
of your passion and sprawl
in the light and shade of your valleys
reminding me clearly
distant sights
can easily become
explosions of a mood;

so let us ride along
through dewy midnights
dewy dawns
and tumble gently into
disemboweled noontides;

—you need not look just the way I want.

Dennis Brutus (1924–   )

Born in what was then Salisbury, Rhodesia, Brutus was educated in South Africa, attending a segregated college as a designated "coloured." He was a vigorous opponent of apartheid and a cofounder of the South African Non-Racial Olympic Committee. Banned from teaching in 1961, Brutus tried to make a living in journalism but was soon banned from that as well. He was arrested in 1963 for contravening his banning order, and spent eighteen months in the notorious prison on Robben Island (where he broke rocks with Nelson Mandela). He accepted enforced exile on his release and now teaches at the University of Pittsburgh.

≈ On the Island

I

Cement-grey floors and walls
cement-grey days
cement-grey time
and a grey susurration
as of seas breaking
winds blowing
and rains drizzling

A barred existence
so that one did not need to look
at doors or windows
to know that they were sundered by bars
and one locked in a grey gelid stream
of unmoving time.

II

When the rain came
it came in a quick moving squall
moving across the island

murmuring from afar
then drumming on the roof
then marching fading away.

And sometimes one mistook
the weary tramp of feet
as the men came shuffling from the quarry
white-dust-filmed and shambling
for the rain
that came and drummed and marched away.

III

It was not quite envy
nor impatience
nor irritation
but a mixture of feelings
one felt
for the aloof deep-green dreaming firs
that poised in the island air
withdrawn, composed and still.

IV

On Saturday afternoons we were embalmed in
        time
like specimen moths pressed under glass;
we were immobile in the sunlit afternoon
waiting;
Visiting time:
until suddenly like a book snapped shut
all possibilities vanished as zero hour passed
and we knew another week would have to pass.

≈ *from* Poems About Prison

Cold

the clammy cement
sucks our naked feet

a rheumy yellow bulb
lights a damp grey wall

the stubbled grass
wet with three o'clock dew
is black with glittery edges;

we sit on the concrete,
stuff with our fingers
the sugarless pap
into our mouths

then labour erect;

form lines;

steel ourselves into fortitude
or accept an image of ourselves
numb with resigned acceptance;

the grizzled senior warder comments:
"Things like these
I have no time for;

they are worse than rats;
you can only shoot them."

Overhead
the large frosty glitter of the stars
the Southern Cross flowering low;

the chains on our ankles
and wrists
that pair us together
jangle

glitter.

We begin to move
        awkwardly.

Colesberg: en route to Robben Island

≈ Under House Arrest

For Daantjie—on a New Coin envelope

On a Saturday afternoon in summer
greyly through net curtains I see
planes on planes in blocks of concrete masonry
where the biscuit factory blanks out the sky

Cézanne clawing agonisedly at the physical world
wrested from such super-imposed masses
a new and plangent vocabulary
evoking tensions, spatial forms and pressures
almost tactile on the eyeballs,
palpable on the fingertips,
and from these screaming tensions wrenched
new harmonies, the apple's equipoise
the immobility of deadlocked conflicts
—the cramp, paralyses—more rich
than any rest, repose.

And I, who cannot stir beyond these walls,
who shrink the temptation of any open door
find hope in thinking that repose
can be wrung from these iron-hard rigidities.

≈ Prayer

O let me soar on steadfast wing
that those who know me for a pitiable thing
may see me inerasably clear:

grant that their faith that I might hood
some potent thrust to freedom, humanhood
under drab fluff may still be justified.

Protect me from the slightest deviant swoop
to pretty bush or hedgerow lest I droop
ruffled or trifled, snared or power misspent.

Uphold—frustrate me if need be
so that I mould my energy
for that one swift inenarrable soar

hurling myself swordbeaked to lunge
for lodgement in my life's sun-targe—
a land and people just and free.

3 July 1966

SIPHO SEPAMLA (1932–   )

Born in Krugersdorp, South Africa, Sepamla trained as a teacher. A prizewinning writer of fiction as well as poetry, he is director of the Federated Union of Black Arts in Johannesburg.

≈ The Odyssey

explore the beauty of our land

discover where the sun shines
where shadows linger eternally
where peace sits ready to walk away
where wild game waits to sniff at your presence
and scamper away

discover the lie of our mountain humps
where low and where high
the drakensberg and its inns
where the tugela falls and then flows
and gives rise to a rich promise

by all means make these discoveries
but don't be in haste
                    to climb
                    to tumble
                and to pronounce

discover the vast empty spaces
that go a-begging for settlement
and the silence in between
where the taste of seasoned waters
can bewitch the mind and make one
succumb to a blabbering of sorts

discover these spaces and feel excited
but don't be amazed
                    they are rushed by some
                    they are rationed by others
                yet they are crowded by none

discover the many nations of our land
for ours is the land of tribes

                                the african
                        the english
                    the afrikaner
                the coloured
            the indian
the jew
and etc, etc and etc

discover that we are far from being an ignorant people
for ours is a land of many tribal universities
where many read unbiased tribal newspapers
for ours is the land of the sabc
the guardian of modern-day twists

discover the thirst of our wonderful land
and the hungered mind fed on human experiments

discover the love that is there
sitting awake waiting to be used
and the hate
that swells and flows as it feeds on fear

and when the feet begin to ache
blisters about to burst

and when the ears begin to itch
the hearing wounding the soul

don't grumble
don't groan

discover how people distrust one another in the room
discover how people talk round the point
discover how people are made to live a lie

and when the flesh begins to twitch
feeling failing to unknot a fear
and when the eyelids begin to whistle
tease those tears
squeeze
but don't cry

and when you feel the pain begin to understand
how i sink it at times
in sweetened streams that flow my way

and when you marvel at how i fall on knees to pray
take it you are right
you haven't begun to understand how i was made before
                                                    time was

discover the hope that lives with despair

discover the rats gnawing at this hope

discover the concern of all non-tribal people

discover the land that has gone sulky to a vision

≈ Measure for Measure

go measure the distance from cape town to pretoria
and tell me the prescribed area i can work in

count the number of days in a year
and say how many of them i can be contracted around

calculate the size of house you think good for me
and ensure the shape suits tribal tastes

measure the amount of light into the window
known to guarantee my traditional ways

count me enough wages to make certain that i
grovel in the mud for more food

teach me just so much of the world that i
can fit into certain types of labour

show me only those kinds of love
which will make me aware of my place at all times

and when all that is done
let me tell you this
you'll never know how far i stand from you

≈ Silence: 2

The silence I speak of
stretches the moment to Pretoria
Bloemfontein and Cape Town
it is the same silence
that has walled in
tense remembrances of days
making of each moment
pebbles of time

the silence I speak of
tends to confound my tongue
I gurgle speech sounds
like a river sipping
the marrow of aged rocks

the silence I speak of
crouches the night
to make shadows that terrorize
even the illusions I fabricate

daily I collide with ghosts
that walk day-night steets
hourly I feel the howling of
their wintered hearts
break into the ease
I've learnt to pace

I've sought to read
the brooding silence
that betrays itself with
dry coughs
or unfolding wrinkles

sometimes I've gone down
on all fours
raking the earth with one ear
to pick what murmurs
may glide down there
beneath the roots

how this silence
I hear
breeds
on avenues of despair
I'll never know

I speak
of a silence
I fear

≈ I Remember Sharpeville

On the 21st March 1960
on a wrath-wrecked
ruined-raked morning

a black sea surged onward
its might ahead
mind behind
it had downed centuries-old containment
one goal fed its dazed loyalty
to shed debris
on an unwilling shore
like a sponge
it sucked into its core
the aged and the young
school-children fell helter-skelter
into its body-might
as it rolled over
crushing the cream
and the scum of its make-up
into a solid compound
of black oozing energy

in a flash
of the eye
of gun-fire
like spray flayed
they fled they fell
the air fouled
the minute fucked
and life fobbed

our heads bowed
our shame aflame
our faith shaken

we buried them for what they were
our fallen heroes and our history

for orations we had the religious
for gun-carriers we had a string of hearses
for flags half-mast tear-soaked hankies

We craned necks to raise voices higher still
for them that lay row upon row crammed
a regiment under the blazing bloodied sun

they had lain deserted around and upon their original graves
left alone to bleed and plead for forgiveness
like the mangled bodies of their warrior forbears

the dust grit we ground as we gnashed teeth
the mournful wail of salt-stained faces
the groan and grouse of aggrieved relations
shall be our pledge to the dead

a monument in our hearts we shall mount
their unheard-of names to engrave
on time's sturdy wings their ideal we shall pin
Africa's priceless heritage to mankind

≈ The Law That Says

The law that says
claws the flesh
leaving imprints
that scar my habit to do

The law that says
constricts the breath-line
causing a gasping
that bends the lie I let out

The law that says
drags a bad mood
into the sugared cup
then I taste poison gall

I should like to reach out my hand
once more
the touch may suppress
the bad breath that snakes into the air
as you say the apology
or maybe, maybe I should rather
watch these things

eyes hollowed
hear them
ears clamped
vices biting the evil
as the law says

WOLE SOYINKA (1934–   )

A Nigerian, Soyinka was the first African to win the Nobel Prize for Literature (1986). He was arrested in 1967 for attempting to effect a compromise between the Hausa government of Nigeria and the rebelling Ibo leaders of the Biafran secession movement, and was imprisoned for almost two years, one of which was spent in solitary confinement. As chair of literature at the University of Lagos, he was later accused of trying to seize the radio station and dismissed. He chose political exile from Nigeria, and spent time with the Royal Court Theatre in London and the Yale Repertory Theater in New Haven, Connecticut. A fierce defender of personal freedom, he has written poetry, novels, autobiography, and essays, with major themes of exile and return.

≈ I Think It Rains

I think it rains
That tongues may loosen from the parch
Uncleave roof-tops of the mouth, hang
Heavy with knowledge

I saw it raise
The sudden cloud, from ashes. Settling
They joined in a ring of grey; within,
The circling spirit

Oh it must rain
These closures on the mind, binding us

In strange despairs, teaching
Purity of sadness

And how it beats
Skeined transparencies on wings
Of our desires, searing dark longings
In cruel baptisms

Rain-reeds, practised in
The grace of yielding, yet unbending
From afar, this your conjugation with my earth
Bares crouching rocks.

≈ Harvest of Hate

So now the sun moves to die at mid-morning
And laughter wilts on the lips of wine
The fronds of palm are savaged to a bristle
And rashes break on kernelled oil

The hearth is pocked with furnacing of teeth
The air is heavy with rise of incense
For wings womb-moist from the sanctuary of nests
Fall, unfledged to the tribute of fire.

Now pay we forfeit on old abdications
The child dares flames his fathers lit
And in the briefness of too bright flares
Shrivels a heritage of blighted futures

There has been such a crop in time of growing
Such tuneless noises when we longed for sighs
Alone of petals, for muted swell of wine-buds
In August rains, and singing in green spaces.

≈ Massacre, October '66

Written in Tegel

Shards of sunlight touch me here
Shredded in willows. Through stained-glass
Fragments on the lake I sought to reach
A mind at silt-bed

The lake stayed cold
I swam in an October flush of dying leaves
The gardener's labour flew in seasoned scrolls
Lettering the wind

Swept from painted craft
A mockery of waves remarked this idyll sham
I trod on acorns; each shell's detonation
Aped the skull's uniqueness.

Came sharper reckoning—
This favoured food of hogs cannot number high
As heads still harshly crop to whirlwinds
I have briefly fled

The oak rains a hundred more
A kind confusion to arithmetics of death:
Time to watch autumn the removal man
Dust down rare canvases

To let a loud resolve of passion
Fly to a squirrel, burnished light and copper fur
A distant stance without the lake's churchwindows
And for a stranger, love.

A host of acorns fell, silent
As they are silenced all, whose laughter
Rose from such indifferent paths, oh God
They are not strangers all

Whose desecration mocks the word
Of peace—salaam aleikun—not strangers any

Brain of thousands pressed asleep to pig fodder—
Shun pork the unholy—cries the priest.

I borrow seasons of an alien land
In brotherhood of ill, pride of race around me
Strewn in sunlit shards. I borrow alien lands
To stay the season of a mind.

≈ Civilian and Soldier

My apparition rose from the fall of lead,
Declared, 'I'm a civilian.' It only served
To aggravate your fright. For how could I
Have risen, a being of this world, in that hour
Of impartial death! And I thought also: nor is
Your quarrel of this world.

                    You stood still
For both eternities, and oh I heard the lesson
Of your training sessions, cautioning—
Scorch earth behind you, do not leave
A dubious neutral to the rear. Reiteration
Of my civilian quandary, burrowing earth
From the lead festival of your more eager friends
Worked the worse on your confusion, and when
You brought the gun to bear on me, and death
Twitched me gently in the eye, your plight
And all of you came clear to me.

                    I hope some day
Intent upon my trade of living, to be checked
In stride by *your* apparition in a trench,
Signalling, I am a soldier. No hesitation then
But I shall shoot you clean and fair
With meat and bread, a gourd of wine
A bunch of breasts from either arm, and that
Lone question—do you friend, even now, know
What it is all about?

BREYTEN BREYTENBACH (1939–   )

Breytenbach, early recognized as a leading poet in Afrikaans, left South Africa in 1959 and settled in Paris, where he became a painter and married a Vietnamese woman. In 1964, when Breytenbach was to return to South Africa, the government refused to give his wife a visa, and continued to refuse for ten years. By that time, however, Breytenbach had joined the struggle against apartheid; he returned to South Africa alone and with a false passport. He was arrested and eventually charged with "terrorism." Even though the public prosecutor and the Security Police requested the minimum sentence, Breytenbach was imprisoned for seven years, and spent two years in solitary confinement. He was released in 1982 and went into exile in France.

≈ Dar es-Salaam: Harbour of Peace

Dar es-Salaam: it's when night is darkest,
just before morning, that the muezzin calls the faithful
because they are all asleep
and his sad complaint flies over minaret forefingers,
            rooftops, and lovers and flowers and docks
and his sad complaint dawns over the city

one proverb goes: 'the cock that crows at night
                    without waiting for daybreak
brings misfortune, slaughter it immediately'; but according to a
                                        second:
'it is unwise to react when you are called
only once in the heart of the night'

you can let that bird loose as often as the sun:
but it always returns
—I think of you, brothers in exile, with only bitterness
                                    for earth

the day comes to dig a sweet earth: a sea full of ships and shells and
                                        coral,
the shells so young they're white—beaches,
and coconut palms very proud and slender with small firm breasts,
banana plantations, mangoes and paw-paws;
the city has sparkling clouds and crows weep in the wind,
'caw! caw!' prophecy the windpolished whitebreasts,
the other birds whistle through their wings: to whistle, so the
                                        saying goes,

is to call on the devil:
under fans in offices, sit bureaucrats
with boils on their lips and flies on their hands:
'wash clothes without water and you invite poverty'

I think of you, freedom-fighters, with the thin vomit
                        of a present that cannot be stomached
with weapons and fear somewhere far out on the foggy borders—
'if a man bites you rub chickenshit into the wound
and his teeth will rot'

with low tide and dusk the Indians come down to the sea
the moon a pale conch glistening in the creases of the void
where stars also swim—
to chat, savour the low tide and the twilight
and grow quieter, sitting cross-legged
and when it's dark enough
seek out an India far across the waters

I think of you, exiled brothers struggling with us for freedom,
I think of you who try to follow the sun:
if you point at the new moon with your finger
then your finger will be cut, but the finger
that picks out the moon is no moon
and if you blow over the pustules on your hands
then it is the moon which becomes a wart

I have heard: 'he who eats chicken's feet will become a wanderer';
'if you walk bare-headed under the moon your brain will dry up
and one day you will go crazy';

'a lunatic who always enjoys his meals
will never regain understanding'

Ukichomeka kisu ndani ya ala anaposema mwenye
kigugumizi basi hataweza kuendelea na kusema tena:
'stick a knife in its sheath while the stutterer talks
and you deprive him of all speech'—
here in Dar es-Salaam night has already fallen

TR. DENIS HIRSON

≈ Exile, Representative

For F.M. and M.K.

you grow less agile, more compliant
fat comes heaping onto your body
like ants deep inside a dead animal
one day you are finished off
your eyes burn all the more desolate

you live as if you'd never die
because this is not where you lead your life
yet death walks in your body
death comes down the trails of your guts
death is knotted into your wings

and holes form in the earth behind your eyes
the hills grow silent, their greenness fades
hands and smiles cave in
photographs and pamphlets are pasted
over memories: *experience is a dream*

you learn to beg
and feed the raw contrition of your people
to the insatiable bureaucrats
and all Officials of the World's Conscience
you look into the gaps of their hearts: deep into the mirror

so that in the morning you are still awake
with a grey mutter in your mouth

words swarming
like parasites around your tongue
and in your throat your words make nests

you're a full-time fugitive in the crowd
you don't smoke you don't drink
because your life is a weapon
you die miserably poisoned by despair
shot down like a dog in a dead-end street

and by the time you want to smash the day with your fist
and say: look my people are rising up!
here it comes, blinding! *Maatla!*
you've forgotten the silences of the language
ants creep from the cry
from belching entrails come blind freedom fighters

TR. DENIS HIRSON

≈ Journey

(: I have died a little)

I

ringing out from our blue heavens
but our heavens are charged with leaping fires
in the trees that slant up against the mountain
a silver light and other things which blind the eyes
a sudden taste like the electric shock of what has
no beginning and no end
: I have died a little

from our deep seas breaking round
the sea no longer has sympathy for the white man
the scum spreads from Europe
oil tankers in their thousands like festering whales
the milkwood stands utterly twisted with fear
nothing rinses the rot out any longer
: I have died a little

valleys and plains and then only flies
and then the desert
in the desert you have no need for a name
you are your own name
you are the nameless one
God, engulf us!
: I have died a little

when the fire burns out the hills are scorched black
to the edge of the night
go lead your eyes between the stars
like water between trees spitting blossoms
and the wind shakes loose concealing nothing
the wind empty houses
: I have died a little

game-reserves for the animals of the land
homelands for tame people
we saw a man in rags following the trail
without descent or refuge spools of flesh on a skeleton
a native an inland exile endlessly moving
deeper inward there was room enough in his eyes
: I have died a little

come all you gods like squawking chickens
unity is strength
farms townships towns suburbs
cities where music gets a grip
and dogs which know nothing but Afrikaans
born and bred to claw people open
: I have died a little

my land my land o anus full of blood
and love like a stiff body within the body . . .
that day we rode out like the blind
crossing the land again and again
the flames of the sky licking through the panes
we are blue and dying and life lies outside
: I have died a little

II

the day rises in the east
from behind the blue mould of white breakers
from the soft sugar-cane plantations
the day is light

all things which inhabit the skies
and are born out of light
below on earth
belong to people

in the mountains there are no longer gods
at night the moon is an empty house
the gods have always been human
our love is a kingdom of the gods

the day raises all the mountains
and goes like fire through the desert
our people stagger drunk with light
each one taking shelter in his own shadow

across the rank towers of the city
across the white trees of the farms
one human being screams out *oo-aa*
and another replies

across climates and seasons
across sorrows and harvests
across flat lands and slopes
and hunter and grass

the day blows
until evening falls
until the cold sea
and the coast of the dead are reached

the night rises high in the east
like breakers rolling towards the land
engulfing vineyards and orchards
the day that butterfly unable to swim

oo-aa one human being screams outside
and another human being replies
grace grace grace revealed in this place
death is the blood in our veins

III

such is man
such is his striving to be human
pressing for love
and acceptance by his fellows
you call and hear no echo

there will be a massacre
blood from the gardens and streets
firebrands freedom flags,

vultures across the bright floors
in the air-conditioned hotel lounges
smiles split eyes threaded onto a silver needle
there are beetles in the soup

soldiers by the lorry-load children on the roof-tops
a white god floating white in the bunker up above
cries shots the screech of teeth

like great pink animals stockinged up to the knees
the cows chew on carcasses houses burst into dust
sirens moan,

and the mine-shafts are taken over by ants
in the factories the orange-trees turn grey
you call and do not hear
such is man, o my love,
you call and do not hear
such is death this blood in our veins:
freedom or death,

TR. DENIS HIRSON

≈ **First Prayer for the Hottentotsgod**

they say, little beast, little creator, the elders say
that the fields of stars, the earth-dwellers and all things
that turn and rise up and sigh and crumble
were brought forth by you, that you planted an ostrich-feather
in the darkness and behold!   the moon!
o most ancient one,
                   you who fired by love
consume your lover, what led you to forsake
the children of those—the human stuff—
remember?   summoned by you
from the mud?
there are fires in the sky, mother, and the moon
cold as a shoe, and a black cry like smoke
mixed with dust—for your black people, people maker, work
like the dust of knives in the earth that the money
might pile up elsewhere
for others—
grassyellow lady of prayer,
                     hear our smoke and our dust—
chastise those who debased your people to slavery

    TR. DENIS HIRSON

≈ **The Struggle for the Taal**

'Clean as the conscience of a gun'
   —Miroslav Holub

We ourselves are aged.
Our language is a grey reservist a hundred years old and more
his fingers stiff around the triggers—
and who will be able to sing as we sang
when we are no longer there?
As we did when alive we will spurn the earth
and the miracles of the flesh which grows
throbbing and flowing like words—
It is you who will serve as bodies for our thoughts
and live to commemorate our death,
you will conjure up tunes from the flutes of our bones . . .

From the structure of our conscience
from the stores of our charity
we had black contraptions built for you, you bastards—
schools, clinics, post-offices, police-stations—
and now the plumes blow black smoke
throbbing the flowing like a heart.

But you have not fully understood.
You have yet to master the Taal.
We will make you say the ABC all over again,
we will teach you the ropes
of Christian National Education . . .

You will learn to be submissive
submissive and humble.
And you will learn to use the Taal,
with humility you will use it
for it is we who possess the mouths
with the poison in the throb and the flow of the heart.

You are the salt of the earth—
with what will we be able to spice our dying
if you are not there?
you will make the earth glint, bitter and brackish
with the sound of our lips . . .

For we are Christ's executioners.
We are on the walls around the townships
gun in one hand
machine-gun in the other:
we, the missionaries of Civilization.

We bring you the grammar of violence
and the syntax of destruction—
from the tradition of our firearms
you will hear the verbs of retribution
stuttering.

Look what we're giving you, free and for nothing—new mouths,
red ears with which to hear red eyes with which to see
pulsing, red mouths

so that you can spout the secrets of our fear:
where each lead-nosed word flies
a speech organ will be torn open . . .

And you will please learn to use the Taal,
with humility use it, abuse it . . .
because we are down already, the death-rattle's
throb and flow
on our lips . . .

As for us, we are aged . . .

TR. DENIS HIRSON

JACK MAPANJE (1944–   )

A well-known theoretical linguist, Jack Mapanje was born in Malawi
and started publishing in 1965. He was one of the founding members
of the Writers' Group at Chancellor College at the University of
Malawi, a group dedicated to creating an authentic postcolonial culture.
Many of Mapanje's poems are, by his own admission, enigmatic (as a
way, perhaps, of evading Malawi's extensive censorship laws), and his
first book, published in England, was "withdrawn" in his native coun-
try. The book was finally banned in 1987 when Mapanje was arrested
and held incommunicado. He was released in 1991, in part because of
international efforts on his behalf.

≈ After Wiriyamu Village Massacre by Portuguese

No, go back into your exile, go back quick.
When those Portuguese soldiers abducted
Falencha's baby quietly strapped on her back
And scattered its precious brain on Falencha's
Own maize grinding stone, when those soldiers
Grabbed and hacked Dinyero's only son
With Dinyero herself stubbornly watching
Or when they burnt down Faranando in his own

Hut as he tried to save Alefa his senile wife—
Where, where was your hand? Tell me that!
And if you helped Adrian Hastings report
The Portuguese atrocities to humans, where,
Where is your verse? You have no shame!
No, go back until our anger has simmered.

≈ On His Royal Blindness Paramount Chief Kwangala

I admire the quixotic display of your paramountcy
How you brandish our ancestral shields and spears
Among your warriors dazzled by your loftiness
But I fear the way you spend your golden breath
Those impromptu, long-winded tirades of your might
In the heat, do they suit your brittle constitution?

I know I too must sing to such royal happiness
And I am not arguing. Wasn't I too tucked away in my
Loin-cloth infested by jiggers and fleas before
Your bright eminence showed up? How could I quibble
Over your having changed all that? How dare I when
We have scribbled our praises all over our graves?

Why should I quarrel when I too have known mask
Dancers making troubled journeys to the gold mines
On bare feet and bringing back fake European gadgets
The broken pipes, torn coats, crumpled bowler hats,
Dangling mirrors and rusty tin cans to make their
Mask dancing strange? Didn't my brothers die there?

No, your grace, I am no alarmist nor banterer
I am only a child surprised how you broadly disparage
Me shocked by the tedium of your continuos palaver. I
Adore your majesty. But paramountcy is like a raindrop
On a vast sea. We should not wait for the children to
Tell us about our toothless gums or our showing flies.

≈ On Being Asked to Write a Poem for 1979

Without kings and warriors occasional verse fails

Skeletal Kampuchea children staring, cold
Stubborn Irish children throwing grenades
These are objects too serious for verse,
Crushed Soweto children clutching their entrails
Then in verse bruised, mocks

Today no poet sufficiently asks why dying children
Stare or throw bombs. And why should we
Compute painful doubts that will forever occupy us?
Talking oil-crises in our eight-cylinder cars
Is enough travesty . . .

The year of the child must make no difference then
Where tadpoles are never allowed to grow into frogs!

JEREMY CRONIN (1949–   )

Cronin was educated in Cape Town and at the Sorbonne. On returning
from France to South Africa, he lectured in philosophy and political
science. He was arrested in 1976 for working for the African National
Congress and sentenced to seven years. He spent three of these years
with prisoners on death row. His wife died during his incarceration. He
was released in 1983.

≈ The Naval Base (Part III)

I cannot disclaim that string-thin, five-year-old boy
with big ears and bucked teeth from thumbsucking late,
who woke to dockyard hooters on mornings of mackerel-green sea
that cast up sea-eggs, argonauts, unexplained white rubber balloons.
A soft sea full of cutting things, of sharkstooth, barnacles, and
        ultramarines.
Who polished with envy and Silvo his pa's ceremonial sword.

Who dreamt of mama and the ocean's lap-lap,
and that one day the tide would ride out,
yes ride oh right out, uncovering bedclothes.
That boy, that endless earache, who knew at five,
because learnt by heart, the naval salute, the sign of the cross,
the servant's proper place, and our father who art.
—This five-year-old boy, this shadow,
this thing stuck to my feet.

≈ **Motho Ke Motho Ka Batho Babang**
(A Person Is a Person Because of Other People)

By holding my mirror out of the window I see
Clear to the end of the passage.
There's a person down there.
A prisoner polishing a doorhandle.
In the mirror I see him see
My face in the mirror,
I see the fingertips of his free hand
Bunch together, as if to make
An object the size of a badge
Which travels up to his forehead
The place of an imaginary cap.
        (This means: A *warder.*)
Two fingers are extended in a vee
And wiggle like two antennae.
        (He's being watched.)
A finger of his free hand makes a watch-hand's arc
On the wrist of his polishing arm without
Disrupting the slow-slow rhythm of his work.
        (Later. Maybe, later we can speak.)
Hey! Wat maak jy daar?
        —a voice from around the corner.
No. Just polishing baas.
He turns his back to me, now watch
His free hand, the talkative one,
Slips quietly behind
        —*Strength brother,* it says,
In my mirror,
        A black fist.

≈ Group Photo from Pretoria Local on the Occasion of a Fourth Anniversary (Never Taken)

An uprooted tree leaves
        behind it a hole in the ground
But after a few months
You would have to have known
        that something grew here once.
And a person's uprooted?
Leaves a gap too, I suppose, but then
        after some years . . .
There we are
        seated in a circle,
Mostly in short pants, some of us barefoot,
Around the spot where four years before
When South African troops were repulsed before
        Luanda

Our fig tree got chopped
        down in reprisal.—That's Raymond
Nudging me, he's pointing
At Dave K who looks bemusedly
Up at the camera. Denis sits on an upturned
Paraffin tin. When this shot was taken
He must have completed
        seventeen years of his first
Life sentence.
        David R at the back is saying
Something to John, who looks at Tony who
Jerks his hand
        So it's partly blurred.
There we are, seven of us
        (but why the grinning?)
Seven of us, seated, in a circle,
The unoccupied place in the center
        stands for what happened
Way outside the frame of this photo.
So SMILE now, hold still and
        click
            I name it: Luanda.

For sure an uprooted tree
      leaves behind a hole in the ground.
After a few years
You would have to have known
      it was here once. And a person?
There we are
      seated in our circle, grinning,
      mostly in short pants,
      some of us barefoot.

Revolutions and the Struggle for Democracy in China

(1911-1991)

The Manchu Dynasty's 260-year rule ended in 1911, when uprisings throughout China forced the Manchus to cede power to Yuan Shih-k'ai, who served as prime minister and then provincial president after the abdication of the young emperor, Hsuan T'ung. Sun Yat-sen founded the Kuomintang (Chinese National Party) in 1912, serving briefly as the first provincial president of the new republic, then as its most important statesman. At his death in 1925, his party, which ruled southern China, was split into Communist and rightist factions, while military commanders vied for power in the north. As Sun Yat-sen's legacy had been advocation of unity, the Kuomintang forces, under the command of General Chiang Kai-shek, marched north and were victorious, partly because the Kuomintang soldiers, trained to be respectful of civilians, were welcomed by the citizenry.

After World War II, the Communists in the north and the Kuomintang in the south attempted to capture territory that had been Japanese-occupied during the war. A civil war ensued, which brought the Communists to power in 1949, under the leadership of Mao Tse-tung, who attempted to revolutionize Chinese society. The "Great Leap Forward" of the 1950s was his ambitious program of industrialization and social reform (which substituted the commune for the traditional family). During political power struggles of the 1960s, Mao, whose power base was the military, tried to seize control of the highly developed bureaucracy of Chinese society by initiating the "Great Proletarian Cultural Revolution." Militant young people converged on Peking and marched in Tiananmen Square. In their fervor to display patriotism, they destroyed art works and historical archives, burned books, denounced intellectuals, and attacked dissidents. The violence grew chaotic as warring "Red Guards," fighting even among themselves, battled other Chinese factions in the provinces until schools and most factories were forced to close. Order was gradually restored, and while the "Cultural Revolution" is credited by some with having eroded class differences, its cost was high: lives and livelihoods were lost, education interrupted, and Chinese society terrorized.

Mao's death in 1976 brought with it economic liberalization, but political reforms did not keep pace. In April 1989, students at the University of Beijing began to demand greater democracy within the People's Republic of China. This agitation gained force during a memorial rally in Tiananmen Square. Several days after the students were attacked in the government press, a protest was mounted that is said to have included one million people. Pro-democracy demonstrations were held in other major cities in China. By the middle of May, several hundred began a hunger strike to press for reforms, and their supporters again congregated in Tiananmen Square. Martial law was declared on May 20, but the large public demonstrations continued. On the night of June 3, troops were sent into Beijing to clear Tiananmen Square.

The resistance to the army was as heroic (in one of the most famous instances, a young man tried to stop a column of tanks by standing in front of it) as it was impossible: at least one thousand people, including children and the elderly, were shot or otherwise killed by the military.

In the aftermath of the massacre, more than ten thousand people were arrested in Beijing alone. Those leaders of the demonstrations who managed to escape the police were forced to flee the country. It is not known how many people were executed for their participation in the pro-democracy movement.

Bei Dao (1949–   )

Born in Beijing the year the Communists took power, Bei Dao, whose real name is Zhao Zhenkai, joined the Red Guard movement during the Cultural Revolution but soon became disillusioned; like others of his generation, he began developing a poetry that challenged the aesthetic and political orthodoxies of Maoist China. He became famous on April 5, 1976, when at a demonstration against dictatorship in Tiananmen Square some of his poems were read. He was one of the leaders of the Democracy Movement in the late 1970s. Although he escaped arrest, his works were vilified by authorities, and he has since lived in exile.

≈ The Answer

Debasement is the password of the base.
Nobility the epitaph of the noble
See how the gilded sky is covered
With the drifting twisted shadows of the dead.

The Ice Age is over now.
Why is there ice everywhere?

The Cape of Good Hope has been discovered.
Why do a thousand sails contest the Dead Sea?

I came into this world
Bringing only paper, rope, a shadow,
To proclaim before the judgement
The voice that has been judged:

Let me tell you, world,
I—do—not—believe!
If a thousand challengers lie beneath your feet,
Count me as number one thousand and one.

I don't believe the sky is blue;
I don't believe in thunder's echoes;
I don't believe that dreams are false;
I don't believe that death has no revenge.

If the sea is destined to breach the dikes
Let all the brackish water pour into my heart;
If the land is destined to rise
Let humanity choose a peak for existence again.

A new conjunction and glimmering stars
Adorn the unobstructed sky now;
They are the pictographs from five thousand years.
They are the watchful eyes of future generations.

TR. BONNIE S. MCDOUGALL

≈ Stretch out your hands to me

Stretch out your hands to me
don't let the world blocked by my shoulder
disturb you any longer
if love is not forgotten
hardship leaves no memory
remember what I say
not everything will pass
if there is only one last aspen

standing tall at the end of the road
like a gravestone without an epitaph
the falling leaves will also speak
fading paling as they tumble
slowly they freeze over
holding our heavy footprints
of course no one knows tomorrow
tomorrow begins from another dawn
when we will be fast asleep

TR. BONNIE S. McDOUGALL

≈ An End or a Beginning

For Yu Luoke

Here I stand
Replacing another, who has been murdered
So that each time the sun rises
A heavy shadow, like a road
Shall run across the land

A sorrowing mist
Covers the uneven patchwork of roofs
Between one house and another
Chimneys spout ashy crowds
Warmth effuses from gleaming trees
Lingering on the wretched cigarette stubs
Low black clouds arise
From every tired hand

In the name of the sun
Darkness plunders openly
Silence is still the story of the East
People on age-old frescoes
Silently live forever
Silently die and are gone

Ah, my beloved land
Why don't you sing any more
Can it be true that even the ropes of the Yellow River towmen

Like sundered lute-strings
Reverberate no more
True that time, this dark mirror
Has also turned its back on you forever
Leaving only stars and drifting clouds behind

I look for you
In every dream
Every foggy night or morning
I look for spring and apple trees
Every wisp of breeze stirred up by honey bees
I look for the seashore's ebb and flow
The seagulls formed from sunlight on the waves
I look for the stories built into the wall
Your forgotten name and mine

If fresh blood could make you fertile
The ripened fruit
On tomorrow's branches
Would bear my colour

I must admit
That I trembled
In the death white chilly light
Who wants to be a meteorite
Or a martyr's ice-cold statue
Watching the unextinguished fire of youth
Pass into another's hand
Even if doves alight on its shoulder
It can't feel their bodies' warmth and breath
They preen their wings
And quickly fly away

I am a man
I need love
I long to pass each tranquil dusk
Under my love's eyes
Waiting in the cradle's rocking
For the child's first cry
On the grass and fallen leaves
On every sincere gaze

I write poems of life
This universal longing
Has now become the whole cost of being a man

I have lied many times
in my life
But I have always honestly kept to
The promise I made as a child
So that the world which cannot tolerate
A child's heart
Has still not forgiven me

Here I stand
Replacing another, who has been murdered
I have no other choice
And where I fall
Another will stand
A wind rests on my shoulders
Stars glimmer in the wind

Perhaps one day
The sun will become a withered wreath
To hang before
The growing forest of gravestones
Of each unsubmitting fighter
Black crows the night's tatters
Flock thick around

TR. BONNIE MCDOUGALL

≈ Résumé

Once I goosestepped across the square
my head shaved bare
the better to seek the sun
but in that season of madness
seeing the cold-faced goats on the other side
of the fence I changed direction
when I saw my ideals
on blank paper like saline-alkaline soil

I bent my spine
believing I had found the only
way to express the truth, like
a baked fish dreaming of the sea
Long live . . . ! I shouted only once, damn it
then sprouted a beard
tangled like countless centuries
I was obliged to do battle with history
and at knife-point formed a
family alliance with idols
not indeed to cope with
the world fragmented in a fly's eye
among piles of endlessly bickering books
calmly we divided into equal shares
the few coins we made from selling off each star
in a single night I gambled away
my belt, and returned naked again to the world
lighting a silent cigarette
it was a gun bringing death at midnight
when heaven and earth changed places
I hung upside down
on an old tree that looked like a mop
gazing into the distance

TR. BONNIE MCDOUGALL

≈ Accomplices

Many years have passed, mica
gleams in the mud
with a bright and evil light
like the sun in a viper's eyes
in a jungle of hands, roads branch off and disappear
where is the young deer
perhaps only a graveyard can change
this wilderness and assemble a town
freedom is nothing but the distance
between the hunter and the hunted
when we turn and look back
the arc drawn by bats

against the vast background of our fathers' portraits
fades with the dusk

we are not guiltless
long ago we became accomplices
of the history in the mirror, waiting for the day
to be deposited in lava
and turn into a cold spring
to meet the darkness once again

TR. BONNIE MCDOUGALL

DUODUO (1951–   )

Born Li Shizheng in Beijing, Duoduo trained as an opera singer. He
began writing poetry during the Cultural Revolution in the early 1970s
and became prominent after the liberalization of Chinese politics at the
end of the 1970s. His work is controversially "modernist." He has
worked as a journalist in Beijing.

≈ *from* Thoughts and Recollections

When the People Stand Up out of the Hard Cheese

The sound of gunfire—dilutes the bloody terror of revolution.
August is stretched like a cruel bow.
The poisonous man-child walks out of a peasant hovel
with tobacco and a parched throat.
The cattle have been brutally blinkered
and remains hang in the hair from their haunches, like swollen
    clappers.
Now even the sacrifice behind the bamboo fence is obscured:
far off, the troops keep coming through the cloud.

1972

TR. GREGORY LEE AND JOHN CAYLEY

≈ Wishful Thinking Is the Master of Reality

And we, are birds beak to beak
in time's story
with people
engaged in proving our differences for the last time:

The key is turned in the ear,
shadows have broken away from us.
The key turns incessantly.
We have degenerated into people,
we have become unrecognizable people.

1982

TR. GREGORY LEE AND JOHN CAYLEY

≈ At Parting

The green fields are like constructions of the mind which have
        suddenly
collapsed, like an unending, boundless twilight
where the future's serried ranks keep marching on.
You, you are like someone pushed onto an unfamiliar path,
walking down a side alley, grown older
—those lights from countless family dwellings
and one shadow of loneliness.
There is only a shepherd, tightly gripping his scarlet switch:
    —he is watching the darkness,
                he is watching over the darkness.

1972

TR. GREGORY LEE AND JOHN CAYLEY

≈ Untitled

Statements 8

Thousands of images have suddenly brightened in the emptiness
the hope of freedom has been given over to cultivation

dreams have been carried off,
   the serenity of the night is shattered.
Not even a mountain will be moved any more,
only the train, like a nerve, electric with anxiety,
moves forward blindly
towards the deeply buried city of memory . . .

Things past have constantly slipped into silence
while those dreams set out in books
and the principles of the sun's impartial rays survive.
Before, they appeared subjective, and were lost
in the immortal graveyard of time.
Still, today, we have only the many worlds
as always, serenely, secretly
spinning, behind the high wall,
the web of their hidden agenda.

1976

TR. GREGORY LEE AND JOHN CAYLEY

≈ Looking Out from Death

Looking out from death you will always see
those whom all your life you ought not to see.
One can always be buried somewhere at one's leisure
sniff around at one's leisure, then bury oneself there
in a place that makes them hate.

They shovel dirt in your face.
You should thank them. And thank them again.
For your eyes will never again see your enemy.
Then from death will come,
when they are consumed by enmity, a scream
although you will never hear again:
Now that is the absolute scream of anguish!

1983

TR. GREGORY LEE AND JOHN CAYLEY

Selected Bibliography

This bibliography includes selected books of poetry and pertinent memoirs written by poets whose work appears in this anthology. As this is a gathering of works in English and in translation, I have not included books in other languages.

Adonis [Ali Ahmad Sa'id]. *Modern Poetry of the Arab World.* Selected and introduced by Abdullah al-Udhari. Harmondsworth, England: Penguin, 1986.

Aichinger, Ilse. *Selected Poetry and Prose.* Translated by Allen H. Chappel. Durango, Colo.: Logbridge-Rhodes, 1983.

———. *Ilse Aichinger.* Translated by James C. Alldridge. Chester Springs, Penn.: Dufour Editions, 1969.

Akhmatova, Anna Andreevna. *Poems without a Hero and Selected Poems.* Translated by Lenore Mayhew and William McNaughton. Field Translation Series, no. 14. Oberlin, Ohio: Oberlin College Press, 1989.

———. *You Will Hear Thunder: Poems.* Translated by D. M. Thomas. Athens, Ohio: Ohio University Press, 1985.

———. *Twenty Poems.* Translated by Jane Kenyon and Vera Sandomirsky Dunham. St. Paul: Eighties Press and Ally Press, 1985.

———. *Poems.* Translated by Lyn Coffin. New York: Norton, 1983.

———. *Way of All the Earth.* Translated by D. M. Thomas. Athens, Ohio: Ohio University Press, 1979.

———. *Requiem and Poem without a Hero.* Translated by D. M. Thomas. Athens, Ohio: Ohio University Press, 1976.

———. *Selected Poems.* Ann Arbor, Mich.: Ardis Publishers, 1976.

———. *A Poem without a Hero.* Translated by Carl R. Proffer and Assya Humesky. Ann Arbor, Mich.: Ardis Publishers, 1973.

———. *Poems of Akhmatova.* Translated by Max Hayward and Stanley Kunitz. Boston: Little, Brown, 1973.

Akhmatova, Anna Andreevna, Marina Tsvetayeva, and Bella Akhmadulina. *Three Russian Poets: Anna Akhmatova, Marina Tsvetayeva, Bella Ahkmadulina.* Translated by Mary Maddock. Trumansburg, N.Y.: Crossing Press, 1983.

Alberti, Rafael. *Ballads and Songs of the Parana.* Van Nuys, Calif.: C'est moi-meme, 1988.

———. *The Other Shore: 100 Poems.* Translated by Kosrof Chantikian, Jose A. Elgorriaga, and Paul Martin. Modern Poets in Translation Series, vol. 1. San Francisco: Cosmos, 1981.

———. *The Owl's Insomnia.* Translated by Mark Strand. New York: Atheneum, 1973.

―――. *Concerning the Angels*. London: Rapp & Carroll, 1967. Translated and with an introduction by Geoffrey Connell. Denver, Colo.: A. Swallow, 1967.

―――. *Selected Poems*. Edited and translated by Ben Belitt. Berkeley, Calif.: University of California Press, 1966.

―――. *Selected Poems of Rafael Alberti*. Translated by Lloyd Malan. New York: New Directions, 1944.

―――. *A Spectre Is Haunting Europe: Poems of Revolutionary Spain*. Translated by Angel Flores and Ira Wallach. New York: Critics Group, 1936.

Alegría, Claribel. *Woman of the River*. Translated by Darwin Flakoll. Pittsburgh: University of Pittsburgh Press, 1989.

―――. *Flowers from the Volcano*. Translated by Carolyn Forché. Pittsburgh: University of Pittsburgh Press, 1982.

Amichai, Yehuda. *Even a Fist Was Once a Palm with Fingers*. Translated by Barbara Harshav and Benjamin Harshav. New York: Harper & Row, 1991.

―――. *Poems of Jerusalem*. New York: Harper & Row, 1988.

―――. *The Early Books of Yehuda Amichai*. Translated by Ted Hughes, Assia Gutmann, and Harold Schimmel. Riverdale-on-Hudson, N.Y.: Sheep Meadow Press, 1988.

―――. *The Selected Poetry of Yehuda Amichai*. Translated by Chana Block and Stephen Mitchell. New York: Harper & Row, 1986.

―――. *Love Poems: A Bi-Lingual Edition*. New York: Harper & Row, 1981.

―――. *Time: Poems*. New York: Harper & Row, 1979.

―――. *Amen*. New York: Harper & Row, 1977.

―――. *Songs of Jerusalem and Myself*. Translated by Harold Schimmel. New York: Harper & Row, 1973.

―――. *Selected Poems of Yehuda Amichai*. Translated by Harold Schimmel and Assia Gutmann. Penguin Modern European Poets. Harmondsworth, England: Penguin, 1971.

―――. *Poems*. Translated by Assia Gutmann. London: Cape Goliard Press, 1968.

Apollinaire, Guillaume. *Apollinaire—Selected Poems*. Translated by Bernard Oliver. London and Dover, N.H.: Anvil Press Poetry, 1986.

―――. *Mirror*. Translated by Carolee Campbell and Anne Hyde Greet. Sherman Oaks, Calif.: Ninja Press, 1986.

―――. *Calligrammes: Poems on Peace and War 1913–1916*. Translated by Anne Hyde Greet. Berkeley, Calif.: University of California Press, 1980.

―――. *Bestiary, or, The Parade of Orpheus*. Translated by Raoul Dufy. Boston: Godine, 1980.

―――. *Color of Time*. New York: Zone Books, 1980.

―――. *Zone*. Translated by Samuel Beckett. Dublin: Dolman Press; London: Calder & Boyars, 1972.

―――. *Hunting Horns: Poems of Apollinaire*. Translated by Barry Morse. South Hinksey Oxon, England: Carcanet Press, 1970.

―――. *Selected Writings*. Edited and translated by Roger Shattuck. New York: New Directions, 1950.

―――. *Alcools: Poems 1898–1913*. Translated by William Meredith. New York: Doubleday, 1964.

Arghezi, Tudor. *Selected Poems of Tudor Arghezi.* Translated by Brian Swann and Michael Impey. Princeton, N.J.: Princeton University Press, 1976.

Auden, W. H. [Wystan Hugh]. *Collected Poems.* Edited by Edward Mendelson. New York: Random House, Vintage Books, 1991. All that W. H. Auden wished to preserve.

―――. *The Complete Works of W. H. Auden.* Edited by Edward Mendelson. Princeton, N.J.: Princeton University Press, 1988.

―――. *Auden—Five Poems.* Cedar Falls, Iowa: Labyrinthe Editions, 1983.

Baca, Jimmy Santiago. *Immigrants in Our Own Land and Selected Early Poems.* New York: New Directions, 1990.

―――. *Black Mesa Poems.* New York: New Directions, 1989.

―――. *Poems Taken from My Yard.* Fulton, Mont.: Timberline Press, 1986.

―――. *What's Happening.* Willimantic, Conn.: Curbstone, 1982.

―――. *Swords of Darkness.* San Jose, Calif.: Mango Publications, 1981.

Bachmann, Ingeborg. *In the Storm of Roses: Selected Poems.* Translated by Mark Anderson. Princeton, N.J.: Princeton University Press, 1986.

Balaban, John. *Remembering Heaven's Face: A Moral Witness in Vietnam.* New York: Poseidon Press, 1991. A memoir.

―――. *Words for My Daughter: Poems.* Port Townsend, Wash.: Copper Canyon, 1991.

―――. *Coming Down Again.* New York: Simon & Schuster, 1989.

―――. *Blue Mountain.* Greensboro, N.C.: Unicorn Press, 1982.

―――. *Ca Dao Viet Nam: A Bi-Lingual Anthology of Vietnamese Folk Poetry.* Edited and translated by John Balaban. Greensboro, N.C.: Unicorn Press, 1980.

―――. *After Our War.* Pittsburgh: University of Pittsburgh Press, 1974.

―――. *Vietnamese Poems.* Oxford, England: Carcanet Press, 1970.

Baraka, Amiri. *The Leroi Jones / Amiri Baraka Reader.* Edited by William J. Harris. New York: Thunder's Mouth, 1991.

―――. *Reggae or Not! Poems.* New York: Contact II Publications, 1981.

―――. *Selected Poetry of Amiri Baraka / Leroi Jones.* New York: William Morrow, 1979.

―――. *Black Magic: Sabotage, Target Study, Black Art, Collected Poetry 1961–1967.* Indianapolis: Bobbs-Merrill, 1969.

Baranczak, Stanislaw, and Clare Cavanaugh, eds. *Polish Poetry of the Last Two Decades of Communist Rule: Spoiling Cannibals' Fun.* Evanston, Ill.: Northwestern University Press, 1991.

―――. *Selected Poems. The Weight of the Body.* Evanston: Triquarterly Books, Northwestern University; Chicago: Another Chicago Press, 1989.

―――. *Under My Own Roof: Verses for a New Apartment.* Forest Grove, Oreg.: Mr. Cogito Press, 1980.

Bei Dao. *The August Sleepwalker.* Translated by Bonnie S. McDougall. New York: New Directions, 1988.

Benn, Gottfried. *Poems, 1937–1947.* Translated by Simona Draghici. Washington, D.C.: Plutarch Press, 1991.

―――. *Prose, Essays, Poems.* Translated by Sander Volkmar and Richard Paul Becker. New York: Continuum, 1987.

————. *Selected Poems.* Translated by Friedrich Wilhelm Wodtke. London: Oxford University Press, 1970.

Berrigan, Daniel. *Poetry, Drama, Prose.* Maryknoll, N.Y.: Orbis Books, 1988.

————. *Lights on in the House of the Dead: A Prison Diary.* Garden City, N.Y.: Doubleday, 1974.

————. *Prison Poems.* New York: Viking, 1973.

————. *Selected and New Poems.* Garden City, N.Y.: Doubleday, 1973.

————. *Encounter: Poems.* New York: World Publishing, 1971.

————. *Night Flight to Hanoi: War Diary with 11 Poems.* New York: Harper & Row, 1971.

————. *The Trial of the Catonsville Nine.* Boston: Beacon Press, 1970.

————. *Trial Poems.* Illustrated by Lewis Thomas. Boston: Beacon Press, 1970.

Bienek, Horst. *Selected Poems.* Greensboro, N.C.: Unicorn Press, 1989.

————. *Time without Bells.* New York: Atheneum, 1988.

————. *Earth and Fire.* New York: Atheneum, 1988.

————. *Selected Poems.* Penguin Modern European Poets Series. Harmondsworth, England: Penguin, 1971.

————. *Horst Bienek: Poems.* Translated by Ruth Mead and Matthew Mead. Santa Barbara, Calif.: Unicorn Press, 1969.

Bobrowski, Johannes. *Shadow Lands: Selected Poems.* London: Anvil Press Poetry, 1984.

————. *Johannes Bobrowski.* Translated by Brian Keith-Smith. London: Wolff, 1970.

Bobrowski, Johannes, and Horst Bienek. *Selected Poems: Johannes Bobrowski and Horst Bienek.* Penguin Modern European Poets Series. Harmondsworth, England: Penguin, 1971.

Borowski, Tadeusz. *The Selected Poems of Tadeusz Borowski.* Lafayette, Calif.: Tech Prose, 1990.

————. *This Way for the Gas, Ladies and Gentlemen.* New York: Penguin, 1976.

Brecht, Bertolt. *Poems.* Translated by John Willett, Erich Fried, and Ralph Manheim. New York: Methuen, 1980.

————. *Selected Poems.* New York: Harcourt Brace Jovanovich, 1975.

Breton, André. *Poems of André Breton: A Bi-Lingual Anthology.* Translated by Jean Pierre Cauvin and Mary Ann Caws. Austin, Tex.: University of Texas Press, 1982.

Breytenbach, Breyten. *The True Confessions of an Albino Terrorist.* New York: McGraw-Hill, 1986.

————. *In Africa Even the Flies Are Happy: Selected Poems 1964–1977.* London: Collings, 1978.

Brodsky, Joseph. *To Urania.* New York: Farrar, Straus, & Giroux, 1988.

————. *A Part of Speech.* New York: Farrar, Straus, & Giroux, 1980.

————. *Three Slavic Poets: Joseph Brodsky, Tymoteusz Karpowicz, Djordje Nikolic.* Chicago: Elpenor, 1975.

————. *Selected Poems.* Translated by George Louis Kline. New York: Harper & Row, 1973.

————. *New Underground Russian Poets: Poems.* Translated by George Reavey. Calcutta: Dialogue Calcutta; New York: Stechert-Hafner, 1969.

Brutus, Dennis. *Airs and Tributes.* Camden, N.J.: Whirlwind Press, 1989.

————. *Salutes & Censures.* Enuga, Nigeria: Fourth Dimension, 1984.

————. *Stubborn Hope: New Poems and Selections from China Poems and Strains.* Washington, D.C.: Three Continents, 1983.

————. *Strains.* Austin, Tex.: Troubadour Press, 1975.

————. *Thoughts Abroad: Poems.* Austin, Tex.: Troubadour Press, 1975.

————. *China Poems.* Austin, Tex.: African and Afro-American Studies & Research Center, 1975.

————. *A Simple Lust: Selected Poems including Sirens Knuckles Boots, Letters to Martha, Poems from Algiers, Thoughts Abroad.* London: Heinemann, 1973.

Caraion, Ion. *Ion Caraion: Poems.* Translated by Marguerite Dorian and Elliott Urdang. Athens, Ohio: Ohio University Press, 1981.

Cassian, Nina. *Life Sentence: Selected Poems.* Edited and with an introduction by William Jay Smith. New York: Norton, 1990.

————. *Blue Apple.* Translated by Eva Feiler. Merrick, N.Y.: Cross Cultural Communications, 1981.

Castillo, Otto Rene. *Let's Go!* Translated by Margaret Randall. Willimantic, Conn.: Curbstone, 1984.

————. *Tomorrow Triumphant: Selected Poems of Otto Rene Castillo.* Translated by Magaly Fernandez and David Volpendesta. San Francisco: Night Horn Books, 1984.

Cavafy, Constantine P. *The Greek Poems of C. P. Cavafy.* Translated by Memas Kolaitis. New Rochelle, N.Y.: Caratzas, 1989.

————. *A Selection of Poems.* Translated by Philip Sherrard, Eileen Hogan, and Edmund Keeley. Introduction by W. H. Auden. London: Camberwell Press, 1985.

————. *Voices of Modern Greece: Selected Poems.* Translated by Edmund Keeley and Philip Sherrard. Princeton, N.J.: Princeton University Press, 1981.

————. *Three Poems of Cavafy.* Translated by Lawrence Durrell. Edinburgh: Tragara Press, 1980.

————. *The Complete Poems of Cavafy.* Translated by Rae Dalven. New York: Harcourt Brace Jovanovich, 1976.

————. *C. P. Cavafy, Collected Poems.* Translated by Philip Sherrard and Edmund Keeley. Edited by Georgios Savvides. Princeton, N.J.: Princeton University Press, 1975.

————. *Selected Poems.* Princeton, N.J.: Princeton University Press, 1972.

————. *Passions and Ancient Days.* Translated by Edmund Keeley. Edited by Georgios Savvides. New York: Dial Press, 1971.

————. *Poems.* Translated by John Mavrogordata. London: Hogarth Press, 1971, 1951.

————. *The Complete Poems of Cavafy.* New York: Harcourt, Brace & World, 1961.

————. *The Poems of C. P. Cavafy.* Translated by John Mavrogordata. New York: Grove Press, 1952.

Cavafy, Constantine P., et al. *The Dark Crystal: An Anthology of Modern Greek Poetry.* Translated by Edmund Keeley and Philip Sherrard. Athens, Greece: D. Harvey, 1981.

Celan, Paul. *Halo: Poems.* Minneapolis: Coffee House, 1991.

————. *Poems of Paul Celan.* Translated by Michael Hamburger. New York: Persea Books, 1989.

————. *Last Poems.* San Francisco: North Point Press, 1986.

————. *Speech-Grille and Selected Poems.* New York: Dutton, 1971.

Char, René. *No Seige Is Absolute.* Translated by Franz Wright. Providence, R.I.: Lost Roads, 1984.

————. *Poems of René Char.* Translated by Mary Ann Caws and Jonathan Griffin. Princeton, N.J.: Princeton University Press, 1976.

————. *Leaves of Hypnos.* New York: Grossman, 1973.

————. *Hypnos Waking: Poems and Prose.* New York: Random House, 1956.

Cronin, Jeremy. *Inside.* Johannesburg: Raven Press, 1983.

cummings, e.e. *Complete Poems, 1904–1962.* New York: Norton, 1991.

Dalton, Roque. *El Salvador at War: A Collage Epic.* Translated by Marc Zimmerman. Minneapolis: MEP Publications, 1988.

————. *Poemas Clandestinas. Clandestine Poems.* Translated by Eric Weaver, Jack Hirschman, and Barbara Paschke. San Francisco: Solidarity Productions, 1986.

————. *Poems.* Willimantic, Conn.: Curbstone, 1984.

Darwish, Mahmoud. *The Music of Human Flesh: Poems of the Palestinian Struggle.* Translated by Denys Johnson-Davies. London: Heinemann; Washington, D.C.: Three Continents, 1980.

Desnos, Robert. *The Selected Poems of Robert Desnos.* Translated by Carolyn Forché and William Kulik. New York: Ecco Press, 1991.

————. *The Voice: Selected Poems of Robert Desnos.* Translated by William Kulik. New York: Grossman, 1972.

————. *22 Poems.* Translated by Michael Benedikt. Santa Cruz: Kayak Books, 1971.

Djogo, Gojko, et al. *Child of Europe.* Edited by Michael March. London and New York: Penguin, 1991.

Dorfman, Ariel. *Last Waltz in Santiago and Other Poems of Exile and Disappearance.* Translated by Edith Grossman. New York: Viking, 1988.

————. *Missing: Poems.* London: Amnesty International British Section, 1981.

Dugan, Alan. *Poems Six.* New York: Ecco Press, 1989.

————. *New and Collected Poems 1961–1983.* New York: Ecco Press, 1983.

Duoduo. *Statements.* London: Wellsweep, 1989.

Eich, Günter. *Pigeons and Moles: Selected Writings of Günter Eich.* Translated by Michael Hamburger. Columbia, S.C.: Camden House, 1990.

————. *Valuable Nail: Selected Poems.* Translated by Stuart Friebert, David Waller, and David Young. Oberlin, Ohio: Oberlin College Press, 1981.

————. *Günter Eich.* Translated by Teo Savory. Santa Barbara, Calif.: Unicorn Press, 1971.

Eich, Günter, et al. *Four German Poets: Günter Eich, Hilda Domin, Erich Fried and Günter Kunert.* Translated by Agnes Stein. New York: Red Dust, 1979.

Éluard, Paul. *Selected Poems.* Translated by Gilbert Bowen. London: John Calder, 1988.

————. *Last Love Poems of Paul Éluard.* Translated by Marilyn Kallet. Baton Rouge, La.: Louisiana State University Press, 1980.

————. *Paul Éluard: The Selected Writings.* Translated by Lloyd Alexander. New York: New Directions, 1951.

Elytis, Odysseas. *Odysseas Elytis: Selected Poems.* Translated by Edmund Keeley and Phillip Sherrard. Harmondsworth, England: Penguin, 1981.

————. *The Little Mariner.* Translated by Olga Broumas. Port Townsend, Wash.: Copper Canyon, 1988.

————. *What I Love.* Translated by Olga Broumas. Port Townsend, Wash.: Copper Canyon, 1986.

Evans, George. *Sudden Dreams: New and Selected Poems.* Minneapolis: Coffee House, 1991.

Faiz, Faiz Ahmad. *The True Subject.* Translated by Naomi Lazard. Princeton, N.J.: Princeton University Press, 1988.

————. *An Elusive Dawn: Selections from the Poetry of Faiz Ahmad Faiz.* Translated by Mahbub ul Haq. Islamabad, Pakistan: Pakistan National Commission for UNESCO, 1985.

————. *Selected Poems of Faiz in English.* Translated by Daud Kamal. Karachi, Pakistan: Pakistan Publishing House, 1984.

————. *Poems by Faiz.* Translated by V. G. Kiernan Victor Gordon. UNESCO Collection of Representative Works: Pakistan Series. London: Allen & Unwin, 1971.

————. *Poems.* Translated by V. G. Kiernan Victor Gordon. New Delhi: People's Publishing House, 1958.

Fenton, James. *Partingtime Hall: Poems.* Hardmondsworth, England: Viking Salamander, 1987.

————. *Children in Exile: Poems 1968–1984.* New York: Random House, 1984.

Fried, Erich, et al. *Poems: 1913–1956.* Poetry by Bertolt Brecht, John Willett, and Erich Fried. Translated by Ralph Manheim. New York: Methuen, 1980.

————. *100 Poems without a Country.* Translated by Stuart Hood. New York: Red Dust, 1980.

————. *On Pain of Seeing: Poems.* Translated by George Rapp. Chicago: Swallow Press, 1969.

García Lorca, Federico. *Four Lorca Suites.* Translated by Jerome Rothenberg. Los Angeles: 20 Pages, 1989.

————. *Poet in New York.* Translated by Steven E. White and Greg Simon. New York: Farrar, Straus, & Giroux, 1988.

————. *The Poetical Works of Federico García Lorca.* Translated by Christopher Maurer. New York: Farrar, Straus, & Giroux, 1988.

————. *Ode to Walt Whitman and Other Poems.* Translated by Carlos Bauer. San Francisco: City Lights, 1988.

————. *Poem of the Deep Song.* San Francisco: City Lights, 1987.

————. *Poet in New York.* Translated by Ben Belitt. New York: Grove Press, 1983.

————. *Lorca/Blackburn: Poems of Federico García Lorca.* Translated by Paul Blackburn. San Francisco: Momo's Press, 1979.

————. *Tree of Song.* Translated by Alan Brilliant. Greensboro, N.C.: Unicorn Press, 1973.

————. *The Lieutenant Colonel and the Gypsy.* Garden City, N.Y.: Doubleday, 1971.

————. *Lament for the Death of a Bullfighter and Other Poems.* Philadelphia: Dufour Editions, 1962.

————. *Selected Poems.* Norfolk, Conn.: New Directions, 1955.

————. *The Gypsy Ballads.* Translated by Rolfe Humphries. Bloomington, Ind.: Indiana University Press, 1953.

————. *Selected Poems of Federico García Lorca.* Translated by J. L. Gili and Stephen Spender. New York: Transatlantic Arts, 1947.

García Lorca, Federico, and Juan Ramon Jimenez. *Lorca and Jimenez: Selected Poems.* Translated and compiled by Robert Bly. Boston: Beacon Press, 1973.

Goll, Yvan. *Yvan Goll, Poems.* Translated by Galway Kinnell. Fremont, Mich.: Sumac Press, 1970

Gorbanevskaya, Natalya. *Selected Poems.* Translated by Daniel Weissbort. London: Carcanet Press, 1972.

Grass, Günter. *In the Egg and Other Poems.* New York: Harcourt Brace Jovanovich, 1977.

————. *New Poems. Ausgefragt.* New York: Harcourt Brace Jovanovich, 1968.

Graves, Robert. *Poems about War.* Mount Kisco, N.Y.: Moyer Bell, 1990.

————. *Goodbye to All That.* New York: Doubleday, 1990. A memoir.

————. *Collected Poems, 1975.* New York: Oxford University Press, 1988.

————. *New Collected Poems.* Garden City, N.Y.: Doubleday, 1977.

H.D. [Hilda Doolittle]. *Selected Poems.* Edited by Louis Lohr Martz. New York: New Directions, 1988.

————. *Collected Poems.* Edited by Louis Lohr Martz. New York: New Directions, 1983.

Hecht, Anthony. *The Transparent Man: Poems.* New York: Alfred A. Knopf, 1990.

————. *Collected Earlier Poems: The Complete Texts of the Hard Hours, Millions of Strange Shadows, and the Venetian Vespers.* New York: Alfred A. Knopf, 1990.

————. *The Seven Deadly Sins: Poems.* Northampton, Mass.: Gehenna Press, 1958.

————. *A Summoning of Stones.* New York: Macmillan, 1954.

Herbert, Zbigniew. *Selected Poems.* Translated by Czeslaw Milosz and Peter Dale Scott. New York: Ecco Press, 1986.

————. *Report from the Besieged City and Other Poems.* Translated by Bogdana Carpenter and John Carpenter. New York: Ecco Press, 1985.

Hernandez, Miguel. *Selected Poems.* Translated by Timothy Baland. Buffalo, N.Y.: White Pine Press, 1989.

————. *Songbook of Absences: Selected Poems.* Translated by Tom Jones. Washington, D.C.: Charioteer, 1980.

Hernandez, Miguel and Blas de Otero. *The Unending Lightning: Selected Poems of Miguel Hernandez.* Translated by Edwin Honig. Riverdale, N.Y.: Sheep Meadow Press, 1990.

————. *Miguel Hernandez and Blas de Otero: Selected Poems.* Translated by Timothy Baland and Hardie St. Martin. Boston: Beacon Press, 1972.

Hikmet, Nazim. *Selected Poetry.* Translated by Randy Blasing and Mutlu Konuk. New York: Persea Books, 1986.

————. *Rubaiyat.* Providence, R.I.: Copper Beech, 1985.

————. *Human Landscapes.* Translated by Randy Blasing and Mutlu Konuk. New York: Persea Books, 1982.

Holan, Vladimir. *Mirroring: Selected Poems of Vladimir Holan.* Translated by C. G. Hanzlicek and Dana Habova. Middletown, Conn.: Wesleyan University Press, 1985.

Huchel, Peter. *The Garden of Theophrastus and Other Poems.* Translated by Michael Hamburger. Manchester, England: Carcanet New Press; Dublin: Raven Arts Press, 1983.

————. *Selected Poems.* Cheadle, England: Carcanet Press, 1974.

Hughes, Langston. *The Panther and the Lash: Poems of Our Time.* New York: Random House, Vintage Books, 1992.

————. *Selected Poems of Langston Hughes.* With drawings by E. McKnight Kauffer. New York: Random House, Vintage Books, 1990.

————. *Let America Be America Again.* Berkeley, Calif.: Okeanos Press, 1990.

————. *The Dream Keeper and Other Poems.* New York: Alfred A. Knopf, 1986.

————. *The Weary Blues: Poems.* Ann Arbor, Mich.: University Microfilms, 1981.

Hugo, Richard. *Making Certain It Goes On: The Collected Poems.* New York: Norton, 1984.

————. *The Hitler Diaries.* New York: William Morrow, 1983.

————. *Death and the Good Life.* New York: St. Martin's Press, 1981.

————. *The Right Madness on Skye: Poems.* New York: Norton, 1980.

————. *Selected Poems.* New York: Norton, 1979.

————. *Road Ends at Tahola.* Pittsburgh: Slow Loris Press, 1978.

————. *31 Letters and 13 Dreams.* New York: Norton, 1977.

————. *What Thou Lovest Well, Remains American.* New York: Norton, 1975.

————. *The Lady in Kicking Horse Reservoir.* New York: Norton, 1973.

————. *Good Luck in Cracked Italian.* New York: World Publishing, 1969.

————. *Death of the Kapowsin Tavern.* New York: Harcourt, Brace & World, 1965.

————. *A Run of Jacks.* Minneapolis: University of Minnesota Press, 1961.

Jabès, Edmond. *Imitations, the Desert.* Middletown, Conn.: Wesleyan University Press; Hanover, N.H.: University Press of New England, 1991.

————. *The Book of Resemblances.* Middletown, Conn.: Wesleyan University Press, 1990.

————. *From the Desert to the Book.* Translated by Marcel Cohen. Barrytown, N.Y.: Station Hill Press, 1990.

————. *The Book of Shares.* Chicago: Chicago University Press, 1989.

————. *If There Were Anywhere But Desert: The Selected Poems of Edmond Jabès.* Translated by Keith Waldrop. Barrytown, N.Y.: Station Hill Press, 1988.

————. *The Book of Dialogue.* Middletown, Conn.: Wesleyan University Press, 1987.

————. *The Book of Questions: El, or The Last Book.* Middletown, Conn.: Wesleyan University Press, 1984.

————. *The Book of Questions: Yael, Elya, Aely.* Middletown, Conn.: Wesleyan University Press, 1983.

―――. *A Share of Ink.* Translated by Anthony Rudolf. London: Menard Press, 1979.

―――. *The Book of Questions.* Middletown, Conn.: Wesleyan University Press, 1976.

Jacob, Max. *The Dice Cup: Selected Prose Poems.* Translated from the French by John Ashbery, David Ball, Michael Brownstein, Ron Padgett, Zack Rogow, and Bill Zauctsky. Edited and with an introduction by Michael Brownstein. New York: SUN, 1979.

Jastrun, Tomasz, et al. *Child of Europe.* Edited by Michael March. London, and New York: Penguin, 1990. Anthology of Eastern European Poetry.

de Jesús, Teresa. *De Repente.* Willimantic, Conn.: Curbstone, 1979.

József, Attila. *Perched on Nothing's Branch: Selected Poetry of Attila József.* Translated by Peter Hargitai. Tallahassee, Fla.: Alalachee Press, 1986.

―――. *Poems of Attila József.* Translated by Anton N. Nyerges. Buffalo, N.Y.: Hungarian Cultural Foundation, 1973.

―――. *Selected Poems and Texts.* Translated by John Batki. Cheadle, England: Carcanet Press, 1973.

Kharms, Daniil. *The Man in the Black Coat: Russia's Literature of the Absurd.* Translated by George Gibian. Evanston, Ill.: Northwestern University Press, 1987.

Khlebnikov, Velimir. *Collected Works of Velimir Khlebnikov.* Translated by Charlotte Douglas. Cambridge: Harvard University Press, 1987.

―――. *The King of Time: Selected Writings of the Russian Futurian.* Translated by Paul Schmidt. Edited by Charlotte Douglas. Cambridge: Harvard University Press, 1985.

―――. *Snake Train: Poetry and Prose.* Translated by Gary Kern. Ann Arbor, Mich.: Ardis Publishers, 1976.

Kinnell, Galway. *When One Has Lived a Long Time Alone.* New York: Alfred A. Knopf, 1990.

―――. *The Past.* Boston: Houghton Mifflin 1985.

―――. *Selected Poems.* Boston: Houghton Mifflin, 1983.

―――. *Mortal Acts, Mortal Words.* Boston: Houghton Mifflin, 1980.

―――. *The Book of Nightmares.* London: Omphalos Press, 1978; Boston: Houghton Mifflin, 1971.

―――. *The Avenue Bearing the Initial of Christ into the New World.* Boston: Houghton Mifflin, 1974.

―――. *First Poems: 1946–1954.* Mount Horeb, Wis.: Perishable Press, 1970.

―――. *Body Rags.* Boston: Houghton Mifflin, 1968.

―――. *Poems of Night.* London: Rapp & Carroll, 1968.

―――. *Flower Herding on Mount Monadnock.* Boston: Houghton Mifflin, 1964.

―――. *What a Kingdom It Was.* Boston: Houghton Mifflin, 1960.

Kirsch, Sarah. *Conjurations: The Poems of Sarah Kirsch.* Translated by Wayne Kvam. Athens, Ohio: Ohio University Press, 1985.

―――. *Catlives.* Translated by Marina Roscher and Charles Fishman. Lubbock, Tex.: Texas Tech University Press, 1990.

Knight, Etheridge. *The Essential Etheridge Knight.* Pittsburgh: University of Pittsburgh Press, 1986.

————. *Born of a Woman: New and Selected Poems*. Boston: Houghton Mifflin, 1980.

————. *Belly Song and Other Poems*. Detroit: Broadside Press, 1973.

————. *Poems from Prison*. Detroit: Broadside Press, 1968.

Komunyakaa, Yusef. *Dien Cai Dau*. Middletown, Conn.: Wesleyan University Press, 1988.

————. *I Apologize for the Eyes in My Head*. Middletown, Conn.: Wesleyan University Press, 1986.

————. *Copacetic: Poems*. Middletown, Conn.: Wesleyan University Press, 1984.

————. *Dedication and Other Dark Horses*. Laramie, Wyo.: R.M.C.A.J. Books, 1977.

Kovner, Abba. *My Little Sister and Selected Poems*. Oberlin, Ohio: Oberlin College Press, 1986.

————. *A Canopy in the Desert: Selected Poems*. Translated by Shirley Kaufman. Pittsburgh: University of Pittsburgh Press, 1973.

————. *Selected Poems of Abba Kovner*. Translated by Nurit Orchan, Michael Hamburger and Shirley Kaufman. Compiled by Stephen Spender. Penguin Modern European Poets. Harmondsworth, England: Penguin, 1971.

Kunitz, Stanley. *Next-To-Last-Things*. Boston: Atlantic Monthly Press, 1985.

————. *The Wellfleet Whale and Companion Poems*. New York: Sheep Meadow Press, 1983.

————. *The Poems of Stanley Kunitz*. Boston: Little, Brown, 1979.

————. *The Lincoln Relics: A Poem*. Port Townsend, Wash.: Graywolf, 1978.

————. *The Testing Tree*. Boston: Little, Brown, 1971.

————. *Selected Poems*. Boston: Little, Brown, 1958.

————. *Passport to the War: A Selection of Poems*. New York: Henry Holt, 1944.

Levertov, Denise. *A Door in the Hive*. New York: New Directions, 1989.

————. *Breathing the Water*. New York: New Directions, 1987.

————. *Poems: 1968–1972*. New York: New Directions, 1987.

————. *Candles in Babylon* New York: New Directions, 1982.

————. *Light Up the Cave*. New York: New Directions, 1981.

————. *Collected Earlier Poems: 1940–1960*. New York: New Directions, 1979.

————. *Life in the Forest*. New York: New Directions, 1978.

————. *The Freeing of the Dust*. New York: New Directions, 1975.

————. *Footprints*. New York: New Directions, 1972.

Levi, Primo. *Collected Poems*. Translated by Ruth Feldman and Brian Swann. London and Boston: Faber & Faber, 1988.

————. *Survival in Auschwitz and the Reawakening: Two Memoirs*. New York: Summit Books, 1985.

Lowell, Robert. *Life Studies, and, For the Union Dead*. New York: Farrar, Straus, & Giroux, 1980.

————. *Lord Weary's Castle, and, The Mills of The Kavanaughs*. San Diego: Harcourt Brace Jovanovich, 1979.

————. *Selected Poems*. New York: Farrar, Straus, & Giroux, 1977.

————. *Day by Day*. New York: Farrar, Straus, & Giroux, 1977.

————. *History*. New York: Farrar, Straus, & Giroux, 1973.

————. *The Dolphin*. New York: Farrar, Straus, & Giroux, 1973.

————. *For Lizzie and Harriet.* New York: Farrar, Straus, & Giroux, 1973.

————. *Notebook.* New York: Farrar, Straus, & Giroux, 1970.

————. *Notebook: 1967–1968.* New York: Farrar, Straus, & Giroux, 1969.

————. *Near the Ocean.* New York: Farrar, Straus, & Giroux, 1967.

Lysohorsky, Ondra. *In the Eye of the Storm: Fifty Years of Poetry.* Translated by David Lawrence William Gill. Bakewell, England: Hub Publications, 1976.

————. *Selected Poems.* Translated by Ewald Osers. London: Cape, 1971.

McDonald, Walter. *Night Landings: Poems.* New York: Harper & Row, 1989.

————. *After the Noise of Saigon.* Amherst, Mass.: University of Massachusetts Press, 1988.

————. *Rafting the Brazos.* Denton, Tex.: University of North Texas Press, 1988.

————. *The Flying Dutchman.* Columbus, Ohio: Ohio State University Press, 1987.

————. *Witching on Hardscrabble.* Granite Falls, Minn.: Spoon River Poetry Press, 1985.

————. *Burning the Fence.* Lubbock, Tex.: Texas Tech University Press, 1981.

————. *Anything, Anything.* Seattle: L'Epervier Press, 1980.

————. *Caliban in Blue and Other Poems.* Lubbock, Tex.: Texas Tech University Press, 1976.

McGrath, Thomas. *Death Song.* Port Townsend, Wash.: Copper Canyon, 1991.

————. *Selected Poems: 1938–1988.* Edited by Sam Hamill. Port Townsend, Wash.: Copper Canyon, 1988.

————. *The Gates of Ivory, The Gates of Horn.* Chicago: Another Chicago Press, 1987.

————. *Letter to an Imaginary Friend, Parts III and IV.* Port Townsend, Wash.: Copper Canyon, 1985.

————. *Echoes Inside the Labyrinthe.* New York: Thunder's Mouth, 1983.

————. *Passages Toward the Dark.* Port Townsend, Wash.: Copper Canyon, 1982.

————. *The Movie at the End of the World: Collected Poems.* Chicago: Swallow Press, 1980.

————. *Waiting for the Angel.* Menominie, Wis.: Uzzano Press, 1979.

————. *Open Songs: Sixty Short Poems.* Mount Carroll, Ill.: Uzzano Press, 1977.

————. *Voices from beyond the Wall.* Moorhead, Minn.: Territorial Press, 1974.

————. *Letter to an Imaginary Friend, Parts I and II.* Chicago: Swallow Press, 1970.

————. *New and Selected Poems.* Denver, Col.: A. Swallow, 1964.

Machado, Antonio. *Solitudes, Galleries, and Other Poems.* Durham, N.C.: Duke University Press, 1987.

————. *Times Alone: Selected Poems of Antonio Machado.* Translated by Robert Bly. Middletown, Conn.: Wesleyan University Press, 1983.

————. *Times Alone; Twelve Poems from Soledades.* Port Townsend, Wash.: Graywolf, 1983.

————. *Antonio Machado: Selected Poems and Prose.* Translated by Dennis Maloney and Robert Bly. Buffalo, N.Y.: White Pine Press, 1983.

————. *Selected Poems.* Translated by Alan S. Trueblood. Cambridge: Harvard University Press, 1982.

————. *The Dream below the Sun: Selected Poems of Antonio Machado.* Translated by Willis Barnstone. Trumansburg, N.Y.: Crossing Press, 1981.

————. *I Never Wanted Fame: Ten Poems and Proverbs.* St. Paul: Ally Press, 1979.

————. *Selected Poems of Antonio Machado.* Translated by Betty Jean Craige. Baton Rouge, La.: Louisiana State University Press, 1978.

————. *Eighty Poems of Antonio Machado.* Translated by Willis Barnstone. New York: Las Americas, 1959.

Machado, Antonio, et al. *Still Waters of the Air: Poems by Three Modern Spanish Poets.* Compiled by Richard Lewis. Illustrated by Arvis L. Stewart. New York: Dial Press, 1970. Includes the works of Federico García Lorca, Juan Ramon Jimenez, and Antonio Machado.

MacNeice, Louis. *Selected Poems of Louis MacNeice.* Edited by Michael Longley. Winston-Salem, N.C.: Wake Forest University Press, 1990.

————. *The Collected Poems of Louis MacNeice.* New York: Oxford University Press, 1967.

————. *The Burning Perch.* New York: Oxford University Press, 1963.

————. *Solstices.* New York: Oxford University Press, 1961.

————. *Visitations.* New York: Oxford University Press, 1958.

————. *Ten Burnt Offerings.* New York: Oxford University Press, 1953.

————. *Holes in the Sky: Poems, 1944–1947.* New York: Random House, 1945.

————. *Springboard: Poems, 1941–1944.* New York: Random House, 1945.

————. *Poems: 1925–1940.* New York: Random House, 1940.

Mandelstam, Osip Yemilyevich. *Selected Poems.* New York: Atheneum, 1989.

————. *Poems.* Translated by James Greene. London: Elek, 1977.

————. *Moscow Trefoil; Poems from the Russian of Anna Akhmatova and Osip Mandelstam.* Translated by David Watt Ian Campbell. Akhmatova, Anna. Translated by Rosemary Dobson. Canberra: Australian National University Press, 1975.

Mapanje, Jack. *Of Chameleons and Gods.* London: Heinemann, 1981.

Mapanje, Jack, et al. *Summer Fires: New Poetry of Africa.* London: Heinemann, 1983.

Mayakovsky, Vladimir. *Listen! Early Poems.* Translated by Maria Enzensberger. Pocket Poets Series, no. 47. San Francisco: City Lights, 1991.

————. *How Are Verses Made? With a Cloud in Trousers; and To Sergey Esenin.* Bristol, England: Bristol Classical Press, 1990.

————. *Selected Works in Three Volumes.* Moscow: Raduga, 1985.

————. *Poems.* Moscow: Progress Publishers, 1976.

————. *The Bedbug a Play and Selected Poetry.* Bloomington, Ind.: Indiana University Press, 1975.

————. *The Bedbug and Selected Poetry.* Translated by George Reavey, Patricia Blake and Max Hayward. New York: World Publishing, 1970.

Milosz, Czeslaw. *Provinces.* New York: Ecco Press, 1991.

————. *The Captive Mind.* New York: Random House, Vintage Books, 1990. A memoir.

————. *The World.* Contributions from Jim Dine, Helen Hennessy Vendler, and Andrew Hogem. San Francisco: Arion Press, 1989.

————. *Collected Poems.* New York: Ecco Press, 1988.

————. *Unattainable Earth.* New York: Ecco Press, 1986.

Montale, Eugenio. *Mottetti: Poems of Love: The Motets of Eugenio Montale*. Translated by Dana Gioia. St. Paul: Graywolf, 1990.

———. *The Occasions*. Translated by William Arrowsmith. New York: Norton, 1987.

———. *The Storm and Other Things*. Translated by William Arrowsmith. New York: Norton, 1985.

———. *Otherwise: Last and First Poems of Eugenio Montale*. Translated by Jonathan Galani. New York: Random House, Vintage Books, 1984.

———. *New Poems: A Selection from Satura and Diario Del '71 e Del '72*. Translated and with an introduction by G. Singh. New York: New Directions, 1976.

———. *Provisional Conclusions: A Selection of the Poetry of Eugenio Montale*. Translated by Edith Farnsworth. Chicago: H. Regnery, 1970.

———. *Selected Poems*. New York: New Directions, 1966.

Mphahlele, Es'kia, et al. *When My Brothers Come Home: Poems from Central and Southern Africa*. Middletown, Conn.: Wesleyan University Press, 1985.

Nemerov, Howard. *Trying Conclusions: New and Selected Poems: 1961–1991*. Chicago: University of Chicago Press, 1991.

———. *War Stories: Poems about Long Ago and Now*. Chicago: University of Chicago Press, 1987.

———. *Inside the Onion*. Chicago: University of Chicago Press, 1984.

———. *Sentences*. Chicago: University of Chicago Press, 1980.

———. *The Collected Poems of Howard Nemerov*. Chicago: University of Chicago Press, 1977.

———. *The Western Approaches: Poems 1973–1975*. Chicago: University of Chicago Press, 1975.

———. *Gnomes and Occasions: Poems*. Chicago: University of Chicago Press, 1973.

———. *The Blue Swallows: Poems*. Chicago: University of Chicago Press, 1967.

———. *New and Selected Poems*. Chicago: University of Chicago Press, 1963.

Neruda, Pablo. *The Book of Questions*. Port Townsend, Wash.: Copper Canyon, 1991.

———. *Elemental Odes*. London: Libris, 1990.

———. *The House in the Sand*. Minneapolis: Milkweed Editions, 1990.

———. *Selected Poems*. Translated by Nathaniel Tarn and Anthony Kerrigan. Boston: Houghton Mifflin, 1990.

———. *Selected Odes of Pablo Neruda*. Translated by Margaret Sayers Peden. Berkeley, Calif.: University of California Press, 1990.

———. *Canto General*. Translated by Jack Schmidt. Berkeley, Calif.: University of California Press, 1990.

———. *The Yellow Heart*. Port Townsend, Wash.: Copper Canyon, 1990.

———. *Let the Rail Splitter Awake and Other Poems*. London: Journeyman Press; New York: International Publishers, 1988.

———. *Poems: Late and Posthumous 1968–1974*. Translated by Ben Belitt. New York: Grove Press, 1988.

———. *The Sea and the Bells*. Port Townsend, Wash.: Copper Canyon, 1987.

———. *Stones of the Sky*. Port Townsend, Wash.: Copper Canyon, 1987.

———. *100 Love Sonnets*. Translated by Stephen Tapscott. Austin, Tex.: University of Texas Press, 1986.

————. *Winter Garden.* Translated by William O'Daly. Port Townsend, Wash.: Copper Canyon, 1986.

————. *The Stones of Chile.* Translated by Dennis Maloney. Fredonia, N.Y.: White Pine Press, 1986.

————. *Art of Birds.* Translated by Jack Schmidt. Austin, Tex.: University of Texas Press, 1985.

————. *The Separate Rose.* Port Townsend, Wash.: Copper Canyon, 1985.

————. *Still Another Day.* Port Townsend, Wash.: Copper Canyon, 1984.

————. *Elegy: Pablo Neruda Presente.* San Francisco: David Books, 1983.

————. *Twenty Love Poems and a Song of Despair.* New York: Penguin, 1976.

————. *Song of Protest.* New York: Quill, 1976.

————. *Residence on Earth and Other Poems.* New York: Gordian Press, 1976.

————. *Selected Poems.* Translated by Nathaniel Tarn and Anthony Kerrigan. Harmondsworth, England: Penguin, 1975.

————. *Fully Empowered.* New York: Farrar, Straus, & Giroux, 1975.

————. *The Heights of Macchu Picchu.* Translated by Nathaniel Tarn. New York: Farrar, Straus, & Giroux, 1974.

————. *Pablo Neruda: Five Decades, a Selection. Poems 1925–1970.* Translated by Ben Belitt. New York: Grove Press, 1974.

————. *Extravagaria.* Translated by Alastair Reid. New York: Farrar, Straus, & Giroux, 1974.

————. *Selected Poems: A Bi-Lingual Edition.* Translated by Nathaniel Tarn, Anthony Kerrigan and W. S. Merwin. New York: Dell, 1972.

————. *The Captain's Verses.* New York: New Directions, 1972.

————. *New Poems: 1968–1970.* Translated by Ben Belitt. New York: Grove Press, 1972.

————. *Pablo Neruda: The Early Poems.* New York: New Rivers Press, 1969.

————. *A New Decade: Poems 1958–1967.* Translated by Ben Belitt and Alastair Red. New York: Grove Press, 1969.

Nezval, Vítězslav. *Three Czech Poets.* Harmondsworth, England: Penguin, 1971.

Oppen, George. *Primitive.* Santa Barbara, Calif.: Black Sparrow, 1975.

————. *The Collected Poems of George Oppen.* New York: New Directions, 1975.

————. *Alpine: Poems.* Mount Horeb, Wis.: Perishable Press, 1969.

————. *Of Being Numerous.* New York: New Directions, 1968.

————. *This in Which: Poems.* New York: New Directions, 1965.

————. *The Materials.* New York: New Directions, 1962.

Orten, Jirí. *Elegie. Elegies.* Translated by Lyn Coffin. Washington, D.C.: SVU Press, 1980.

Owen, Wilfred. *The Poems of Wilfred Owen.* New York: Norton, 1986.

————. *The Complete Poems and Fragments.* Edited by Jon Stallworthy. New York: Norton, 1984.

————. *The Collected Poems of Wilfred Owen.* Edited by C. Day Lewis and Edmund Blunden. New York: New Directions, 1965.

————. *Thirteen Poems.* Illustrated by Ben Shahn. Northampton, Mass.: Gehenna Press, 1956.

Padilla, Heberto. *Legacies: Selected Poems by Heberto Padilla.* Translated by Alastair Reid and Andrew Hurley. New York: Farrar, Straus, & Giroux, 1982.

Pagis, Dan. *Variable Directions: The Selected Poetry of Dan Pagis.* San Francisco: North Point Press, 1989.

———. *Points of Departure.* Translated by Stephen Mitchell. Philadelphia: Jewish Publication Society of America, 1981.

Parra, Nicanor. *Antipoems: New and Selected.* New York: New Directions, 1985.

———. *Emergency Poems.* Translated by Miller Williams. New York: New Directions, 1972.

———. *Poems and Antipoems.* New York: New Directions, 1967.

Pasternak, Boris Leonidovich. *The Zhivago Poems.* Translated by Barbara Everest. Huntington, W.Va.: Aegina Press, 1988.

———. *Selected Poems.* Translated by Peter France and Jon Stallworthy. New York: Norton, 1983.

———. *Seven Poems.* Translated by George Louis Kline. Santa Barbara, Calif.: Unicorn Press, 1972

———. *Poems.* Ohio: Kent State University Press, 1964.

———. *The Poetry of Boris Pasternak: 1914–1960.* Edited and translated by George Reavey. New York: Putnam, 1960.

———. *Poems.* Ann Arbor, Mich.: University of Michigan Press, 1959.

Pavese, Cesare. *Hard Labor.* Translated by William Arrowsmith. New York: Ecco Press, 1979.

———. *The Moon and the Bonfires.* Westport, Conn.: Greenwood, 1975.

———. *The Burning Brand: Diaries 1935–1950.* New York: Walker, 1961.

Péret, Benjamin. *Death to the Pigs and Other Writings.* Translated by Rachel Stella. Lincoln, Nebr.: University of Nebraska Press, 1988.

———. *A Marvelous World: Poems.* Baton Rouge, La.: Louisiana State University Press, 1985.

———. *From the Hidden Storehouse: Selected Poems.* Translated by Keith Hollaman. Field Translation Series, no. 6. Oberlin, Ohio: Oberlin College Press, 1981.

Pilinszky, János. *Selected Poems.* Translated by Ted Hughes and János Csokits. New York: Persea Books, in association with the Iowa Writers Program, University of Iowa, Iowa City, Iowa, 1977.

Polkowski, Jan, et al. *Child of Europe.* Edited by Michael March. London: Penguin, 1990.

Ponge, Francis. *Vegetation.* Translated by Lee Fahnestock. New York: Red Dust, 1987.

———. *Things: Selected Writings.* Translated by Cid Corman. Fredonia, N.Y.: White Pine Press, 1986.

———. *The Power of Language: Texts and Translations.* Berkeley, Calif.: University of California Press, 1979.

———. *The Making of the Pré.* Translated by Lee Fahnestock. Columbia, Mo.: University of Missouri Press, 1979.

———. *The Sun Placed in the Abyss and Other Texts.* Translated by Serge Gavronsky. New York: SUN, 1977.

———. *The Voice of Things.* Translated by Beth Archer Brombert. New York: McGraw-Hill, 1972.

———. *Things.* Selected and translated by Cid Corman. New York: Grossman, 1971.

Pound, Ezra. *Personae: The Shorter Poems of Ezra Pound.* Edited by Lea Baechler and A. Walton Litz. New York: New Directions, 1990.

———. *Collected Early Poems of Ezra Pound.* New York: New Directions, 1976.

———. *The Cantos of Ezra Pound.* New York: New Directions, 1972.

Prévert, Jacques. *Paroles: Selected Poems.* Translated by Lawrence Ferlinghetti. San Francisco: City Lights, 1990.

———. *Selected Poems of Jacques Prévert* Translated by Carol Poster. Fredonia, N.Y.: White Pine Press, 1987.

———. *Blood and Feathers: Selected Poems of Jacques Prévert.* New York: Schocken, 1987.

———. *Words for All Seasons: Collected Poems of Jacques Prévert.* Translated by Teo Savory. Greensboro, N.C.: Unicorn Press, 1980.

———. *To Paint the Portrait of a Bird: Pour Faire le Portrait d'un Oiseau.* Translated by Lawrence Ferlinghetti. Garden City, N.Y.: Doubleday, 1971.

Quasimodo, Salvatore. *Complete Poems.* Translated by Jack Bevan. New York: Schocken, 1984.

———. *The Tall Schooner: A Poem.* Translated by Michael Egan and Janet Morgan. New York: Red Ozier Press, 1980.

Radnóti, Miklós. *Under Gemini: A Prose Memoir and Selected Poetry.* Translated by Kenneth McRobbie, Jascha Frederick Kessler, and Zita McRobbie. Athens, Ohio: Ohio University Press, 1985.

———. *The Complete Poetry.* Translated by Emery George. Ann Arbor, Mich.: Ardis Publishers, 1980.

———. *Subway Stops: Fifty Poems.* Translated by Emery George. Ann Arbor, Mich.: Ardis Publishers, 1977.

———. *Clouded Sky.* Translated by S. J. Marks, Steven Polgar, and Steven Berg. New York: Harper & Row, 1972.

———. *Postcard.* Translated by S. Polgar, S. Berg, and S. Marles. West Branch, Iowa: Cummington Press, 1969.

Ratushinskaya, Irina. *In the Beginning.* London: Sceptre, 1991.

———. *Selections. English & Russian.* Evanston, Ill.: Northwestern University Press, 1987.

———. *Poems.* Ann Arbor, Mich.: Hermitage, 1984.

Ritsos, Yannis. *Exile and Return: Selected Poems, 1967–1974.* Translated by Edmund Keeley. New York: Ecco Press, 1985.

———. *Subterranean Horses.* Translated by Minas Savvas. International Poetry Series, vol. 3. Columbus, Ohio: Ohio State University Press, 1980.

———. *Ritsos in Parentheses.* Translated by Edmund Keeley. Princeton, N.J.: Princeton University Press, 1979.

———. *The Land of the Vineyards.* Modern Greek Poetry Series, no. 4. New York: Pella Publishing, 1978.

———. *Scripture of the Blind.* Columbus, Ohio: Ohio State University Press, 1978.

———. *The Fourth Dimension: Selected Poems of Yannis Ritsos.* Translated by Rae Dalven. Boston: Godine, 1977.

———. *Chronicle of Exile.* San Francisco: Wire Press, 1977.

———. *Corridor and Stairs.* Curragh, Ireland: Goldsmith, 1976.

————. *Yannis Ritsos, Selected Poems.* Translated by Nikos Stangos. Penguin Modern European Poets Series. Harmondsworth, England, and Baltimore: Penguin, 1974.

————. *Gestures, and Other Poems.* London: Cape Goliard Press, in association with Grossman, New York, 1971.

Rózewicz, Tadeusz. *Conversations with the Prince and Other Poems.* Translated by Adam Czerniawski. London: Anvil Press Poetry, 1982.

————. *Unease.* Translated by Victor Contoski. St. Paul: New Rivers Press, 1980.

————. *The Survivor and Other Poems.* Translated by Robert A. Maguire and Magnus Jan Krynski. Princeton, N.J.: Princeton University Press, 1976.

————. *Selected Poems: Tadeusz Rozewicz.* Translated by Adam Czerniawski. Harmondworth, England, and Baltimore: Penguin, 1976.

————. *Faces of Anxiety: Poems.* Translated by Adam Czerniawski. Poetry Europe Series, no. 12. Chicago: Swallow Press, 1969.

Rukeyser, Muriel. *The Collected Poems.* New York: McGraw-Hill, 1978.

————. *The Gates.* New York: McGraw-Hill, 1976.

————. *Breaking Open.* New York: Random House, 1973.

Sachs, Nelly. *The Seeker and Other Poems.* Translated by Matthew Mead, Ruth Mead, and Michael Hamburger. New York: Farrar, Straus, & Giroux, 1970.

————. *O the Chimneys: Selected Poems.* Translated by Michael Hamburger. New York: Farrar, Straus, & Giroux, 1967.

Sassoon, Siegfried. *Collected Poems.* New York: Viking, 1949.

————. *Rhymed Ruminations. Poems.* New York: Viking, 1941.

————. *Counter-Attack and Other Poems.* New York: Dutton, 1918.

Seferis, George. *George Seferis, Collected Poems.* Translated by Edmund Keeley and Philip Sherrard. Princeton, N.J.: Princeton University Press, 1992.

————. *Days of 1945–1951, A Poet's Journal.* Translated by Athan Anagnostopoulus. Cambridge: Belknap Press of Harvard University Press, 1974.

————. *George Seferis: Collected Poems 1924–1955.* Translated by Edmund Keeley and Philip Sherrard. Princeton, N.J.: Princeton University Press, 1971, 1969, 1967.

————. *Three Secret Poems.* Cambridge: Harvard University Press, 1969.

————. *Poems.* Translated by Rex Warner. Boston: Little, Brown, 1964.

Seifert, Jaroslav. *A Wreathe of Sonnets.* Translated by Eva Stucke and J. K. Klement. Toronto: Larkwood Books, 1987.

————. *The Selected Poetry of Jaroslav Seifert.* Translated by Ewald Osers and George Gibian. New York: Macmillan, Collier Books, 1987.

————. *Eight Days: An Elegy for Thomas Masaryk.* Translated by Paul Jagosich and Tom O'Grady. Iowa City: Spirit That Moves, 1985.

————. *The Casting of Bells.* Translated by Paul Jagasich and Tom O'Grady. Iowa City: Spirit That Moves, 1984.

————. *An Umbrella from Picadilly.* Translated by Ewald Osers. London: London Magazine Editions, 1983.

————. *The Plague Column.* Translated by Ewald Osers. London and Boston: Terra Nova Editions, 1979.

Sepamla, Sipho. *Selected Poems.* Craighall, South Africa: Donker, 1984.

————. *The Blues Is You and Me.* Johannesburg: Donker, 1976.

Serge, Victor. *Resistance.* San Francisco: City Lights, 1989.

Simic, Charles. *Selected Poems.* New York: Braziller, 1990.

———. *The Book of Gods and Devils.* San Diego: Harcourt Brace Jovanovich, 1990.

———. *The World Doesn't End.* San Diego: Harcourt Brace Jovanovich, 1989.

———. *Undending Blues. Poems.* San Diego: Harcourt Brace Jovanovich, 1986.

———. *Selected Poems: 1963–1983.* New York: Braziller, 1985.

———. *Weather Forecast for Utopia and Vicinity: Poems 1967–1982.* Barrytown, N.Y.: Station Hill Press, 1983.

———. *Austerities.* New York: Braziller, 1982.

———. *Classic Ballroom Dances: Poems.* New York: Braziller, 1980.

———. *White.* Durango, Colo.: Logbridge-Rhodes, 1980.

———. *Charon's Cosmology.* New York: Braziller, 1977.

———. *Return to a Place Lit by a Glass of Milk.* New York: Braziller, 1974.

———. *Dismantling the Silence.* New York: Braziller, 1971.

Simpson, Louis Aston Marantz. *In the Room We Share.* New York: Paragon House, 1988.

———. *Collected Poems.* New York: Paragon House, 1988.

———. *People Live Here: Selected Poems, 1949–1983.* Brockport, N.Y.: BOA Editions, 1983.

———. *The Best Hour of the Night.* New Haven: Ticknor & Fields, 1983.

———. *Caviare at the Funeral: Poems.* Oxford: Oxford University Press, 1981.

———. *Armidale.* Brockport, N.Y.: BOA Editions, 1979.

———. *Search for the Ox.* New York: William Morrow, 1976.

———. *Selected Poems.* New York: Harcourt, Brace & World, 1965.

Soupault, Philippe. *I'm Lying: Selected Translations of Philippe Soupault.* Translated by Paulette Schmidt. Providence, R.I.: Lost Roads, 1985.

———. *Last Nights of Paris.* Translated by William Carlos Williams. New York: Full Court Press, 1982.

Soyinka, Wole. *Mandela's Earth and Other Poems.* New York: Random House, 1988.

———. *The Man Died: The Prison Notes of W.S.* New York: Farrar, Straus, & Giroux, Noonday, 1988.

———. *Idanre and Other Poems.* New York: Hill & Wang, 1987.

———. *Poems of Black Africa.* London: Heinemann, 1975.

Spender, Stephen. *Collected Poems, 1928–1985.* New York: Oxford University Press, 1987.

Stein, Gertrude. *Tender Buttons: Objects, Food, Rooms.* Los Angeles: Sun and Moon Press, 1990.

———. *Really Reading Gertrude Stein: A Selected Anthology with Essays.* Edited by Judy Grahn. Freedom, Calif.: Crossing Press, 1989.

———. *Useful Knowledge.* Barrytown, N.Y.: Station Hill Press, 1988.

———. *The Yale Gertrude Stein.* Edited by Richard Kostelanetz. New Haven: Yale University Press, 1980.

Swirszczynska, Anna. *Happy As a Dog's Tail.* Translated by Leonard Nathan and Czeslaw Milosz. San Diego: Harcourt Brace Jovanovich, 1985.

Szymborska, Wislawa. *People on the Bridge: Poems.* Translated by Adam Czerniawski. London and Boston: Forest Books, 1990.

————. *Sounds, Feelings, Thoughts: Seventy Poems.* Translated by Robert Mac-Guire and Magnus Jan Krynski. Princeton, N.J.: Princeton University Press, 1981.

Tekeyan, Vahan. *Sacred Wrath: The selected Poems of Vahan Tekeyan.* T. by Diana Der Hovanessian and Marzbed Margossian. New York: Ashod Press, 1982.

Thomas, Dylan. *The Collected Poems of Dylan Thomas.* Edited by Daniel Jones. New York: New Directions, 1971.

Thomas, Edward. *The Collected Poems of Edward Thomas.* Edited by George R. Thomas. New York and Oxford: Oxford University Press, 1981.

————. *Collected Poems.* New York: Norton, 1974.

Trakl, Georg. *Autumn Sonata. Selected Poems of Georg Trakl.* Translated by Daniel Simko. Mt. Kisco, N.Y.: Moyer Bell, 1989.

————. *Song of the West: Selected Poems of Georg Trakl.* Translated by Robert Firmage. San Francisco: North Point Press, 1988.

————. *Winter Night: Four Prose Poems.* Birmingham, Ala.: Thunder City Press, 1979.

————. *Poems.* Athens, Ohio: Mundus Artium Press, 1973.

————. *Selected Poems.* London: Cape, 1968.

Troupe, Quincy. *Weather Reports: New and Selected Poems.* New York: Harlem River Press, 1991.

Tsvetayeva, Marina. *In the Inmost Hour of the Soul.* Translated by Nina Kossman. Clifton, N.J.: Humana Press, 1989.

————. *Starry Sky to Starry Sky: Poems.* Translated by Mary Jane White. Stevens Point, Wis.: Holy Cow! Press, 1988.

————. *Selected Poems.* Translated by David McDuff. Newcastle upon Tyne, England: Bloodaxe Books, 1988.

————. *Selected Poems of Marina Tsvetayeva.* Translated by Elaine Feinstein. New York: Dutton, 1987.

————. *How Many Have Fallen.* Translated by Herbert Marshall and Michael Christopher Caine. London: London College of Printing, 1984.

Tuquan, Fadwa. *A Mountainous Journey.* Translated by Salma Khadra Jayyusi. St. Paul: Graywolf, 1990.

Tzara, Tristan. *Primele Poeme: First Poems.* New York: New Rivers Press, 1976.

————. *Approximate Man and Other Writings.* Detroit: Wayne State University Press, 1973.

Vallejo, Cesar. *The Black Heralds.* Pittsburgh: Latin American Literary Review Press, 1990.

————. *Cesar Vallejo, A Selection of His Poetry.* Translated by James Higgins. Liverpool: Cairns, 1987.

————. *Selected Poems.* Translated by H. R. Hays Hoffman Reynolds and Louis Hammer. Old Chatham, N.Y.: Sachem Press, 1987.

————. *Battle in Spain: Five Unpublished Poems.* Translated by Jose Rubia Barcia and Clayton Eshleman. Santa Barbara, Calif.: Black Sparrow, 1978.

————. *Cesar Vallejo: The Complete Posthumous Poetry.* Translated by Clayton Eshleman and Jose Rubia Barcia. Berkeley, Calif.: University of California Press, 1978.

————. *The Selected Poems of Cesar Vallejo.* Translated by Gordon Brotherston and Edward Dorn. Penguin Latin American Poets. Harmondsworth, England, and Baltimore: Penguin, 1976.

————. *Trilce.* Translated by David Smith. New York: Grossman, 1976.

————. *Spain, Take This Cup from Me.* New York: Grove, 1974.

————. *Cesar Vallejo: An Anthology of His Poetry.* Translated by James Higgins. Oxford and New York: Pergamon, 1970.

Vallejo, Cesar, and Pablo Neruda. *Neruda and Vallejo: Selected Poems.* Translated by Robert Bly, John Knoepfle, and James Arlington Wright. Boston: Beacon Press, 1971.

Wat, Aleksander. *With the Skin.* Translated by Leonard Nathan and Czeslaw Milosz. New York: Ecco Press, 1989.

————. *Mediterranean Poems.* Translated by Czeslaw Milosz. Ann Arbor, Mich.: Ardis Publishers, 1977.

Weigl, Bruce. *Song of Napalm: Poems.* New York: Atlantic Monthly Press, 1988.

————. *The Monkey Wars: Poems.* Athens, Ga.: University of Georgia Press, 1985.

————. *A Romance.* Pittsburgh: University of Pittsburgh Press, 1979.

Wright, Richard. *Richard Wright Reader.* New York: Harper & Row, 1978.

————. *Snake-Back Solos: Selected Poems, 1969–1977.* New York: I. Reed Books, 1978.

————. *Embryo.* New York: Balenmir House, 1972.

Young Bear, Ray. *The Invisible Musician.* Duluth, Minn.: Holy Cow! Press, 1990.

Permissions

Grateful acknowledgment is made to the following authors, publishers, translators, heirs, and agents for their permission to reprint poems in *Against Forgetting: Twentieth-Century Poetry of Witness.*

ADONIS (ALI AHMAD SA'ID): From *Transformations of the Lover:* "Elegy for the Time at Hand." Translated by Samuel Hazo. Reprinted by permission of the International Poetry Forum. From *Modern Poetry of the Arab World,* selected and introduced by Abdullah al-Udhari: "A Mirror for the Twentieth Century" and "The New Noah." Reprinted by permission of Penguin Books Ltd.

AICHINGER, ILSE: From *Ilse Aichinger: Selected Poetry & Prose:* "Enumeration," "Glimpse from the Past," and "In Which Names." Translated by Allen H. Chappel. Reprinted by permission of Logbridge-Rhodes.

AKHMATOVA, ANNA: From *Poems of Akhmatova:* "Requiem." Translated by Stanley Kunitz and Max Hayward. Reprinted by permission of Stanley Kunitz.

ALBERTI, RAFAEL: From *Concerning the Angels:* "Punishments," "The Angels of the Ruins," and "The Warlike Angels." Reprinted by permission of Andre Deutsch Ltd.

ALEGRÍA, CLARIBEL: From *Flowers from the Volcano:* "We Were Three." Translated by Carolyn Forché. Reprinted by permission of Claribel Alegría and Carolyn Forché. From *Woman of the River:* "From the Bridge." Translated by Darwin Flakoll. Reprinted by permission of Claribel Alegría and Darwin Flakoll.

AMICHAI, YEHUDA: From *Poems by Yehuda Amichai:* "God Has Pity on Kindergarten Children," "Ibn Gabirol," "If I Forget Thee, Jerusalem," "Like Our Bodies' Imprint," and "Two Songs of Peace." Translated by Assia Gutmann. Reprinted by permission of Yehuda Amichai.

APOLLINAIRE, GUILLAUME: From *Selected Poems: Apollinaire:* "Post Card" and "The Little Car." Translated by Oliver Bernard. Reprinted by permission of Oliver Bernard. From *Calligrammes: Poems of Peace and War (1913–1916),* translated and edited by Anne Greet: "Shadow." Copyright © 1980 by The Regents of the University of California. Reprinted by permission of the University of California Press. "Stanzas Against Forgetting." Translated by Carolyn Forché. Reprinted by permission of Carolyn Forché.

BOBROWSKI, JOHANNES: "Kaunas 1941," "Pruzzian Elegy," "Latvian Songs," and "Elderblossom." Public Domain.

BOROWSKI, TADEUSZ: From *The Selected Poems of Tadeusz Borowski:* "Project: Flag," "The Sun of Auschwitz," and "Two Countries." Translated by Larry Rafferty, Meryl Natchez, and Tadeusz Pioro. Reprinted by permission of Larry Rafferty.

BRECHT, BERTOLT: From *Bertolt Brecht: Poems 1913–1956:* "The God of War." Translated by Michael Hamburger. "Motto" ("In the dark times . . ."), "Motto" ("This, then, is all . . ."), and "When Evil-Doing Comes Like Falling Rain." Translated by John Willett. "From a German War Primer," "The World's One Hope," and "To Those Born Later." Translated by John Willett, Ralph Manheim, and Erich Fried. Reprinted by permission of Routledge, Chapman and Hall, Inc.

BRETON, ANDRÉ: From *Poems of André Breton:* "More than Suspect" and "War." Copyright © 1982 by the University of Texas Press. Translated by Mary Ann Caws and Jean-Pierre Cauvin. Reprinted by permission of the University of Texas Press.

BREYTENBACH, BREYTEN: From *In Africa Even the Flies Are Happy:* "Dar es-Salaam," "Exile, Representative," "First Prayer for the Hottentotsgod," "Journey," and "The Struggle for the Taal." Copyright © 1976, 1977 by Yolande Breytenbach and Meulenhoff Nederland, Amsterdam. Translated by Denis Hirson. Translation copyright © by John Calder (Publishers) Ltd., London. Reprinted by permission of The Calder Educational Trust, London, and Riverrun Press, Inc., New York.

BRODSKY, JOSEPH: From *To Urania:* "Elegy," "The Berlin Wall Tune," and "To Urania." Copyright © 1988 by Joseph Brodsky. Reprinted by permission of Farrar, Straus, and Giroux, Inc.

BRÜCK, EDITH: Translations originally published in *Milkweed Chronicle:* "Childhood," "Equality, Father," and "Pretty Soon." Translated by Ruth Feldman. Reprinted by permission of Ruth Feldman.

BRUTUS, DENNIS: From *A Simple Lust:* from "Poems About Prison," "On the Island," "Prayer," and "Under House Arrest." Reprinted by permission of Dennis Brutus.

CARAION, ION: From *Ion Caraion: Poems:* "Remember," "Song from the Occupation Time," "The Enveloping Echo," "Tomorrow the Past Comes," and "Ultimate Argument." Translated by Marguerite Dorian and Elliott B. Urdang. Reprinted by permission of Ohio University Press.

CASSIAN, NINA: "Temptation" and "Vowel." Translated by Brenda Walker and Andrea Deletant. Reprinted by permission of Forest Books.

CASTILLO, OTTO RENE: From *Let's Go:* "Apolitical Intellectuals" and "Distances." Translated by Margaret Randall. Reprinted by permission of Curbstone Press. From *Tomorrow Triumphant,* edited by David Volpendesta and Magaly Fernandez: "Before the Scales, Tomorrow." Translated by Barbara

Paschke and David Volpendesta. Reprinted by permission of Barbara Paschke and David Volpendesta.

CAVAFY, CONSTANTINE P.: From *C. P. Cavafy: Collected Poems,* Princeton University Press: "The City" and "Waiting for the Barbarians." Translated by Edmund Keeley. Reprinted by permission of Edmund Keeley.

CELAN, PAUL: "Death Fugue" (*"Todesfuge"*). Translated by John Felstiner. Reprinted by permission of John Felstiner. From *Poems of Paul Celan:* "A Leaf," "I Hear That the Axe has Flowered," "Night Ray," and "There Was Earth Inside Them." Translations copyright © 1988 by Michael Hamburger. Reprinted by permission of Persea Books, Inc.

CHAR, RENÉ: "Leaves of Hypnos No. 128." Translated by Cid Corman. Reprinted by permission of Cid Corman. From *The Dog of Hearts:* "Disdained Apparitions." Translated by Paul Mann. Reprinted by permission of Green Horse Press. From *Poems of Rene Char:* "Argument," "Man flees suffocation," and "Unbending Prayer." Translated by Mary Ann Caws. Reprinted by permission of Princeton University Press.

CRONIN, JEREMY: From *TriQuarterly* ("From South Africa"): "Group Photo from Pretoria Local on the Occasion of a Fourth Anniversary (Never Taken)," "Motho Ke Motho Ka Batho Bebang (A Person Is a Person Because of Other People)," and "The Naval Base (Part III)." Reprinted by permission of *TriQuarterly,* a publication of Northwestern University.

CUADRA, ANGEL: "Brief Letter to Donald Walsh (in memoriam)" and "In Brief." Translated by Katherine Rodriguez Nieto. Reprinted by permission of Angel Cuadra.

cummings, e. e.: From *Complete Poems, 1913–1962:* "am was. are leaves few this. is these a or" and "(i sing of Olaf glad and big)." Copyright © 1923, 1925, 1931, 1935, 1938, 1939, 1940, 1944, 1945, 1946, 1947, 1948, 1949, 1950, 1951, 1952, 1953, 1954, 1955, 1956, 1957, 1958, 1959, 1960, 1961, 1962 by the Trustees for the E. E. Cummings Trust. Copyright © 1961, 1963, 1968 by Marion Morehouse Commings. Reprinted by permission of Liveright Books.

DALTON, ROQUE: From *Poems:* "Love Poem" and "My Neighbor." Translated by Richard Schaaf. Reprinted by permission of Curbstone Press.

DARWISH, MAHMOUD: From *The Music of Human Flesh: Poems of the Palestinian Struggle:* "Prison" and "Psalm 2." Translated by Denys Johnson-Davies. Reprinted by permission of Denys Johnson-Davies. From *Modern Poetry of the Arab World,* selected and introduced by Abdullah al-Udhari: "Earth Poem" and "We Travel Like Other People." Translations copyright © 1986 by Abdullah al-Udhari. Reprinted by permission of Penguin Books Ltd.

DESNOS, ROBERT: From *The Selected Poems of Robert Desnos:* "Ars Poetica." Translated by Carolyn Forché. Reprinted by permission of The Ecco Press. "Letter to Youki" and "The Night Watchman of Pont-au-Change." Translated by Carolyn Forché. Reprinted by permission of Carolyn Forché.

FRIED, ERICH: From *On Pain of Seeing:* "Exile," "My Girlfriends," "One Kind of Freedom Speaks," and "What Things Are Called." Translated by Georg Rapp. Reprinted by permission of Andre Deutsch Ltd.

GARCÍA LORCA, FEDERICO: From *Selected Poems: Lorca and Jimenez,* Beacon Press: "Casida of Sobbing," "Little Infinite Poem," "Rundown Church," and "The Quarrel." Translated by Robert Bly. Reprinted by permission of Robert Bly.

GOLL, YVAN: From *Lackawanna Elegy:* "Lackawanna Elegy." From *Yvan Goll, Poems:* "The Last River" and "Your Sleep." Translated by Galway Kinnell. Reprinted by permission of Galway Kinnell.

GORBANEVSKAYA, NATALYA: From *Selected Poems:* "Sukhanovo." Translated by Daniel Weissbort. Reprinted by permission of Carcanet Press Ltd.

GRASS, GÜNTER: From *Selected Poems (Die Verzuge Der Windhuhner),* translated by Christopher Middleton: "Music for Brass." Copyright © 1956 by Hermann Luchterhad Verlag. English translation copyright © 1966 by Martin Secker & Warburg Ltd. From *Selected Poems (Gleisdreieck),* translated by Michael Hamburger and Christopher Middleton: "In the Egg" and "Saturn." Copyright © 1960 by Hermann Luchterhad Verlag GmbH. English translation copyright © 1966 by Martin Secker and Warburg Ltd. Reprinted by permission of Harcourt Brace Jovanovich, Inc.

GRAVES, ROBERT: From *Poems About War:* "Recalling War." Reprinted by permission of A. P. Watt Ltd. on behalf of The Trustees of the Robert Graves Copyright Trust.

H.D. (HILDA DOOLITTLE): From *H.D.: Collected Poems 1912–1944:* from "The Walls Do Not Fall." Copyright © 1982 by the Estate of Hilda Doolittle. Reprinted by permission of New Directions Publishing Corp.

HECHT, ANTHONY: From *Collected Earlier Poems:* "It Out-Herods Herod. Pray You, Avoid It" and "More Light! More Light!" Copyright © 1990 by Anthony Hecht. Reprinted by permission of Alfred A. Knopf, Inc.

HERBERT, ZBIGNIEW: From *Report from the Besieged City and Other Poems,* The Ecco Press: "Report from the Besieged City" and "What I Saw." From *Zbigniew Herbert: Selected Poems,* Oxford University Press: "Painter," "The Trial," and "The Wall." Translated by John Carpenter and Bogdana Carpenter. Reprinted by permission of John Carpenter.

HERNANDEZ, MIGUEL: From *Selected Poems: Miguel Hernandez and Blas de Otero:* "I go on in the dark lit from within," "July 18, 1936–July 18, 1938," and "Waltz Poem of Those in Love and Inseparable Forever." Translated by Timothy Baland. Reprinted by permission of Beacon Press. From *Songbook of Absences:* "Tomb of the Imagination." Translated by Tom Jones. Reprinted by permission of Tom Jones. From *Miguel Hernandez: Selected Poems:* "Lullabye of the Onion." Translated by Robert Bly. "War." Translated by Hardie St. Martin. Reprinted by permission of White Pine Press.

HIKMET, NAZIM: From *Selected Poetry:* "The Evening Walk," "Letters from a Man in Solitary," "Since I Was Thrown Inside," and "Things I Didn't Know I

Loved." Translations copyright © 1986 by Randy Blasing and Mutlu Konuk. Reprinted by permission of Persea Books, Inc.

HOLAN, VLADIMIR: From *Mirroring: Selected Poems of Vladimir Holan:* "Children at Christmas in 1945," "In the Yard of the Policlinic," "Resurrection," and "To the Enemies." Translated by C. G. Hanzlicek and Dana Habova. Translations copyright © 1985 by C. G. Hanzlicek and Dana Habova. Reprinted by permission of the University Press of New England.

HUCHEL, PETER: "Landscape Beyond Warsaw," "Psalm," "Roads," and "The Garden of Theophrastus." Translated by Daniel Simko. Reprinted by permission of S. Fischer Verlag.

HUGHES, LANGSTON: "Let America Be America Again," "Letter to the Academy," and "Madrid—1937." Reprinted by permission of Harold Ober Associates.

HUGO, RICHARD: From *Making Certain It Goes On: The Collected Poems of Richard Hugo:* "A View from Cortona," "Napoli Again," and "The Yards of Sarajevo." Copyright © 1984 by The Estate of Richard Hugo. Reprinted by permission of W. W. Norton & Company, Inc.

JABÈS, EDMOND: From *The Book of Dialogue:* "Notebook, II," "The Beginning of the Book," "The Book," "The Desert," and "The Desert, II." Translated by Rosemarie Waldrop. Translations copyright © 1987 by Rosemarie Waldrop. Reprinted by permission of the University Press of New England.

JACOB, MAX: From *The Dice Cup: Selected Prose Poems:* "In Search of the Traitor," "Moon Poem," and "War." Translated by Michael Brownstein. Reprinted by permission of Michael Brownstein. "The Horrible Today." Translated by Ron Padgett. Translation copyright © 1979 by Ron Padgett. Reprinted by permission of Ron Padgett.

JASTRUN, TOMASZ: From *Child of Europe,* edited by Michael March: "Hat" and "Scrap." Translated by Daniel Bourne. "The Polish Knot" and "The Seed." Translated by Michael March and Jaroslaw Anders. Reprinted by permission of Michael March.

DE JESÚS, TERESA: From *De Repente:* "Curfew," "Proverbs," and "The Flag of Chile." Translated by Maria Proser, Arlene Scully, and James Scully. Reprinted by permission of Curbstone Press.

JÓZSEF, ATTILA: From *Attila József: Selected Poems and Texts:* "Attila József," "Freight Trains," "The Seventh," and "To Sit, to Stand, to Kill, to Die." Translated by John Batki. Reprinted by permission of the International Writing Program, University of Iowa.

KHARMS, DANIIL: From *The Man in the Black Coat: Russia's Literature of the Absurd,* Northwestern University Press: "An Event on the Street," "Symphony No. 2," and "The Beginning of a Beautiful Day (A Symphony)." Translated by George Gibian. Reprinted by permission of George Gibian.

KHLEBNIKOV, VELIMIR: From *The King of Time: Selected Writings of the Russian Futurian,* translated by Paul Schmidt and edited by Charlotte Douglas: "It has

NERUDA, PABLO: From *Neruda and Vallejo: Selected Poems,* Beacon Press: "America, I Do Not Call Your Name Without Hope," "Letter to Miguel Otero Silva, in Caracas," and "The Dictators." Translated by Robert Bly. "They Receive Instructions Against Chile." Translated by Robert Bly and James Wright. Reprinted by permission of Robert Bly.

NEZVAL, VÍTĚZSLAV: From *Three Czech Poets:* "Moon over Prague," "Prague in the Midday Sun," "The Lilac by the Museum on St. Wenceslas Square," and "Walker in Prague." Translated by Ewald Osers. Reprinted by permission of Ewald Osers.

OPPEN, GEORGE: From *The Collected Poems of George Oppen:* "Route." Copyright © 1975 by George Oppen. Reprinted by permission of New Directions Publishing Corp.

ORTEN, JÍRÌ: From *Elegies:* "The Last Poem" and "Whispered." Translated by Lyn Coffin. Reprinted by permission of Lyn Coffin.

OWEN, WILFRED: From *The Collected Poems of Wilfred Owen:* "Anthem for Doomed Youth," "Dulce et Decorum Est," and "Exposure." Copyright © 1963 by Chatlo & Wendeis, Ltd. Reprinted by permission of New Directions Publishing Corp.

PADILLA, HEBERTO: From *Legacies: Selected Poems by Heberto Padilla:* "History," "In Trying Times," "Nuclear Umbrella," "Sometimes I plunge into the ocean ..." and "Song of the Juggler." Translation copyright © 1969, 1971, 1978, 1979 by Alastair Reid. Translation copyright © 1982 by Alastair Reid and Andrew Hurley. Reprinted by permission of Farrar, Straus, and Giroux, Inc.

PAGIS, DAN: From *Variable Directions,* North Point Press: "A Lesson in Observation," "Autobiography," "Draft of a Reparations Agreement," and "Written in Pencil in the Sealed Railway-Car." Translated by Stephen Mitchell. Reprinted by permission of Stephen Mitchell.

PARRA, NICANOR: From *Emergency Poems:* "Inflation," "Letters from the Poet Who Sleeps in a Chair," "Manifesto," "Modern Times," "Sentences," and "Warnings." Translated by Miller Williams. Copyright © 1972 by Nicanor Parra and Miller Williams. Reprinted by permission of New Directions Publishing Corp.

PASTERNAK, BORIS: From *Boris Pasternak: Selected Poems:* "Fresco Come to Life" and "Hamlet." Translated by Jon Stallworthy and Peter France. Translations copyright © 1983 by Peter France. From *Pasternak: Fifty Poems:* "Mary Magdalene (I)." Translated by Lydia Pasternak Slater. Reprinted by permission of Unwin Hyman.

PAVESE, CESARE: From *Hard Labor:* "August Moon" and "Words from Confinement." Translated by William Arrowsmith. Reprinted by permission of The Ecco Press.

PÉRET, BENJAMIN: From *From the Hidden Storehouse: Selected Poems:* "Hymn of the Patriotic War Veterans" and "Nungesser und Coli Sind Verreckt." Translated by Keith Hollaman. Reprinted by permission of the Field Translation Series, Oberlin College Press.

RÓZEWICZ, TADEUSZ: From *Faces of Anxiety,* "Massacre of the Boys," "Pigtail," "Questions about Poetry since Auschwitz," and "What Happens." Reprinted by permission of Andre Deutsch, Ltd.

RUKEYSER, MURIEL: From *Breaking Open,* Random House: "Breaking Open." Copyright © by Muriel Rukeyser. Reprinted by permission of William L. Rukeyser.

RYUICHI, TAMURA: From *Dead Languages: Selected Poems 1946–1984:* "My Imperialism," "October Poem," "Spiral Cliff," and "Standing Coffin." Translated by Christopher Drake. Reprinted by permission of Katydid Books.

SACHS, NELLY: From *O the Chimneys:* "But Look," "O Sister," "O the Chimneys," and "You." Translation copyright © 1967 by Farrar, Straus, and Giroux, Inc. Reprinted by permission of Farrar, Straus, and Giroux, Inc.

SASSOON, SIEGFRIED: From *Collected Poems:* "A Working Party." Copyright © 1918 by E. P. Dutton. "Repression of War Experience" and "The Death-Bed." Copyright © 1918, 1920 by E. P. Dutton. Copyright © 1936, 1946, 1947, 1948 by Siegfried Sassoon. Reprinted by permission of Viking Penguin, a division of Penguin Books USA Inc.

SEFERIS, GEORGE: From *George Seferis: Collected Poems,* Princeton University Press: "A Word for Summer" and "Last Stop." Translated by Edmund Keeley and Philip Sherrard. Reprinted by permission of Edmund Keeley. From *George Seferis: Collected Poems:* "Our Sun" and "The Last Day." Translated by Edmund Keeley and Philip Sherrard. Reprinted by permission of Princeton University Press.

SEIFERT, JAROSLAV: From *Selected Poetry of Jaroslav Seifert:* "Never Again" and "The Candlestick." Translated by Ewald Osers. Reprinted by permission of DILIA Agency on behalf of the heirs of Jaroslav Seifert.

SEPAMLA, SIPHO: From *The Blues Is You in Me,* A. D. Donker (PTY) Ltd.: "I Remember Sharpeville," "Measure for Measure," "Silence: 2," "The Law That Says," and "The Odyssey." Reprinted by permission of Sipho Sepamla.

SERGE, VICTOR: From *Resistance:* "Constellation of Dead Brothers," "Dialectic," "Hands," and "The Asphyxiated Man." Translated by James Brook. Reprinted by permission of City Lights Books.

SIAMANTO: "Grief" and "The Dance." Translated by Peter Balakian and Nevart Yaghlian. Reprinted by permission of Peter Balakian.

SIMIC, CHARLES: From *Charon's Cosmology,* George Braziller, Inc.: "The Lesson." From *Classic Ballroom Dances,* George Braziller, Inc.: "Begotten of the Spleen," "Prodigy," and "Toy Factory." From *Dismantling the Silence,* George Braziller, Inc.: "Butcher Shop." Reprinted by permission of Charles Simic.

SIMPSON, LOUIS: From *A Dream of Governors:* "The Runner." Copyright © 1959 by Louis Simpson. Published by Wesleyan University Press. Reprinted by permission of the University Press of New England.

SOUPAULT, PHILIPPE: From *I'm Lying: Selected Translations of Philippe Soupault:* "Condemned," "One o'Clock," "Poems from Saint Pelagia Prison," and "You Who Sleep." Translated by Paulette Schmidt. Reprinted by permission of Lost Roads.

SOYINKA, WOLE: From *Idanre and Other Poems:* "Civilian and Soldier," "Harvest of Hate," "I Think It Rains," and "Massacre, October '66." Copyright © 1967 by Wole Soyinka. Reprinted by permission of Hill & Wang, a division of Farrar, Straus, and Giroux, Inc.

SPENDER, STEPHEN: From *Collected Poems 1928–1985* by Stephen Spender: "Rejoice in the Abyss." Copyright © 1953 by Stephen Spender. From *Selected Poems by Stephen Spender:* "Air Raid Across the Bay at Plymouth" and "Epilogue to a Human Drama." Copyright © 1942, 1949 by Stephen Spender. "Ultima Ratio Regum." Copyright © 1942 by Stephen Spender. Reprinted by permission of Random House, Inc.

STEIN, GERTRUDE: From *Useful Knowledge:* "Scenes from the Door." Reprinted by permission of Station Hill Press.

SWIR, ANNA: Originally published in *American Poetry Review:* "We Survived Them" and "White Wedding Slippers." From *Happy as a Dog's Tail:* "A Conversation Through the Door" and "I Am Afraid of Fire." Translated by Czeslaw Milosz. Reprinted by permission of Czeslaw Milosz.

SZYMBORSKA, WISLAWA: "Children of the Epoch" and "Hunger Camp at Jasło." Translated by Grazyna Drabik and Austin Flint. "Any Case" and "Once we knew the world well." Translated by Grazyna Drabik and Sharon Olds. Reprinted by permission of Grazyna Drabik. From *Sounds, Feelings, Thoughts: Seventy Poems by Wislawa Szymborska:* "Still" and "The Terrorist, He Watches." Translated by Magnus Krynski and Robert McGuire. Reprinted by permission of Princeton University Press.

TEKEYAN, VAHAN: From *Sacred Wrath: The Selected Poems of Vahan Tekeyan:* "Dream," "Forgetting," "Prayer on the Threshold of Tomorrow," and "The Country of Dust." Translated by Diana Der Hovanessian and Marzbed Margossian. Reprinted by permission of Diana Der Hovanessian.

THOMAS, DYLAN: From *The Collected Poems of Dylan Thomas:* "A Refusal to Mourn the Death, by Fire, of a Child in London" and "Ceremony after a Fire Raid." Copyright © 1945 by the Trustees for the Copyrights of Dylan Thomas. Reprinted by permission of New Directions Publishing Corp.

THOMAS, EDWARD: From *Collected Poems:* "The Owl." Reprinted by permission of Myfanny Thomas.

TRAKL, GEORG: From *Autumn Sonata*, Moyer Bell Ltd.: "A Romance to Night," "Downfall," "Grodek," and "In the East." Translated by Daniel Simko. Reprinted by permission of Daniel Simko.

TROUPE, QUINCY: From *Weather Reports: New and Selected Poems,* Harlem River Press: "Boomerang: A Blatantly Political Poem" and "Poem for my Father." Reprinted by permission of Quincy Troupe.

Index